World Yearbook of Education 2021

Providing a comprehensive introduction to the topic of accountability and datafication in the governance of education, the *World Yearbook of Education 2021* considers global policy dynamics and policy enactment processes. Chapters pay particular attention to the role of international organizations and the private sector in the promotion of performance-based accountability (PBA) in different educational settings and at multiple policy scales.

Organized into three sections, chapters cover: the global/local construction of accountability and datafication; global discourse and national translations of performance-based accountability policies; and enactments and effects of accountability and datafication, including controversies and critical issues.

With carefully chosen international contributions from around the globe, the *World Yearbook of Education 2021* is ideal reading for anyone interested in the future of accountability and datafication in the governance of education.

Sotiria Grek is Professor in European and Global Education Governance at the School of Social and Political Science, University of Edinburgh, UK.

Christian Maroy is Emeritus Professor of Sociology at UCLouvain, Belgium and a researcher for GIRSEF, a research centre of which he is the co-founder and former director.

Antoni Verger is Associate Professor of Sociology at the Universitat Autònoma de Barcelona (UAB), Spain and a research fellow at the Catalan Institution for Research and Advanced Studies (ICREA).

World Yearbook of Education Series

Examining a different topical subject each year, these fascinating books put forward a wide range of perspectives and dialogue from all over the world. With the best and most pivotal work of leading educational thinkers and writers from 1965 to the present day, these essential reference titles provide a complete history of the development of education around the globe. Available individually or in library-ready sets, this is the indispensable atlas of education, mapping ever changing aspects of theory, policy, teaching and learning.

Series editors:
Julie Allan, University of Birmingham, UK.
Terri Seddon, La Trobe University, Australia.
Gita Steiner-Khamsi, Teachers College, Columbia University, USA.
Antoni Verger, Universitat Autònoma de Barcelona, Spain.

Titles in the series:
World Yearbook of Education 2016
The Global Education Industry
Edited by Antoni Verger, Christopher Lubienski and Gita Steiner-Khamsi

World Yearbook of Education 2017
Assessment Inequalities
Edited by Julie Allan and Alfredo J. Artiles

World Yearbook of Education 2018
Uneven Space-Times of Education: Historical Sociologies of Concepts, Methods and Practices
Edited by Julie McLeod, Noah W. Sobe and Terri Seddon

World Yearbook of Education 2019
Comparative Methodology in the Era of Big Data and Global Networks
Edited by Radhika Gorur, Sam Sellar and Gita Steiner-Khamsi

World Yearbook of Education 2020
Schooling, Governance and Inequalities
Edited by Julie Allan, Valerie Harwood and Clara Rübner Jørgensen

World Yearbook of Education 2021
Accountability and Datafication in the Governance of Education
Edited by Sotiria Grek, Christian Maroy and Antoni Verger

For more information about this series, please visit: www.routledge.com/World-Yearbook-of-Education/book-series/WYBE

World Yearbook
of Education 2021

Accountability and Datafication
in the Governance of Education

Edited By
**Sotiria Grek, Christian Maroy
and Antoni Verger**

Routledge
Taylor & Francis Group

LONDON AND NEW YORK

First published 2021
by Routledge
2 Park Square, Milton Park, Abingdon, Oxon OX14 4RN

and by Routledge
52 Vanderbilt Avenue, New York, NY 10017

Routledge is an imprint of the Taylor & Francis Group, an informa business

British Library Cataloguing-in-Publication Data
A catalogue record for this book is available from the British Library

Library of Congress Cataloging-in-Publication Data
A catalog record has been requested for this book

ISBN: 978-0-367-85650-2 (hbk)
ISBN: 978-1-003-01416-4 (ebk)

Typeset in Minion Pro
by SPi Global, India

Contents

Figures

Tables

Contributors

Camilla Addey is a Marie Curie Research Fellow at GEPS (the Globalisation, Education and Social Policies research centre) in the Department of Sociology at the Autonomous University of Barcelona (Spain). Formerly, Camilla was lecturer in Comparative and International Education at Teachers College, Columbia University (USA), and a researcher at Humboldt University in Berlin (Germany). She researches international large-scale assessments, global educational policy, and education privatization. Currently, she is carrying out a European Commission-funded, interdisciplinary research project (ILSAINC) on the privatization of international assessment (see the Facebook page ILSA Inc. The ILSA industry). Camilla is also a director of the Laboratory of International Assessment Studies.

Andreas Breiter is Professor in Information Management and Educational Technologies at the University of Bremen (Germany) in the Department for Mathematics and Informatics. He is Scientific Director of the Institute for Information Management Bremen (www.ifib.de/en) and currently Chief Digital Officer of the University of Bremen. His research work centres around interdependent processes of deep mediatization, datafication and technological and organizational change within the educational system.

Luís Miguel Carvalho is Professor in Education Policy at the Instituto de Educação of the Universidade de Lisboa, and Coordinator of Research Center on Education (UIDEF). He works in the area of education policy. His research focuses on education policy. His main scholarly interests include education governance, international large-scale assessments, and the making and transnational flows of education models and reforms.

Thokozani Chilenga-Butao is a lecturer and researcher. Her research interests include decentralization, public administration, public policy and the governance of education. Her PhD focuses on national government interventions in South Africa's provincial education departments. Her ongoing research examines South Africa's national education department and its decentralized relationship with provinces and schools.

Vincent Dupriez is Full Professor of Education at the Université of Louvain and member of the Interdisciplinary Research Group in Socialization, Education and Training (GIRSEF-IACCHOS). His research focuses on educational policies and organizations, with a strong interest for the new forms of governance and their impact on teachers, schools and students.

Melanie Ehren is a Professor in the Governance of Schools and Education systems at the Free University Amsterdam, director of the research institute LEARN! and honorary professor at University College, Institute of Education. Her academic work focuses on the effectiveness of accountability and evaluation systems and aims to contribute to a greater understanding of the interplay between accountability and the broader education system in tackling inequality and improving student outcomes.

Gerard Ferrer-Esteban has a PhD in Sociology and a BA in Pedagogy (Autonomous University of Barcelona). His main fields of research are comparative education, education policy, and equity in school systems. Dr. Ferrer-Esteban is part of the ERC-funded REFORMED project as a Marie Curie Research Fellow, and complements the existing qualitative approach with quantitative analyses to disentangle the effects of school autonomy and performance-driven accountability policies on relevant outcomes, such as learning outcomes, equity, and other non-cognitive domains. He aims to articulate relevant policy implications to inform global and local education policy agendas.

Clara Fontdevila is a PhD candidate at the Department of Sociology of the Universitat Autònoma de Barcelona, with a thesis focusing on the negotiation of the SDG4 global education agenda and the development of associated global learning metrics. Over the years, she has collaborated with various educational and research organizations, including Education International, UNESCO and the Open Societies Foundation. Her areas of interest are education markets, the global governance of education, and the global governance of education.

Radhika Gorur is an Associate Professor at Deakin University, and a Director of the Laboratory for International Assessment Studies. Engaging with the sociology of quantification and critical data studies, she explores the social and political lives of data and metrics in education. Her research interests include education policy, regulation and reform; global networks, aid and development; and data infrastructures, data cultures and quantification.

Sotiria Grek is Professor in European and Global Education Governance at the School of Social and Political Science, University of Edinburgh. Her research focuses on education, with a particular focus on the relationship between knowledge and policy. Further, she has worked in-depth on analysing quantification as a form of governance. She has co-authored (with Martin Lawn) *Europeanising education: governing a new policy space* (2012) and co-edited (with Joakim Lindgren) *Governing by Inspection* (Routledge, 2015). She is currently working on a European Research Council Starting Grant (ERC-StG-2016) that studies 'International Organisations and the Rise of a Global Metrological Field' (2017–2022).

Sigrid Hartong is professor in sociology with a focus on the transformation of governance in education and society at the Helmut Schmidt University (HSU) Hamburg, Germany. Her main scholarly interests include global–local reform mobilies, from both single-case and international comparative perspectives, as well as the growing datafication and digitalization of education policy, governance and practice. She is Principal Investigator for different research projects on new (big) data infrastructures, actor constellations and data practices in schooling.

Jessica Holloway is an Australian Research Council DECRA Fellow within the Research for Educational Impact (REDI) Centre at Deakin University (Melbourne, Australia). Her DECRA project, entitled "The Role of Teacher Expertise, Authority and Professionalism in Education," investigates the role of education in modern democratic societies, with a particular focus on teachers and teacher expertise. Her work has appeared in journals such as the *Journal of Education Policy* and *Critical Studies in Education*. She is currently writing a book called *Metrics, Standards and Alignment in Teacher Policy: Critiquing Fundamentalism and Imagining Pluralism* (2021).

Priya Goel La Londe is an Assistant Professor at the University of Hong Kong in the Faculty of Education. A former teacher and school leader, she holds cross-disciplinary training in sociology, early childhood education, and education leadership and policy. Dr. La Londe's research examines the relationships between school reform and school improvement. Currently, she is investigating how performance accountability shapes teachers and teaching and leaders and leadership. Dr. La Londe's research is supported by the Hong Kong Research Grants Council and the China Confucius Institute, and she has assisted on projects funded by the Spencer and William T. Grant Foundations.

Bob Lingard is a Professorial Fellow in the Institute for Learning Sciences & Teacher Education at Australian Catholic Education and Emeritus Professor at The University of Queensland. He is a Fellow of the Academy of Social Sciences in Australia and also of the Academy of Social Sciences in the UK. His research focuses on education policy. His most recent books include *Globalisation and Education* (Routledge, 2021); *Globalizing Educational Accountabilities* (Routledge, 2016); *National Testing in Schools: An Australian Assessment* (Routledge, 2016) and *Politics, Policies and Pedagogies in Education* (Routledge, 2014).

Eric Mangez is Professor of Sociology at UCLouvain, a researcher for Girsef/ IACCHOS, and former lead editor of the *European Educational Research Journal*. Before being appointed as professor, he was a postdoctoral fellow at the University of Edinburgh. He has developed a special interest in the sociology of Niklas Luhmann and its relevance for our understanding of the globalization and Europeanization of education. He collaborated with many researchers across Europe as director of a European project on knowledge and policy (FP6, *knowandpol project*). He is currently co-directing a large-scale research project on normative indeterminacy and the global governance of education.

Christian Maroy is Emeritus Professor at UCLouvain and a researcher for GIRSEF, a research centre, of which he was the co-founder and the former director. He is also Associate Professor at the University of Montreal and former holder of the Canada Chair of Research on Education Policies. His research focuses on education policies, governance and regulation in a comparative perspective. He has recently published *Accountability Policies in Education* (2019, with X. Pons), *Professionnalisme enseignant et politiques de responsabilisation* (2017, with Yves Dutercq) and *Les marchés scolaires. Sociologie d'une politique publique d'éducation* (2013, with Georges Felouzis and Agnès van Zanten).

Romuald Normand is Professor at the Faculty of Social Sciences at the University of Strasbourg, Research Unit SAGE (Societies, Actors and Government in Europe), France. He is leading the French–Chinese Chair on Education Policies in Europe and he is visiting associate professor at the Beijing Normal University, China. His research interests are on comparative education and policies. His recent publications include *Shaping Policy Agendas: The Micro-Politics of Economic International Organizations* (2020, with D. Dolowitz and M. Hadjiisky) and *Education Policies and the Restructuring of the Educational Profession: Global and Comparative Perspectives* (2018, co-edited with M. Liu, L.M. Carvalho, D.A. Oliveira and L. Vasseur).

Dalila Andrade Oliveira is Professor of the Federal University of Minas Gerais and on the Federal University of Paraíba (Brazil). PhD in Education from the University of São Paulo (USP, Brazil). Post-doctorate at the State University at the Université de Montréal (Canada) and at the University of London (UK). President (2009/2013) of the National Association of Postgraduate and Research in Education (ANPEd). She develops studies and research projects with an emphasis on public policy in education, school management and teaching work in Brazil and Latin America. Researcher at the National Research Council (PQ 1A – CNPq).

Nomancotsho Pakade is a researcher at the Public Affairs Research Institution. Her work experience involves advocacy and documentation work in NGOs and research posts, with a focus on education, gender and sexual rights. Currently, she is a Doctoral candidate at the Department of History and Heritage Studies, University of Pretoria.

Aaron M. Pallas is Arthur I. Gates Professor of Sociology and Education and Chair of the Department of Education Policy and Social Analysis at Teachers College, Columbia University. He educates stakeholders – including representatives of the media – about the complexities and unexpected consequences of account-ability and resource distribution policies in public schools. His current work illuminates these dynamics across New York City, New York State and beyond. His most recent book, with Anna Neumann, is *Convergent Teaching: Tools to Spark Deeper Learning in College* (2019).

Lluís Parcerisa is a Research Fellow at the Department of Sociology of the *Universitat Autònoma de Barcelona* (UAB). Since 2013, he has been a member of the Globalization, Education and Social Policies (GEPS) research group, where he participates in the ERC-funded project 'Reforming Schools Globally: A Multiscalar Analysis of Autonomy and Accountability Policies in the Education Sector' (REFORMED). His research interests include global governance, education policy, political sociology, policy enactment, perfor-mance-based accountability reforms, and datafication.

Xavier Pons is an Associate Professor at the University of Paris-Est Créteil (UPEC), France. A member of several comparative research projects since 2006, his work in the sociology of educational policies focuses on transforma-tions of governance of education systems, school administrations, and educat-ing States in Europe and on the logics of public debates in education. Winner of the 2011 Jean-Claude Eicher Prize for the Development of Educational Research, he is the co-editor of the *Revue française de pédagogie*. He recently co-edited with Christian Maroy the book entitled *Accountability Policies in Education: A Comparative and Multilevel Analysis in France and Quebec*.

Linda Rönnberg is a Professor at the Department of Applied Educational Science, Umeå University, Sweden and a Senior Research Fellow at the Department of Education, University of Turku, Finland. Her research focuses on education governance and politics with a particular focus on evaluation, privatization and internationalization in compulsory and higher education. She is a co-editor of *Education Inquiry*, the executive editor of the *European Educational Research Journal* and Principal Investigator of the project "Going Global: Swedish school companies and their international operations," funded by the Swedish Research Council.

Guri Skedsmo is Professor at Institute for Research on Professions and Professional Learning, Schwyz University of Teacher Education, Switzerland and Associate Professor at Department of Teacher Education and School Research, University of Oslo, Norway. Her research focuses on governance and leadership in education. Currently, she is Principal Investigator of the project Professional Actors' Work on Retaining Students in Secondary Education, funded by the Norwegian Research Council and she is involved in research on types of knowledge that inform decision-making processes in schools. She is also editor-in-chief for the journal *Educational Assessment, Evaluation and Accountability* (*EAEA*).

Pieter Vanden Broeck is a postdoctoral researcher in sociology at the University of Louvain. His research draws on the systems theory of Niklas Luhmann to address the intertwining processes of globalization and Europeanization in the domain of education (and beyond). Recent publications have appeared in *Journal of Education Policy*, *Educational Philosophy and Theory* and *The American Sociologist*. He currently participates in a large-scale research project on normative indeterminacy and the global governance of education, funded by the *Action Concertée de Recherche* (ARC) programme of the French Community of Belgium.

Antoni Verger is an associate professor at the Department of Sociology of the *Universitat Autònoma de Barcelona* (UAB) and a research fellow at the Catalan Institution for Research and Advanced Studies (ICREA). With a cross-disciplinary training in sociology and education studies, his research examines the relationship between globalization, governance institutions, and education policy – i.e. how education policies are internationally disseminated and enacted in different settings, and how this impacts education quality and equity. Since 2016, he has studied school autonomy with accountability reforms from this perspective in the context of the ERC-funded project REFORMED (www.reformedproject.eu).

Annelise Voisin is a postdoctoral research fellow (Quebec Research Council funded-FRQSC) at CIAE, University of Chile (Santiago, Chile) and the National Institute for Scientific Research (Montreal, Canada). She is also part of the ERC-funded Teachers Careers project (GIRSEF – UCL, Belgium) and was a member of the Canada Research Chair in Education Policies (Canada). She works in the areas of comparative education and education policy. Her main research interests include education governance and policies, the international dissemination of education policy models and effects on actors, the regulation of the teaching profession and the transformations of teacher careers, social and school inequalities.

Ben Williamson is a Chancellor's Fellow in the Centre for Research in Digital Education at the University of Edinburgh. His research focuses on the relations between digital technologies and education policy and governance, with a current emphasis on Higher Education data infrastructures and new computational learning sciences. He wrote *Big Data in Education: The Digital Future of Learning, Policy and Practice*, and is an editor of the journal *Learning, Media and Technology*.

Christian Ydesen is a professor (WSR) at Aalborg University, Denmark. He is the Principal Investigator of the project 'The Global History of the OECD in education' funded by the Aalborg University talent programme and the project 'Education Access under the Reign of Testing and Inclusion' funded by the Independent Research Fund Denmark. He has been a visiting scholar at Edinburgh University (2008–2009, 2016), Birmingham University (2013), Oxford University (2019), and the University of Milan (2021). He has also published several articles on topics such as educational testing, international organizations, accountability, educational psychology and diversity in education from historical and international perspectives.

Xingguo Zhou holds a PhD in Educational Sciences at University of Turku (Finland) and a MA in Pedagogy at Xiamen University (China). Previously, she worked in a transnational comparative research project on the quality assurance and evaluation in Brazil, China and Russia. She is also the co-author of the book *Politics of Quality in Education: a comparative study of Brazil, China, and Russia* (Routledge, 2018). Her research interest is in area of the transformation of Chinese educational politics and she is currently working on a project dealing with the implementation of VR technology in Finnish and Chinese schools.

Introduction:
Accountability and datafication in education: Historical, transnational and conceptual perspectives

Sotiria Grek, Christian Maroy and Antoni Verger

Introduction[1]

Accountability has become a buzzword used not only in media and academic debates, but also at the political, regulatory and legislative levels (Espeland and Vannebo, 2007; Lindberg, 2013). The proliferation of the notion of accountability goes hand in hand with its polysemy, its 'catch-all' character and its – often willingly – normative use. It is mobilized both to increase transparency and hence the legitimacy of democratic institutions, and to improve 'good governance' and the achievement of the objectives of effectiveness, efficiency or equity of (public) organizations (Mattei, 2012; Veselý, 2013). The purpose of this book is to reconceptualize the notion of accountability as part and parcel of the increasing datafication in education, understood as the processes and effects of quantifying education, from education policymaking to pedagogy and education practice in all its physical and digital manifestations.

If the notion of accountability is often normatively referred to as a 'virtue', it can also be considered analytically as an institutional mechanism that can take various forms depending on the actors involved, and the fields or the objects it covers (Bovens, 2010). In this perspective, Bovens proposes a narrow, yet useful definition of accountability as 'a relationship between an actor and a forum, in which the actor has an obligation to explain and to justify his or her conduct, the forum can pose questions and pass judgments, and the actor may face consequences' (Bovens, 2007: 450). The definition aims at distinguishing between different types of accountability, by answering the following questions: who is accountable?; to whom?; about what?; with reference to what evaluation criteria and on the basis of what information?; finally, with what consequences? One can thus distinguish between different types of accountability: *democratic* (from elected representatives to their electorate); *bureaucratic* (or administrative, from an executive to his or her hierarchical superior); *professional* (from a professional to his or her peers); *legal* (from a subject of law to a court of justice); and *social* (from individuals to the communities to which they belong). Moreover, the object of accountability (the decisions or behaviours of an individual or collective actor, its results or impacts, etc.), the evaluation criteria used (legality, appropriateness, effectiveness, equity, transparency, etc.), or its consequences (symbolic, material, legal, severe or mild) can vary greatly. Finally, the knowledge bases on which accountability is based also differ: formal hearings and testimony in a parliamentary committee, written and documentary traces, quantified data, or media communications, for example.[2]

Beyond this panorama of forms of accountability, accountability as an institutional mechanism is more broadly embedded in the imaginary and cultural referents inscribed in the modernity and long history of societies, mainly Western societies: as a result, it interacts with other institutional arrangements of democratic political regimes and contributes to constructing their very content (Olsen, 2017; Rosanvallon, 2008). Moreover, as a bureaucratic or professional requirement, accountability is based on a rationality horizon (procedural, instrumental, epistemological) associated with the increased differentiation of contemporary societies into specific fields, as highlighted by Max Weber in particular (Weber, 2019). At the social level, it can meet the moral requirements of everyday social life, which requires an actor to make his conduct understandable and justifiable by others (accountable), as has been shown by ethnomethodologists (Garfinkel, 2016).

As already suggested, whilst the meaning and forms of accountability vary historically but also according to social fields, and disciplinary and theoretical perspectives, this book focuses on contemporary forms of accountability in education, those developing at the intersection of global, national and local policy spaces at the beginning of the 21st century. In this particular field, accountability is taking on the contemporary form of *performance-based accountability* (PBA) (Carnoy et al., 2003; Figlio & Loeb, 2011), in an increasingly significant, if not unique way.

PBA is an assemblage of formal or informal procedures, various techniques and tools, and normative discourse (on the legitimate societal aims and expectations from the schools or school systems), aimed at making schools accountable and motivating their staff to achieve certain performances in terms of learning or pupil socialization. This form of accountability is sometimes based on a formal institutional mechanism (as in the Bovens definition), but also – and crucially for the purposes of this book – on datafication; that is, on quantified data that originates from standardized external tests and other performance indicators, and from diverse forms of evaluation and comparison. This accountability and these expectations for improvement and performance are exercised at several interlocking scales, such as those of a national or subnational school system, a district or individual schools.

It is thus important to note that performance-based accountability schemes participate in and rely to varying degrees on the datafication of education (Jarke & Breiter, 2019; Williamson, 2017). Datafication 'refers to the transformation of different aspects of education (such as test scores, school inspection reports, or clickstream data from an outline course) into digital data. Making information about education into digital data allows it to be inserted into data bases, where it can be measured, calculations can be performed on it, and through which it can be turned into charts, tables and other forms of graphical presentations' (Williamson, 2017: 5).

More broadly, the processes of accountability and datafication are underpinned by the process of quantification that has been developing in modern societies for a long time (Desrosières, 1998; Diaz-Bone & Didier, 2016; Mennicken & Espeland, 2019; Porter, 1995; also Mangez & Vanden Broeck in this volume).

As the chapters of this book will eloquently explicate, PBA lies currently at the crossroads of two socio-technical, historical currents that have gained more and more momentum: on the one hand, PBA relates to the ever-increasing demand for results-based accountability on the part of schools; on the other hand, it has become the vehicle of an expanding and all-encompassing process of educational datafication. In this introduction, we will first develop a historical background and the genealogy of various forms of accountability in education, in relation with various other key societal, economic, political and technological changes that have influenced either the global/local nexus or the process of datafication. Although accountability has a much longer history than can be accommodated and meaningfully discussed in this introduction, our focus will be on account-ability forms and effects that began in the 1980s. As we shall see, the 1980s was the decade during which, for the first time, the measurement of education perfor-mance, locally, nationally or internationally, became a key component of educa-tional accountability, or what we call in this book performance-based accountability (PBA). Secondly, we will summarize in conceptual terms the notion of PBA and elaborate how and why it could be considered as a policy instrument, that is related to data and quantification, from a political sociology perspective. Finally, we will present the main inquiry lines in the configuration of a comprehensive research agenda on accountability, datafication and education, and how the book's contents relate to it.

The long-lasting development of accountability and quantification in education

1980s–1990s: New Public Management and the emergence of high stakes testing

During the 1980s, accountability in public services adopted a performance-ori-ented rationale. This shift was brought about by the consolidation of New Public Management (NPM) as a paradigm of public sector reform. With NPM, business management ideas and techniques, such as outcomes-based management, decen-tralization and greater competition and choice, gained currency in the public administration reform agenda (Vigoda, 2003).

NPM first took ground in the 1980s, in a context characterized by a fiscal global crisis and the critique that ensued against the inefficiency and uniformity of pub-lic services (Soguel and Jaccard, 2008). The early adopters of NPM included the neoliberal governments of several Anglo-Saxon countries, including the UK and the USA, but also Chile. In the 1990s, NPM expanded to many Southern regions via the loan conditionality of international financial institutions, and to Continental Europe through the active promotion of NPM doctrines by the Organization for Economic Cooperation and Development (OECD) and the

European Union (EU) (Pal, 2012). In the 1990s, NPM saw further expansion and rooting in public administration, as it was also embraced by social democratic parties under the tenets of the Third Way. However, in contrast to emphasizing the economizing function of NPM, social democratic forces put more emphasis on the NPM promises of modernizing public services by making them more diverse and responsive to citizens' demands (Gunter et al., 2016).

It was precisely NPM's efficiency and equity arguments that rendered it conducive to the promotion of PBA in education. As the discursive change was coupled with the development of sophisticated data-intensive instruments, PBA soon rose to a key policy instrument in the governance of education. First, by placing greater emphasis on public services being managed through smaller managerial units, educational authorities were seen as needing to equip themselves with new control technologies to steer educational providers at a distance. Second, by replacing inputs- and process-based management with an outcomes-based management style, governments had to publicize performance data, as the means via which both improved management would occur. Third, to promote diversification and choice, which are some of the central tenets of NPM, governments had to share school performance data in the form of 'naming and shaming' league tables, school rankings or school browsers (Maroy, 2009).

Nonetheless, few of these developments were completely novel. What we can observe is that overall, in those countries where NPM became crystallized as a governing mode, national assessments and performance data were not newly introduced (Kamens and McNeely, 2010). What NPM brought about was the recalibration of standardized testing, learning standards and related tools as managerial devices made to steer schools' behaviour at a distance, increase peer pressure, and actively construct a more competitive *ethos* among a broad range of school actors – including teachers, principals, school owners and families (Lingard et al., 2016).

Under the aegis of NPM, and under the increasing presence of performance data in all sorts of policy fields, accountability loses – to an extent – its previous democratic and professional manifestations and emerges as a concept primarily defined by its role and function in bureaucratic and managerial systems. Accountability becomes measurable, statistical and evidence-based, a tool to surveil, penetrate and organize public services (Le Galès, 2016). The concept of accountability is stripped of its democratic and political roots and connected to forms of critique and proliferating programmes of organizational improvement.

2000s–now: International comparative assessments and the rise of datafication

In the 2000s, methodological and technological advances in psychometrics and in the digitization of testing have contributed to intensify and scale up learning assessments and learning analytics (Gorur, 2013). The Programme for International Students Assessment (PISA) of the OECD, as well as other international large-scale assessments (ILSAs), have become instrumental in transferring data-gathering techniques and frameworks of indicators to national large-scale assessment systems (Meyer and Benavot, 2013) and enhance capacities for assessment and datafication at the national level (Lingard et al., 2016).

Nonetheless, beyond technology transfer, the most significant way ILSAs promote PBA as a key governance instrument consists in the promotion of a global competition between countries for better learning outcomes (Grek, 2009). To become competitive in the 'global education race' (cf. Sellar et al., 2017), the enactment of national PBA systems becomes a key, strategic tool towards achieving improved education performance: that is, PBA is seen as a necessary condition for national governments to control the level of learning achievement of subnational territories and schools, and to activate school improvement dynamics at different scales of governance (see Skedsmo et al. in this volume). Through international competition and country comparisons, ILSAs also disseminate an implicit message about what constitutes 'good governance' in education. Specifically, they construct powerful discourses about comparative and datafied approaches to educational performance as being both effective and appropriate governance mechanisms to improve educational systems. In the ILSA era, there is no control without comparison (Lawn, 2008), but at the same time comparison itself becomes a *de facto* form of control and coercion in the educational domain.

Economic interests are also behind the current shift towards datafication and PBA in education. The industry focusing on educational testing, learning analytics and/or school performance improvement is not only expanding its economic activity under the auspices of PBA, but is also a core constituency behind the international spread of PBA (see Williamson in this volume). Companies like Pearson, Educational Testing Services or the Australian Council for Educational Research are strongly embedded within policy networks and 'have a vested economic interest to have education systems and schools change what they define as academic knowledge or even useful knowledge to fit the particular test they sell' (Carnoy, 2016: 36). The OECD (2013: 51) itself admits that the fact that 'standardized student assessment becomes a more profitable industry' means that 'companies have strong incentives to lobby for the expansion of student standardized assessment as an education policy therefore influencing the activities within the evaluation and assessment framework'. Overall, the increasing involvement of private interests within education testing regimes contributes to testing practices expanding towards new areas of education activity, educational levels and scales of governance (Verger, Parcerisa and Fontdevila, 2019b).

The changes described so far are broadly driven by factors of a political and economic nature, but they have evolved in parallel to changing notions of quality in education, evidence-based policy and the role of learning achievement therein. Today, policymakers do not conceive taking policy decisions or evaluating the success of educational programmes without resorting to learning achievement data. Learning achievement data has become a key, and to a great extent hegemonic, indicator to track school improvement and measure school effectiveness. In fact, in policy and research circles, many have conflated 'educational quality' and 'quality assurance' with students' improved learning outcomes (Kauko, Rinne and Takala, 2018; Smith, 2016). Education research has played its part, too.

For example, school effectiveness research or related work on pedagogical effectiveness (Hargreaves, 1996) has given growing credibility to the use of 'learning technology' and 'evidence-based practices'. As a result, efficient data production, handling and analysis are supposed to then trigger the improvement of the learning processes by schools and teachers, as it is argued by accountability apologists (see Fullan, 2007).

Beyond its growing centrality in the field of education, learning achievement has also become a key proxy to assess countries' economic success, potential economic growth, (un)employment behaviour, and foreign investment attractiveness (De Mello and Padoan, 2010; Hanushek and Woessmann, 2008). In a globalized economy, thus, both the important direct and indirect effects attributed to learning achievement increase the pressure on education authorities and institutions to improve their performance. Among others, this shows that the power acquired by PBA as a policy instrument cannot be disentangled from the power of the measurement tools PBA depends upon.

A policy instrument approach to accountability and datafication

One originality of this book is the interrogation of contemporary PBA as a core governance mechanism in education in the 21st century in increasingly datafied education policy spaces. PBA is a policy instrument, interweaving accountability mechanisms with tools as external testing, data, numbers and comparisons, promoted by various policy actors at various scales. As shown above, these instruments and tools, in its current configuration, emerged with NPM reforms and consolidated with the increasing relevance of internal comparative assessments and other sources of performance data. However, this is only part of the PBA story. What we are witnessing is a broader shift towards new forms of regulatory governance in which the state is endowed with the necessary instruments to find new ways to orientate, penetrate, discipline and change social behaviour (Le Galès, 2016). The reconfiguration of the state through a new generation of data-intensive and incentivizing policy instruments, among which PBA stands out, is usually justified by noble goals such as efficacy, equity and transparency. However, the analysis of the emergence of PBA, its multiple trajectories and translations, from a policy instruments perspective contributes to the depiction of a much more nuanced and multilayered reality.

In this section, we analyse PBA as a policy instrument or a policy technology (Ozga, 2013), adopting a conceptual perspective derived from the political sociology of policy instruments (Halpern et al. 2012; Lascoumes and Le Galès, 2004; Le Galès, 2016). We also reflect on the increasing embeddedness between datafication and accountability instruments in the reconfiguration of educational governance.

PBA *as a policy instrument*

A political sociology perspective to policy instruments, in contrast to a functionalist perspective, does not see policy instruments as neutral and technical devices that politicians can 'pragmatically' choose from a toolbox to solve policy problems according to effectiveness criteria (Lascoumes and Simard, 2011). On the contrary, it conceives policy instruments as conveying values, as instituting or condensing a certain type of power and relations between those who govern and those who are governed, a perspective freely derived from Foucault's approach to the technologies of power and governmentality (Lascoumes, 2004; Le Galès, 2016). For Lascoumes and Le Galès (2004: 13), a policy instrument is defined as 'an apparatus that is both technical and social, that organizes specific social relations between the state and those it is addressed to, according to the representations and meanings it carries. It is a particular type of institution, a technical device with the generic purpose of carrying a concrete concept of the politics/ society relationship and sustained by a concept of regulation'.[3] This definition invites us to grasp the political, normative and cognitive, and not just the technical dimension of the instrumentation of a policy.

A key issue in the analysis of public action is indeed its instrumentation, defined as 'the set of problems posed by the choice and use of techniques, means of operation, and devices that make it possible to materialize and operationalize government action' (Lascoumes and Le Galès, 2004: 12). It is a question of looking at the processes of construction of the tools, the interests of the actors involved in their choices, and the way in which they were chosen (historical perspective), but also looking at the functions they fulfil (or are expected to fulfil), the effects they produce (in terms of opportunities, but also of redefining identities or power relations) and their evolution over time (Mennicken and Espeland, 2019).

Following this perspective, we could thus consider PBA as a policy instrument, an apparatus, composed of various tools, discourses, generating new regulations among actors, at different inter-related scales.

PBA as an assemblage of old and new tools

The instrumentation of PBA consists first of all of an assemblage of techniques and tools, whose precise configuration and historical genesis may vary from country to country, but which is found more or less comprehensively in most policies and systems. Institutional and political factors matter indeed in the global/national/local making of each specific assemblage. Some of these tools exist sometimes for long in certain countries (e.g. external exams, curricular standards), however their assemblage tends to redefine their function (retooling) in relation with PBA. These tools and techniques include:

- The definition of *curricular standards and objectives* to be followed by educational institutions, which specify the key knowledge and skills to be mastered at different stages by students. (Darling-Hammond, 2006; O'Neill, 2015)
- *Contracts* or agreements between a supervisory authority and a school organization (school, district, etc.), specifying the quantified targets to be aimed at by the latter, in relation to the political objectives of the state (e.g. graduation rates, success rates, averages in external examinations, etc.); related often to *strategic or operational action plans*, specifying the means and strategies

developed to achieve these targets or to improve the performances, taking into account the context. (Bezes, 2005)

- *External, standardized tests*, organized on a regular basis, for different subjects which are considered central (literacy, mathematics, science, second languages, etc.) and years of study. These tests, organized in a variety of ways, constitute a key tool for standardizing the evaluation of the quality of pupils' learning. These tests are one key source of the data necessary for the definition of the targets set by schools and the evaluation of their progress. (Kamens and McNeely, 2010; Lingard et al., 2016)
- The development at various degrees of *data infrastructure and database*, related to various *indicators* of progress or performances to be reached by school organizations or systems. (Sellar, 2015; Williamson, 2017)
- Regular *(self)-assessments* of the achievement of targets and the realizations of the strategic action plans, with *reports* to the supervisory authorities, users or stakeholders of the organizations concerned. (Altrichter and Kemethofer, 2015; Hall and Sivesind, 2014; Ozga and Grek, 2012)
- These self-evaluation reports are followed by some *'rectifying' measures*: these are *high or low stakes*, incentivizing or coercive, symbolic or material, aimed at improving the effectiveness of the organization concerned; for example, financial incentives for staff, school on probation, publication of results and comparison of schools, managerial or pedagogical monitoring, self-evaluation and external pedagogical support. (Figlio and Loeb, 2011; Fullan et al., 2015)

PBA tools and techniques have often been promoted or formalized by various political doctrines (NPM, for example) or scientific discourses (school effectiveness research). However, the genesis of policy instruments like PBA is never the consequence of a single discourse, epistemic of policy agenda; rather, as the empirical chapters of this book will show, policy instruments are assemblages of historic and social constructions, the result of a trajectory, that leads to the selection, bricolage and translation of these tools in a singular education policy (Maroy and Pons, 2019).

PBA as (a) transformative discourse of education

Not only does PBA as a policy instrument provide the tools of its operationalization, but it also constructs a new vision of education, based on legitimizing discourses and noble goals that are articulated and deployed in novel ways. Several discursive registers could in fact be mobilized to justify PBA in various ways depending on the history of each education system, namely; the register of social and school justice, under the particular species of a discourse of school inclusion and success for all pupils; the register of local and participatory 'democracy' via 'opening' schools to parents, pupils and other users; the discursive register of the transparency of school professionals and administrators, and their accountability to the political and supervisory authorities; and, finally, the register of effectiveness and efficiency that must be ensured by qualified professionals, specialized in a sector considered key, such as education.

PBA as (a) new form of governance and regulation

The performance-based accountability mechanisms are the bearers of a redefinition of governance and regulations existing between the state and the organizations and actors in the field of education. They redefine the relationships and roles between governors and governed, establishing new objects, new modalities and new accountability and responsibility relationships within the school sector. Further, at the global and international levels, through international comparisons and the active strategy of some global actors such as the OECD (Grek, 2009; Mundy et al., 2016; Gorur in this volume), some national jurisdictions see their symbolic status and image redefined, while the making of their education policy is influenced and the education system restructured at different degrees (Lingard et al., 2016). At other scales of schools' systems, the relationship between the state, intermediate authorities, and schools is changing, often in favour of a growing cognitive or coercive power of the state or intermediate authorities (see Skedsmo et al.; Maroy et al. in this volume). Within school systems, with various tools and mechanisms and stakes, schools and professionals are accountable to their administrative hierarchy not only on what used to traditionally be the object of school accounting (their 'good' use of the budget or their conformity to the formal rules), but also for their actual performance or progress concerning the pupil's learning. This bureaucratical accountability goes hand in hand with a growing public accountability to parents and the public at large through the dissemination of school report cards and/or the publication of school/system performances and their rankings (Landri, 2018, Hartong and Breiter in this volume).

Moreover, the definition of what matters as education and learning is also evolving, and potentially narrowing, with the association of pupil's success with instruction or specific topics or curricular subjects. The definition of professionalism is evolving and the key actors in charge of their evaluation is changing; these are no longer teachers' peers, but instead school principals or a renewed professional elite – with sometimes old institutional actors as inspection or new professional groups as 'pedagogic counsellors', educational scientists and others.

Finally, analysing PBA as a policy instrument means that we look at the same time at the threefold dimension of this apparatus: an assembly of tools, associated with a different register of transformative discourse, which carry new forms of governance and regulation of the domain.

However, it is important to highlight the hybrid character of the PBA apparatus and its malleable nature. As we discussed above, PBA may both address learning gaps and thus strengthen the democratic control of education, whilst simultaneously promoting school choice and competition. This malleability contributes to PBA's widespread and politically transversal adoption, as well as to the incremental evolution of its constitutive tools and their uses. From the perspective of instrumentation, external evaluations and accountability mechanisms are appealing and convenient choices. The seductive power of PBA as an instrument relies not only on the fact that it contributes to the commensuration of complex educational realities into numerical categories, but also on the fact that it constructs the perception that deep educational problems (learning gaps, quality issues) can be addressed by setting up predefined patterns of conduct, measuring actors' performance, and distributing incentives accordingly (Barbana, Dumay and Dupriez, 2014; Falabella, 2020; Verger, Fontdevila and Parcerisa, 2019).

Moreover, as this book will show, this hybridization of managerial and pedagogical discourse on school effectiveness and equity comes at the price of ambiguities and contradictions that could be deconstructed. Indeed, in the face of the dominance of the PBA paradigm, it is necessary and possible to reaffirm the existence of other forms of accountability, whether democratic, professional, or both, that pre-exist it or could replace it. The fact that the school and its professionals are subject to a form of accountability is an old one, of course; nonetheless, PBA alters not only the modes of accounting but also the very meaning and function of accountability itself. In other words, PBA as a policy instrument, is a social and historical construct amongst others possible. The future of the instrumentation related to accountability in education could thus further evolve. The paramount place of performativity could decline and the policy instruments really 'progress' in relation with the normative ideals of 'democracy' and 'reason' (Biesta, 2004; Olsen, 2017; Ranson, 2003).

The accountability–datafication nexus

From a larger public policy perspective, since the turn of the century, PBA has become central to many attempts to control and develop both private and public organizations, their performance and products, as indicated by the proliferation of terms such as audit, 'quality assurance', performance measurement and so on. Datafication, or in other words the explosion of the production and use of statistical data to govern organizational action, has enabled accountability to become an overarching and integrating function in organizations, determining operations across the board; in that sense, we are experiencing a further evolution of PBA as 'datafied'. In terms of content, 21st-century PBA continues to carry multiple layers of meaning. Although an important element of assessing organizations' operation and performance, datafied PBA is no longer a singular moment; rather, it tends to become a much more all-encompassing, standardizing and integrating organizational specialization. Indeed, processes of digitalization and automatization in the provision and assessment of all types of public services have reinforced this trend.

Datafied accountability is no longer simply a property of the service offered. Data allow both the further abstraction of the concept of accountability *and* its huge expansion. The explosion of quantified and standardized accountability tools and sanctions enable them to travel from organization to organization within nations but also transnationally; as a result, the influence of accountability specialists increases (Power, 2003). Datafied accountability is applied to service management, and later to services delivered by the public sector, and includes a broader range of performance indicators than ever. School browsers in numerous educational settings offer data not only about learning achievement, but also about effective leadership, school climate, family involvement or levels of trust. Schools, universities and hospitals become datafied, measurable organizations in the abstract, and, in that capacity, they are expected to be perpetually accountable.

Not only key decisions, but also the core functions of these organizations are increasingly shaped by accountability and performance analytics tools.

The integration of accountability into organizational – and especially statistical and managerial – thinking has interesting implications. In the datafication era, accountability clearly becomes something which cannot be left to chance. It cannot simply be left to the teaching profession either. It is no longer an afterthought, a question of whether organizations that spend taxpayers' money are doing their job satisfactorily or not. Rather, PBA becomes a question of good leadership and organization. In the era of datafication, accountability must now be represented statistically at all times. It is no longer extra-ordinary, a moment in the cycle of good governance. It becomes simply what can be continuously expected by all organizations. PBA in the era of datafication relates closely to horizontal governance processes; it is closely linked to quality assurance; and it is guaranteed through the collection, analysis and communication of robust statistical evidence and a thorough conformity with standards.

Research perspectives

Under these new datafied and increasingly commercialized conditions of producing education policy, we need the application of interdisciplinary theorizations of accountability in order to make sense of the landscape.

While we accept that a global education policy field may be emerging (Ozga and Lingard, 2007), we suggest that more attention needs to be paid to the levers or mechanisms through which accountability processes and effects are produced in 'local' states (Dale, 1999), along with exploration of how global accountability agendas may be mediated by local and national history and politics. We explore accountability types and regimes as sites for the interaction of 'global', 'regional' and 'local' policy in education/learning that capture the influence of historically embedded assumptions and beliefs on the mediation of global policy trends and pressures (Ozga, 2005; Newman and Clarke, 2009). Linked to this is also our approach to the reshaping of governance as challenging nation-states' sovereignty (Sassen, 2007), and operating as a 'mobius web' top-down, bottom-up and side by side all at once (Rosenau, 2005: 145). In these new education governance forms, datafication plays a highly significant role: data make the spaces to be governed visible and comparable, and they allow for the operation of the new networked, horizontal and flexible accounting forms that are replacing conventional 'systems' with their hierarchical ordering of activity.

In considering new governing forms, the book engages with the ways in which national processes adapt and work with datafied accountability. These developments are tracked through different levels in national and regional systems, but also at the level of large global monitoring programmes, illustrating divergent and convergent responses to accountability demands. The book therefore reports on very rich data, at all levels across and within the education systems under study, and with reference to transnational policy actors and networks.

The book is organized around the key themes of *Accountability* and *Datafication* and their interdependency, as illustrated by rich analysis of cases developed from all the book's authors. We are preoccupied with the interrelationships between transnational demands and national 'translations' of these accountability demands, with negotiations between and across levels and contexts, with the emergence of networks that challenge ideas of vertical organizational forms in education governance, and with the simultaneous development of constant comparison of performance and the role of private and philanthropic actors. At the heart of this edited collection is a consideration of the ways these processes relate to one another, and the extent to which they form a coherent governing technology.

Next, we present in more detail the three main lines of inquiry of the book, namely, the global production of PBA; trajectories and translations; and enactment dynamics.

The global production of PBA and performance metrics

Scholarship on the role of data in governing societies has been burgeoning and has attracted multiple fields of study, including sociology, history, political science, geography, anthropology, philosophy, science and technology studies, and others. Prominent authors have written lucidly about the role of numbers in the making of modern states and the governing role of performance metrics in various areas of public policy and social life (Alonso and Starr, 1987; Desrosières, 1998; Espeland and Stevens, 2008; Hacking, 1990, 2007; Porter, 1995; Power, 1997; Rose, 1999). Similarly, anthropologies of numbers suggest that datafication has had fundamental effects not only on public policy but on our lived experience, too: 'our lives are increasingly governed by – and through – numbers, indicators, algorithms and audits and the ever-present concerns with the management of risk' (Shore and Wright, 2015: 23; see also influential work by Merry, 2011; Sauder and Espeland, 2009; Strathern, 2000; Mangez and Vanden Broeck in this volume).

Nonetheless, despite the increasing number of publications on global datafication, our understanding of the relationship of the politics of performance metrics and the making of performance-based accountability is less well examined. What are the properties of datafication that would suggest such a central role in the production of performance-based accountability? By contrasting data to language, Hansen and Porter (2012) suggest that, although it took scholars a long time to recognize the constitutive nature of discourse, we are now well aware of the role of language in shaping reality. However, they suggest that datafication is characterized by additional qualities that make its influence much more pervasive than words: these elements are order; mobility; stability; combinability; and precision. By using the example of the barcode, they lucidly illustrate 'how numerical operations at different levels powerfully contribute to the ordering of the transnational activities of states, businesses and people' (2012: 410). They suggest the need to focus not only on the nominal qualities of the data themselves but also, according to Hacking, on 'the people classified, the experts who classify, study and help them, the institutions within which the experts and their subjects interact, and through which authorities control' (2007: 295) (see Fontdevila and Grek in this volume).

It is precisely on the forms and functions of datafication in PBA that this book focuses. Following the literature on the capacities of global performance metrics to both be stable yet travel fast and without borders, the book casts light on what Latour called 'the few obligatory passage points' (1987: 245): in their movement, data go through successive reductions of complexity until they reach a simplified enough state that can travel back 'from the field to the laboratory, from a distant land to the map-maker's table' (Hansen and Porter, 2012: 412). PBA, in all its forms and effects, represents such a multifaceted and ever-changing 'centre of calculation'. This does not suggest, however, that PBA is significant only in terms of its evaluative and knowledge production capacities. By examining specifically the role of datafication in accountability, this book elucidates PBA's governance effects; consequently, following the extensive analysis above, if we consider datafied PBA as central in the production of organizational action, we can infer that the operation of performance metrics as knowledge gatherers, controllers and distributors must have crucial governing impact (see, for example, Williamson; Hartong and Breiter in this volume). Indeed, Shore and Wright argue that, 'while numbers and 'facts' have both knowledge effects and governance effects, it is also important to consider how these are produced, who designs them, what underlying assumptions about society shape the choice of what to measure, how they deal with missing data, and what interests they serve' (2015: 433).

Trajectories and translations

If datafication and PBA policies are spreading to many regions and nation-states around the world, it is due to the favourable conditions that different forms of globalization create. These include economic globalization, which affects economic interdependencies and forms of competition (around human capital and technological innovations), political globalization, which affects the forms and scales of construction of 'policies' (particularly educational), and, more broadly, the exercise of power and political regulation over societies (multi-governance and multi-regulation). Moreover, globalization is made possible but also accelerates major socio-technical transformations (datafication, digitalization). These multiple transformations accentuate PBA policies, whose testing, benchmarking and accountability tools further embolden the processes of quantifying and measuring the world, as Mangez and Vanden Broeck highlight in this volume. Datafication of education and PBA are therefore mutually reinforcing processes, as global interdependencies between actors or nation-states develop (Lingard et al., 2016).

However, globalization cannot be reduced merely to changes in economic, technological or political structures; it also manifests itself in new forms of global players whose strategies and power are undoubtedly increasingly important. We have thus stressed the importance of international or transnational public action sites and networks, the role of UNESCO (see Grek and Fontdevila in this volume) and the OECD in the production and active circulation of indicators, testing and technical and political infrastructures conducive to the development of a process of PBA (see Lingard in this volume). In this volume, Gorur and Addey show that OECD is actively creating the political and technical conditions that favour an active use of the PISA-D by local experts and decision-makers in Cambodia, a process that they analyse as 'a third translation' changing the local education policy process. The OECD is, in fact, accentuating the quantification and accountability of education through the continuous extension of its data-based regulation tools. Its testing tools extend the coverage of the quantification and comparison of educational results at the geographical level (see Gorur and Addey; Oliveira and Carvalho in this volume), in terms of the skills measured (cognitive and non-cognitive), of the target populations (from young people to adults), but also according to the agent that one wishes to make accountable, which range from individuals to local organizations (with PISA-schools) and national school systems.

Often with the assistance of and in network with transnational state organizations, private companies or philanthropic foundations (national or transnational) also play major roles in the production, circulation and legitimization of the instrumentation of PBA or datafication (see Williamson; Gorur and Addey; Oliveira and Carvalho in this volume).

Do these developments suggest, however, that the dissemination of PBA tools and ideas is linear, mechanical, the sole effect of a 'top-down' coercive mechanism linked to certain transnational agencies? And would this suggest that the dissemination and use of such similar policy tools and assemblages (testing, datafication, PBA) 'naturally' leads to the diagnosis of an apparent convergence of educational policies and practices? The second part of this book shows that, contrary to the normative arguments of isomorphism and policy mimesis, these global trends are modulated, mediated and constrained by various factors that sustain forms of diversity, both in terms of goals, tools and legitimizing discourses but also in terms of the effects of these policies. Indeed, it is important to consider various types of factors and conditions that are at stake in processes of mediation and translation of transnational discourses, tools and models, at various interwoven levels (national, regional, local).

At the level of nation-states, it is necessary to consider the full historical depth and morphology of school systems, the long trajectories of education policies, and more specifically those of accountability per se or testing. Indeed, as historical institutionalism has already pointed out, institutions (understood in the broad sense of formal devices and rules, but also of shared norms, sanctioned by third parties) can indeed draw path-dependencies that constrain the possible paths of reform (Thelen and Conran, 2016), and lead to particular translations (and transformations) of transnational models/tools, in order to favor their local legitimization (Callon, 1986; Campbell, 2004). PBA policies thus develop in specific trajectories, marked by the configurations of the actors involved and several institutional mechanisms of change: processes of sedimentation of the tools mobilized; gradual conversion of existing institutions; and bricolage of policies and tools to make them politically or normatively acceptable are at stake, given the strength of resistance or opposition (Maroy and Pons, 2019). These processes are oriented towards gradual or 'incremental' transformations of the institutional or technical arrangements of each system; more rarely, following more significant external 'shocks' and the mobilization of powerful change entrepreneurs, the transformations may be more 'radical' (Campbell, 2004).

Thus, in this book, Maroy et al. highlight the long-term processes that have led to the development of more or less coherent and influential PBA policies in several French-speaking countries: in France, significant opposition from the teaching profession has led to a very weak institutionalization of testing and accountability, while in Quebec, the relay of school administrators has favoured a greater appropriation and dissemination of results-based management. In Belgium, the PBA policy considers the institutions of the prevailing regime of consociational democracy: the result is a failure to compare the performance of the various networks of school operators, which runs counter to the principles of new public management.

In the Scandinavian countries, Skedsmo et al. emphasize, with the concept of 'instrument constituencies', that the Nordic welfare state model has been variously and partially reworked or preserved, according to the actors who supported the implementation of the new PBA tools. Oliveira and Carvalho, in the case of Brazil, also underline the tensions between the various sources of a 'multi-regulation' that is the bearer of PBA, whose orientations and tools are not always adjusted and compatible according to the sources (regional, federal or transnational). Moreover, depending on the regional states, different types of PBAs are set up according to the very unequal socio-economic contexts, but also according to the contrasting political and ideological orientations of the governments in power. The trajectory of PBA and the changing uses of national assessments are also subject to the veto power of key educational stakeholders such as teachers' unions, as Chilenga-Butao, Ehren and Pakade (in this volume) make clear in their detailed study of the South African case.

Thus, the long trajectory of policies, the historical memory of states and institutions, the political cultures of reference, actors' political games and bricolage of tools, must be considered in order to understand the national mediations of transnational trends and the specific translations of their tools, models or discourses. Finally, cultural practices of even longer duration also have to go through these political and institutional mediations, and translate and adjust, as the study of the Chinese case by Normand and Zhou (in this volume) underlines.

Within each state entity as well, it is also necessary to consider domestic factors of internal diversification and local mediation of global trends, as the latter have already been recontextualized by the political and institutional level of each national (or federal) jurisdiction. At that intermediate (district, regional) or local level, there can be further differentiation to and appropriating national political orientations or tools by local organizations. The latter are in fact conditioned and inscribed in contingent 'local orders' (Ben Ayed, 2009), by local organizational cultures, specific economic and social contexts, or different local community projects (educational or institutional). All these elements play out differently according to their varying logics of appropriation of national PBA policies, as shown in particular in the chapters by Oliveira and Carvalho, Verger et al., or Maroy et al. in this volume.

Enactment dynamics

Although the promises offered by PBA and its apologists are usually high, the evidence on the circumstances and mechanisms under which these policy initiatives generate their intended effects or, otherwise, side-effects or unintended consequences remains inconclusive. A number of studies indicate that standards and accountability have the potential to generate increased awareness and motivation, leading to the adoption of targeted development strategies and changes in instruction (Chiang, 2009) and have a positive impact on student achievement (Hanushek and Raymond, 2005). Nevertheless, there have been numerous studies which, on the contrary, show that the relationship between accountability and performance cannot be taken for granted (Dubnick, 2005) and that PBA has the potential of generating side-effects, gaming strategies and opportunistic behaviours amongst school providers (Au, 2007; Elstad and Turmo, 2011). Up until today, evidence remains inconclusive regarding the specific conditions and mechanisms likely to generate which types of effects on the teaching profession and on school actors' practices and behaviour.

The very disparate results that the existing research on the effects of PBA policies reaches is, to a great extent, the consequence of how diverse PBA systems can be, but also of how diverse the institutional and social contexts where PBA is implemented are. As shown above, PBA can be articulated very differently according to who gives the account, how the account-giver is evaluated and by whom, according to what sources of data and measures, and what are the consequences of the evaluation results. These specific policy options, together with contrasting programme ontologies that might prevail behind accountability and other data-intensive instruments, which also differs country by country, makes each PBA system unique (Maroy and Voisin, 2013).

Therefore, the adoption of comparative perspectives both between- and intra-countries allow us to reflect on how different accountability designs might generate different effects when enacted at district and school levels in diverse institutional and school settings. As Pallas in this volume eloquently shows, policy design features (such as the level of ambition of the learning goals, whether learning goals are related to proficiency thresholds or to growth models, or the nature of the rewards and sanctions associated to goals' achievement) condition how conducive PBA systems are to learning achievement, but also to score inflation and related educational practices such as item-teaching.

Contributions to this volume also look at the implications of different PBA configurations for educational equity and quality. Voisin examines both high-stakes and lower-stakes accountability systems, enabling a fruitful comparison between both types of accountability regimes and thus explicating the homogenizing and diversifying effects of PBA assemblages and enactments. She concludes that PBA systems that incentivize teachers for performance are related with lower levels of aggregate outcomes and higher inequality in the achievement of basic skills, whereas the association between lower-stakes systems and learning outcomes is rather spurious.

Nonetheless, the effects of PBA systems, given their nature as a policy instrument, are not only understood as contingent to design characteristics or to the technical decisions that regulators take. In real education settings, PBA systems are co-constructed by a range of intermediary and street-level agents, such as local governments, teachers, school principals and families, who are actively involved in the process of transferring, translating and re-contextualizing PBA instruments from regulatory frameworks to everyday practices. This process of co-construction is, at the same time, markedly influenced by the changing social relations that PBA involves both between and across different forms of educational agency. From the enactment perspective, it is thus crucial to understand that PBA systems might differ in how policy actors interpret and re-signify PBA-related instruments, and to analyze how actors' educational views and collective and/or individual interests shape such varying perceptions. Furthermore, when enacted, PBA instruments interact critically with other education policies in place, other forms of accountability (bureaucratic, market, social) and different socio-economic realities. In this sense, not only do PBA systems diverge from country to country, but their final outcomes are also contingent to a broad range of more localized dimensions.

We can therefore infer that the social, educational and institutional effects of PBA instruments are the outcome of the 'sense-making' processes that these instruments trigger among education actors, their creative uses by local school managers and school leaders, and their articulation with specific instructional or pedagogical strategies and educational legacies in socially situated contexts. In this volume, Verger, Ferrer and Parcerisa, by analyzing how teachers and principals experience and make sense of accountability pressures in the highly segmented Chilean educational system, construct a typology of school responses to PBA which goes beyond more conventional alignment-decoupling classifications, and includes a more varying range of options. Amongst the diverse responses to PBA, dissenting voices are also common, as Lingard's rich analysis of parent activist groups against high-stakes testing in New York State shows in this volume.

PBA is not only affecting teachers' behaviour, work and decisions about pedagogy, instruction and evaluation. As Ball (2003) has famously argued, the intensification of PBA also alters teachers' professional subjectivities, identities and their way of being in and understanding the world. Holloway and Goel, in this volume, echo and develop this argument by showing how, currently, performativity and datafication are two complementary technologies of governance that interact in the production of a new kind of teacher subject: the datafied teacher.

Conclusion

The development of accountability as a form of governing is of major significance in understanding education policy and the development of a knowledge society/ knowledge economy as a key policy objective in the ever-changing governance of education in different world regions (Lawn and Lingard, 2002; Novoa and Lawn, 2002). The new, innovative argument introduced in this book is the impact that datafication and the 'performance–evaluation' nexus (Clarke, 2009) has had in the design, trajectory and enactments of performance-based accountability, and on the importance of analysing these trends from a policy instruments perspective. In contrast to most literature which largely understands developments in performance measurement and management in 'common sense' terms (i.e. as vehicles for improved policymaking and better-informed pedagogic practice at school level), the contributions gathered in this volume question the assumption that PBA must, by its very nature, and despite the very significant costs in time and money, contribute to system and individual improvement (Dahler-Larsen, 2004; Segerholm, 2001). On the other hand, as the chapters which follow will extensively show, PBA as a policy instrument is only part (but also parcel) of the wider socio-historical and cultural changes in which it was born; as such, it needs to be disentangled and made sense in relation to the specificity of contexts, time periods and events in which it occurs and perpetuates.

Notes

1   All authors have contributed equally to this work. This work has been supported by the European Research Council under the European Union's 'Horizon 2020 Framework Programme for Research and Innovation' [GA-680172 – REFORMED and GA-715125 METRO].
2   Number of typologies of accountability are available in the education research literature (for example, Dupriez and Mons, 2011; Kogan, 1988; Leithwood et al., 1999; Maroy, 2015; Maroy and Voisin, 2013; Ranson, 2003; West, Mattei and Roberts, 2011) or in political science (Bovens et al., 2014).
3   Our translation; see also, Le Galès (2016).

References

Alonso, W., & Starr, P. (Eds.). (1987). *The Politics of Numbers*. New York: Russell Sage Foundation.
Altrichter, H., & Kemethofer, D. (2015). Does accountability pressure through school inspections promote school improvement? *School Effectiveness and School Improvement*, 26(1), 32–56.
Au, W. (2007). High-stakes testing and curricular control: A qualitative metasynthesis. *Educational Researcher*, 36(5), 258–267.
Ball, S. J. (2003). The teacher's soul and the terrors of performativity. *Journal of Education Policy*, 18(2), 215–228.
Barbana, S., Dumay, X., & Dupriez, V. (2014). Perceptions et usages des instruments d'accountability. Enquête exploratoire dans l'enseignement secondaire en Belgique francophone. *Éducation Compare*, 12, 21–44.
Ben Ayed, C. (2009). *Le nouvel ordre éducatif local*. Paris: Presses universitaires de France.
Bezes, P. (2005). Le renouveau du contrôle des bureaucraties. L'impact du New Public Management. *Informations sociales*, 126(6), 26–37.
Biesta, G. J. J. (2004). Education, accountability, and the ethical demand: Can the democratic potential of accountability be regained? *Educational Theory*, 54(3), 233–250.
Bovens, M. (2007). Analysing and assessing accountability: A conceptual framework. *European Law Journal*, 13(4), 447–468.
Bovens, M. (2010). Two concepts of accountability: Accountability as a virtue and as a mechanism. *West European Politics*, 33(5), 946–967.

Bovens, M., Goodin, R. E., & Schillemans, T. (Eds.). (2014). *The Oxford Handbook of Public Accountability*. Oxford: Oxford University Press.

Callon, M. (1986). Some elements of a sociology of translation: Domestication of the scallops and the fisherman in St Brieuc Bay. In K. Knorr-Cetina & A. V. Cicourel (Eds.), *Advances in Social Theory and Methodology: Toward an Integration of Micro and Macro-Sociologies* (pp. 196–223). Boston, MA: Routledge & Kegan Paul.

Campbell, J. L. (2004). *Institutional Change and Globalization*. Princeton, NJ: Princeton University Press.

Carnoy, M. (2016). Educational policies in the face of globalization: Whither the Nation State? In K. Mundy, A. Green, R. Lingard, & A. Verger (Eds.), *Handbook of Global Policy and Policy-Making in Education* (pp. 27–42). West Sussex, UK: Wiley-Blackwell.

Carnoy, M., Elmore, R., & Siskin, L. (2003). *The New Accountability: High Schools and High-Stakes Testing*. New York: Routledge.

Chiang, H. (2009). How accountability pressure on failing schools affects student achievement. *Journal of Public Economics*, 93(9), 1045–1057.

Dale, R. (1999). Specifying globalization effects on national policy: a focus on the mechanisms. *Journal of Education Policy*, 14(1), 1–17. Retrieved from http://www.informaworld.com/10.1080/026809399286468

Darling-Hammond, L. (2006). *Standards, Assessments, and Educational Policy: In Pursuit of Genuine Accountability*. Princeton, NJ: Educational Testing Service.

De Mello, L., & Padoan, P. (2010). Promoting potential growth: The role of structural reform. OECD Economics Department Working Papers, No. 793, OECD Publishing, Paris.

Desrosières, A. (1998). *The Politics of Large Numbers: A History of Statistical Reasoning*. Cambridge, MA: Harvard University Press.

Diaz-Bone, R., & Didier, E. (2016). The sociology of quantification – Perspectives on an emerging field in the social sciences. *Historical Social Research*, 41(2), 7–26.

Dupriez, V., & Mons, N. (2011). Les politiques d'accountability. Du changement institutionnel aux transformations locales. *Education Comparée* (5), 7-16.

Elstad, E., & Turmo, A. (2011). Obeying the rules or gaming the system? Delegating random selection for examinations to head teachers within an accountability system. *Education, Knowledge and Economy*, 5(1-2), 1–15.

Espeland, W., & Stevens, M. L. (2008). A sociology of quantification. *Archives Europeennes de Sociologie*, 49(3), 401–436.

Espeland, W. N., & Vannebo, B. I. (2007). Accountability, quantification, and law. *Annual Review of Law and Social Science*, 3(1), 21–43.

Falabella, A. (2020). The ethics of competition: accountability policy enactment in Chilean schools' everyday life. *Journal of Education Policy*, 35(1), 23–45.

Figlio, D., & Loeb, S. (2011). School accountability. In E. A. Hanushek, S. Machin, & L. Woessmann (Eds.), *Handbooks in Economics* (Vol. 3, pp. 383–421). Amsterdam, the Netherlands: North-Holland.

Fullan, M. (2007). *The New Meaning of Educational Change* (4th ed.). New York: Teachers College Press.

Fullan, M., Rincon-Gallardo, S., & Hargreaves, A. (2015). Professional capital as accountability. *Education Policy Analysis Archives*, 23(15), 1–17.

Garfinkel, H. (2016). *Seeing Sociologically: The Routine Grounds of Social Action*. Abingdon, Oxon: Routledge.

Gorur, R. (2013). My school, my market. *Discourse: Studies in the Cultural Politics of Education*, 34(2), 214–230

Grek, S. (2009). Governing by numbers: The PISA 'effect' in Europe. *Journal of Education Policy*, 24(1), 23–37.

Gunter, H. M., Grimaldi, E., Hall, D., & Serpieri, R. (2016). NPM and the dynamics of education policy and practice in Europe, in H. M. Gunter, E. Grimaldi, D. Hall, & R. Serpieri (Eds.), *New Public Management and the Reform of Education: European Lessons for Policy and Practice* (pp. 3–17). London: Routledge.

Hacking, I. (1990). *The Taming of Chance*. Cambridge: Cambridge University Press.

Hacking, I. (2007). Kinds of people: Moving targets. *Proceedings of the British Academy*, 151, 285–318.

Hall, J. B., & Sivesind, K. (2014). State school inspection policy in Norway and Sweden (2002–2012): A reconfiguration of governing modes? *Journal of Education Policy*, 30(3), 429–458.

Halpern, C., Lascoumes, P., & Le Galès, P. (Eds.). (2012). *L'instrumentation de l'action publique*. Paris: SciencePo. Les Presses.

Hansen, K., & Porter, T. (2012). What do numbers do in transnational governance? *International Political Sociology*, 6, 409–426.

Hanushek, E. A., & Raymond, M. E. (2005). Does school accountability lead to improved student performance? *Journal of Policy Analysis and Management*, 24(2), 297–327.

Hanushek, E. A., & Woessmann, L. (2008). The role of cognitive skills in economic development. *Journal of Economic Literature*, 46(3), 607–668.

Hargreaves, D. H. (1996). *Teaching as a Research-Based Profession: Possibilities and Prospects*. London: TTA.

Jarke, J., & Breiter, A. (2019). Editorial: The datification of education. *Learning, Media and Technology*, 44(1), 1–6.

Kamens, D. H., & McNeely, C. L. (2010). Globalization and the growth of International Educational Testing and National Assessment. *Comparative Education Review*, 54(1), 5–25.

Kauko, J., Rinne, R., & Takala, T. (Eds.). (2018). *Politics of Quality in Education: A Comparative Atudy of Brazil, China, and Russia*. London: Routledge.

Kogan, M. (1988). *Education Accountability: An Analytic Overview*. London: Dover, NH, USA Hutchinson Education.

Landri, P. (2018). *Digital Governance of Education: Technology, Standards and Europeanization of Education*. London: Bloomsbury Publishing.

Lascoumes, P. (2004). La Gouvernementalité: de la critique de l'Etat aux technologies du pouvoir. *Le Portique (En ligne)*, 13–14.

Lascoumes, P., & Le Galès, P. (2004). *Gouverner par les instruments*. Paris: Presses de la fondation nationale des sciences politiques.

Lascoumes, P., & Simard, L. (2011). L'action publique au prisme de ses instruments. *Revue française de science politique*, 61(1), 5–22.

Latour, B. (1987). *Science in Action: How to Follow Scientists and Engineers through Society*. Cambridge: Harvard University Press.

Le Galès, P. (2016). Performance measurement as a policy instrument. *Policy Studies*, 37(6), 508–520.

Leithwood, K., Edge, K., & Jantzi, D. (1999). *Educational Accountability: The State of the Art International Network of Innovative School Systems (INIS)*. Gütersloh: Bertelsmann Foundation Publishers.

Lindberg, S. I. (2013). Mapping accountability: Core concept and subtypes. *International Review of Administrative Sciences*, 79(2), 202–226.

Lingard, B., Martino, W., Rezai-Rashti, G., & Sellar, S. (2016). *Globalizing Educational Accountabilities*. New York: Routledge.

Maroy, C. (2009). Convergences and hybridization of educational policies around 'post-bureaucratic' models of regulation. *Compare*, 39(1), 71–84.

Maroy, C. (2015). Comparing accountability policy tools and rationales: Various ways, various effects? In H.-G. Kotthoff, & E. Klerides (Eds.), *Governing Educational Spaces : Knowledge, Teaching and Learning in Transition* (pp. 35–58). Boston; Rotterdam; Taipei: Sense Publishers.

Maroy, C., & Voisin, A. (2013). Les transformations récentes des politiques d'accountability en éducation: enjeux et incidences des outils d'action publique. *Educaçao & sociedade*, 34(124), 881–901.

Maroy, C., & Pons, X. (Eds.). (2019). *Accountability Policies in Education. A Comparative and Multilevel Analysis in France and Quebec*. Basel: Springer.

Mattei, P. (2012). Market accountability in schools: Policy reforms in England, Germany, France and Italy. *Oxford Review of Education*, 38(3), 247–266.

Mennicken, A., & Espeland, W. N. (2019). What's new with numbers? Sociological approaches to the study of quantification. *Annual Review of Sociology*, 45(1), 223–245.

Merry, S. E. (2011). Measuring the world. Indicators, human rights, and global governance. *Current Anthropology*, 52, S83–S95.

Meyer, H. D., and A. Benavot, eds (2013), *PISA, power, and policy: The emergence of global educational governance*, Oxford: Symposium Books

Mundy, K., Green, A., Lingard, B., & Verger, A. (Eds.). (2016). *The Handbook of Global Education Policy*. Chichester, UK; Malden, MA: Wiley Blackwell.

Nóvoa, A., & Lawn, M. (2002). *Fabricating Europe. The formation of an education space*. Dordrecht: Kluwer academic publishers.

OECD. (2013), *Synergies for Better Learning: An International Perspective on Evaluation and Assessment*. Paris: OECD

O'Neill, A.-M. (2015). The New Zealand experiment: Assessment-driven curriculum – Managing standards, competition and performance to strengthen governmentality. *Journal of Education Policy*, 30(6), 831–854.

Olsen, J. (2017). *Democratic Accountability, Political Order, and Change: Exploring Accountability Processes in an Era of European Transformation*. Oxford: Oxford University Press.

Ozga, J. (2013). Accountability as a policy technology: Accounting for education performance in Europe. *International Review of Administrative Sciences*, 79(2), 292–309.

Ozga, J., & Grek, S. (2012). Governing through learning. School self-evaluation as a knowledge-based regulatory tool. *Recherches Sociologiques et anthropologiques*, 43(2), 35–52.

Pal, L. (2012). *Frontiers of Governance: The OECD and Global Public Management Reform*. Dordrecht, the Netherlands: Springer.

Porter, T. (1995). *Trust in Numbers: The Pursuit of Objectivity in Science and Public Life*. Princeton, NJ: Princeton University Press.

Power, M. (1997). *The Audit Society: Rituals of Verification*. Oxford: Oxford University Press.

Power, M. (2007). *The Audit Society*. Oxford: Oxford University Press.

Ranson, S. (2003). Public accountability in the age of neoliberal governance. *Journal of Education Policy*, 18(5), 459–480.

Rosanvallon, P. (2008). *La légitimité démocratique. Impartialité, réflexivité, proximité*. Paris: Seuil.

Rose, N. (1999). *Powers of Freedom: Reframing Political Thought*. Cambridge: Cambridge University Press.

Sassen, S. (2007). *La globalisation. Une sociologie*. Paris: Gallimard.

Sauder, M., & Espeland, W. (2009). The discipline of rankings: Tight coupling and organizational change. *American Sociological Review*, 74, 63–82.

Sellar, S. (2015). Data infrastructure: A review of expanding accountability systems and large-scale assessments in education. *Discourse: Studies in the Cultural Politics of Education*, 36(5), 765–777.

Sellar, S., Thompson, G., & Rutkowski, D. (2017). *The Global Education Race: Taking the Measure of PISA and International Testing*. Toronto: Brush Education.

Shore, C., & Wright, S. (2015). Audit culture revisited: Ratings, rankings and the reassembling of society. *Current Anthropology*, 56(3), 421–444.

Soguel, N. C., & Jaccard, P. (2008). *Governance and Performance of Education Systems*. Dordrecht, the Netherlands: Springer.

Smith, W.C. (2016). *The Global Testing Culture: Shaping Education Policy, Perceptions, and Practice*. Oxford: Symposium.

Strathern, M. (Ed.). (2000). *Audit Cultures: Anthropological Studies in Accountability, Ethics, and the Academy*. London: Routledge.

Thelen, K., & Conran, J. (2016). Institutional change. In O. Fioretos, T. G. Faletti, & A. Sheingate (Eds.), *The Oxford Handbook of Historical Institutionalism*. Oxford: Oxford University Press.

Verger, A., Parcerisa, L., & Fontdevila, C. (2019a). The growth and spread of large-scale assessments and test-based accountabilities: A political sociology of global education reforms. *Educational Review*, 71(1), 5–30.

Verger, A., Fontdevila, C., & Parcerisa, L. (2019b). Reforming governance through policy instruments: How and to what extent standards, tests and accountability in education spread worldwide. *Discourse: Studies in the Cultural Politics of Education*, 40(2), 248–270.

Veselý, A. (2013). Accountability in Central and Eastern Europe: Concept and reality. *International Review of Administrative Sciences*, 79(2), 310–330.

Vigoda, E. (2003). New public management. In *Encyclopedia of Public Administration and Public Policy* (Vol. 2, pp. 812–816). New York: Marcel Dekker.

Weber, M. (2019). *Economy and Society: A New Translation*. Cambridge, MA: Harvard University Press.

West, A., Mattei, P., & Roberts, J. (2011). Accountability and sanctions in English schools. *British Journal of Educational Studies*, 59(1), 41–62.

Williamson, B. (2017). *Big Data in Education: The Digital Future of Learning, Policy and Practice*. London: SAGE Publications.

Part I

The global/local construction of accountability and datafication

1 The construction of worlds: On the function and fiction of quantified data in education policy

Eric Mangez and Pieter Vanden Broeck

This article is part of a research project funded by the Concerted Research Action (ARC) programme of the French Community of Belgium.

Introduction

'Educational reform movements would not have been able to get started without quantitative comparisons', the German sociologist Niklas Luhmann (1981/2010) once remarked, pointing out concisely and not without irony how the warm intentions of well-meaning reformers go hand in hand with stone-cold numbers. In this chapter, we present an overview of how Luhmann's systems theory, and in particular a subsequent generation of scholars working within his theoretical framework, deals with the issues of quantification and educational reform. The ambition is thus to unearth its rather distinctive position on the sociological land-scape – one all too often left unheard – which offers a different vista on reform efforts and the role of numbers, challenging many of the accounts currently more in vogue.

As a first taste, it is worth mentioning that systems theory cannot readily sub-scribe to the ubiquitous mantra of 'governance by numbers'. By such an assertion we do not so much mean that systems theory necessarily remains blind to the transition to (usually supranational) governance mechanisms and how these dif-fer greatly from the conventional governing-via-government practised on a national scale (for more or less recent examples, *cf.* Thornhill 2011 or Kjaer 2015). Rather, such a conclusion takes stock of the extensive body of literature in which systems theory has put some welcome question marks next to explanations that, perhaps precisely in their all too eager attempt to unmask latent sources of power, blindly re-affirm the ability to steer society according to political specifications. Especially in the domain of education, it is widely assumed and accepted that policy is capable of shaping, indeed of governing educational praxis. That such an assumption is commonly contradicted by reforms failing to live up to their own ambitions, is then usually remedied by speaking of flawed implementations or diverging policy enactments. Seldom, if ever, have such outcomes led the schol-arly debate to question with more radicality the implied causality between policy and education. Systems theory, as we wish to demonstrate in this chapter, might bring a valuable contribution here.

Like so many things today, the reform of education systems is a worldwide phenomenon and, as we will show later on, one of systems theory's acknowledged merits indeed lies in the elaboration of that observation. What sets educational reforms apart, however, is their particularly recurrent nature: 'reforming again, again, and again', as Larry Cuban (1990) has famously summarized the idea. Even beyond the differences that might characterize its numerous national settings, education as a whole appears to be deeply marked by the conviction that changing how instruction is structured or organized is necessary, virtuous and, above all, feasible. As Giancarlo Corsi (1998) has commented, we are facing a *syndrome* of sorts – a curious tendency towards continuous self-negation, which stretches well beyond isolated cases or conjunctural trends. However, contrary to what the literature around the aforementioned Cuban and David Tyack (1995) has concluded, systems theory does not refer to a fixed, unshakeable 'grammar of schooling' in order to explain the often-disappointing results of so much reform fervour.

This, of course, raises the question as to what systems theory *can* say about quantification and educational reform. If numbers are not depicted as steering education and if the latter's inertia is not explained by implementation effects or by the tenacious hold that an immutable grammar of school exerts, how is the relationship between the two to be understood? Surveying how systems theory has answered this question, we will argue in this chapter that the theory's overall contribution consists in the subtle inversion already visible in the quotation we began with: numbers are not so much a tool for decision-makers to wield power with, as they are a historically situated mechanism by which the social world increasingly opens up for decision-making. Quantification itself, the thesis goes, fuels a need for decisions and action. It drives society away from an institutional order based on invariable being towards a 'cosmology of contingency' (Luhmann 2005, p. 39), where everything that is shown by numbers, at once reveals the promise of difference and change – more, less, better or worse, but above all no longer necessarily the same. In order to make this argument, we will first review how the historical emergence of statistics since the 17th century has been dealt with as an instrument to double reality, offering a probable duplicate of reality from where to address future uncertainties. Next, we will step to the more current usage of numbers in education, and review how they establish education as a global affair. In both cases, we argue, systems theory shows quantification as the construction of worlds – *speculum* and *artifex mundi* at once. In conclusion, we return to the steering question and elucidate Luhmann's theorem of functional differentiation, together with its implications for educational policy.

Doubling reality

Today, we are largely accustomed to the ubiquity of numbers and their statistical elaboration into rates, estimates and rankings. We depend on them in the most diverse situations of our lives, ranging from deciding where to live or work up to even more mundane tasks, such as pondering what clothes to wear tomorrow or which groceries (not) to buy. In the domain of education too, of course, quantification is omnipresent, where it is used to express how pupils, but increasingly also teachers, individual schools or national schooling regimes, have been evaluated. We will return to this given later. It is easy to forget, we should underline first, that from a historical perspective such abundant presence of numbers is a rather curious novelty. Many of the statistical measures we routinely rely on were developed less than two centuries ago, Theodore Porter (1986) reminds us. The current numerical abundance – in electoral polls, economic growth rates, climate forecasts and many more – is hence a typically *modern* phenomenon and one of the more original contributions systems theory has made to the scholarly debate starts precisely from this simple observation.

In her work on the improbable success of probability theory, Elena Esposito (2008a) points out with a rich and detailed historical analysis how the birth of chance theory, followed later by modern statistics, intriguingly coincides with the emergence of the modern novel and the deployment of perspective in the visual arts. What such parallel changes have in common, she argues, is that they all constitute instances of an unexpected upheaval in which reality gives way to elaborate fictitious constructions, which rebuild that reality and, strangely enough, often become regarded as more informative than reality itself. The case of statistics is a particularly telling one: today, surveys and numeric revelations of various kinds are considered as referring to the reality of the world. But at its origins, statistical calculations served to unravel the obscure realm of uncertainty and opinions, the non-real sphere par excellence, Esposito (2008a, p. 8) points out and hence asks: 'How can we explain this shift of accent whereby the unreal takes the place of the real?'

At its core, the question boils down to modernity's changed conception of reality and, in a fashion characteristic of systems theory, Esposito approaches such a shifting conception of the real by addressing its opposite – its fictions – in order to understand how the difference between the two is established. Before we turn to this reshuffling distinction between what is real and not real, the reasons Esposito advances for this shift are worth mentioning, since they highlight the rise of statistics as an expression of (if not a coping mechanism for) the radical changes with which systems theory characterizes modernity. These changes can be summarized as the following double movement. First, as Luhmann's oeuvre extensively elaborates, modernity is in many ways the historical moment wherein a normative concept of nature starts to wane. The nature of things denotes no longer necessarily 'an invariant basis of being' (Luhmann 2013a, p. 248) and, as a result, nature itself can no longer provide us with sufficient orientation for our knowledge of the world. For science, empiricism thus came to replace blind faith in the nature of things as declared by religious authority. But, Esposito (2008a, p. 16) rightly remarks, that also implied that assertions on the state of things could no longer justify themselves by reference to an idealized nature. Instead, they now have to include their own legitimation. The classic distinction between truth and opinion (dogma versus scepticism, certainty versus uncertainty) thus lost its self-evidence and centrality, since it was mainly the twilight zone between the two that now gained in interest: the (inflating) space where there can be no certainty, but where decisions nonetheless impose themselves. How is one to decide then? The modern interest in probability calculus, and hence statistics, emerged against such a background as the study of human ignorance – of *not* knowing – and materialized as the wish to yet establish reasonable certainty in those areas of high uncertainty. Second, systems theory understands modernity as the historical transition away from societal stratification. With this today still provocative stance, Luhmann characterized modern society as defined no longer by social hierarchies, but instead by a heterarchy of different functional domains. We will return to this characterization. For now, it is more important to underline that this socio-historical evolution has broken the cosmological compactness of the classical world. The once-stable relationship between the facts (what), the opinions of observers (who) and their moment of observation (when) begins to falter: not only does the world no longer appear as an invariant point of reference, but personal idiosyncrasies and particularities gain more acceptance too: we all become strongly 'individualized individuals' (Luhmann 2013a, p. 156). Time, of course, becomes uncertain too, since increasingly dominated by a future that we necessarily and ineluctably ignore (Luhmann 1976). Precisely the resulting loss of congruence or unity between those various dimensions of meaning, observes Esposito, fostered new techniques that seek to expose new regularities and so, in extremis, restore order within what seemed mere chaos at first.

> The order of modern society, which can no longer rely on a single authority or a single Reason, must somehow recognize the multiplicity of individual perspectives and reasons, and yet successfully establish itself. The calculus of probability, and the Gauss curve in particular, seem to accomplish the miracle of combining specificity with generalization, idiosyncrasy with normality, and of legitimizing an order that admits and encourages individual diversity and unpredictability.
>
> (Esposito 2008a, p. 33)

While probability theory and statistics, Esposito argues, search for the so-called laws of chance, seeking certainty in the quantitative formalization of uncertainty, they promote and enable a social order based on sheer contingency (*cf.* Luhmann 1998, pp. 44–62), emancipated from earlier impossibilities or necessities that are increasingly unable to dictate the limits of what is possible now. The central mechanism behind this evolution, Esposito suggests, is a *doubling of reality*.

With this Luhmannian concept, she underlines how numbers – but the same goes for novels or paintings – duplicate within reality a *new* reality, different from the reality they depict. The notion of reality doublings offers, in many ways, a very condensed entry point to Luhmann's particular re-articulation of constructivism. The point of this is not that our observations of the world produce mere fictions, as cruder versions of radical constructivism might advocate. Rather, in an attempt to leave behind the sterile discussions between realists and constructivists, it is argued that systems *operate* whenever they *observe* and vice versa. An extensive elaboration lies far beyond the scope of this chapter. But we could summarize the position as follows: via their operations, systems are both constructed and constructing reality, since they establish themselves while observing their environment. The world itself, then, remains inaccessible and that is precisely why 'there is no possibility other than to construct reality'. The sociological task at hand, hence, is 'to observe observers as they construct reality' (Luhmann 2000, p. 6), as an observer among others.

Two traits need to be underlined. First, reality doubles are *necessarily* fictitious, since in order to convince, they have to construct an imaginary world with its own rules and necessity, as if it were reality. In other words, statistics, novels or any other duplicate reality have to construct a fictitious world that is able to compete with the realistic character of the actual world (*cf.* Blumenberg 1969). They have to produce the conditions for their own existence. Only then can they succeed in telling us something about the world (from which they differ). Secondly, such competition between realities cannot be understood as the sheer antagonism between what represents and what is represented. Duplicate realities cannot be reduced to merely faithful depictions of the world – and if they could, they would not work. Neither do reality doubles control or model the world to their likeness. As Gustave Flaubert's *Madame Bovary* illustrates painfully, duplicate realities do not steer the world in their direction. Much to the contrary: regardless of all her efforts, the tedium and tragedy of Emma Bovary's life remains diametrically opposed to the much more exciting adventures depicted in the contraband romances she devoured. Similarly, and in more general terms, it can be said that the effects of reality doublings are much less direct than the univocal causality that is implied when speaking of governing or other concepts to express a steering control. The relationship between real and duplicate reality is much less straightforward. With the idea of duplicate realities, systems theory seeks to show how 'a special (let us call it a *real*) reality is generated through the existence of something that is different/distinguished from it' (Luhmann 2013b). Duplicate realities – whether sacral, fictional or statistically probable realities – produce the world as *real* and we could call that their 'performative' effect. But then on the understanding that such reality doublings do not simply force the world to conform to their image. Rather, while constructing a different, *sui generis* reality, they draw a line, as it were, from behind which the real world appears and thus can be distinguished from what that real world is not.

If we now transpose the above to the surge of quantification in and around the classroom, it is clear that the contemporary scholarly debate has neglected much of these facets. There seems to be more enthusiasm to condemn numeric excess than a sociological interest in understanding why such excessive quantification emerges in the first place. That is precisely why we considered it fruitful to bring up the work of Esposito and its underlying theorization of reality doubles, since the two undoubtedly shed light on a lacuna in the present literature on educational reform and the role of numbers within it. Vice versa, however, the same holds true as well: systems theory has hitherto paid little attention to the specificity of statistics in the educational domain. This chapter cannot, of course, bridge such a gap. But we can indicate, in line with the main tenets of Esposito's historical reconstruction, from where future research that takes up such a task could begin.

If the modern fascination with numbers answers above all a lack of certainty, studying the statistical quantification of education then should above all have more eye for the classroom and why it has become, too, an *area of uncertainty*. It is easy to see, in light of the above, how educational numbers, rankings and figures establish a statistical duplication of reality that appears both more informative and certain, or at least more controllable than the reality of classrooms itself. The question then is: why is this the case? What kind of evolution are we witnessing in the domain of education to which this quantification reacts? Easy and tired explanations that propagate monocausal accounts of this change, mistaking quantification for either the politicization or the economization of education, simply miss this point. They remain blind to the much more spectacularly growing indeterminacy and uncertainty that education is currently facing. What should schools teach today? Are all pupils learning what they will need later in life? How should education prepare for or engage with a future of which we know nothing, except that it will probably be different? What role does a professional teacher play in these questions? To speak of quantification should imply more engagement with these and similar questions. It should lend space to this increased uncertainty and education's institutional change – or decline, as others have termed it (Dubet 2002). From such a viewpoint, the question of numbers, as we could summarize the above, is hardly any longer a mere question of governance and power. Instead, such research would observe how educational quantification works much like the images produced by mirrors. It does not depict reality itself, but instead it is asked to guide reality by reflecting back to the world a version that is at once *less* and *more* than the world itself:

> one does not see oneself in the mirror but only the countenance that one composes for the mirror and shows to it. But this is not all. In addition, by looking over one's own shoulder, one sees others who also act before the mirror.
>
> (Luhmann 2010, p. 180)

Reality doublings such as numbers, to conclude with the metaphor, offer just like mirrors a different view on reality. They allow one to observe oneself and others, but in return demand a certain distance from reality in order to succeed. They simplify and complexify at once. One is no longer 'glued' to reality (Luhmann 1990, p. 97) and can resort to a simpler version of it, which more easily accepts manipulation. At the same time, however, they increase the available options by adding a fictious, incongruent perspective on the world and that, as we have tried to show in this paragraph, affects the complexity of reality – and not only its fictious duplicates.

Creating world society

The simultaneously reductive and productive qualities of numbers have, of course, been recurring themes in much of the sociology of quantification, far beyond systems theory. Alain Desrosières (1998, p. 236), for example, indicates in a similar vein that the aim of statistical work 'is to make a priori separate things hold together, thus lending reality and consistency to larger (...) objects'. Wendy Espeland and

Mitchell Stevens (2008, p. 406) add that this remarkable achievement is due to the faculty to transform 'all difference into quantity', an operation they name 'commensuration' and which, they explain, brings distinct 'objects' together and unites them, while simultaneously distinguishing them by assigning to each one a certain quantity (a score, a price, a grade, a performance, etc.). The constructed nature of statistics, resulting from many choices that could have turned out differently, has also been emphasized in this branch of the literature, notably with regard to the construction of the categories and equivalences (like occupational categories or age cohorts) without which counting would simply not be possible in the first place. But systems theory brings a specific contribution to this discussion.

With the help of a rather unusual conceptual opposition, Luhmann (1990, pp. 399–401) characterized *quantity* as the medium science developed for its internal purposes. Borrowing the distinction from the *Gestalt* psychologist Fritz Heider, he opposed media to form so as to explain the connectivity among phenomena – the succession of forms – by the presence of a medium that itself always remains invisible. Much as a series of sounds always relies on silent air to be heard or a variation of colours needs invisible light in order to be seen, Luhmann theorized, numbers and their scientific calculations, too, exist only by virtue of an invisible medium, quantity, in which they can be expressed.

As Luhmann remarks, 'numbers (and the same applies to all kinds of quantities) are indifferent to the concrete constellation of their application' (1990, p. 399). There exists no necessary link between context and numbers, which enjoy their own operative autonomy. They are thus capable of extracting information from the thickness of concrete events. It is sufficient, for example, to calculate how many students passed or failed, or how well they performed on this or that test, in this or that school, in this or that country. The rest – everything else that happened simultaneously, the full scope of the present – is easily forgotten. For statistics to exist and obtain meaning, all remnants of the thick present *must* be neglected.

By relying on Esposito's work on social memory, one may further conceive the role of numbers from a temporal perspective.[1] Memory, she suggests, never does full justice to the past. Most of the 'past present' must be sacrificed for it to translate into a 'present past'.[2] Remembering all that happened simply amounts to a mere impossibility: the present would immediately suffocate and choke on such an unbearable accumulation of information. In order to remember, it is necessary to forget almost everything. Without the ability to forget, a system could actually not observe its own past, let alone learn from it. The function of memory is therefore not to passively preserve the past, but to forget most of it in order to reconstruct it in such a way that it can productively be connected to further operations in the present.

While this is not a privilege of statistics, it is easy to see how quantification functions as a specific and productive, indeed fecund, forgetting technique. As the surge in large-scale international assessments in education illustrates, the forgetfulness of statistics even allows new global realities to emerge, showing correlations or causalities while connecting remote places, drawing statistical analysis between distinct variables on a worldwide scale. Thus, numbers do more than achieving the necessary task of forgetting the past. Their amnesia simultaneously establishes the ground for other versions of reality to arise. This leads us to the second contribution systems theory brings to the debate on numbers and education: it understands quantification as a medium for the genesis of world society.

In dialogue with the current literature on quantification, Bettina Heintz (2010) further elaborated on this characterization so as to sketch out the first contours of a sociological history of comparison. Central to her account is the observation of a societal evolution towards mechanisms (or indeed media) that allow for increasingly abstract, decontextualized comparisons, culminating in the birth of official statistics. If comparison involved for centuries the actual presence of what was compared, first writing, but since the second half of the 18th century, above all, publicly available statistics, freed comparison from the requirement of co-presence, thus extending its scope towards a largely anonymous audience. In that regard, Kaat Louckx and Raf Vanderstraeten (2014) note how statistics was first and foremost an exercise in 'state-istics, the empirical study of the state'. Indeed, numbers not only enabled comparison across a wide range of variables, they simultaneously uncovered an overarching comparative context and homogenized the previous administrative differences (among dioceses, counties or kingdoms) into a uniform social body: national society. As Vanderstraeten (2006) points out, such 'discovery' of society has been accompanied not only by the generation of ever more numbers, but by a close linking to the schemata and patterns ingrained in the statistical processing of national data.

If several studies operating within the framework of systems theory hence largely concur with the tenets of the mainstream literature, underlining the coincident emergence of national society and official statistics, the extension of that line of thought to the genesis of a *world society* is much less common. As Heintz argued, though, quantification 'helps to relate events far away in time and space, regardless of the context in which they took place'. The construction of such a comparative order, she continues, 'is an – or even: the – essential moment of globalization' (2008, p. 124, our translation). The case studies on which Heintz relies to make her point include external evaluation, international comparisons, rankings and league tables. It is not difficult to see how such new realities establish comparative orders of a potentially worldwide scale.

> By means of publicly communicated comparisons, individual events are related and brought into an overarching context that is visible to all. Every university, every sporting achievement, every publication and every state can now be observed in the light of such potentially worldwide comparative contexts and evaluated with regard to its past and future development. [...] It is this integrating and at the same time differentiating effect that makes comparisons – and especially quantitative comparisons – a globalization mechanism in its own right
>
> (Heintz 2010, pp. 177–178)

The conviction that (quantitative) comparison sets in motion dynamics on a global scale via processes of reciprocal observation constitutes one of systems theory's most fruitful lines of research. Especially in the domain of education, this very idea has been extensively explored and documented, even well beyond purely quantitative comparisons. As Jurgen Schriewer (1989) argued in his seminal text on the role of comparison, international survey data are an essential part of the " 'frames of reference' within which to specify appropriate reform policies".

> Their function, accordingly, is not to present 'models for emulation'; rather this function is to establish on 'firmer grounds', to give 'greater depth' to, to increase the 'problem awareness' needed in, and, in sum, to 'enrich', by means of 'supplementary meaning' as derivable from external points of reference, the system-internal debates on policies adapted to the needs of the time.
>
> (Schriewer 1988, p. 66)

With as its well-known conclusion, that such externalizations establish a globally operating education system:

> As a result of that, a kind of 'social construction of internationality' flowing from recurrent externalizations to world situations, as well as 'main-streaming', along the lines of internationality, help shape the 'standardized world model of education', or 'transnational ideology', that correspond, as its semantic corre-lates, to the emerging world society.
>
> (Schriewer 1988, p. 70)

Rather than denoting a global sameness, such world education then points towards the jumbled 'socio-logic of externalizations' (Schriewer & Martinez 2004, p. 51) by which reform movements outsource the legitimacy for their own deci-sions to examples from abroad. Instead of uniformity or integration, it denotes the global attainability and connectivity of the education system against the backdrop of a worldwide horizon of possibilities (Luhmann 1971).

The governance of an ungovernable world

Modern education has always, even routinely, relied on doubling the complex reality of its classrooms by means of numbers. In the last decades, however, as has been widely noticed and regularly lamented, the quantification of education began to play a new role: numbers became a central component of education pol-icy, where large-scale assessments developed with a view to holding teachers, schools and even national systems accountable for their own success or lack thereof. Such accountability measures initially merely intended to inform stake-holders, policymakers or the wider public about the performances of those thus evaluated, as Michael Power (1994) reconstructs in his overview of the phenom-enon. Only later arose the idea that, beyond their merely informative function, such measures could be turned into means of steering practices. Notwithstanding their differences, these more recent modern accountability policies all rest on the same assumption that information does not simply describe, but instead affects the world it depicts (Espeland & Sauder 2007).[3] In education, the expectation is that providing professionals and organizations with feedback regarding their per-formance will drive them to reflect, to process and account for their results, ulti-mately leading to responses and strategies to improve them (Verger & Parcerisa 2017).[4] Unsurprisingly, research on accountability policies became primarily interested in assessing their effects: do they actually work and meet their targets? Do teachers, schools, systems perform better as a result? Many research efforts have gone into answering this question; yet the findings remain stubbornly incon-sistent. The scholarly debate suggests distinguishing between various types of accountability policies in order to examine how each distinctively affects those held accountable (Maroy & Voisin 2015).[5] But even such refinements do not pro-duce firmer conclusions. The argument that high-stakes accountability, for exam-ple, would be more likely to realign education and policy, while low-stakes accountability would be more efficient in bringing about reflexivity, is not sup-ported by clear evidence (Barbana, Dumay & Dupriez 2020). All in all, from the literature results a rather ambiguous picture: effects are often moderate, uncer-tain, multiple, sometimes contradictory, regularly unexpected and even counter-productive (Mons 2009; Maroy & Pons 2019).

Systems theory, we wish to show in this section, suggests a different under-standing of the relation between these policies and what happens on the ground as a result of their implementation. We have already alluded to this problem in the first section by underlining that systems theory considers the relation between reality doubles and the world they mirror and inhabit to be much less straightfor-ward than what is presumed when one speaks of power relations in causal terms.

To better grasp the position of systems theory on the matter, one may follow Luhmann's hint that steering necessarily involves distinct strands of operations: 'one has to distinguish the operation of steering, which produces its own effects, from the operation of observing this operation, which produces for its own part its own effects' (1997, p. 45). As the long history of education reforms illustrates, the mere attempt to steer the world, simply by virtue of being visible to that world, tends to produce effects that cannot be steered. Indeed, Luhmann notes, 'steering always creates an additional effect by being observed and by the reactions of the observer in the one or the other way' (1997, p. 49). The well-known difficulties of reform ambitions then result from the given that both the political intent to steer and its intended addressee observe and process this steering event usually very *differently*.[6] As a consequence, the very question of policy effects appears as, how-ever understandable, simply ill-conceived. It assumes and silently reproduces causal attribution schemes between policy and the societal domain that policy addresses, thus effectively concealing the latter's autonomy and ignoring the much more paradoxical nature of decision-making (Luhmann 2019, pp. 98–121). In contrast to both difficulties, systems theory starts from the *self-referentiality* of observing systems (Luhmann 1995). Reform or decision-making is hence not framed in causal or hierarchical terms (*cf.* Vanderstraeten 1997). Instead, each system is observed as recursively and selectively processing the information it distinguishes in its environment.[7]

The outcome of this ensemble, the contingent coexistence of the most diverse societal domains autonomously processing information according to their own standards, constitutes the centrepiece of systems theory's observation of modern society and is commonly abridged as the latter's *functional differentiation*. This means that for systems theory, function and not (hierarchical) rank, is the dominant principle organizing modern society. From its viewpoint, since each societal domain accepts for its organization only the primacy of its own function and subordinates everything else as a purely secondary matter, society becomes *ungovernable*.

> Like every system, politics cannot transcend itself and act on higher orders; [it is] only able to steer itself by a specific political construction of the difference between system and environment. That this happens and how it happens has without doubt tremendous effects on the society because the other functional systems must orient themselves along the differences thus produced. *But this effect is certainly not steering and it is not possible to steer it* because it depends on the construction of differences in the context of other systems and because it falls under the [self]steering programmes operating in these systems.
>
> (Luhmann 1997, pp. 47–48, emphasis in original)

Such characterization, which has been addressed by various scholars (see, e.g., Willke 1986; Andersen & Pors 2016; Wansleben 2020), should of course not be read as a thinly veiled invitation for more laissez-faire. Rather, it highlights the limits of political steering and the highly paradoxical constellation wherein modern politics operates: a society that requires and institutionalizes the production of collectively binding decisions, but is structurally unable to abide by them. Accountability policies, then, make for an interesting case in point, since they can be said to *reflect* and *react to* much of the above. Together with practices such as evidence-based policy, evaluation policy, benchmarking, best practices or peer learning, accountability policies belong to a range of tools for which the umbrella concept of *governance* is usually reserved (as, for example, Kjaer 2010), so as to express a withdrawal from firm state government towards more nimble mechanisms to exert power. According to systems theory scholars, what such governance structures have in common is that they do not rely on the normative power of the law or political decision-making – in contrast with traditional governing techniques. Rather, as Anders Esmark (2009) points out, they attempt to mobilize the functional logic of other domains instead. They do not confront individuals and organizations with rules or hierarchy but offer (and request) *information* as a substitute. Schools, universities, teachers, or even national systems are given feedback on their own performances, practices or outputs, compared with others, or showered with examples of 'best practices' from abroad.

In that light, two remarks can be made. The *first* remark starts from the above observation that information plays a central role in accountability policies. The quantification implied by its 'governance by numbers' is expected to produce numbers that inform. Adopting Gregory Bateson's (1972) canonical definition, Luhmann defines information as a 'difference that makes a difference': information necessarily adds something new, otherwise it simply fails to inform. Today's prevalence of ratings and rankings can be explained that way (Esposito & Stark 2019).

They order and chart evolutions, thus translating numbers into information necessary to guide us through uncertain choices. But, Luhmann warns, information 'is a concept with two sides. It helps – and it troubles' (Luhmann 2005, p. 28). Information, in other words, is a profoundly ambivalent matter.

> It contains, so to speak, its own counter-concept. It reproduces knowledge and ignorance ever anew from moment to moment. As information, it provides connectivity options, but in so doing – on the other side, the 'unmarked space' of its form – it always renews the background knowledge that there are other possibilities too.
>
> (Luhmann 2013a, pp. 311–312)

The ambivalent nature of information leads straight into paradox: we hope to take better decisions when gaining information, but simultaneously more information fuels the need to make more decisions. Or phrased differently: as long as we remain unaware of alternatives, there is no room for decisions in the first place. Once those alternatives become present, however, choices become necessary and the initial problem returns: how to decide? It should hence not surprise that the use of quantified information in accountability policies says nothing about how its addressees will react, which remains an empirical matter, but certainly participates in and perpetuates what Ian Hacking (1983) so aptly described as the endless avalanche of numbers. The latter, Sotiria Grek (2013) points out, coincides with the emergence of dense networks of calculating experts, who, together with a series of new governance mechanisms (like benchmark-setting), redefine governing as the examination of such quantitative information (*cf.* Verschraegen 2015).

As the previously mentioned relevance of information and knowledge accentuates, *secondly*, accountability policies rely primarily on cognitive processes, rather than on legal norms or political authority. They can be said to belong, together with other governance mechanisms, to a *post-sovereign* steering mode (*cf.* Esmark 2009). What such characterization seeks to make clear, is that accountability policies have often been adopted, or even initiated and developed, by non-state actors (such as the European Commission or the OECD) in order to intervene in domains where they lack formal power. Of course, such policies have also been implemented by formal governments which, in some cases, have mobilized their binding power to associate the observed performances with incentives and sanctions. But even that cannot hide from sight the plain truth that the turn to governance designates primarily a restructuring or reshaping of the political: what is being steered, is indeed the political system itself, nothing beyond it.

Coda: Irritating numbers?

In the previous pages, we have sketched out the various ways in which systems theory can be and has been used to rethink the role of quantification in today's world. In line with previous research continuing on the precepts of Luhmann's systems theory, we have put emphasis on how quantification yields *new worlds*: either as a doubling of reality that sets out the probable against the real, or as the emergence of world society, resulting from the comparisons enabled by the thus created statistical reality. With our contribution, we have sought to relate this world-constructing capacity of quantified data to the debate on transnational governance and education policy. Unlike an overwhelming portion of the scholarly debate on the role of quantification in contemporary education, we have emphasized that systems theory cannot simply portray, let alone criticize, numbers as a steering mechanism. Rather than seeing it as mere technocratic aid (as official discourse might present it) or as an instrument of the powers-that-be (as many social scientists insist), we have discussed quantification against the background of steering limits. That is: as a repercussion of the paradoxical necessity of governing a world that appears ungovernable.

To conclude this chapter, let us return a last time to the topic of accountability policies in the domain of education. Together with other governance techniques, such policies rely on quantity as a medium to extract information from concrete situations, allowing ever more benchmarks and comparisons to be drawn, circulated and fed back to professionals and organizations. Whether and how the latter may be affected, we have argued, cannot be causally deduced from the characteristics of the steering attempt itself. Such a lack of control should naturally not be confused with an absence of effects (*cf.* Luhmann 2019, p. 280). Steering efforts do not leave the world unchanged, Luhmann acknowledges (1997, p. 47) – quite the contrary: more intentional steering, he reckons, might 'lead to more (and more rapid) unintentional evolution'[8] (Luhmann 1982, p. 134). Indeed, such proliferation multiplies the possibilities for systems to become irritated by, and to react to, the circulation of (quantified) information in their environment. Irritations introduce discontinuities in the course of time. They create the present as the time when reactions must occur, and decisions be made in the face of new uncertainties: should we change our habits or hide our failures? Should we game the system or improve our practices? Should we transform our image or train our staff? Should we imitate our successful neighbour or find our own way? Points of bifurcation that would otherwise not emerge now become subject to decision-making.

The fundamental mechanism behind quantification processes in accountability policies, we argue, is that the statistical realities thus produced allow for differentiating between the past and the future:[9] what has been could become different. In the thus emerging 'cosmology of contingency', as Luhmann (2005, p. 29) dubbed it, we all become decision-makers. And, as we, or others, measure and observe ever more new aspects of our practices, they too become perceived as contingent, which further fuels the need for new decision-making. Building on a conclusion Luhmann (1992) formulated in the early 1990s, Heintz (2008) illustrates with her analysis of accountability policies in higher education how the new focus on quantifiable outputs and results transforms the way universities understand themselves. From *institutions* merely executing established scripts, the expectation to rationally decide and plan towards future goals turns them into (textbook) *organizations*.[10] The issue is thus not an impending economic colonization of higher education, as many critics of the so-called New Public Management lament, but unfolds at a different level of analysis: that of the self-understanding and self-steering of organizations.

We have linked this mutually reinforcing dynamic between numbers and decision-making to the changing shape of the political, underlining how accountability policies and the broader turn to governance amount primarily to the steering and restructuring of the political system itself. Be that as it may, such a dynamic, and the movement from institution to organization that we have sketched out, strongly echo an even deeper evolution, which Luhmann had already identified in the early 1970s, when he hypothesized that an increased preference for cognitive, rather than normative expectations would characterize the crystallizing world society (Luhmann 1971). This Luhmannian twist on what others have called the 'knowledge society' or 'globalization' is not so much based on shifting economic production relations or technological innovation. Although one could draw lines to such evolutions, the trend that Luhmann observes goes deeper. It observes how normative, counter-factual expectation structures gradually lose their grasp. As so often, such evolution is above all a matter of time: with the exhaustion of normative control, the stable future that norms project is also increasingly undermined. Quantification, then, gives both visibility and grip to the thus emerging cosmology of contingence, where our future increasingly appears indeterminate.

Notes

1   See Esposito (2008b) for an accessible introduction to the matter. Luhmann himself elaborates on the sociological relevance of memory in his two-volume magnum opus, *Die Gesellschaft der Gesellschaft* (1997/2012, pp. 348–358), published shortly before his death. As so often, the underlying intuition actually goes back to the field of cybernetics and in particular to Heinz von Foerster's (1948) mathematical phenomenology of forgetting, which described memory, the retaining of what we deem important, as the outcome of a forgetting process that increasingly clouds the remembered experience. Esposito (2001) later extended this line of thought into a stand-alone inquiry on social memory, featuring particular attention to the evolutionary path leading to the emergence of digital media.

2   As Sven Opitz and Uwe Tellman (2015, p. 110) concede, this Luhmannian "game of words might be confusing at first sight, but it turns out to be a disarmingly simple and yet effective conceptual pairing". The term "present past" refers to the present observation of the past, while the "past present" refers to the (today inaccessible) present as it occurred in the past. The "present future", for its part, denotes our present understanding of the future(s), while the "future present" points to the (as-yet inaccessible) present that will come when it comes.

3   The notion that people change their ways in reaction to being observed and compared is not new to the social sciences. Initially, it was considered a methodological problem: if mere observation changes the behaviour of the observed entity, how could scientific observation ever be valid? Campbell's (1957) seminal paper on the matter elaborates the notion of reactivity (later narrowed down and rebranded as "performativity") and distinguishes non-reactive observations from reactive ones. Accountability policies build on such reactivity to turn a methodological problem into a policy solution. For systems theory, however, the distinction between reactive and non-reactive observations is slightly misleading as it seems to attribute their difference to the nature of the observation, while it would be more accurate to attribute them to the observer: one does or does not observe that one is being observed.

4 Evaluation of performance can be geared to assess various criteria (equity, efficiency or inclusiveness, for example) and with regard to many different disciplines or competences. Some have therefore argued that such policies are void of any content and that their potential use relies on such 'emptiness': "their success as tools of regulation depends on their being empty of substantive content," Michael Power (2002, p. 195) writes. The theme is further explored in a special issue of *Soziale Systeme* (volume 8, issue 2), guest-edited by Dirk Baecker.

5 A great number of typologies have been produced, distinguishing many types of accountability policies according to various criteria (such as the actors involved, the presence/absence of sanctions/incentives, or the publicity of results). For a detailed review, see in particular the recent volume edited by Christian Maroy and Xavier Pons (2019).

6 "The observation of steering can, and typically will, use other distinctions than steering itself, for instance will carry out the imputation of successes and failures in a different manner than he to whom the steering is imputed as action" (Luhmann 1997, p. 45).

7 The already cited work by Corsi (1998) illustrates how such analysis proceeds when reform movements are observed as a strictly educational affair – and not as a policy or its mere effect.

8 In the original quotation Luhmann uses the notion of planning, not steering: "more intentional planning", he writes, "will lead to more (and more rapid) unintentional evolution". The point remains, however, that intentions take part in a much wider process of evolution which does not conform to them. Once an intention is put in the world, the argument goes, its very presence induces reactions and effects which escape its control, and eventually lead to its own disappointment. Reforms then do not shape the world as they intend to; instead, evolution does. In his book *Organization and Decision*, Luhmann (2019) dedicates a chapter (pp. 273–298) to the distinction between "the poetry of reform" and "the reality of evolution" so as to emphasize how reality never obeys intentions, but results instead from a non-governable, non-predictable process of becoming, which he refers to under the aforementioned Darwinian vocabulary of evolution. Obviously, steering attempts play their part in, but ultimately fail to control, evolution.

9 On how our changing understanding of time plays out in the field of education, see Vanden Broeck (2019, 2020); Mangez and Vanden Broeck (2020).

10 Raimund Hasse and Georg Krücken have developed a similar argument, even if they nuance that this evolution is well advanced in universities while schools remain "more profoundly imprinted by institutional factors" (2015, p. 209).

References

Åkerstrøm Andersen, N. & Grønbæk Pors, J. (2016). *Public Management in Transition: The Orchestration of Potentiality*. Chicago, IL: Policy Press.

Barbana, S., Dumay, X. & Dupriez, V. (2020). Accountability policy forms in European educational systems: An outro. *European Educational Research Journal*, 19(2), 165–169.

Bateson, G. (1972). *Steps to an Ecology of Mind*. New York: Ballantine.

Blumenberg, H. (1969). Wirklichkeitsbegriff und Möglichkeit des Romans. In H. R. Jauß (Ed.), *Nachahmung und Illusion* (pp. 9–27). München: Fink.

Campbell, D. T. (1957). Factors relevant to the validity of experiments in social settings. *Psychological Bulletin*, 54(4), 297–312.

Corsi, G. (1998). *Sistemi che apprendono*. Lecce: Pensa.

Cuban, L. (1990). Reforming again, again, and again. *Educational Researcher*, 19(1), 3–13.

Desrosières, A. (1998). *The Politics of Large Numbers: A History of Statistical Reasoning*. Cambridge, MA: Harvard University Press.

Dubet, F. (2002). *Le déclin de l'institution*. Paris: Seuil.

Esmark, A. (2009). The functional differentiation of governance: Public governance beyond hierarchy, market and networks. *Public Administration*, 87(2), 351–370.

Espeland, W. N., & Stevens, M. L. (2008). A Sociology of Quantification. *European Journal of Sociology*, 49(03), 401–436.

Esposito, E. (2001). *La memoria sociale*. Roma: Laterza. (Translated in 2002 as: Soziales Vergessen. Frankfurt am Main: Suhrkamp.)

Esposito, E. (2008a). *Probabilità improbabili*. Roma: Meltemi. (Translated and revised version of the German original published in 2007 as Die Fiktion der wahrscheinlichen Realität. Frankfurt am Main: Suhrkamp.)

Esposito, E. (2008b). Social forgetting: A systems-theory approach. In A. Erll & A. Nünning (Eds.), *Media and Cultural Memory* (pp. 181–189). Berlin/Boston, MA: De Gruyter.

Esposito, E. & Stark, D. (2019). What's observed in a rating? Rankings as orientation in the face of uncertainty. *Theory, Culture & Society*, 36(4), 3–26.

Grek, S. (2013). Expert moves: International comparative testing and the rise of expertocracy. *Journal of Education Policy*, 28(5), 695–709.

Hacking, I. (1983). Biopower and the avalanche of printed numbers. *Humanities in Society*, 5(3-4), 279–295.

Hasse, R. & Krücken, G. (2015). Decoupling and coupling in education. In B. Holzer, F. Kastner & T. Werron (Eds.), *From Globalization to World Society: Neo-Institutional and Systems-Theoretical Perspectives* (pp. 197–214). New York: Routledge.

Heintz, B. (2008). Governance by Numbers. Zum Zusammenhang von Quantifizierung und Globalisierung am Beispiel der Hochschulpolitik. In G. F. Schuppert and A. Voßkuhle (Eds.) *Governance von und durch Wissen* (pp. 110–129). Baden-Baden: Nomos.

Heintz, B. (2010). Numerische Differenz. Überlegungen zu einer Soziologie des (quantitativen) Vergleichs. *Zeitschrift für Soziologie*, 39(3), 162–181.

Kjaer, P. F. (2010). *Between Governing and Governance*. Oxford: Hart.

Kjaer, P. F. (2015). Context construction through competition: The prerogative of public power, intermediary institutions, and the expansion of statehood through competition. *Distinktion*, 16(2), 146–166.

Louckx, K., & Vanderstraeten, R. (2014). State-Istics and Statistics: Exclusion Categories in the Population Census (Belgium, 1846-1930). *The Sociological Review*, 62(3), 530–546.

Luhmann, N. (1971). Die Weltgesellschaft. *Archiv für Rechts- und Sozialphilosophie*, 57(1), 1–35.

Luhmann, N. (1976). The future cannot begin: Temporal structures in modern society. *Social Research*, 43(1), 130–152.

Luhmann, N. (1982). The World Society as a social system. *International Journal of General Systems*, 8(3), 131–138.

Luhmann, N. (1990). *Die Wissenschaft der Gesellschaft*. Frankfurt am Main: Suhrkamp.

Luhmann, N. (1992). *Universität als Milieu* (A. Kieserling, Ed.). Bielefeld: Haux.

Luhmann, N. (1995). *Social Systems*. Stanford, CA: Stanford University Press.

Luhmann, N. (1997). Limits of steering. *Theory, Culture & Society*, 14(1), 41–57.

Luhmann, N. (1998). *Observations on Modernity*. Stanford, CA: Stanford University Press.

Luhmann, N. (2000). *The Reality of the Mass Media*. Stanford, CA: Stanford University Press.

Luhmann, N. (2005). Entscheidungen in der "Informationsgesellschaft". In G. Corsi & E. Esposito (Eds.), *Reform und Innovation in einer unstabilen Gesellschaft* (pp. 27–40). Berlin: De Gruyter.

Luhmann, N. (2010). Societal complexity and public opinion. In J. Gripsrud, H. Moe, A. Molander & G. Murdock (Eds.), *The Idea of the Public Sphere* (pp. 173–183). Lanham, MD: Lexington Books.

Luhmann, N. (2012). *Theory of Society*. Volume 1. (R. Barrett, Trans.). Stanford, CA: Stanford University Press.

Luhmann, N. (2013a). *Theory of Society*. Volume 2. (R. Barrett, Trans.). Stanford, CA: Stanford University Press.

Luhmann, N. (2013b). *A Systems Theory of Religion*. (A. Hermann & D. Brenner, Trans., A. Kieserling, Ed.). Stanford, CA: Stanford University Press.

Luhmann, N. (2019). *Organization and Decision* (D. Baecker, Ed.). Cambridge: Cambridge University Press.

Mangez, E. & Vanden Broeck, P. (2020). The history of the future and the shifting forms of education. *Educational Philosophy and Theory*, 52(6), 676–687.

Maroy, C. & Pons, X. (2019). *Accountability Policies in Education*. Berlin/Heidelberg: Springer.

Maroy, C. & Voisin, A. (2015). Comparing accountability policy tools and rationales: various ways, various effects? In H.-G. Kotthoff & L. Klerides (Eds.), *Governing Educational Spaces: Knowledge, Teaching, and Learning in Transition*. Rotterdam: Sense.

Mons, N. (2009). Effets théoriques et réels des politiques d'évaluation standardisée. *Revue française de Pédagogie*, (169), 99–139.

Opitz, S. & Tellmann, U. (2015). Future emergencies: Temporal politics in law and economy. *Theory, Culture & Society*, 32(2), 107–129.

Porter, T. M. (1986). *The Rise of Statistical Thinking*. Princeton, NJ: Princeton University Press.

Power, M. (1994). *The Audit Explosion*. London: Demos.

Power, M. (2002). Standardization and the regulation of management control practices. *Soziale Systeme*, 8(2), 191–204.

Sauder, M., & Espeland, W. N. (2009). The Discipline of Rankings: Tight Coupling and Organizational Change. *American Sociological Review*, 74(1), 63–82.

Schriewer, J. (1988). The method of comparison and the need for externalization: Methodological criteria and sociological concepts. In J. Schriewer & B. Holmes (Eds.), *Theories and Methods in Comparative Education* (pp. 25–83). Frankfurt am Main: Peter Lang Publishing.

Schriewer, J. (1989). The twofold character of comparative education: Cross-cultural comparison and externalization to world situations. *Prospects*, 19(3), 389–406.

Schriewer, J. & Martinez, C. (2004). Constructions of internationality in education. In G. Steiner-Khamsi (Ed.), *The Global Politics of Educational Borrowing and Lending* (pp. 29–53). New York: Teachers College Press.

Thornhill, C. J. (2011). The future of the state. In P. F. Kjaer, G. Teubner & A. Febbrajo (Eds.), *The Financial Crisis in Constitutional Perspective* (pp. 357–394). Portland, OR: Hart.

Tyack, D. & Cuban, L. (1995). *Tinkering toward Utopia*. Cambridge, MA: Harvard University Press.

Vanden Broeck, P. (2019). Beyond school: Transnational differentiation and the shifting form of education in world society. *Journal of Education Policy*, 1–20.

Vanden Broeck, P. (2020). The problem of the present: On simultaneity, synchronisation and transnational education projects. *Educational Philosophy and Theory*, 52(6), 664–675.

Vanderstraeten, R. (1997). Circularity, complexity and educational policy planning: A systems approach to the planning of school provision. *Oxford Review of Education*, 23(3), 321–332.

Vanderstraeten, R. (2006). Soziale Beobachtungsraster: Eine wissenssoziologische Analyse statistischer Klassifikationsschemata. *Zeitschrift Für Soziologie*, 35(3), 193–211.

Verger, A. & Parcerisa, L. (2017). A difficult relationship: Accountability policies and teachers. International evidence and key premises for future research. In M. Akiba & G. LeTendre (Eds.), *International Handbook of Teacher Quality and Policy* (pp. 241–254). New York: Routledge.

Verschraegen, G. (2015). Fabricating social Europe: From neo-corporatism to governance by numbers. In E. Hartmann & P. F. Kjaer (Eds.), *The Evolution of Intermediary Institutions in Europe* (pp. 101–119). Basingstoke: Palgrave Macmillan.

von Foerster, H. (1948). *Das Gedächtnis*. Wien: Franz Deuticke.

Wansleben, L. (2020). "Ghost in the Machine". Der Staat in Luhmanns Theorie politischer Systeme. *Soziale Systeme*, 21(2), 279–306.

Willke, H. (1986). The tragedy of the state: Prolegomena to a theory of the state in polycentric society. *Archiv für Rechts- und Sozialphilosophie*, 72(4), 455–467.

2 The construction of SDG4: Reconciling democratic imperatives and technocratic expertise in the making of global education data?

Clara Fontdevila and Sotiria Grek

Introduction

Datafication in education governance has become established in recent decades as the prime mode of knowing and reforming complex education systems around the world. The rise of large international assessments created a wealth of statistical information and thus allowed states and transnational agencies for the first time to construct comparative knowledge about education performance. One of these global education monitoring exercises is the construction of the Education 2030 agenda, otherwise the Sustainable Development Goal 4 (SDG4), which promises to 'ensure inclusive and equitable quality education and promote lifelong learning opportunities for all' (United Nations General Assembly, 2015, p. 14). SDG4 represents the single biggest attempt to bring together a vast array of actors and countries in order to construct universal education indicators, as well as to decide on the appropriate methodologies and data sources. It is a country-led, global exercise – led by UNESCO, but with the collaboration and close involvement of all major international organizations (IOs). Given its global and collaborative scope, it presents its leaders and participants with enormous technical and political problems.

Through an in-depth analysis of texts and interviews, this chapter will discuss the conundrum of securing accountability of this global performance monitoring project through ensuring the objective validity of its measurement tools, whilst promoting the democratic and equal participation of all actors. UNESCO, as the custodian agency of SDG4, has a double accountability obligation to participating countries: first, the robust and objective monitoring of progress towards the SDG4 goals; and secondly, the participatory and democratic, equitable process in which all member countries have a voice and stake in the project. As a result, although the UNESCO Institute of Statistics has been significantly reinvigorated in relation to its statistical capacity, it has also put great emphasis on the participatory, inclusive and consensual aspects of the agenda – a process that some of the participants see sometimes as taking place at the expense of the robustness of the data produced. As this chapter will show, this double responsibility does not always happen without friction; on the contrary, it has been causing a significant amount of tension in the relationship between and within some of the major IOs, as well as between IOs and other stakeholders, including developing nations.

One of the key questions that this chapter aims to answer is where the account-ability of these large performance monitoring projects lies. As education gover-nance by data continues expanding from cradle to grave, can governing through data secure both technocratic legitimacy and political legitimation at the same time? Does the democratic expansion of participating actors pose threats to tech-nocracy as a scientific, robust endeavour? This chapter grapples with the question of how expertise and trust in objectivity can be maintained in political processes that aspire to greater inclusion and the set-up of common, global objectives. How do the processes of indicator development change as they are increasingly subject to democracy and transparency demands? Which compromises are needed in order to reconcile international and national data sources relying on different sources of expertise? Ultimately, how can we theorize on the relationship of elite, expert, technocratic objectivity-making with the inclusive, participatory and ever-expanding process of making consensus?

This chapter will begin with a short overview of the main theoretical underpin-nings of the notions of accountability and transparency and their relationship with the growing role of datafication in education. We will continue with a focus on the historical trajectory of the initial inception, followed by the first steps and the decisive moments that made the SDG4 the kind of monitoring instrument that it is today. Next, we will offer a short description of the research design and methods, before moving on to the analysis of interview data.[1] The chapter will show how the notions of mediation and instrumentation, as they emerge from actors' accounts, point towards a better understanding of the uneasy coexistence of different accountabilities in the transnational governance of education.

Accountability and transparency in the age of governing by numbers

Since the 1990s, both transparency and accountability have become dominant tools in the education governing arsenal; indeed, Meyer et al. (1997) see them having been imposed as a new world society norm. Especially in the field of the transnational governance of education, rituals of comparison and performance measurement as well as the economization of education discourses have become integral modes of the universal panacea of governing by a distance (Ozga, 2013). New forms of accountability and audit have transformed national education gov-erning regimes, too, and in doing so, they have directly impacted on the transna-tional architecture of education.

Indeed, Power has insightfully written about the rise of the audit society (1999) and the enabling of calculative technologies that allow for decision-making and action at a distance (Porter, 1996). Although these accountability structures are power-laden and hierarchical, these hierarchies are not rigid or stable (Djelic & Sahlin-Andersson, 2006). The endless 'treadmill of accountability' (Bostrom & Garsten 2008, p. 242) requires that actors and alliances are permanently in movement and are always incomplete. Thus, accountability can arguably by equated to a norma-tive shell through which audit, standards and deregulation are pushed in education.

Given the increasing pervasiveness and centrality of accountability and datafication in education governance, a number of theoretical tools have been developed to understand such transformations. A recent contribution to this scholarship
– that proves particularly apposite to the objectives of this chapter – is Maroy and
Pons' (2019) tripartite schema for the examination of the *practice* of accountability. The relevance of this work lies in the fact that it goes beyond the performativity perspective that has dominated education scholarship from the 1990s onwards.
Through the application of the theoretical tools of the *sociologie de l'action publique*, Maroy and Pons invite us to examine not only the accountability policies *per
se*, but in fact pay attention to the notions of *trajectory*, *mediation* and *instrumentation* in school accountability:

–   The notion of *trajectory* is used to make sense of the emergence and imple-
    mentation of a given policy instrument. According to Maroy and Pons (2019),
    this needs to be understood in relation to three intertwined processes and
    factors: namely, an element of path-dependency; bricolage practices through
    which available tools are recombined; and the translation and recontextual-
    ization of tools and ideas developed elsewhere and, particularly, those circu-
    lating at a transnational level.
–   The concept of *mediation*, in turn, captures process of transformation and
    mutation. This is a consequence of the co-construction work performed by
    actors operating at different levels and in different settings. The notion throws
    light on the interplay and the combined impact of a wide range of organiza-
    tions and individuals – whose action contributes to (re)define the meaning of
    policy tools.
–   Finally, the process of *instrumentation* borrows from political science debates
    on the making and role of policy instruments, i.e. 'an apparatus that is both
    technical and social, that organizes specific social relations between the state
    and those it is addressed to, according to the representations and meanings it
    carries' (Lascoumes & Le Galès, 2004, p. 13). It captures thus the dynamics
    through which policy instruments come into being.

Before moving on to a short description of our methodology and the examination
of actors' accounts, the next section will focus on a description of the historical
context of the emergence of the SDG4. Through exploring the trajectory of an
idea initially devised by a small set of people to the major monitoring instrument
that it has now become, the following account shows the degree to which a certain
path dependency, coupled by some bricolage work, gave birth to the core conundrum surrounding the SDG4: technical or democratic?

Negotiating and producing metrics for Sustainable Development Goal 4: A historical trajectory

2015 was a crucial year for the global education community. In May, a World
Education Forum (WEF) was celebrated in Incheon (Republic of Korea) with the
participation of over 1,500 participants, including 120 Ministries of Education

and representatives from a wide range of international governmental and non-governmental organizations. The gathering was devised (and touted) as a successor or the Jomtien and Dakar meetings celebrated respectively in 1990 and 2000 – both of them widely acknowledged as milestones in the development and consolidation of the Education for All movement. The main product of WEF 2015 was the so-called Incheon Declaration, along with the Framework for Action adopted by UNESCO Member States in November 2015. In conjunction, both documents established an ambitious and highly aspirational education agenda for the 2015–2030 period, condensed in the overarching goal 'Ensure inclusive and equitable quality education and promote lifelong learning opportunities for all' and a number of associated targets (UNESCO, 2016).

What is important here is that both documents were the product of a long, multilayered and multi-sited negotiation process that involved numerous meetings and consultations, largely led by UNESCO under the auspices of the EFA Steering Committee. At the same time, it should be noted that efforts towards the development of this agenda were in turn paralleled by the negotiation of the Sustainable Development Goals – one of the cornerstones of the 2030 Agenda adopted by the General Assembly of the United Nations in September 2015 and devised as a follow-up of the Millennium Development Goals. In fact, the EFA-led process and the debates facilitated by the UN Open Working Group on Sustainable Development Goals reinforced and informed one another through an intricate political process, eventually crystallizing in a single agenda conventionally known as SDG4/Education 2030 – a denomination reminiscent of the dual origins of the new set of goals.

Education 2030/SDG4 represented simultaneously a form of continuity and a departure from previous instances of goal-setting such as EFA and the Millennium Development Goals. As a programmatic document oriented at nurturing and securing a form of collective commitment towards a shared set of aspirations, the new agenda builds on a well-established tradition that has come to be recognized as a procedural hallmark of the UN system. However, Education 2030 entails a certain discontinuity regarding education goal-setting practices – in both content and procedural terms.

First, and as different scholars have noted, the new set of goals is characterized by an unprecedented degree of ambition – shifting away from the focus on primary education and gender equality that characterized the MDG era, but also expanding on the vision set up by the EFA program; and establishing a truly universal agenda that contrasts with the prior focus on developing countries (King, 2017; Unterhalter, 2019). Secondly, the very *making* of Education 2030 (and of the SDGs more in general) represents a path-breaking development in the long history of goal-setting practices and UN summitry. The open, inclusive and participatory nature of the consultative process facilitated by UNESCO and the EFA architecture was in many ways unprecedented, and the openly-negotiated and improvisatory character of the SDG debate contrasted with the technocratic origins of the MDGs (cf. Fukuda-Parr & McNeill, 2019).

In addition to these normative and procedural shifts, the SDGs agenda introduced also a greater emphasis on accountability and transparency – increasingly portrayed as key operating principles and as governance challenges directly influencing the implementation of the SDG framework (Bowen et al., 2017). Such commitment contrasts with the diffuse lines of responsibility that characterized the MDG era (Clegg, 2015). It is significant, for instance, that the notion of accountability features prominently in the roadmap sketched by the Education 2030 Framework for Action. At the same time, it should be noted that the policy translation of such principle remains largely undefined. The notion of accountability seems to be equated to an emphasis or commitment to transparency, and to efforts to improve monitoring, reporting and follow-up practices. The focus on shared responsibility makes it difficult to ascertain who should be accountable to whom, and over which outcome. In practice, the implementation of the accountability principle in relation to the SDG agenda has materialized in the adoption of a series of monitoring and review mechanisms – most notably, the delivery of formalized and periodic reviews at the national, regional and international levels (Bowen et al., 2017). In this new scenario, data-collection efforts have only been gaining prominence – with two of the targets of SDG17 explicitly aiming to affect and improve the availability of data, to develop new measurements of progress on sustainable development, and to strengthen the statistical capacity of developing countries.

Although, as noted above, 2015 was much of a turning point for the global education community, it left a number of issues open – among them, the so-called *indicator debate*. The fact that the measurement of SDG4 remained an instance of 'unfinished business' is all the more relevant given the centrality placed on data-collection, monitoring and tracking efforts. Over the last years, the datafication of transnational education governance has come to be perceived as the sole means through which the so-called 'learning crisis' can be solved. Brought to the fore by the 2013/2014 EFA Global Education Monitoring, the idea of a global learning crisis aims at capturing and exposing the limited academic progress made by schooled children in a number of low- and middle-income countries. As noted by Barrett (2016), the emergence of this notion was in fact made possible by the proliferation of learning assessments. The author goes on to argue that the so-called testing culture and the learning crisis narrative have tended to reinforce each other – for solving the crisis requires data, and such data only renders more evident the extent of the crisis.

Reflecting the primacy given to data-collection and monitoring efforts, the Framework for Action established four levels of indicators (global, thematic, regional and national) associated to different reporting strategies. In the light of the unequal development of global indicators, and their availability and coverage, a tier classification tool was implemented for the whole SDG framework. Importantly, a number of custodian agencies became responsible for the development and refinements of such indicators. In the case of education, the UNESCO Institute for Statistics (UIS) became responsible for 9 out of 11 indicators – sharing the responsibility with UNICEF and the OECD for the other remaining two. Given the initial classification of a number of metrics as Tier 2 and Tier 3 indicators (e.g. indicators not regularly produced by countries or for which measurement standards are not available yet), their refinement and production rapidly become a priority for UIS, which, as discussed below, perceived their organizational legitimacy or prestige as closely tied to the fate of these global indicators (cf. UIS, 2017a).

Global indicators were in turn complemented by a thematic indicator framework, originally developed by the Technical Advisory Group on Education Indicators (TAG) established by UNESCO in 2014 and included in a draft form in the Framework for Action. This document proposed up to 43 indicators and, more importantly, established the leading role of the UIS in developing and refining this initial list – in collaboration with Member States and other education stakeholders and SDG4 partners.

Given the complexity of such endeavours, but also in order to guarantee the participation of a wide range of stakeholders, two ad hoc mechanisms were created with a view to advance the development and production of SDG4 global and thematic indicators – namely, the Technical Cooperation Group (TCG) and the Global Alliance to Monitor Learning (GAML). The former was established in 2016, being conceived as a space for discussion as well as a technical platform to support UIS in the implementation of the thematic indicator framework, and to assist other bodies and countries in their data-collection and reporting efforts. Chaired by the UIS and the UNESCO Education Sector's Division for Education 2030 Support and Coordination, the TCG is composed by regionally-representative UNESCO Member States, as well as representatives of different IOs, civil society organizations and the co-chair of the Education 2030 Steering Committee (see UIS-TCG, 2017).

The GAML, in turn, was created in 2016, being originally defined as an 'umbrella initiative to monitor and track progress towards all learning-related Education 2030 targets' (UIS, 2016, p. 49), and tasked with the development of tools, methodologies and shared standards to measure learning outcomes in the context of SDG4. The GAML is also expected to support and strengthen country-level capacities to generate and use learning data (see UIS, 2017b). Its membership is open to any individual or organization willing to contribute to the work of the GAML. Representatives of Member States have been gaining prominence since 2018, with the engagement of countries being increasingly perceived as central to the GAML's success and legitimacy. With the UIS hosting the Secretariat, the GAML operates by definition in an open and participatory manner, with decisions being made through consensus.

Importantly, these mechanisms did not emerge in a vacuum. Quite the contrary, and as the notion of policy trajectory helps establish, both of them were born out of already existing initiatives launched during the run-up towards the approval of Education 2030. More specifically, the TCG represents a continuation of the TAG established in 2014. The GAML, in turn, was a successor of the Learning Metrics Task Force (LMTF), launched in 2012 as a multi-stakeholder partnership co-convened by the Center for Universal Education at the Brookings Institution and the UIS. However, both the TCG and the GAML entailed a procedural shift vis-à-vis their own precedents. Both initiatives are explicitly articulated as subject to a transparency mandate, and are expected to operate through democratic, equitable and inclusive dynamics. In this sense, both spaces are subject to a dual form of accountability; they are held responsible over the results of their work, but judged also over the quality and inclusive character of their delibera-tions. To put it differently, both spaces are characterized by a built-in tension between a democratic imperative and the technical and specialized nature of the work they are tasked with.

In the following section, we examine the manifestations and implications of this tension between a democratic and a technical ideal. To this end, we draw on data from semi-structured interviews with representatives of different organiza-tions partaking in the SDG4 indicator development efforts – including IOs, but also civil society organizations and technical partners actively involved in such endeavour. The interviews were conducted during the 2017–2019 period in the context of two separate, but complementary studies.[2] Such data-collection efforts were in turn complemented with the documentary analysis of publicly-accessible reports, technical notes and declarations produced in the context of the SDG4 negotiations and, specifically, indicator-development efforts as those that centred the activity of the GAML and the TCG.

From mediation to instrumentation: Producing data and consensus for the SDG4

As the overview above suggests, the negotiation and production of SDG4 indica-tors has been guided from the outset by a double imperative – preserving techni-cal sophistication while ensuring political legitimacy. Even if (theoretically) such principles are not mutually exclusive, as we will show below, this double impera-tive has frequently translated into a form of tension or duality. Thus, the everyday practice of turning these principles into actionable strategies and plans is often associated with different courses of action, different (and sometimes competing) forms of expertise and different valuation standards and consensus-making prac-tices. Making decisions often means prioritizing among these competing logics – deciding on a division of labour and an agenda, but also determining who is brought to the table, whose proposals are selected and whose proposals are ruled out. It is in these *mediation* practices that the tension between technocratic and political legitimacy crystallizes and becomes evident. In this section, we inquire into the different manifestations of such mediations and translations in bridging concerns of the apparent contradiction of a highly technical process, being also a democratic one.

Whose voices? Opportunities and costs of 'getting everyone on board'

Debates around the role of country representatives are particularly illustrative of such tensions and mediations. The inclusion of country representatives to the Technical Advisory Group,[3] and the transition from the TAG to a TCG explicitly geared towards the incorporation of national voices, constitute revelatory epi-sodes of the frictions created by this democratization ideal. The unease generated by the incorporation of country representatives among UN agencies appears to stem partially from the (perceived) risk of politicization of what would otherwise constitute a dispassionate, technical debate. An additional source of concern is the nature of the expertise exhibited by those representing the national perspective. Country representatives are thus perceived as lacking the necessary preparation to effectively contribute to TCG debates:

> There's of course the other issue of people who come tend to be illiterate sta-tistically. Not always, because some countries send bureaucrats. But there are enough people. But the question is how are these people linked, and how well do they represent first of all not just their own country, but the region
>
> (UNESCO 1)

The evolution of GAML suggests similar dynamics. Widening the membership of the platform (and especially incorporating country representatives) was seen as necessary to secure the buy-in and cooperation on the part of the Member States that, ultimately, should produce and developed the indicators, and report them according to the procedures and standards discussed in GAML:

> The first meeting of GAML only had technical partners around the table. And I would say to an extent this is understandable. It's such a technical question, you can't quite open the discussion to everybody, you need to find a common language, and share common objectives, and then you can present that to the political level. Now, this seems to have open up a little bit more. … I guess it's a realization that things can move quickly, so you don't want to present a solu-tion completely all of a sudden.
>
> (Interviewee/UIS)

At the same time, such democratization efforts were perceived as problematic by those participants with a more technical profile – or more concerned by the statis-tical and psychometric sophistication of data-collection efforts:

> We can't consult everyone, everywhere, we've gone through this whole tech-nical consultation. Is there some value in saying these are the technical stan-dards? … And it keeps going back to this theme of democracy and voice. Is there such a thing as too much democracy, too much consultation? At what stage do you say we just have to run with this, this is what it is?
>
> (Interviewee/World Bank)

Paradoxically, what was perceived as *excessive* consultation among certain GAML members, was deemed insufficient among others – especially those representing civil society more explicitly driven by a principled agenda privileging openness and coun-try ownership. The inclusion of these domestic actors was sometimes perceived as a performative exercise motivated by formalist concerns. Given that it is unclear how the preoccupations or motions put forward by countries do effectively inform the work or decisions made by GAML, some interviewees pointed to a risk of tokenism:

> And then what the GAML did last time was that they actually supported representatives from the Global South, but they were flown in to give

presentations about what they are already doing. Which isn't a bad thing to do, but in practice it meant that we had about six hours of uninterrupted PowerPoint presentations and no real participation of these people in the actual meeting. ... It was a bizarre setup.

(Interviewee/Civil society)

Whose data?

When it comes to the production of indicators, the selection or prioritization of specific data sources has also brought to the fore the tension between democratic and technocratic ideals. While both of them are expected to equally inform the measurement labour of UIS, the selection of one dataset or another frequently entails a de facto prioritization of one principle over the other. Disputes on the measurement of learning through large-scale assessments are particularly illustrative of such tension. While some IOs and assessment consortia claim that the need for global reporting in an argument in favour of the in-built comparability enjoyed by *international* large-scale assessments (ILSAs), other actors have called into question such notions – arguing that the value of data lies in its *usability for domestic policymakers* and that, in consequence, national large-scale assessments (NLSAs) represent equally valid (if not more appropriate) data sources when it comes to measuring learning. Ultimately, the ILSAs vs. NLSAs debate echoes a more fundamental disagreement on what constitutes valuable or trustworthy knowledge:

> We [*at the OECD*] are working with UNESCO, and the UIS, to help fill capacity for measuring progress at the end of primary. And there's a proposal to use national assessment systems, as far as possible, but a lot of these national assessment systems ... the quality of these assessments is not good
>
> (Interviewee/OECD)

> I would say that global metrics in their purest sense, and by the highest standards of psychometrics, are impossible. So the question is, can we do them well enough that they are fit for purpose, right? [...] And I fear that there will be some people who see the imperfections, and see a glass half-empty rather than a glass half-full. And so that's what I fear. And the consequence of that is to go to something like PISA or TIMSS or PIRLSS, or you know, one of the international studies
>
> (Interviewee/ACER)

Negotiating organizational legitimacy

One of the direct consequences of the existence of two (potentially conflict) principles expected to guide data production has been the emergence of competing sources of organizational legitimacy or authority. Since such forms of authority are enjoyed to differing degrees by the concerned IOs, disagreements over the hierarchization of democratic vs. technocratic demands should be read in connection with the competition for dominant positions in the measurement field. As a consequence, a number of inter-organizational tensions have unfolded – with some organizations privileging technical robustness and others putting a premium on procedural values such as inclusion, democracy and consensus. Among the former, the OECD features prominently. Representatives of the orga-nization have thus argued that the technical expertise of the organization is unmatched in the education measurement realm. Conversely, representatives of UNESCO emphasize their own mandate as the custodian agency for SDG4, as well as their capacity (and responsibility) to represent the interests of all Member States:

> The OECD really doesn't have a mandate to work with Sub Saharan Africa. This is the mandate of the UNESCO institute of statistics. So OECD shouldn't come now and tell even UNESCO for example, you were talking about the relationship between OECD and UNESCO. OECD shouldn't go to UNESCO in Paris and say oh we can do all these things for you, why don't you work with us? There is an Institute of Statistics that's part of UNESCO that should be doing this.
>
> (Interviewee/UIS)

Importantly, the technocratic-political tension manifests itself in the form of fric-tion or dissent not only *between* organizations, but also *within* organizations. Thus, technocratic and democratic imperatives are likely to translate into conflict-ing demands that pull certain organizations toward opposite directions. Such dynamics have been particularly visible in the case of the UIS – which, as noted above, is held accountable over the technical robustness of the data produced and reported, but also over the democratic and inclusive character of data-collection and data-production processes. This frequently translates into the need for some form of compromise. It is precisely in this form of compromise (both internally and externally) that UIS as an actor has had an important mediating role; with UNESCO being the lead organization, that UIS as an actor has had an important mediating role. With UNESCO being the lead organization, the UIS needs to mediate between the technical experts of other IOs, the numerous public and private research agencies that contribute with data, and national representatives and civil society actors who are interested in the democratic legitimation and equal representation of all countries involved. Although brokerage efforts for finding some kind of equilibrium between technical superiority and plurality of voice are to be found in all IOs involved, the UIS – with its proclaimed indepen-dence from UNESCO – is the key institution mediating and acting as the buffer in this unusual epistemic vs. political tug-of-war. In the following interview extracts, UIS actors discuss the opportunities but also difficulties of having this role:

> It has always been very difficult to have a global conversation about these tools that are being used to measure learning in different regions [...] And the UIS neutrality in the global governance agenda, plus its mandate, positions the UIS as the natural convener for the discussion. And many

stakeholders do agree that the UIS is neutral and has this mandate, that gives the UIS the leverage to engage with this discussion. So I think it would have been unfortunate for the UIS to let this opportunity go

(Interviewee/UIS)

So OECD has a TCG, but the world has not a TCG of the same calibre, where countries lead the decision. And I'd say it's very, very difficult. To the credit of the UIS for having established it … but the amount of effort it would take to do that at a global level is very difficult, is very high. So the problem is the effort it takes. You know, the UIS is not a particularly well-funded organization … It has a convening power, but it doesn't have the resources.

(Interviewee/UNESCO)

At the same time, the reliance on consensus-making and the participatory, inclusive nature of UIS-led debates could come at a cost. The UIS risks being perceived as inefficient as a result of its own democratization efforts. Such reputation is considered to negatively impact the volume of resources available for measuring and monitoring SDG4:

My take on that, and I could be wrong, but my take is the funding will be available … and the funding is out there, provided GAML is clear about their governance and what it wants to achieve. So I think that among the funders and government agencies and philanthropic agencies and so on, there's plenty of money to do this. That would be my take. But, these people are gonna keep their hands in their pockets, not pull the cash, you know, until it's not absolutely clear what's gonna be done, by whom it's gonna be done, and where's gonna be done.

(Interviewee/Technical partner)

Discussion

After decades of education scholarship examining accountability as fluid, chameleonic and all-pervasive (Sinclair, 1995), SDG4 represents a clear case of a new era in the role and practices of accountability – at least at the level of the transnational governance in education. The chapter has discussed the tensions arising from the coexistence of two, separately demarcated, types of accountability logics. As we have seen above, these are the political and the technical types of accountability, which, at least in the governing of the SDG4, appear to be stirring uneasy discussions amongst the main players in the field. The chapter has shown actors' apprehensiveness about whether they can maintain the legitimacy of their expertise, when faced with the demand for technocracy to be politically accountable, too. On the other hand, those actors who strive for more inclusive and diverse decision-making, do not want to be seen as less rigorous, or as compromising the validity and robustness of the data produced. It has to be stressed that although, in the quotations above, the divergence between the UNESCO versus the OECD and World Bank perspectives seem to frame a discussion of contrasting organizational cultures and ways of working, a deeper look into the controversy shows that organizations do not take monolithic or single views on this, but that there is also a great deal of internal organizational struggle and contest.

How to make sense of this open disagreement over which type of accountability ought to prevail in the process of producing monitoring for SDG4? First, our data purport that the making of the SDG4 offers a particularly opportune moment in which to enter the organizational agendas and practices of the major international organizations, whose work has been defining in many ways the trends in global education governance for at least two decades. Both projects are focused on exploring the workings of producing data for education policy; by entering the laboratory of the making of numbers, one can acquire a much better grasp of the political nature of the decisions in relation to the production of data.

Secondly, and perhaps more importantly, the examination of the making of the SDG4 as the first collaborative endeavour to produce a measurement agenda for global governance is a unique opportunity to examine how the major IOs come together and drift apart in the making of data for policy. In many ways, the politics of data production has so far been part of the black box of organizational processes that, in their majority, remain hidden from public (and researchers') view. The interdependency of IOs in producing monitoring for the SDG agenda allows for a more nuanced understanding of the politics of the making of quantification, since it reveals the knowledge and value conflicts that large IOs have.

However, beyond IOs' interdependency and the challenges that come with it, what is it about the SDG4 that unravels the accountability conundrum and requires that different kinds of accountability are treated equally in the governing of the transnational space of education? For a long time, the accountability that large international comparative assessments faced was one that related solely to their robustness and trustworthiness. Thus, comparative assessments have long been challenged primarily on technical grounds – with much of the debate revolving around solidity and validity (see Rutkowski, 2018 for an overview of such limitations). Despite the emergence of more politically-driven criticisms focusing on the (mis)uses and effects of such comparative exercises, the debate on international assessments has tended to develop in a bifurcated way – with political and technical discussions neatly separated one from another, taking place in different spaces and relying on different parlances (Gorur, 2017). What is it about the SDG4 that has unearthed this conflict of political and technical accountabilities? The chapter, through a careful and detailed examination of the historical trajectory and the developments that led to the birth of the SDG4, in addition to actors' own voices, has shown how it was precisely the close collaboration of different IOs that contributed to a large extent to these tensions.

All three key organizations that take part, OECD, UNESCO and the World Bank, bring their knowledge expertise and networks to the table. With the datafication of transnational education governance as a given, the struggle now moves to a different plane: as we have seen in this chapter, some of these IOs see their function as primarily the guarantors of the legitimacy of the whole global education governing agenda as fair and democratic. Thus, UNESCO, at least, appears to be using its capital as a trustworthy defender of a more humanistic face of education, while the OECD and the World Bank, although protecting their technical expertise, also use their networks and tried-and-tested methods of managing consensus. In this new, global game of the datafication of education governance, the concerns of legitimizing the process move now beyond the mere argument of 'trust in numbers'. As shown above, the struggle of individual and organizational actors is to maintain the scientific authority and technical objectivity of the exercise, whilst ensuring that this is a politically and democratically fair process – and not another colonial endeavour into building new data empires in the Global South.[4]

This chapter argues that Maroy and Pons' (2019) tripartite schema of the examination of *trajectory, mediation* and *instrumentation* represents a promising approach to understand the challenges faced by SDG4 it its attempt to bring the two accountabilities together: the political and the technocratic one. Thus, and as shown in detail above, the historical trajectory of the SDG4 played a key role in how it was shaped from the beginning, as well as where it would move towards. Whilst maintaining some of the features of all such monitoring instruments, for example, the defining and setting of an architecture of quantitative measures of performance to be achieved by a totemic time point (2030), SDG4's trajectory also saw the introduction of quite a new governing style: an open, inclusive, participatory mode of organizing the work, which has involved (and continues to involve) extensive consultations. It was precisely this specific trajectory that meant that translation and brokering work would become such as an essential part of the IOs' work.

The notion of mediation as advanced by the authors has also been key for the discussion of the continuous co-construction of accountabilities, at different settings and times and by different actors. Remarkably, although all relevant IOs need to do this kind of mediating work both for their internal as well as their external audiences, the UIS appears as the main actor tasked with the role to find a middle ground between the centrifugal forces of statistical robustness and democratic legitimacy. We have shown above the challenges and opportunities of this political work (Lagroye, 1997), as the Institute navigate the risks and perform the (maybe impossible) task of trying to satisfy such a diverse array of stakeholders and interests.

Indeed, in order to understand the ability of IOs to validate their work through being both technically and politically accountable, we need to understand the core condition that makes any accountability process successful. Thus, there is never a single space or time that any decisions of this kind are taken. The informality, multiplicity and dynamism of the epistemic and policy networks that bring the SDG4 into being is built precisely on the ability to simultaneously use different discourses and accountabilities, depending on the context and participant actors. Therefore, although there may be meetings and spaces where the complex technical statistical work of validating data for indicators takes place, there are also parallel meetings where these data are presented to national representatives for their approval. These represent the essential consensus-making and mediating work that is a sine qua non for the approval not only of countries, but crucially of funders and donors too.[5]

Finally, the making of SDG4 is in essence the manifestation of an 'apparatus' as Lascoumes and Le Galès (2004) describe – and, consequently, can be productively analysed as an instance of an instrumentation process as conceptualized by Maroy and Pons (2019). Both technical and social, SDG4 could be seen as a prime example of a transnational soft regulatory instrument (in the tradition of soft law, i.e. best practices, expert standards, rankings, ratings, audits, quality assurance and the like). As such, it creates competitive and reputational pressures on those participating – including pressures for countries to set up (or invigorate) their statistical infrastructure and educational management information (EMIS) systems. In this sense, the SDG4 represents a singular exercise in that it weaves together two forms of accountability that have traditionally been perceived as disparate, if not irreconcilable – that is, political and administrative accountability (see Bovens, 2007; Verger and Parecerisa, 2017 for a discussion of different forms of accountability in education). This is so as the possibility for countries to engage in a form of political accountability (by reporting on and answering for their progress against the SDGs) is made conditional on their engagement with administrative forms of accountability (through which public administrations collect and analysed data on performance or behaviour of a range of education stakeholders).

Finally, the chapter has shown how the SDG4 does not merely set broad global measurement agendas, but crucially politically legitimizes the endeavour by claiming that it gives participating actors equal say – putting different countries and IOs on an equal footing. Therefore, it is interventionist in nature, leading effectively to a mutually constitutive relationship of the statistics and the countries they are meant to represent. More importantly, it represents a leap in the practice of transnational soft regulation in education because, although prescriptive, it also appears as transparent, pluralistic, open and developmental. In the end, little will it matter whether the targets will be met or not. In having set up such a complex, yet fluid, governing infrastructure, the SDG4 has been successful already.

Funder acknowledgement

This manuscript is part of a project that has received funding from the European Research Council (ERC) under the European Union's Horizon 2020 research and innovation program, under grant agreement No 715125 METRO (ERC-2016-StG) ('International Organisations and the Rise of a Global Metrological Field', 2017-2022, PI: Sotiria Grek).

Notes

1 This publication is informed by two separate research projects: (a) it is part of a project that has received funding from the European Research Council (ERC) under the European Union's Horizon 2020 research and innovation programme under grant agreement No. 715125 METRO (ERC-2016-StG) ('International Organisations and the Rise of a Global Metrological Field', 2017–2022, PI: Sotiria Grek); and (b) it draws on the data collected in the context of a PhD project funded by the Spanish Ministry of Education and Science under the Programme for University Lecturer Formation (FPU) (grant FPU014/0611, awarded to Clara Fontdevila).

2 Please see note 1.

3 Originally formed exclusively from representatives from IOs and technical agencies.
4 This preoccupation echoes recent debates on the specific impact of datafication on middle- and low-income in the reproduction of power asymmetries between the Global North and the Global South. See, for instance, Arora's (2016) insights into the parallels between ambitious data projects unfolding in the South and colonial regimes of surveillance; or Couldry and Mejías' (2019) discussion on data colonialism and the extractive nature associated to contemporary data-collection practices.
5 Thus, the UIS has received financial support from a variety of bilateral aid programs and philanthropic organizations – relevant donors include the Bill & Melinda Gates Foundation, the UK Department for International Development and the Norwegian Agency for Development Cooperation. While such organizations expect the UIS to make significant, rapid progress in the measurement of SDG4, they also place a high value on an inclusive and participatory modus operandi – one open to the input of a variety of development partners, as opposed to one tightly controlled by international bureaucracies.

References

Arora, P. (2016). Bottom of the data pyramid: Big data and the global south. *International Journal of Communication*, 10(2016), 1681–1699.

Barrett, A. M. (2016). Measuring learning outcomes and Education for Sustainable Development: The new education development goal. In W. C. Smith (Ed.), *The Global Testing Culture: Shaping Education Policy, Perceptions, and Practice* (pp. 101–114). Oxford, UK: Symposium Books.

Bostrom, M., & Garsten, C. (2008). *Organising Transnational Accountability*. Cheltenham, UK: Edward Elgar Publishing.

Bovens, M. (2007). Analysing and assessing accountability: A conceptual framework. *European Law Journal*, 13(4), 447–468.

Bowen, K. J., Cradock-Henry, N. A., Koch, F., Patterson, J., Häyhä, T., Vogt, J., & Barbi, F. (2017). Implementing the 'Sustainable Development Goals': Towards addressing three key governance challenges – collective action, trade-offs, and accountability. *Current Opinion in Environmental Sustainability*, 26–27, 90–96.

Clegg, L. (2015). Benchmarking and blame games: Exploring the contestation of the Millennium Development Goals. *Review of International Studies*, 41(5), 947–967.

Couldry, N., & Mejias, U. A. (2019). Data colonialism: Rethinking big data's relation to the contemporary subject. *Television & New Media*, 20(4), 336–349.

Djelic, M. L., & Sahlin-Andersson, K. (2006). *Transnational Governance: Institutional Dynamics of Regulation*. Cambridge, UK: Cambridge University Press.

Fukuda-Parr, S., & McNeill, D. (2019). Knowledge and politics in setting and measuring the SDGs: Introduction to Special Issue. *Global Policy*, 10(Suppl. 1), 5–15.

Gorur, R. (2017). Towards productive critique of large-scale comparisons in education. *Critical Studies in Education*, 58(3), 341–355.

King, K. (2017). Lost in translation? The challenge of translating the global education goal and targets into global indicators. *Compare: A Journal of Comparative and International Education*, 47(6), 801–817.

Lagroye, J. (1997). *Sociologie politique*. Paris: Dalloz-Presses de la FNSP.

Lascoumes, P., & Le Galès, P. (2004). *Gouverner par les instruments*. Paris: Presses de la Fondation Nationale des Sciences Politiques.

Maroy, C., & Pons, X. (2019). Introduction. In C. Maroy & X. Pons (Eds.), *Accountability Policies in Education: A Comparative and Multilevel Analysis in France and Quebec* (pp. 1–12). Cham, Switzerland: Springer.

Meyer, J. W., Boli, J., Thomas, G. M., & Ramirez, F. O. (1997). World society and the nation-state. *American Journal of Sociology*, 103(1), 144–181.

Ozga, J. (2013). Accountability as a policy technology: Accounting for education performance in Europe. *International Review of Administrative Sciences*, 79(2), 292–309.

Porter, T. M. (1996). *Trust in Numbers: The Pursuit of Objectivity in Science and Public Life.* Princeton, NJ: Princeton University Press.

Power, M. (1999). *The Audit Society*. Oxford, UK: Oxford University Press.

Rutkowski, D. (2018). Improving international assessment through evaluation. *Assessment in Education: Principles, Policy & Practice*, 25(1), 127–136.

Sinclair, A. (1995). The chameleon of accountability: Forms and discourses. *Accounting, Organisations and Society*, 20(2/3), 219–237.

UNESCO. (2016). *Education 2030: Incheon declaration and framework for action for the implementation of Sustainable Development Goal 4* (ED-2016/WS/28). Retrieved from: https://unesdoc.unesco.org/ark:/48223/pf0000245656

UNESCO Institute for Statistics (UIS). (2016). *Sustainable Development Data Digest. Laying the Foundation to Measure Sustainable Development Goal 4*. Montreal, Canada: UNESCO-UIS.

UNESCO Institute for Statistics (UIS). (2017a). *SDG 4 monitoring: Framework development* (GAML4/REF/18). Retrieved from: http://uis.unesco.org/sites/default/files/documents/gaml4-sdg4-monitoring-framework-development.pdf

UNESCO Institute for Statistics (UIS). (2017b). Global Alliance to Monitor Learning (GAML): Concept paper. Retrieved from: http://gaml.uis.unesco.org/wp-content/uploads/sites/2/2018/10/gaml-concept_paper-2017-en2_0.pdf

UNESCO Institute for Statistics (UIS)/Technical Cooperation Group (TCG). (2017). *Technical Cooperation Group on the SDG 4 – Education 2030 indicators (TCG)*. Terms of Reference – Draft. Retrieved from: http://tcg.uis.unesco.org/wp-content/uploads/sites/4/2018/08/TCG_ToRdraft_20170929.pdf

United Nations General Assembly. (2015). *Transforming our world: The 2030 agenda for sustainable development.* Resolution A/RES/70/1. Retrieved from: http://www.un.org/ga/search/view_doc.asp?symbol=A/RES/70/1&Lang=E

Unterhalter, E. (2019). The many meanings of quality education: Politics of targets and indicators in SDG 4. *Global Policy*, 10(Suppl. 1), 39–51.

Verger, A., & Parecerisa, L. (2017). *Accountability and education in the post-2015 scenario: International trends, enactment dynamics and socio-educational effects*. Background paper prepared for the 2017/8 Global Education Monitoring Report. Retrieved from: https://unesdoc.unesco.org/ark:/48223/pf0000259559

3 Re-engineering the infrastructure of performance-based accountability: For-profit philanthropy, learning sciences, and automated education at the Chan–Zuckerberg Initiative

Ben Williamson

Accountability systems driven by performance on standardized achievement tests have become central to education reform, at national and international scales, over the past three decades. Since the 1990s, accountability systems focused on quantitative performance measures, high-stakes incentives and sanctions have steadily evolved and consolidated to become centralized mechanisms of control, and have made testing and the reporting of results into a dominant form of educational policy and governance (Lingard, Martino & Rezai-Rashti, 2013). Variously termed 'test-based', 'results-based' or 'performance-based' accountability, these systems of measurement have both political and technical aspects. In political terms, accountability systems have been developed at the level of states and nations (Anagnostopoulos, Rutledge & Bali, 2013a; Mintrop & Sunderman, 2013), as well as internationally through the involvement of organizations including the OECD, World Bank and UNESCO (Anderson, 2005; Ozga, 2013).

Understood in technical terms, performance-based accountability has been made possible by the creation of large-scale information systems that enable test results and performance data to be collected, connected together, analysed and diffused (Gulson & Sellar, 2018). The data required for test-based accountability are 'the products of complex assemblages of technology, people, and policies' that stretch across education systems (Anagnostopoulos, Rutledge & Jacobsen, 2013b, p. 2). Data infrastructures consist of technologies, analytics and standards of data collection produced by networks of actors that include policy centres, technical organizations, experts in measurement practices, and funding and advocacy from institutions such as philanthropic foundations (Hartong, 2018). Data infrastructures also encode particular desires, values, and morals, dictating the evaluative and classificatory criteria for assessing school performance, defining what gets counted and thereby determining what makes a 'good school', a 'good teacher' or a 'good student' (Sellar, 2015).

Influential philanthropic foundations have played central roles in building and promoting the data systems that support performance-based accountability, especially in the United States (Scott & Jabbar, 2013). However, these philanthropies are now beginning to shift their emphasis from test-based forms of accountability to 'personalized learning' centred on the use of digital technologies in teaching, learning and assessment. The focus of this chapter is the Chan–Zuckerberg Initiative (CZI), established in 2015 by Facebook founder Mark Zuckerberg with paediatrician Priscilla Chan as a 'for-profit philanthropy' that makes charitable donations, invests in profit-making companies, and engages in political activity in the areas of science, education and justice (Reiser, 2018). Along with other philanthropies originating from the wealth of technology sector entrepreneurs, notably the Bill and Melinda Gates Foundation established by Microsoft founder Bill Gates, CZI views previous education reform strategies – test-based accountability, school choice, curriculum standardization, and teacher improvement – as policy failures in need of radical reform (Matthews, 2018). Instead of test-based accountability, CZI promotes digital technologies and science to narrow the achievement gap between students at the top and bottom of the socio-economic scale, improve the evidence base for policymaking, and 'personalize' educational experiences around the unique profile of the individual student (Wexler, 2019).

The central argument presented in this chapter is that CZI, together with other tech philanthropies, is attempting to re-engineer the 'infrastructure of test-based accountability' that has been integral to US schooling policies and practices for two decades (Anagnostopoulos, Rutledge & Jacobsen, 2013b). An analysis of CZI's 'Education Initiative' reveals how it is: (1) 'disrupting' educational philanthropy as a for-profit mode of 'impact investing' and thereby introducing new 'market accountabilities' into education systems; (2) prioritizing the scientific measurement of learning and how to improve it through 'learning engineering'; and (3) driving advanced technologies into schools to enable automated measurement and improvement through 'personalized learning'. CZI is seeking to distantiate itself from regimes of standardized testing and performance-based accountability by creating new models of measurement and intervention. The CZI's Education Initiative directors claim, 'Our increasing knowledge about developing minds, technological advances, and evidence-based approaches … allow us to know more than ever before about what works' (Stafford-Brizard & Saxberg, 2019). As the chapter demonstrates, CZI is prototyping a novel infrastructure of accountability based less on test-based performance measurement and more on digital 'big data', new scientific methods of measuring learning, and automated interventions. Drawing on an 'infrastructure studies' approach to 'map the assemblages of technologies, people and policies that must be created to build and operate the information infrastructure' (Anagnostopoulos et al., 2013b, p. 8), the analysis presented in this chapter draws on the CZI website, its grants and ventures database, public materials from its funded projects, and associated media commentary, in order to map out the ways CZI is seeking to re-engineer the infrastructure of accountability in US education.

Philanthropy and performance-based accountability

Internationally, school accountability has become a key feature of education policy and governance since the 1980s, with the massification, marketization, decentralization, standardization, and increased documentation of education raising questions concerning the quality and responsibilities of schools and teachers (Smith & Benavot, 2019). Consequently, many schooling systems have introduced standardized testing to hold schools and teachers to account through the publication of comparative performance data (Lingard et al., 2013). Policymakers have turned attention to ensuring high-quality education as measured by student outcomes and results, and to ongoing monitoring and auditing of the performance of institutions and staff (Hopmann, 2008). The result is that teaching is treated as test preparation; test scores as indicators of school quality and accountability; and schools are subjected to managerialist techniques of performance management (Smith, 2014).

Although these are international developments, the US education system has been a particularly intense site of performance accountability measurement. The mid-1990s was a period of significant growth in advocacy for performance-based accountability in US schools, including incentivist policies (financial rewards) and punitive sanctions based on student test outcomes (King & Mathers, 1997). Test-based accountability consolidated with the federal No Child Left Behind (NCLB), the main law for US education from 2002 to 2015, which established clear targets based on quantitative information about student performance as the dominant way of incentivizing and measuring for school improvement (Mintrop & Sunderman, 2013). The Obama-era Race to the Top programme introduced further 'value-added teacher assessments' to existing accountability mechanisms (Holloway & Brass, 2018), while the introduction of the Every Student Succeeds Act (ESSA) in 2015 returned authority for implementing accountability systems to states, but introduced new indicators (including non-academic measures of performance) as part of a more 'holistic' approach to accountability (Jimenez & Sargrad, 2017).

Education philanthropies have developed their involvement in performance-based school accountability over the two decades since NCLB was introduced (Scott, 2009; Reckhow & Snyder, 2014). Across education systems in Europe and worldwide too, working alongside experts, edu-businesses, consultants, advocacy networks, and financial organizations, philanthropies are key players in new 'network governance' structures and relations (Lawn & Grek, 2012; Ball, Junemann & Santori, 2017). Under network governance, wealthy elites, foundations, corporate leaders, and non- and for-profit organizations increasingly shape policy and are paid for direct services to public education (Au & Lubienski, 2016). As influential network actors, philanthropies both act on the demand side of policy and reform, by pursuing change through political advocacy, lobbying and media, and on the supply side, by developing new reformatory technologies (Saltman, 2010), thereby creating new market spaces in which 'for profit solutions, outside or over and against state provisions, are given possibility and legitimacy' (Santori, Ball & Junemann, 2016, p. 204).

In this context, philanthropies have helped import managerial models of performance measurement from the private sector into public education, redirecting attention from 'strong accountability' around social goals and democratic processes to performance accountability through quantitative market comparison (Ozga, 2013). These business-aligned philanthropies are 'privatizing the policymaking process itself, as philanthropists such as Gates re-write the rules in their own favor, and then distribute resources in ways that advance their agendas in those new policy landscapes', while simultaneously 'contributing to the nurturing of a global education industry' (Au & Lubienski, 2016, p. 38). They have shifted the functions and position of philanthropy from charitable giving to active design, negotiation, promotion and delivery of policy processes, both by 'giving back' profit from their businesses to social causes, and by using 'their donations in a business-like way – that is, in the form of strategic investments that should lead to "good" measurable results' (Olmedo, 2016, p. 47). Their activities have been captured in terms such as 'philanthrocapitalism' and 'venture philanthropy', characterized by the application of business terms – investment, impact, efficiency, returns, performance measurement, and so on – to education reforms and policies (Saltman, 2010). The key claim of the philanthrocapitalist version of philanthropy 'is that markets and morals are not distinct phenomena, but rather commensurate goods', which 'resonates with long-held economic assumptions of the moral advantages of capitalism' (McGoey, 2012, p. 186).

Accountability is a key concern of philanthrocapitalism because it focuses on the measurable performance of its investments and their outcomes. Wealthy philanthropists have also combined strategic investment with 'big data', enabling 'tech experts' to 'manipulate the data and help entrepreneurs more efficiently "fix" institutions' through 'business-tech theory' inspired 'experiments' in testing, rating and ranking schools by performance (Rasseger, 2020, n.p.). As such, philanthropies have been integrally involved in the infrastructural construction and maintenance necessary to performance-based accountability, through funding programmes, defining data interoperability standards, and political lobbying (Scott & Jabbar, 2013). The Chan–Zuckerberg Initiative has become a leading philanthropic organization in education over the past five years, using the wealth of its founders to advocate new models of accountability based on an increasingly pervasive collection of intimate data about student performance rather than the periodic testing that has characterized accountability regimes in the US and internationally for more than two decades.

Disruptive philanthropy

The Chan–Zuckerberg Initiative was established in 2015 by the paediatrician Priscilla Chan and billionaire Facebook founder Mark Zuckerberg with a pledge to give 99% of their net worth (US$45 billion) to 'personalized learning, curing disease, connecting people and building strong communities' (Zuckerberg, 2015). These moral ambitions have consolidated into CZI 'Initiatives' in Science, Education, Justice and Opportunity, all supported by technology engineering:

> We are a new kind of philanthropy focused on engineering change at scale. Our engineering team partners with issue experts across our Science, Education, and Justice & Opportunity Initiatives, to help bring technology to the table in new ways that drive solutions.
>
> (https://chanzuckerberg.com/technology/)

In its first three years, CZI made $1.6 billion in grants and $110 million in investments in organizations and initiatives seeking to pair engineering to 'change at scale' in its three key 'mission' areas, positioning it as one of the top five US philanthropic donors. CZI represents a pairing of moral ambition and engineering expertise, aspiring not just to 'doing good' while generating capital, but to producing moral, mission-led markets for technological goods. As a high-profile technology entrepreneur, Zuckerberg developed links into political, financial, media, philanthropic and scientific networks too, enabling him to increase his power by brokering common goals and sharing resources across these networks (Moran, 2018).

Rather than setting up as a traditional non-profit, tax-exempt foundation, CZI was established as a Limited Liability Company (LLC), a legally-defined entity giving it capacity to engage in grantmaking, investment, and political action with few restrictions and enhanced personal control for its founders. LLCs have become an increasingly common model for 'Silicon Valley philanthropy' or 'for-profit philanthropy', with organizations including eBay founder Pierre Omidyar's Omidyar Network, Laurene Powell Jobs' Emerson Collective, and ex-Google CEO Eric Schmidt's Schmidt Futures.

> The philanthropy LLC structure offers donors the flexibility to bolster charitable grantmaking with impact investment and political advocacy, free of the restrictions, penalties, and transparency requirements applied to tax-exempt vehicles. The LLC form also provides donors complete control over the organizations they found, including an ability to reclaim donated assets that is absolutely prohibited in traditional forms …, at relatively little tax cost.
>
> (Reiser, 2018, p. 921)

Zuckerberg claimed CZI would mirror Bill Gates's 'Giving Pledge' to commit tech wealth to social problems (Cassidy, 2015). Saltman (2018) notes that the Gates Foundation is typical of a 'nonprofit venture philanthropy foundation' that applies business ideals, corporate culture, and a private sector approach to charity while still qualifying as a philanthropic 'giver'. By contrast, CZI operates as a 'for-profit company' that raises a 'serious question as to whether CZI functions philanthropically at all or whether its activities are only profit seeking and "philanthropy" is a label intended to project an image of "corporate social responsibility"' (Saltman, 2018, n.p.). Reiser (2018, pp. 926–927) terms CZI a 'disruptive philanthropy' that 'can make both grants to non-profit entities like a traditional foundation and equity investments and acquisitions like a venture capital or private equity fund'. The LLC philanthropy model is well suited to the culture of 'disruption' in Silicon Valley: it transposes ideals of risky technological innovation on to philanthropy, privileging entrepreneurs who want to manage 'gift-giving' in commensurate ways to personal profit-making (Reiser, 2018).

CZI represents a 'third wave' of philanthropy. The traditional philanthropies of the twentieth century – the Rockefeller, Carnegie and Ford foundations – were challenged by aggressive 'venture philanthropic' strategies of the Gates Foundation, Eli and Edythe Broad Foundation, and the Walton Family Foundation

(Scott, 2009; Au & Lubienski, 2016). In its for-profit, impact-investing and 'disruptive' mode, CZI acts more like a Silicon Valley business, investing in risky innovations and technical engineering as a template for policy solutions. Third wave philanthropy combines commitments to moral purposes, market-making, and advanced computational product development with the aspiration of making measurable social and public impact and a return on investment. 'By demanding that philanthropy be impact-oriented, market-savvy and cost-effective, the new philanthropy explicitly assumes a moral hierarchy of philanthropic value that is structured according to measurable financial benefit' (McGoey, 2012, p. 193). In other words, as the next section demonstrates, disruptive philanthropies such as CZI have begun introducing new market accountabilities into education, where investees are accountable to their investors to perform in ways that produce both measurably beneficial social outcomes (moral values) and produce a return on investment (market values).

Measuring impact

The Chan–Zuckerberg Initiative is reconfiguring performance-based account-ability through funding programmes focused specifically on the measurement of human development and learning progress rather than standardized tests. Reflecting its emphasis on engineering innovations across its philanthropy and investments portfolio, CZI's Education Initiative focuses on technological solutions, data and evidence:

> We build tools that help teachers tailor learning experiences to the needs of every student, with an emphasis on using evidence-based practices from the fields of learning science and human development … We believe in a data-driven approach … [and] that students need to learn more in school than what is measured on standardized tests. Our tools help students set and track progress towards short- and long-term goals, make plans, demonstrate mastery when ready, and reflect on their learning.
>
> (https://chanzuckerberg.com/technology/education/)

By countering standardized tests, CZI is seeking to re-engineer the ways learning is measured and reported—as temporally continuous performance traces that indicate progress in learning and development. This evidence is to be captured using new data tools that CZI builds and supports.

In its more conventional grant-giving capacity, CZI has funded over 80 education projects aligned with its 'data-driven' mission since 2018, according to its grants database (https://chanzuckerberg.com/grants-ventures/grants/?initiative=education), plus earlier grants not visible on its grants database (Barnum & Zhou, 2018). The grants exemplify the educational mission of CZI, many focused on charter schools, scientific research on learning and child development, evidence-based policy, digitally-enhanced 'personalized learning', and reducing inequality. CZI's largest grant to date is $23 million awarded to Summit Public Schools, a network of public charter schools, 'to enhance the quality of student-teacher interactions and tailor learning to meet individual student needs through the Summit Learning Program – a person-alized approach to teaching and learning shared at more than 300 district-run, public charter, and independent schools nationwide'. It gifted a further $2 million to TLP Education (Teachers, Learners & Partners) to scale up the Summit Learning Program – the personalized learning software used across the schools' network – to 'reach schools nationwide'.

Through support for Summit and other charter school operations, CZI is firmly committed to 'disruptive' philanthropic provision of personalized learning as a private service alternative to state schooling. Venture philanthropic support for charter schools has played a central role in performance-based school accountability, by developing new data systems to measure and report performance outcomes and demonstrate measurable improvements in student learning:

> the new philanthropists have come to favour school choice, privatization, and charter schools, among other deregulatory educational reforms. They often believe that educational reform could greatly benefit from the strategies and principles that contributed to their financial successes in the private sector. As such, they tend to favor market-based hallmarks such as competition, standardization, and high-stakes accountability.
>
> (Scott, 2009, p. 108)

As foundations have invested in charter organizations, systems of accountability have found purchase in national US policies from NCLB to ESSA. CZI's grants for charter networks and the expansion of associated data systems nationwide is a key mechanism for further embedding advanced accountability systems in schools at very large scale, though its emphasis on data-driven personalized learning represents a marked shift away from test-based forms of accountability measurement.

Beyond grant-giving, CZI's Ventures arm is significantly involved in 'impact investing' (https://chanzuckerberg.com/grants-ventures/ventures/). Using finan-cial instruments such as 'social impact bonds', 'results-based financing' or 'pay for success initiatives', impact investing involves injecting capital into enterprises that generate measurable beneficial social outcomes alongside financial returns on the invested capital. Impact investing has become a significant form of educational funding globally, as a way to allow private firms to fund public projects (Srivastava & Read, 2020), and reflects 'the trend toward increasing accountability practices tethered to impact evaluations that use "what works" criteria to judge investments in education and other social service' (Carnoy & Marachi, 2020, p. 7). Such arrangements prioritize efficiency savings, the delivery of low-cost/high-impact outcomes, and are based on calculations about return on investment, made in both moral and marketized terms, which prioritize accountability to investors (Saltman, 2018). As with other impact investors such as the Gates Foundation, the Omidyar Network LLC, 'and other widely known foundations that are heavily steeped in policies that promote both the privatization and datafication of educa-tion in the US', the promise for the investor is to profit from impact outcomes while 'a corollary payoff ... resides in the data extracted as evidence of success' (Carnoy & Marachi, 2020, p. 11).

The switch to outcomes- and performance-based impact investing alongside datafication is significant for existing regimes of performance-based accountability because it builds measures of performance and impact, based on expectations of measurably beneficial social and financial returns, into the initial criteria for investment. CZI is strongly involved in efforts to define the criteria for 'what works' in terms of delivering measurable educational outcomes, which can then be used as a guide to 'what works' in terms of guaranteeing a profitable return on investment. A $1.5 million grant awarded by CZI to the Tides Foundation's Impact Genome Project, for example, is intended to produce 'a free, searchable evidence-base and tools to make use of the data on what works in education':

> Drawing on hundreds of research studies and program evaluations, the Education Genome creates standardized taxonomies or common terminology, for program activities, beneficiaries, contexts and outcomes. This data standard allows social programs to use a common language to describe what they do, who they benefit and what outcomes they produce. The benefit of a common data standard is that it enables the field to compare programs and combine research findings across a field so that we can begin to understand what works and why.
>
> (https://www.impactgenome.org/education/)

The Education Genome funded by CZI 'covers outcomes related to student academic achievement, teacher effectiveness, social & emotional learning, school environment and college persistence', as well as 'secondary or "adjacent" outcomes such as employment, health, crime, youth development, financial stability and entrepreneurship'. By funding the Education Genome 'data standard', CZI is supporting a standardized tool for the performance measurement of the impact of educational initiatives without the need for test results. Instead of test outcomes, the 'impact DNA' standard delimits educational impact investment to proven benchmarks of 'what works' in terms of 'cost-per-outcome', thereby focusing investors' attention on programmes that can be standardized, coded, quantified and analysed in comparative and evaluative terms. The Education Genome data standard is, in other words, a key component in the re-engineered infrastructure of accountability pursued by CZI, because it provides a standard for evaluating the performance of its investments.

Ultimately, then, through mechanisms such as the Education Genome for standardized measurement of 'what works', funded educational programmes are subject to new forms of performance-based accountability, as the criteria for assessment are reduced to cost-per-outcome and return-on-investment calculations determined through standard taxonomies. Such impact calculations are based on accountability to investors rather than solely to the public beneficiaries of educational programmes. By funding the Education Genome, CZI is entrenching impact investing instruments as key ways of measuring outcomes for performance-based accountability purposes, and in so doing is valorizing programmes that help deliver profit to investors. It also shifts the emphasis to market accountability, whereby investees are accountable to their investors' demands for return on investment rather than accountable to the publics their initiatives are supposed to serve. Moreover, it shifts attention in accountability measurement from regimes of testing, to other ways of quantifying student performance.

Learning engineering

The second key way that CZI is reshaping performance-based accountability is through its commitment to 'learning science', which includes the use of data analytics and other innovative forms of 'learning measurement' from the psychological, cognitive and neurological sciences (https://chanzuckerberg.com/education/learning-science/). This is continuous with long-standing efforts in the 'global education industry' to mobilize statistical evidence and the objectivity of science to frame and support services and policy proposals, giving edu-businesses and philanthropies more policy credibility (Verger, Lubienski & Steiner-Khamsi, 2016), and reflects a technicization, scientization and politicization of educational knowledge production (Lubienski & La Londe, 2019).

However, in contrast to existing modes of test-based accountability, CZI supports a shift in focus away from test outcomes to far more intimate tracking of processes of learning, as captured and analysed through the disciplinary lenses of psychology, cognitive science, and neuroscience. The so-called 'learning sciences' have rapidly gained scientific legitimacy over the past decade, as technologies such as learning analytics and other data monitoring systems have become available to capture real-time, long-term, and intimate data about individuals' learning processes (Williamson, 2019). In this context, CZI is one among a growing network of new educational actors advocating learning science approaches based on various aspects of cognitive, neuro- and psy-sciences. The OECD (Organisation of Economic Cooperation and Development) has begun to invest significant institutional resources and advocacy into 'the science of learning'. Focusing on 'the interplay of the biological, physiological, cognitive and behavioural processes supporting the learner', it advocates for 'technological advances, particularly in neuroscience, engineering, and computer and information sciences', to be put to the task of policy-relevant knowledge production in education (Kuhl et al., 2019, p. 16).

CZI has become a generous funder of learning science-based research, as reflected in a $5million fund for 'teams of schools, support organizations, and researchers who want to apply the science of learning and human development to improve existing school-based practices' (https://chanzuckerberg.com/newsroom/5-million-funding-opportunity-to-support-the-whole-child/). Moreover, a high-profile 2019 National Academies for Sciences, Engineering and Medicine 'consensus study report' on how to apply scientific insights about the 'adolescent brain' to public services – education, healthcare, child welfare and youth justice – was co-funded by CZI and strongly advocated personalized learning technologies 'to tailor instruction to meet individual needs' (NASEM, 2019). Its funding for the report exemplifies CZI's ambition to bring neuroscience into educational practice and knowledge production. A further 2018 partnership with the Gates Foundation began to explore the science of 'executive function' and the neural substrates of learning, leading to another 'consensus report' and a blueprint for further research and development (CZI & Gates Foundation, 2019). It catalysed a joint Gates/CZI $50million fund for the five-year EF+Math Program, designed to award basic and applied research in executive function, which is housed within the NewSchools Venture Fund and led by educational neuroscientists at the University of California San Francisco (https://www.efmathprogram.org/). The programme lead of EF+Math is also the Director of Education at Neuroscape at UCSF, a brain-imaging centre awarded a further $2.9 million by CZI to develop 'a free mobile tool to measure child and adult progress in executive functioning skills such as working memory, attention, problem solving, and goal setting'.

As well as funding learning science experts, CZI in-housed expertise by hiring Bror Saxberg to lead its learning science strategy. Saxberg is a high-profile learning scientist within the education technology industry, who has popularized the notion of 'learning engineering' as a multidisciplinary blend of the learning sciences, instructional design and learning analytics:

> getting the most from learning analytics has to be an interdisciplinary effort: computer science, linguistics, education, measurement science, cognitive science, motivational and social psychology, machine learning, cognitive neuroscience among others. These different domains will need to be combined to build out an effective evidence-grounded 'learning engineering' version of learning analytics.
>
> (Saxberg, 2018, p. viii)

In this 'learning engineering' version of education, data gathering and modelling 'ultimately can allow for personalization to interests, capabilities, identity, social-emotional state, and motivation states for individual learners', by using evidence 'at multiple levels, from clickstreams, motion position data, speech streams, gaze data, biometric and brain sensing, to more abstracted feature sets from all this evidence' (Saxberg, 2018, p. viii). The use of this evidence across 'multiple dimensions', he adds, will allow examination of longitudinal and multidimensional trajectories, clusters and patterns of 'learner change', thereby helping to identify 'new opportunities for targeted intervention' and 'precise action' that are analogous to data-scientific 'precision medicine' (Saxberg, 2018, p. x). Through Saxberg and its learning science grants, CZI is promoting learning engineering as an educational parallel to precision medicine, part of a shared imaginary of 'precision education' based on data-scientific methods and interdisciplinary human sciences (Williamson, 2020).

CZI is mobilizing, supporting and advocating learning sciences and learning engineering as evidence-based policy agendas focused on measures of learning, cognition and its neural substrates rather than the test-based outcomes characteristic of existing infrastructures of performance-based accountability. As CZI's Bror Saxberg argues, learning analytics and learning science focus on 'valid and reliable, performance-based measures of learner capabilities' rather than 'just better measures of academic performance' (Saxberg, 2018, p. ix). Through its multimillion dollar grants, partnerships, engineering and support for new research and development programmes, CZI is constructing prototypical components for a re-engineered infrastructure of accountability focused on assessing the performance of the brain, cognitions and affects of students. Key to this precision education and learning engineering approach is the development of data analytics technologies for diverse performance assessments and the personalization of learning experiences.

Automated accountability

The third CZI approach to reengineering the infrastructure of performance-based accountability is through algorithmic data analytics and 'personalized learning' software. Although CZI and its investees present personalized learning software as a transformative technology, the initial growth in such advanced data analytics systems in education was itself driven by concerns to capture information required for accountability:

> shrinking fiscal resources and the expansion of a global competitive education market have fueled this increasing pressure for educational accountability. The offshoot of these economic drivers has been the development in the education sector of standardized scalable, real-time indicators of teaching and learning outcomes.
>
> (Lockyer, Heathcote & Dawson, 2013, p. 1439)

The subsequent proliferation of learning analytics led further to adaptive personalized learning platforms where the real-time measurement of teaching and learning produces predictions of student progress, and an adaptive response by the system itself to ensure measurably beneficial outcomes. For all the transformational hype surrounding them, these educational data analytics are automated engines of accountability, originally designed to provide detailed real-time measures of student performance, and then to 'optimize' the results through personalized adaptations that match the individual.

By adopting the ideal of personalized learning, CZI's Education Initiative reflects the business experience of Zuckerberg as founder of Facebook, a platform built on the capacity of software algorithms to personalize consumer experience online and thereby secure long-term user engagement as a source of capital generation. CZI has extensively trialled and refined learning analytics and personalized learning software through its long-term partnership with Summit Public Schools. Zuckerberg first partnered with Summit in 2014–2015 by seconding a Facebook team to help build its personalized learning software. The platform is part of the Summit Learning school improvement programme now reportedly used in 400 schools across the USA (https://www.summitlearning.org/).

The platform integrates CZI's interests in personalized learning and learning science by deploying an explicit model of cognitive skills development developed at the Stanford Center for Assessment, Learning and Equity:

> Summit developed the Cognitive Skills Rubric built into our Summit Learning Platform in collaboration with the SCALE team at Stanford, whose mission is to improve instruction and learning through the design and development of innovative, educative, state-of-the-art performance assessments and by building the capacity of schools to use these assessments in thoughtful ways, to promote student, teacher, and organizational learning.
>
> (http://info.summitlearning.org/program/program-requirements/)

Through the rubric, Summit's 'state-of-the-art performance assessments' make real-time cognitive assessment into a key accountability mechanism. Summit has also produced a 70-page white paper outlining the learning science research underpinning the platform design. 'The Science of Summit' introduces findings regarding cognitive skills development, content knowledge acquisition, social-emotional learning, 'habits of success', and 'sense of purpose', all of which it defines as 'measurable outcomes' (https://cdn.summitlearning.org/assets/marketing/The-Science-of-Summit-by-Summit-Public-Schools_03052019.pdf).

CZI's commitment to Summit demonstrates its resistance to conventional notions of accountability. Rather than highlighting high-stakes accountability through test scores, CZI emphasizes skills, habits and purposefulness that can be continually assessed in almost invisible ways, through the personalized learning software that tracks progress and outcomes and adapts to ensure future improvement. The Summit platform is a hidden infrastructure of accountability based on automated measurement and feedback. As its most high-profile and well-rewarded project, Summit is paradigmatic of CZI's approach to performance-based accountability. In common with other Silicon Valley-based foundations, venture philanthropies, and edtech businesses, it is based on an imagined 'future of education' that is 'radically customized through technology and mediated by commercial interests. This is education "unbundled" from traditional schools and redistributed in personalized learning "grids" and "ecosystems" created by edu-preneurs and unfettered market forces' (Means, 2018, p. 106). In this approach, personalized learning software becomes 'performance-based accountability 2.0': a socio-technical upgrade to existing infrastructures of test-based measurement, quality evaluation and intervention that promises value both to policymakers and to the market by gathering intimate performance assessment data from students and personalizing education according to the models of learning science.

Conclusion

In conclusion, CZI is intervening in a re-engineering of performance-based school accountability through for-profit disruptive philanthropy, learning engineering interventions, and as a source of automated accountability through personalized learning software. In the context of network governance, CZI is creating new topologies of policy influence, by empowering new organizations, actors and practices through funding and investment. It is making Facebook money a key source of educational investment, and investing it in new governing networks of experts, practitioners, and scientists. By merging its philanthropic outlook with its market ambitions, CZI encodes particular moral concerns into its funding projects and also its technical engineering products. In many ways, CZI is continuous with the activities of other venture philanthropies which have invested in 'jurisdictional challengers' to state education, divested support from more traditional educational institutions, and also injected new perspectives from alternative scientific disciplines into educational policy debates (Reckhow & Snyder, 2014). With its emphasis on disruptive philanthropy and technological disruption through engineering prowess, CZI can be characterized as a 'jurisdictional disruptor' that is both continuous with existing infrastructures of accountability but also 'disrupts' them in specific ways.

Its first disruptive influence is to challenge democratic notions of state schooling by offering for-profit provisions that accrue capital back to the company. Reflecting 'education financialization' in the global education industry (Verger et al., 2016), CZI is both a philanthropic grant-giving organization and a for-profit private investor that openly exploits its charitable mission for profit-making purposes and speculative financialization. In this sense, 'gift-giving' collapses into 'personally profiting' in a new kind of moral economy, since 'what is most novel about the new philanthrocapitalism is the openness of personally profiting from charitable initiatives, an openness that deliberately collapses the distinction between public and private interests in order to justify increasingly concentrated levels of private gain' (McGoey, 2012, p. 188). New kinds of market accountabilities emerge from such arrangements, where the performance of educational initiatives is made measurable both in terms of socially beneficial outcomes and profitable outcomes for investors.

Second, CZI is disrupting test-based accountability by focusing on a wider range of performance assessment measures defined by experts in learning sciences and learning engineering. It is furthering the scientization of education by viewing learning processes, including their neural, affective and cognitive substrates, as objectively measurable and machine-readable. Yet the science here is also subject to moralization, with CZI positioning science as part of its 'mission' and as a solution to 'tough challenges' and 'big problems'. These are part of the encoding of particular desires and moral frameworks in data infrastructures, and a key aspect of political negotiations about what should be counted and valued in education (Sellar, 2015). Ultimately, CZI mobilizes science to reassert its moral authority and organizational values, while reorienting accountability systems to focus on the measurement of students in increasingly intimate detail through real-time performance assessments rather than periodic testing events.

Its aggressive push for engineering solutions to schooling, plus its strategy of rendering performance-based accountability invisible and automatable through personalized learning software, is its third major disruptive influence. This enhances 'systems based on algorithms attached to automatic sanctions' that characterize test-based infrastructures of accountability and separate 'accountability for education from informed judgment by professionals' (Henig, 2013, p. xi). It also advances their recursive power to intervene performatively through personalized feedback in the very educational processes they measure. The technicization of school accountability is hidden inside opaque software systems that deploy sophisticated algorithms and analytics to profile students in terms of real-time measurable performances, and then make automated decisions to customize subsequent courses of instruction. Products such as the Summit Learning Platform act as moral technologies for achieving what CZI defines as desirable and measurable beneficial outcomes as opposed to other criteria for evaluating worth and value in education (Saltman, 2018).

Finally, CZI disrupts understandings of how contemporary philanthropy functions and its strategies of influence over education, science and technology. If the early 2000s were marked by an increasing philanthropization of education – characterized by the Gates Foundation's venture philanthropic efforts to generate capital from gifts awarded to support test-based accountability – then CZI's status as a Limited Liability Company raises fresh questions about the entanglement of philanthropy, impact investment, political advocacy, and technology engineering in new systems of accountability. LLCs magnify elite influence to set policy agendas, and fund initiatives that deliver them, without public debate, transparency, or accountability, while primarily focusing on issues that ensure a rapid return on investment. The subtle shift from philanthropy to LLC empowers and rewards unaccountable technology elites to identify problems and apply technical fixes. School accountability itself, formerly perceived as a problem to be solved through the application of measurable quality standards, has now been reframed by LLCs such as CZI as a problem to be corrected through the application of Silicon Valley expertise. CZI is leading efforts to re-engineer the infrastructure of performance-based accountability, with potentially significant effects on the future of schools' policy and practice.

References

Anagnostopoulos, D. Rutledge, S.A. & Bali, V. 2013a. State education agencies, information systems, and the expansion of state power in the era of test-based accountability. *Educational Policy*, 27(2), 217–247.

Anagnostopoulos, D., Rutledge, S.A. & Jacobsen, R. (eds). 2013b. *The Infrastructure of Accountability: Data Use and the Transformation of American Education*. Cambridge, MA: Harvard Education Press.

Anderson, J.A. 2005. *Accountability in Education*. Brussels: International Academy of Education.

Au, W. & Lubienski, C. 2016. The role of the Gates Foundation and the philanthropic sector in shaping the emerging education market: Lessons from the US on privatization of schools and education governance. In Verger, A., Lubienski, C. & Steiner-Khamsi, G. (eds), *The Global Education Industry*, pp. 27–43. London: Routledge.

Ball, S.J., Junemann, C. & Santori, D. 2017. *Edu.net: Globalisation and Education Policy Mobility*. London: Routledge.

Barnum, M. & Zhou, A. 2018. Mark Zuckerberg's education giving so far has topped $300 million. Here's a list of where it's going. Chalkbeat, 6 September: https://chalkbeat.org/posts/us/2018/09/06/czi-education-donations-list/

Carnoy, M. & Marachi, R. 2020. *Investing for 'Impact' or Investing for Profit?* Boulder, CO: National Education Policy Center. Online: http://nepc.colorado.edu/publication/social-impact-bonds

Cassidy, J. 2015. Mark Zuckerberg and the rise of philanthrocapitalism. *The New Yorker*, 3 December: https://www.newyorker.com/news/john-cassidy/mark-zuckerberg-and-the-rise-of-philanthrocapitalism

CZI/Gates Foundation. 2019. Education Research and Development: Learning from the field. Gates Foundation, March: http://k12education.gatesfoundation.org/index.php?pdf-file=1&filename=wp-content/uploads/2019/03/Education-RD-RFI-Synthesis-Report.pdf

Gulson, K. & Sellar, S. 2018. Emerging data infrastructures and the new topologies of education policy. *Environment and Planning D: Society and Space*, 37(2), 350–366. https://doi.org/10.1177/0263775818813144

Hartong, S. 2018. Towards a topological re-assemblage of education policy? Observing the implementation of performance data infrastructures and 'centers of calculation' in Germany. *Globalisation, Societies and Education*, 16(1), 134–150.

Henig, J. 2013. Foreword. In Anagnostopoulos, D., Rutledge, S.A. & Jacobsen, R. (eds), *The Infrastructure of Accountability: Data Use and the Transformation of American Education*, pp. vii–xiii. Cambridge, MA: Harvard Education Press.

Holloway, J. & Brass, J. 2018 Making accountable teachers: The terrors and pleasures of performativity. *Journal of Education Policy*, 33(3), 361–382.

Hopmann, S.T. 2008. No child, no school, no state left behind: Schooling in the age of accountability. *Journal of Curriculum Studies*, 40(4), 417–456.

Jimenez, L. & Sargrad, S. 2017. A new vision for school accountability. Center for American Progress, 3 March: https://www.americanprogress.org/issues/education-k-12/reports/2017/03/03/427156/a-new-vision-for-school-accountability/

King, R.A. & Mathers, J.K. 1997. Improving schools through performance-based accountability and financial rewards. *Journal of Education Finance*, 23, 147–176.

Kuhl, P.K., Lim, S.-S., Guerriero, S. & van Damme, D. 2019. *Developing Minds in the Digital Age: Towards a Science of Learning for 21st Century Education*. Paris: OECD.

Lawn, M. & Grek, S. 2012. *Europeanizing Education: Governing a New Policy Space*. Oxford: Symposium.

Lingard, B., Martino, W. & Rezai-Rashti, G. 2013. Testing regimes, accountabilities and education policy: Commensurate global and national developments. *Journal of Education Policy*, 28(5), 539–556.

Lockyer, L., Heathcote, E. & Dawson, S. 2013. Informing pedagogical action: Aligning learning analytics with learning design. *American Behavioral Scientist*, 57(10), 1439–1459.

Lubienski, C. & La Londe, P. 2019. Politicized data and spatial methods: Generating understanding of contemporary educational policy environments and interventions. In Gorur, R., Sellar, S. & Steiner-Khamsi, G. (eds), *Comparative Methodology in the Era of Big Data and Global Networks*, pp. 76–95. London: Routledge.

Matthews, D. 2018. Billionaires are spending their fortunes reshaping America's schools. It isn't working. Vox, 30 October: https://www.vox.com/future-perfect/2018/10/30/17862050/education-policy-charity

McGoey, L. 2012. Philanthrocapitalism and its critics. *Poetics*, 40, 185–199.

Means, A.J. 2018. *Learning to Save the Future: Rethinking Education and Work in an Era of Digital Capitalism*. London: Routledge.

Mintrop, H. & Sunderman, G. L. (2013). The paradoxes of data-driven school reform: Learning from two generations of centralized accountability systems in the United States. In Anagnostopoulos, D., Rutledge, S. & Jacobsen, R. (Eds.) *The Infrastructure of Accountability: Data Use and the Transformation of American Education*. Cambridge, MA: Harvard Education Press (23–40).

Moran, R.E. 2018. Examining switching power: Mark Zuckerberg as a novel networked media mogul. *Information, Communication and Society*, 23(4), 491–506. https://doi.org/10.1080/1369118X.2018.1518473

NASEM (National Academies of Sciences, Engineering, and Medicine). 2019. *The Promise of Adolescence: Realizing Opportunity for All Youth*. Washington, DC: The National Academies Press.

Olmedo, A. 2016. Philanthropic governance: Charitable companies, commercialization of education and *that thing* called 'democracy'. In Verger, A., Lubienski, C. & Steiner-Khamsi, G. (eds), *The Global Education Industry*, pp. 44–62. London: Routledge.

Ozga, J. 2013. Accountability as a policy technology: Accounting for education performance in Europe. *International Review of Administrative Sciences*, 79(2), 292–309.

Rasseger, J. 2020. Billionaire power? Two decades of education policy are a cautionary tale. National Education Policy Center, 9 March: https://nepc.colorado.edu/blog/billionaire-power

Reckhow, S. & Snyder, J.W. 2014. The expanding role of philanthropy in education politics. *Educational Researcher*, 43(4), 186–195.

Reiser, D. 2018. Disruptive philanthropy: Chan-Zuckerberg, the limited liability company, and the millionaire next door. *Florida Law Review*, 70(5), 921–970.

Saltman, K. 2010. *The Gift of Education: Public Education and Venture Philanthropy*. New York: Palgrave Macmillan.

Saltman, K. 2018. *The Swindle of Innovative Education Finance*. Minneapolis: University of Minnesota Press. Online ebook edition: https://manifold.umn.edu/projects/the-swindle-of-innovative-educational-finance

Santori, D., Ball, S.J. & Junemann, C. 2016. Financial markets and investment in education. In Verger, A., Lubienski, C. & Steiner-Khamsi, G. (eds), *The Global Education Industry*, pp. 193–210. London: Routledge.

Saxberg, B. 2018. Preface. In Niemi, D., Pea, R.D., Saxberg, B. & Clark, R.E. (eds), *Learning Analytics in Education*, pp. vii–x. Charlotte, NC: Information Age Publishing.

Scott, J. 2009. The politics of venture philanthropy in charter school policy and advocacy. *Educational Policy*, 23(1), 106–136.

Scott, J. & Jabbar, H. 2013. Money and measures: The role of foundations in knowledge production. In Anagnostopoulos, D., Rutledge, S.A. & Jacobsen, R. (eds), *The Infrastructure of Accountability: Data Use and the Transformation of American Education*, pp. 75–92. Cambridge, MA: Harvard Education Press.

Sellar, S. 2015. Data infrastructure: A review of expanding accountability systems and large-scale assessments in education. *Discourse: Studies in the Cultural Politics of Education*, 36(5), 765–777.

Smith, W.C. 2014. The global transformation toward testing for accountability. *Education Policy Analysis Archives*, 22(116), 1–29. https://doi.org/10.14507/epaa.v22.1571

Smith, W.C. & Benavot, A. 2019. Improving accountability in education: The importance of structured democratic voice. *Asia Pacific Education Review*, 20, 193–205.

Srivastava, P. & Read, R. 2020. New education finance. In: Sarangapani, P. & Pappu, R. (eds), *Handbook of Education Systems in South Asia: Global Education Systems*. Singapore: Springer.

Stafford-Brizard, B. & Saxberg, B. 2019. Tackling today's classroom complexities. CZI Education Initiative, 26 February: https://chanzuckerberg.com/story/tackling-todays-classroom-complexities/.

Verger, A., Lubienski, C. & Steiner-Khamsi, G. 2016. The emergence and structure of the global education industry: Towards an analytical framework. In Verger, A., Lubienski, C. & Steiner-Khamsi, G. (eds), *The Global Education Industry*, pp. 3–24. London: Routledge.

Wexler, N. 2019. How classroom technology is holding students back. *MIT Technology Review*, 19 December: https://www.technologyreview.com/s/614893/classroom-technology-holding-students-back-edtech-kids-education/

Williamson, B. 2019. Intimate data infrastructure: Emerging comparative methods of predictive analytics and psycho-informatics. In Gorur, R., Sellar, S. & Steiner-Khamsi, G. (eds), *Comparative Methodology in the Era of Big Data and Global Networks*, pp. 59–75. London: Routledge.

Williamson, B. 2020. Digital policy sociology: Software and science in data-intensive precision education. *Critical Studies in Education*. https://doi.org/10.1080/17508487.2019.16 91030

Zuckerberg, M. 2015. A letter to our daughter. Facebook, 1 December: https://en-gb.facebook.com/notes/mark-zuckerberg/a-letter-to-our-daughter/10153375081581634/

4 Between fairness optimization and 'inequalities of dataveillance': The emergence and transformation of social indices in German school monitoring and management

Sigrid Hartong and Andreas Breiter

Introduction

With the worldwide success of digitalization, society has been undergoing a period of 'deep mediatization' (Hepp et al., 2017), with digital data becoming increasingly relevant for, and present in, governance as well as in everyday life (van Dijck, 2014; Williamson, 2017). Even though the use of data for education governance itself is nothing new, recent years have marked a new era as data is digitally and automatically formatted to a great extent, recoded, stored, manipulated and distributed (Selwyn, 2014: 1). In the field of education, intensifying 'datafication' has also deeply affected teaching and learning as well as the organization, management and supervision of schools (Jarke & Breiter, 2019; Landri, 2018; Selwyn et al., 2017; Williamson 2017). Digital and automated data have thus become integral features of educational governance and practice, while their 'infrastructuring', which is understood here as the complex socio-technical processes of organizing, producing, processing, managing or mediating data, increasingly acts as a set of powerful new tools for shaping data-based representations of schooling (Breiter 2017; Breiter & Ruhe, 2017; Hartong 2016; Hartong & Förschler, 2019; Hartong & Piattoeva, 2019; Landri, 2018; Sellar, 2015; West, 2017).

Despite a growing body of research which critically examines the overall mechanisms and effects of datafication and digitalization in school governance and practice, we still know too little about '[...] how various forms of digital data are [specifically] set to work within educational contexts, including what data is used, what the uses and consequences are, and how data has become embedded within different organizational cultures' (Selwyn, 2014: 13–14). In other words, there remains a pressing need to empirically trace how new entanglements of actors and digital technologies (e.g. State Monitoring Data Systems, School Management Information Systems, Learning Management Software; see Hartong et al. 2019) have been promoting an increasingly *datafied* school through '[…] practices of sorting, naming, numbering, comparing, listing, and calculating' (Lury et al., 2012: 3; see also Selwyn et al., 2017).

In this chapter, we seek to contribute to this research gap, focusing in particular on the rising pressures on school management and school monitoring to increase *fairness*. Fairness is hereby understood, on the one hand, as a general political rationale to foster equality in education systems, ranging from resource allocation to assessment programmes, rankings and accountability systems. Concepts of fairness are never absolute, but rather constantly debated and negotiated within and across education systems. On the other hand, we argue that with the rise of datafication, the focus of negotiation and legitimation has increasingly shifted towards defining or revising 'fairness measures', which also includes the intentional social adjustment or *correction* of performance-relevant school data (e.g. by taking into account the socio-economic background of students). In this contribution, we use the vivid, yet underexplored example of so-called *social indices*, a 'fairness measure' intended to classify the average socio-economic status of a school (or district), which in Germany is increasingly used to inform school monitoring and management (see also Groot-Wilken et al., 2016; Groos, 2019; Klemm & Kneuper, 2019). In particular, our interest hereby lies in showing how such social adjustment actually manifests in the inscription/representation of inequality in and through data as well as how these adjustments have triggered particular dynamics of governance transformation, including school accountability.

Drawing on more than 50 interviews with education agencies' data experts at the state and district level as well as analyses of documents and data tools used in these agencies across different German Federal States,[1] we show that, on the one hand, such manifestations are highly diverse, strongly contextualized and ambivalent, e.g. regarding what socially adjusted metrics digital tools employ. On the other hand, despite this diversity, we also identify an overarching self-enforcing dynamic deriving from a productive tension between increasing objectivity/fairness and performativity/fuzziness (see also Piattoeva & Saari, 2018), which results in continuous data expansion and refinement. In other words, we contend that once data-based inequality representations (usually with the best of intentions) become linked to governmental decision-making, sooner or later this provokes a need for further adjustments in the form of more or better data, often triggered by unintended consequences and/or political or statistical challenges (see also Groos, 2019; Hartong, 2018; Piattoeva & Saari, 2018; Thompson & Sellar, 2018). Simultaneously, this self-reinforcing dynamic, somewhat paradoxically, co-manifests with what we describe as *inequalities of dataveillance*, whereby particular indicators or social indices become *fixed* and thus objectified as representations of inequality. This could mean that further refinements or adjustments might become 'added' to these objectified numbers, but rarely lead to a full replacement. At the same time, a growing number of monitoring and management practices become affected by the indices, including practices of school performance comparison, resource allocation, school choice and accountability. More generally speaking, while school accountability research has often focused on if and how test data are used to hold schools or teachers accountable (e.g. Anagnostopoulos et al., 2013), with this contribution we seek to better understand the rising governmental power of statistical indices, which increasingly form important, yet still underestimated 'backstages' of accountability calculation and classification.

Following this introduction, we explain our conceptual framing, before briefly describing the research background and methodology from which the findings derive as well as some specifications of the datafication of schooling in the German context. Then, we provide empirical insights into the aforementioned dynamics of (re)fabricating inequality in and through datafication, before ending with a discussion of the findings as well as implications for future research.

Conceptual framing

This contribution is informed by a sociology of quantification (Espeland & Stevens, 2008; Gorur, 2014; Mau, 2019) as well as a critical data studies perspective (Iliadis & Russo, 2016; Kitchin, 2014, 2016), both having become increasingly popular approaches to critically examining the ongoing datafication and digitalization, within and beyond the field of education (e.g. Hartong & Förschler, 2019; Landri, 2018; Sellar, 2015; Selwyn, 2014; Williamson, 2017). A central goal of these approaches lies in better understanding how relations enacted with and through growing amounts of (digital) data work in practice and which effects they produce (see also Perrotta & Selwyn, 2019).

As many scholars have convincingly illustrated, in the field of education, there is no linear and thus easy way of understanding 'data at work', but rather a number of highly contextualized, ambivalent and frequently messy ways in which technology and education appear to interact (Selwyn et al., 2017). This particularly accounts for how education (e.g. 'the school', 'the teacher', 'the student') becomes inscribed and thus prefigured in data/software/programming, producing not only one, but often an interplay of multiple black boxes (see also Bucher, 2018). In other words, the design of underlying algorithms or database models (e.g. definition of variables, number of columns, definition of cell relations, primary key indexing, etc.) used in software and data infrastructures[2] is highly *productive* in the sense of shaping the conditions of possibility for how actors can interact with and interpret data (see also Ratner et al., 2019). It is also *reductive* in terms of what is (in)visibilized in the modelling of digital school representations (Bradbury & Roberts-Holmes, 2017). Similarly, this accounts for specifically (pre-)defined stakeholder groups (e.g. school supervisors, headteachers/principals, teachers or parents), which each become specifically targeted and 'programmed in' as potential users of the data. In other words, processes and forms of data 'information' (Sellar, 2015) and visualization create an in-built logic, which constructs particular social realities by influencing how stakeholders interpret data and enact data-based decision-making, including the evaluation of school performance or accountability-related interventions. Consequently, when taking a critical approach to the increasingly datafied school, it is these information and design processes that scholars need to engage with – something which they are increasingly doing (see for example Gray, Gerlitz, & Bounegru, 2018; Ruppert, 2012).

The empirical focus of this contribution is on how, in the German context, datafication has accompanied attempts to increase the fairness of school monitoring and management through (better) representing – or *objectifying* – social inequality in data infrastructures. While such attempts are informed by a more general belief that datafication can increase educational fairness by replacing human (biased) decision-making with data analysis, each data instrument's design necessarily involves sorting, classifying and evaluating (Mau, 2019). Furthermore, such instruments never capture (and actually never claim to capture) *real*, individually contextualized experiences of inequality, but rather numerically informed representations of parts of constructed inequality, which thus enact inequality-related realities as actual objects of government. Scheel, Ruppert and Ustek-Spilda (2019: 581f) use the concept of *onto-politics* to describe the constitutive power of data, transcending the simplistic idea that data are collected about already existing realities 'out there' (such as inequality), which these data represent more or less accurately. Referring to the field of migration management, they state: '[T]he politics of migration management do not happen after knowledge about migration has been produced. They happen in and through the data practices that are mobilized to know (and enact) migration as an actionable reality' (Scheel et al., 2019: 582). Within this fabrication of knowable categories of people are particular problematic groups, which are framed as needing governmental intervention (Grommé & Scheel, 2019: 21).

While the focus of this contribution is mainly on *social indices* – illuminating both the variety and dynamics of their design and transformation – there are many more examples from the datafication of schooling which could be used to discuss similar forms of social categorization (also a core mechanism in the exploding field of learning analytics or adaptive learning tools). Despite this, the (re)productive effects of such classification practices through data which go well beyond assessment data (such as algorithmic bias, which ultimately does not decrease, but instead reinforces existing inequality, as shown in 2020 by the British example of readjusting grades for A-levels and GSCE) still mark an under-researched topic in the field of schooling, particularly in Germany. Nevertheless, algorithmic bias has increasingly been discussed in the fields of news (e.g. DeVito, 2017; Lazer et al., 2018), predictive policing (Brantingham et al., 2018), or political participation in social media (Theocharis & Lowe, 2016). Most of such empirical studies from other fields show an ambivalent relationship between data, algorithms and decision-making. While political participation might increase through social networking sites, automatic news curation relies heavily on deep learning algorithms and their training data, which reproduces biases. Predictive policing meanwhile simultaneously opens up new forms of criminal justice while increasing racial profiling.

Therefore, it seems important to keep in mind that despite their regulatory power, data infrastructures do not determine users' actions (Allert et al., 2018). Instead, as Selwyn et al. (2017) and Landri (2018) have illustrated empirically, educational actors still interpret data differently and with very different effects. This may include bundles of unintended consequences, rejection, but also different types of performativity, which in turn results in efforts to redesign, refine or adjust data infrastructures to increase their objectivity (see also Hartong, 2018; Piattoeva & Saari, 2018). As demonstrated in the following sections, while this tension between objectivity and performativity is clearly visible in the emergence and transformation of socially adjusted data tools, so are the actual (partly counter-)productive effects of this tension, which, instead of undermining their legitimacy, result in an ongoing intensification or optimization. We illuminate this dynamic using the example of school resource distribution in Germany, which (accompanied, of course, by numerous ruptures, setbacks, simultaneities and overlaps) changed from being informed by (self-reported) student numbers per school to automatically generated student numbers per school, then to including laboriously developed social indices, which today continue to be redesigned and refined.

Simultaneously, we argue that this self-reinforcing dynamic has co-manifested with what we describe as *inequalities of dataveillance*. We show how once particular indicators or social indices become 'fixed' and thus objectified as representations of inequality, a growing number of continuous monitoring and management practices may become affected by these indicators, such as practices of school performance comparison or accountability measures. In other words, as schools become increasingly surveilled through the use of (meta)data (= dataveillance), social indices can become a powerful form of such (meta)data, which ultimately inform multiple sorting, classification and ordering practices, and thus stabilize the (datafied) inequality between schools.

Case selection and material

Before detailing our empirical observations, we briefly explain our rationale for case selection, the research background of the material, as well as methodological issues. For this contribution, we drew on past data as well as ongoing research projects, which have focused on the increasing datafication and digitalization of schooling in the German context. Germany provides an interesting case here, given that the turn towards datafication and digitalization did not begin before the 2000s and is still in its initial stages, particularly regarding the use of digital data for school management and educational (performance) monitoring. In this regard, Germany differs from countries such as the United Kingdom, the United States and Australia, which have created extensive (centralized) data infrastructures and systems of e-governance over the past decades (Hogan et al., 2016; Koyama, 2011; Ruppert, 2012).

Germany is notable for having a strongly decentralized education system, in which federal agencies have no direct influence. Instead, responsibility lies with subnational 'units', the Federal States, within which schooling is organized according to a combination of central authority and school autonomy. To some extent, the Federal States have synchronized their education policies via a Standing Commission of the State Education Ministers (the *Kultusministerkonferenz*, KMK) and via cross-State exchange, which includes increasing datafication and digitalization such as the building of monitoring infrastructures and the implementation of school information systems.

In each Federal State, there is an additional division of responsibility for school matters. While the districts are responsible for the infrastructural dimensions of schooling (such as buildings, maintenance and school administration), the pedagogical aspects (teacher education, training, and hiring, curricula and accountability) lie with the State departments of education. This division also explains a common gap between information management systems for administrations (e.g. statistics) and data infrastructures for school improvement and accountability (e.g. test data collection), which is still visible in many German Federal States. Nonetheless, the growing relevance of data infrastructures with its flows and practices has become increasingly visible in Germany and contributes to a gradual reduction in the gap between administrative and performance data.

Over recent years, we have intensively studied instances of rising datafication, including three mixed-method case studies which form the background for the findings illuminated in this contribution. In the first case study, we used a socio-technical system perspective to evaluate the transition process from separate data-bases and spreadsheets to a comprehensive enterprise resource planning system in one German Federal State. We conducted interviews with key stakeholders at the state and school level, scanned and analysed the network server to identify database-like files and modelled the workflows and data delivery processes within the school administration as well as between the administration and schools (Drieling, 2006; Lange & Breiter, 2009). This was later extended to a network analysis of key stakeholders as well as a requirement analysis of their data tool requests.

The second case study, embedded in a larger comparative (United States and Germany) research project on data infrastructures and the digitalization of education policy, focuses on the ongoing transformation of school monitoring infrastructures, from both a national and a state-level perspective. The study includes analyses of (1) policy material, such as national/state monitoring regulations, resolutions and digitalization/datafication programmes; (2) the actors and institutions involved in monitoring and data management at national and state level, using policy network analysis; (3) a closer observation of monitoring infrastructures and their modes of operation in four selected state education agencies; and (4) interviews with national and state-level policy actors, technicians, administrators and data system providers (for a more detailed explanation as well as findings, see Hartong, 2019; Hartong & Förschler, 2019).

The third study is part of an ongoing joint research network (DATAFIED – Data For and In Education).[3] The network not only follows a comprehensive approach by examining (digital) data tools used in teaching and learning but also links these examinations to the operation of data infrastructures within the administration and supervision of schools (which are increasingly made interoperable). In this study, we again use a combination of different qualitative methods, including (1) documentary analysis; (2) interviews with school supervision/consultancy experts, headmasters, school secretaries, software providers, teachers and students; (3) software studies of selected digital tools (e.g. reverse engineering of school information systems); and (4) classroom observations in eight schools/ four different German Federal States. The goal of the network is to trace how ideas of *good* schooling/professionalism/pedagogy become transformed through the growing use of data in school-relevant relationships and systems, which is addressed through four aligned case studies: (1) the interface between school supervision agencies and the school, focusing in particular on practices of evaluation and school quality consultation; (2) a socio-technical analysis of the school management information systems, which also includes the relationship between schools and technology providers; (3) digital tools used in classrooms, which analyse the interface between digital learning software (providers) and classroom practice; and (4) the digital interface between teachers and students in the classroom.

While none of these projects has exclusively focused on the (re)fabrication of inequality through data infrastructures, this de facto appeared as an important element driving datafication and the gradual reshaping of governance and every-day practices in school monitoring and management. This also includes the rise of social indices, which in all three case studies were identified as increasingly pow-erful numbers to inform school governance. It seems important to mention, how-ever, that so far there are four German Federal States which most clearly show a specific social index use, even though there are many other States that use or have started to develop index-like data tools (see Klemm & Kneuper 2019).

The optimization of fairness in school resource distribution and later accountability: Insights into the German context[4]

The dynamics of optimizing fairness started with a rather innocent quest: German Federal States wanted to know exactly how many children and adolescents were registered in schools, in order to inform the annual allocation of resources. For example, the number of domain-specific teachers is commonly based on class size calculation, with a set threshold at which a class must be divided in half. Hence, the number of 'calculated in' students becomes a crucial factor for school princi-pals as they plan resources for each upcoming school year, with individual school management teams responsible for laboriously monitoring and reporting annual student numbers to state agencies. Hence, this procedure has often produced unintended consequences, such as the production of inconsistent data as well as data manipulation, the latter even including the 'invention' of fake students.

While all German Federal States are responsible for overseeing and guarantee-ing compulsory education for every citizen (grade 1–9/10, i.e. ages 6/7 to 16/17, depending on the state), which somewhat contradicts misreported student num-bers, this task is usually delegated to school districts as local administrations are responsible for the obligatory registration of residents as well as the collection of registration data in a centralized database.

With the implementation of digital school management systems and their gradual centralization in many Federal States, data interoperability has become a central topic of debate, resulting in adaptations such as automated interfaces between databases. For example, an interface between the local resident registry and the school information system was established in order to monitor student numbers and school attendance. This often required legal amendments as well as various technical adaptations to manage data flows between the different systems on a (nearly) real-time basis. Such automated data exchange was intended to sig-nificantly increase the fairness of monitoring and management, which included fair(er) resource distribution as well as the provision of education to every regis-tered child.

At the same time, however, it soon produced new conflicts, particularly related to the actual fuzziness regarding socio-economic differences between districts, schools and students, thus once again triggering debates around the need to increase fairness and objectivity by better accounting for social factors. In different Federal States, this redesign included the development of so-called *social indices*, a number intended to classify the average socio-economic status of a school (or district), thus supporting once again fairer resource distribution.

In contrast to synchronization between student records and local resident registries, the calculation/design of social indices appears to be far more complicated and, consequently, so does the inscription of inequality into the various indices. In fact, many of our interviewees in state education agencies were well aware of and even problematized the 'how' of in-valuation, which they described as provoking philosophical, ethical and political considerations (see also Groos 2019: 2):

> The problem is that you might take resources away from someone, which makes it a little difficult. So you have to consider how to distribute what, what concept of justice to rely on, what is meant by fairness [- this] is a highly philosophical question. And a very statistical one, of course [...]. (GER32, translated S.H.)

Consequently, given the different Federal States contexts within which social indices have been developed, we found significant variations in design, including which data are used to frame (and enact) the social categorization of a school or district as an actionable reality source. For example, while to date many Federal States have only used pre-existing data such as the school's location (measured e.g. through geodata) and information about students or their homes (e.g. through addresses), one *Land* (Hamburg) relies on survey data, mainly drawn from a questionnaire for parents, which was specifically designed for the production of the social index. Some Federal States use indicators such as the unemployment rate, the share of people receiving transfer payments, the share of single-parent homes and the share of migrant students – partly collected as district averages, partly as school average data – while others deliberately exclude migration as an indicator.

Similarly, the Federal States differ significantly in terms of modelling and weighting procedures, which refers to the multiple steps (again, often using subindices or the complex interplay of various formula) in which information, in-valuation and index compression is laboriously exercised (Figure 4.1; see also Groos, 2019).

All Federal States that have developed a social index use this index to inform resource distribution, yet again there is significant variation regarding which

$$\text{Budget}_{school\,1} = \frac{\text{student number}_{school\,1} \times \text{Social Index}_{school\,1}}{\Sigma\,(\text{student number}_{all\,schools} \times \text{Social Index}_{all\,schools}} \times total\ budget$$

Figure 4.1 Example of including the social index of a school in budget calculation.

Table 4.1 Comparison of Social Index Usage in four German Federal States

NRW	Hesse	Bremen	Hamburg
Social Index usage: • Allocation of additional teachers (substituting missed lessons + special education) [70% index based]	Social Index usage: • Allocation of additional teachers (only 1% of all teaching positions) • Allocation of new social worker positions	Social Index usage: • Staff allocation • Special education support [88% of special education resources are distributed to the social index] • Language training support • Class size determination • Social worker positions	Social Index usage: • Allocation of financial resources • Staff allocation • Class size determination • Sampling for school inspection • Fair performance comparisons • Subclassification of educational reporting • Selection of schools for special support programmes

kind of funding (e.g. financial resources, additional teachers, social workers or secretary staff, special kinds of teacher training, etc.) as well as what percentage of overall school funding the index becomes linked to (see overview in Table 4.1).

Each allocation dimension is then based on complex weighting/in-valuation procedures, in which the social index now turns into one indicator among others (such as student numbers) (see Figure 4.1).

Here we also see the important, yet often neglected dynamic of the social index, which – as *one* objectified number enacts a specifically modelled reality of inequality – now starts flowing into other types of data practices, while simultaneously and deliberately invisibilizing the complexity of its own production. In other words, the social index becomes an indicator, which, through its *easy* transferability, appears as a highly attractive way to *add fairness* in the form of a numerically enacted, and in this sense fixed, representation of inequality to other monitoring and management procedures.

One example is using the social index of schools as one of many indicators to profile schools on publicly accessible data platforms, thus making it (but not the production procedure behind it) available to other expert (such as researchers) and non-expert (such as parents) user groups. The modes of publication range from unsorted tables (as in North Rhine-Westphalia) to digital school maps (as in Hamburg), in which the social index is actually shown as the very first characteristic of a school (see Figure 4.2).

Figure 4.2 shows an interactive map of all schools in Hamburg. Users can personalize the map view by adjusting the bar on the left-hand side. When clicking on a school, a summary of school data is displayed at the upper right side.

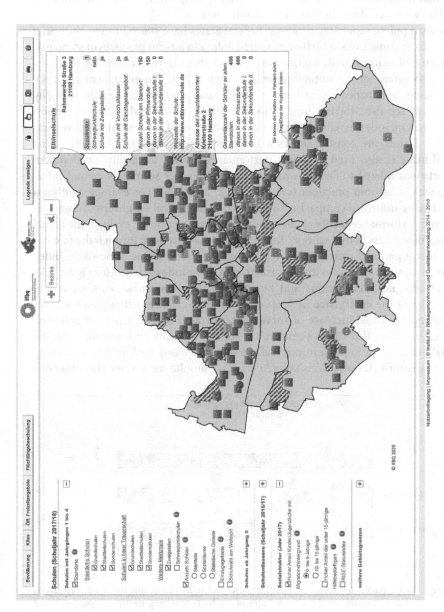

Figure 4.2 Example of social index reporting in Hamburg.
Source: http://bildungsatlas-hamburg.de/Schulen.

These data, inter alia, include the school's name, address, social index (high-lighted) or numbers of students.

However, if and how the published data then goes on to affect, for example, parental school choice has so far remained an open question – one that could not be clearly answered by our state agency interviewees.[5]

Beyond public reporting, different Federal States have started to use the social index (or, in some cases, a further modified index) to inform practices of standardized test evaluation as well as school supervision, thus clearly transferring the index into a 'backstage' of accountability (even though the human judgement of school supervisors and inspectors, at least in the German context, has remained highly important; see also Morris-Lange, 2016: 15). While in some Federal States, schools of a low social index hereby become targeted with special programmes of intervention[6] and, thus, are constructed as a group of schools needing intervention, the social index is also used to adjust performance as well as quality development expectations related to factors which the school/teacher seemingly cannot influence with classroom practices (see also Fiege, 2013: 25). For example, within a social index-informed comparison of test results, numerical subgroups of comparison and performance feedback are modelled, seeking to better evaluate the actual impact of teachers in that school.[7] Fair comparisons thus work through the fabrication of subspaces of commensuration, in which schools of the same social index become compared, but also distinguished from other index groups (see Figure 4.3).

Both special interventions and fair comparisons illuminate what we earlier described as the emergence of *inequalities of dataveillance*: although all schools are facing a gradual increase of surveillance through data in school monitoring and supervision, this varies significantly both in intensity and content, with the social index operating as a numerically condensed fixing tool, which legitimizes these variations (see also Weishaupt, 2016: 23). Simultaneously, we also observe a

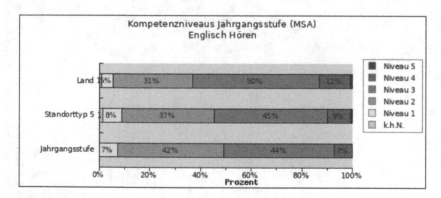

Figure 4.3 Comparing a school's test performance in English Listening using social indices. The figure shows the percentages of students reaching particular performance levels ('niveau'). The figure compares the grade ('Jahrgangsstufe'), the groups of school peers with the same social index (here 'Standorttyp 5') as well as the state average ('Land').

Source: https://www.2019.lernstand8.de/ls8web/ls_sch_pdf.php?schnr=600015&nkklasse= 1&sdatei=outSchulberichtd350e9dd5506859c7869357d99ef6b34.pdf&sname=Schulbericht.

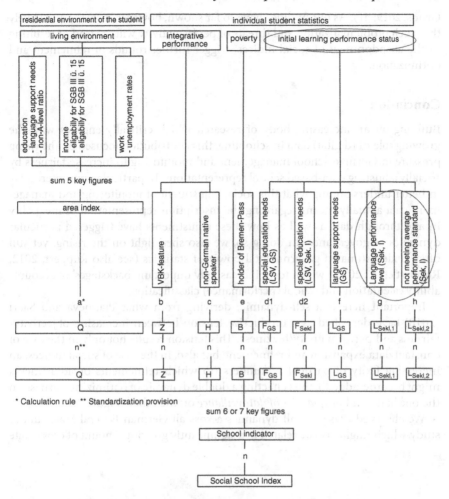

Figure 4.4 Modelling of the social index in Bremen (which includes counting in specific types of school/student performance data; see below).
Source: Makles & Schneider, 2018: 14, translated S.H.

new kind of inverse dynamic, with more available data triggering further remodelling of the social indices, particularly regarding the inclusion of performance metrics (see Figure 4.4).

In other words, the index not only informs more and more data practices but also becomes increasingly infused with other accountability-related numbers.

Finally, it seems important to mention that, as with the synchronization of student records and local resident registries, the rising power of social indices has evoked a number of new conflicts, including people within and beyond state education agencies who still question their suitability to mirror inequality and guide decision-making.[8] This is somewhat linked to concerns about a potential performative reaction from schools that might attempt to manipulate data in order to lower their index and, consequently, receive more funding from the state (see also

Groos, 2019: 4f). As our findings have so far shown, however, it seems quite likely that such problematization and threats of performativity will, instead of resulting in the abandonment of social indices, trigger further rounds of refinement and optimization.

Conclusion

Building on an increasing body of research which critically engages with the growing role of (digital) data in schooling, this contribution focused on the rising pressure in German school management and monitoring to increase fairness by socially adjusting data-based school representations. In particular, our interest lay in better understanding what this social adjustment of monitoring and management data actually means regarding the inscription/representation of inequality in and through data as well as how these adjustments have triggered particular dynamics of governance. In doing so, we also shed light on the rising, yet still often underestimated governmental power of statistics (see also Ruppert, 2012; Ruppert et al., 2017), which form increasingly important 'backstages' of accountability calculation and school (performance) classification.

Important here is a self-dynamic, deriving from what Piattoeva and Saari (2018) have described as a productive tension between increasing objectivity/fairness and performativity/fuzziness. This tension results not only in the case of constant data expansion and refinement, but also, in the case of social indices, an increasing fixity of particular numbers (to which refinements or adjustments might become 'added'), thus enacting a double dynamic of optimizing fairness on the one hand and *inequalities of dataveillance* on the other (Figure 4.5).

We observed these overall dynamics across all German Federal States under study, which might also be related to a significantly growing amount of cross-state

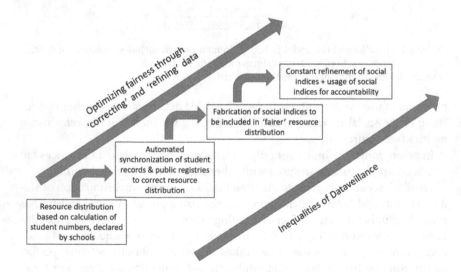

Figure 4.5 The double dynamic of optimizing fairness and inequalities of dataveillance.

datafication activities (e.g. the sharing of data infrastructures or the co-development of monitoring and information systems) as well as national standardization (e.g. promoting national data standards) over the past decade (see also Hartong, 2018; Hartong et al., 2019; Hartong & Förschler, 2019). Nonetheless, despite these similarities, the Federal States still vary significantly with regard to *how* they produce socially adjusted numbers, what becomes accounted for as well as *how* exactly such numbers become linked to resource distribution or accountability (see also Groos, 2019; Groot-Wilken et al., 2016). Closer observations of these variations and linkages may then further contribute to broadening the scope from a still narrowed focus on assessment data to complex accountability operations within constantly transforming data infrastructures.

Regarding the limitations of our contribution, we are well aware that we have only provided some initial thoughts on the actual effects of social indices. In particular, this refers to the potential simultaneity of intended and unintended consequences of social indices, and the consequences of that interplay for either diminishing or reinforcing social inequality between schools. In other words, how might the index-related provision of resources as well as the adjustment of, for example, performance expectation be accompanied by stigmatization, data manipulation, and also effects such as moral hazard, 'cream skimming' or school choice (dis)advantages (Sendzik, 2018)? While we came across interesting ongoing debates on such actual effects, there is still scant knowledge about how small decisions – such as in index design or usage – might produce high-impact differences (see also Diesner, 2015).

Furthermore, our findings illuminated a key problem in ongoing datafication dynamics, namely the *invisibilization* of production logics and, thus, the politics of data (Ruppert et al., 2017). Understanding these politics, however, appears to be of some significance for critical reflection on normativity, which always and somewhat paradoxically plays a key role in the objectivation of inequality. In other words, while we find increasingly complex social measures which (seek to) increase the transparency of schools regarding their social circumstances, we also see decreasing transparency about actual data information (see also Hartong, 2018). We assume that this lack of transparency will further increase with the evolution of digitalization, which, in the case of generating social indices in Germany, is still in its infancy.

Finally, despite the importance of developing a more critical perspective on the datafication of schooling in general, and socially adjusted measures in particular, we must acknowledge the dilemma of developing alternatives. In other words: how, if at all, could a *fair*, data-informed governing of schools be developed, taking into equal account social inequality *and* the (re)productive power of data infrastructures?

Notes

1 In Germany, the subnational level is organized into *Länder* units, very similar to, for example, state units in the United States. For easier understanding in non-German reader communities, in this chapter, we thus use the term Federal States instead of *Länder*.

2 Data infrastructures are taken to be the networks of objects (the data itself, hard- and software, but also policy 'fragments' such as educational standards or funding formulas) and subjects (technicians, administrators, school actors, intermediary agents, etc.) assembled around data and its socio-technical de- and recontextualization practices (see also Hartong & Förschler, 2019; Sellar, 2015; Williamson, 2017).

3 Funded by the German *Federal Ministry of Education and Research* (BMBF) 2018–2021 and based at the Helmut-Schmidt-University in Hamburg (subproject 1), the Institute for Information Management Bremen (ifib) (subproject 2), the Georg-Eckert-Institute (GEI) in Göttingen (subproject 3) and the Leibniz Institute for Research and Information in Education (DIPF) in Frankfurt/Main (subproject 4). See www.datafied.de.

4 We would like to thank Vito Dabisch and Annina Förschler (Helmut-Schmidt-University Hamburg) who have significantly contributed to the data collection and analysis used for this chapter.

5 This reflects the still significant gap in German research on actual effects of data infrastructures in general and social indices in particular, especially in terms of school choice, despite the fact that school choice itself represents a well-researched field of analysis.

6 See, for example, the 23+ program in Hamburg, see https://www.hamburg.de/content blob/10120248/70ec1b9f1d2f7a90d2de36ada2b415bc/data/projektbericht-23-2013-2017.pdf

7 Comparable to value-added models in other countries; see, for example, Amrein-Beardsley, 2008.

8 See, for example, https://www.hamburg.de/contentblob/4458462/5f7d1b2af92c58e732 8be298374bbb05/data/pdf-schulte-und-hartig.pdf, GER03, GER32.

References

Allert, H., Asmussen M., & Richter C. (2018). Formen von Subjektivierung und Unbestimmtheit im Umgang mit datengetriebenen Lerntechnologien – eine praxistheoretische Position. *Zeitschrift für Erziehungswissenschaft, 21*(1), 142–158.

Anagnostopoulos, D., Rutledge, S. A., & Jacobsen, R. (Eds.). (2013). *The infrastructure of accountability: Data use and the transformation of American education.* Cambridge, MA: Harvard Education Press.

Bradbury, A., & Roberts-Holmes, G. (2017). *The datafication of primary and early years education: Playing with numbers.* Abingdon, UK: Routledge.

Brantingham, P. J., Valasik, M. & Mohler, G. O. (2018). Does predictive policing lead to biased arrests? Results from a Randomized Controlled Trial. *Statistics and Public Policy, 5*(1), 1–6.

Breiter, A. (2017). Datafication in education: A multi-level challenge for IT in educational management. In T. Brinda, N. Mavengere, I. Haukijärvi, C. Lewin, & D. Passey (Eds.), *Stakeholders and information technology in education* (pp. 95–103). Berlin, Germany: Springer.

Breiter, A., & Ruhe, A. H. (2017). Paper versus school information management systems: Governing the figurations of mediatized schools in England and Germany. In A. Hepp, A. Breiter, & U. Hasebrink (Eds.), *Communicative figurations: Transforming communications in times of deep mediatization* (pp. 313–339). London, UK: Palgrave Macmillan.

Bucher, T. (2018): *If... then: Algorithmic power and politics.* Oxford: Oxford University Press.

DeVito, M. A. (2017). From editors to algorithms: A values-based approach to understanding story selection in the Facebook news feed. *Digital Journalism, 5*(6), 753–773.

Diesner, J. (2015). Small decisions with big impact on data analytics. *Big Data & Society 2*(2): 1–6.

van Dijck, J. (2014). Datafication, dataism and dataveillance: Big Data between scientific paradigm and secular belief. *Surveillance & Society, 12*(2), 197–208.

Drieling, D. (2006). First steps - setting up an EMIS in German schools in Bremen. In A. Breiter, E. Stauke, N. Büsching, & A. Lange (Eds.), *Educational management information systems - Case studies from 8 countries* (pp. 175–187). Aachen, Germany: Shaker.

Espeland, W. N., & Stevens, M.L. (2008). A sociology of quantification. *European Journal of Sociology 49*(3): 401–436.

Fiege, C. (2013). Faire Vergleiche in der Schulleistungsforschung – Methodologische Grundlagen und Anwendung auf Vergleichsarbeiten. Dissertation. Jena.

Gorur, R. (2014). Towards a sociology of measurement in education policy. *European Education Research Journal, 13*(1): 58–72.

Gray, J., Gerlitz, C., & Bounegru, L. (2018). Data infrastructure literacy. *Big Data and Society 5*(2): 1–13.

Grommé, F., & Scheel, S. (2019). Doing statistics, enacting the nation: He performative powers of categories. Nations and Nationalism, 26 (3): 576–593.

Groos, T. (2019). *Sozialindex für Schulen – Herausforderungen und Lösungsansätze*. Berlin, Germany: Friedrich Ebert Stiftung.

Groot-Wilken, B., Isaac, K., & Schräpler, J.-P. (Eds.) (2016). *Sozialindices für Schulen Hintergründe, Methoden und Anwendung*. Munster, Germany: Waxmann.

Hartong, S. (2016). Between assessments, digital technologies, and big data: The growing influence of 'hidden' data mediators in education. *European Educational Research Journal, Special Issue: Effects of International Assessments in Education – A Multidisciplinary Review, 15*(5), 523–536.

Hartong, S. (2018). 'Wir brauchen Daten, noch mehr Daten, bessere Daten!' Kritische Überlegungen zur Expansionsdynamik des Bildungsmonitorings. *Pädagogische Korrespondenz, 58*(2), 15–30.

Hartong, S. (2019). The transformation of state monitoring systems in Germany and the US: Relating the datafication and digitalization of education to the Global Education Industry. In M. Parreira do Amaral, M. Steiner-Khamsi & C. Thompson (Eds.), *Researching the global education industry commodification, the market and business nvolvement* (pp. 157-180). London, UK: Palgrave Macmillan.

Hartong, S., Breiter, A., Jarke, J., & Förschler, A. (2019). Digitalisierung der staatlichen Schulverwaltung. In T. Klenk, F. Nullmeier, & G. Wewer (Eds.), *Handbuch Staat und Verwaltung im digitalen Zeitalter*. Berlin, Germany: Springer.

Hartong, S., & Förschler, A. (2019). Opening the black box of data-based school monitoring: Data infrastructures, flows and practices in state education agencies. *Big Data & Society, 6*(1): 1–12.

Hartong, S., & Piattoeva, N. (2019). Contextualizing the datafication of schooling – a comparative discussion of Germany and Russia. *Critical Studies in Education, 1–16*

Hepp, A., Breiter, A., & Hasebrink, U. (Eds.). (2017). *Communicative figurations: Transforming communications in times of deep mediatization*. London, UK: Palgrave.

Hogan, A., Sellar, S., & Lingard, B. (2016). Commercialising comparison: Pearson puts the TLC in soft capitalism. *Journal of Education Policy, 31*(3), 243–258.

Iliadis, A., & Russo, F. (2016). Critical data studies: An introduction. *Big Data & Society, 3*(2), 2053951716674238.

Jarke, J., & Breiter, A. (2019). Editorial: The datafication of education. *Learning, Media and Technology, 44*(1), 1–6.

Kitchin, R. (2014). *The data revolution: Big data, open data, data infrastructures and their consequences*. London, UK: Sage.

Kitchin, R. (2016). Thinking critically about and researching algorithms. *Information, Communication & Society, 20*(1), 14–29.

Klemm, K., & Kneuper, D. (2019). *Zur Orientierung von Schulausgaben an Sozialindizes — ein Bundesländervergleich.* Berlin, Germany: Friedrich Ebert Stiftung.

Koyama, J. P. (2011). Generating, comparing, manipulating, categorizing: Reporting, and sometimes fabricating data to comply with No Child Left Behind mandates. *Journal of Education Policy, 26*(5), 701–720.

Landri, P. (2018). *Digital governance of education: Technology, standards and Europeanization of education.* London, UK: Bloomsbury Academic.

Lange, A., & Breiter, A. (2009). Bringing order into chaos. Building an integrated school management information system – A case study from Germany. In A. Tatnall, A. J. Visscher, A. Finegan, & C. O'Mahony (Eds.), *Evolution of information technology in educational management* (pp. 1–14). New York, U.S.A.: Springer.

Lazer, D. M., Baum, M. A., Benklr, Y., Berinsky, A. J., Greenhill, K. M., Menczer, F., Metzger, M. J., Nyhan, B., Pennycook, G., Rothschild, D., & Schudson, M. (2018). The science of fake news. *Science, 359*(6380), 1094–1096.

Lury, C., Parisi, L., & Terranova, T. (2012). Introduction: The becoming topological of culture. *Theory, Culture & Society, 29*(4–5): 3–35.

Makles, A. & Schneider, K. (2018). *Neues Schulranking als Grundlage der Mittelzuweisung in der Stadt Bremen.* Wuppertal: WIB - Wuppertaler Institut für bildungsökonomische Forschung.

Mau, S. (2019). *The metric society: On the quantification of the social.* New York, USA: John Wiley & Sons.

Morris-Lange, S. (2016). *Ungleiches ungleich behandeln! Wege zu einer bedarfsorientierten Schulfinanzierung.* Policy-Brief des Sachverständigenrats der deutschen Stiftungen für Integration und Migration 2016-1.

Perrotta, C., & Selwyn, N. (2019). Deep learning goes to school: Toward a relational understanding of AI in education. *Learning, Media and Technology*, 1–19.

Piattoeva, N., & Saari, A. (2018). The infrastructures of objectivity in standardized testing. In: B. Maddox (Ed.), *International large-scale assessments in education: Insider research perspectives* (pp. 53-68). London: Bloomsbury Academic.

Ratner, H., Andersen, B. L., & Madsen, S. R. (2019). Configuring the teacher as data user: Public–private sector mediations of national test data. *Learning, Media and Technology, 44*(1), 22–35.

Ruppert, E. (2012). The governmental topologies of database devices. *Theory, Culture and Society, 29*(4–5), 116–136.

Ruppert, E., Isin, E., & Bigo, D. (2017). Data politics. *Big Data & Society 4*(2): 1–7.

Scheel, S., Ruppert, E., & Ustek-Spilda, F. (2019). Enacting migration through data practices. *Society and Space, 37*(4): 579–588.

Sellar, S. (2015). Data infrastructure: A review of expanding accountability systems and large-scale assessments in education. *Discourse. Studies in the Cultural Politics of Education 36*(5): 765–777.

Selwyn, N. (2014). Data entry: Towards the critical study of digital data and education. *Learning, Media and Technology 40*(1): 1–18.

Selwyn, N., Nemorin, S., Bulfin, S., & Johnson, N. F. (2017). *Everyday schooling in the digital age: High school, high tech?.* Abingdon, UK: Routledge.

Sendzik, N. (2018). Faire Ungleichbehandlung durch Sozialindizes: Kann Evidenz helfen, Ungleiches ungleich zu behandeln?. In K. Drossel, & B. Eickelmann (Eds.), *Does 'What works' work? Bildungspolitik, Bildungsadministration und Bildungsforschung im Dialog* (pp. 291–310). Berlin, Germany: Waxmann Verlag.

Theocharis, Y., & Lowe, W. (2016). Does Facebook increase political participation? Evidence from a field experiment. *Information, Communication & Society, 19*(10), 1465–1486.

Thompson, G., & Sellar, S. (2018). Datafication, testing events and the outside of thought. *Learning, Media and Technology 43*(2): 139–151.

Weishaupt, H. (2016). Sozialindex-Ein Instrument zur Gestaltung fairer Vergleiche: Einführung. In B. Groot-Wilken, K. Isaac & J.-P. Schräpler (Eds.), *Socialindices für Schulen. Hintergründe, Methoden und Anwendung*. Munster, Germany: Waxmann.

West, J. (2017). Data, democracy and school accountability: Controversy over school evaluation in the case of DeVasco High School. *Big Data & Society 4*(1): 1–16.

Williamson, B. (2017). *Big data in education: The digital future of learning, policy and practice*. Los Angeles, USA: Sage.

Disclosure/Funding Information

The presented research was funded by the *Deutsche Forschungsgemeinschaft* (DFG, German Research Foundation) – project number HA 7367/2 – as well as by the German *Federal Department of Education and Research* (BMBF) – project numbers 01JD1803A and 01JD1803D.

5 Capacity building as the 'Third Translation': The story of PISA-D in Cambodia

Radhika Gorur and Camilla Addey

Introduction

In 2010, two states in India participated in an out-of-cycle round of PISA (PISA 2009+). At this time, India's confidence was high – the IMF was projecting a growth rate of over 9% and India was seen as one of Asia's rising stars (International Monetary Fund, 2010). Many Indians had assumed prominent global positions as CEOs of major companies. There was an expectation that India would perform well. But it did not. In fact, India did rather badly. In the two states that participated in the study, Himachal Pradesh and Tamil Nadu, fewer than 20% of the students attained even the lowest proficiency levels. Overall, India placed second to last on the PISA ladder, doing better only than Kyrgyzstan.

When Germany performed below the OECD average in PISA 2000, it famously triggered 'PISA Shock' (Ertl, 2006). The press coverage and the huge public outcry resulted in a number of reforms in the German system in the ensuing years (OECD, 2010). It was a different story in India. The press hardly acknowledged the results. The central government and the governments of the participating states were more eager to bury the results than learn from them – so the exercise prompted no changes to the system (OECD, Interview notes). Instead, the results were dismissed, claiming that PISA was not culturally appropriate to the Indian context (OECD, Interview notes).

This was a disappointing outcome for the UK's Department for International Development (DFID), which had worked with the World Bank and the EU to put together a technical assistance package worth GBP1.5 million to build capacity for assessment in India. Participation in PISA was part of this package. It had taken 'three years of negotiation and painful step-by-step' to get the two states in India to participate in PISA (OECD, Interview extract). The main goal, that of building technical capacity, was (to some extent) accomplished. But:

> India implemented PISA fine, took one look at the results and said, 'we don't want to own these results'. PISA was a disruption to their narrative.
>
> (OECD, Interview extract)

Clearly, something more than technical capacity was required. When a decision was taken at the OECD to expand PISA to the Global South, and develop a new instrument specifically for 'emerging and developing economies' – PISA for Development, or PISA-D – India held many lessons:

> The lesson we learnt (again, we've internalized it for PISA for development) is that it is not enough to have the country doing PISA for Development. It is not enough to give them the capacity building and the support so that they implement the assessment successfully. You need to be there and help the country collaborate over the analysis of the results, the development basically of a national report, and you also need to be there with the minister, with the ministry, when they are presenting these results. (OECD, Interview extract)

This is clearly reflected in the OECD's Capacity Needs Analysis report on Cambodia, where the aims of PISA-D are defined as supporting evidence-based policymaking, building 'country capacity in assessment, analysis and use of results' (OECD, 2016a, p. 7).

PISA-D, then, was not just about tweaking the cognitive and contextual survey instruments to make them more suited to low-income contexts. There was an explicit concern that the exercise of participating in PISA should have a long-term and meaningful effect; that the results should be analysed and used to inform policy; and that a culture of assessment, accountability and evidence-based policy practices should be enabled and institutionalized – in contrast to what had happened in India. The PISA National Centres were seen as key to this process:

> It's the national centre, that is what it is all about. It's the institutional home of assessment [...]. A big part of the capacity building is building this institutionally, as the centre of expertise and the centre of understanding, of how to measure learning, analyse the results, and then use the results for policy making and then to get more leverage in the policy making sphere.
>
> (OECD, Interview extract)

Indeed, it was also felt that linking national assessments so they aligned with PISA would be useful in PISA-D nations (OECD, 2013; Addey, 2017).

It is this exercise of translating the culture of the participating nations through participation in PISA-D that is the focus of this chapter. Rather than examining how PISA was adapted to low-income contexts, we focus on how the OECD prepared the participating low-income nations to receive PISA-D – and in the process sought to change these nations in significant and enduring ways (Addey & Gorur, 2020). In particular, we focus on the 'capacity needs analysis' (CNA) and the development of the 'capacity building plan' (CBP) as part of effort to make PISA-D nations 'fit' for PISA.

Capacity building: Politics by stealth

Increasingly, 'capacity building' has become 'a core concept of development policy' (Zamfir, 2017, p. 1). It is estimated that a quarter of all development aid – i.e., about US$15bn a year – is spent on capacity building (Guy, 2016).

The World Bank 'supports capacity development in almost all of its work' (Constantinou, 2007). First foregrounded in the decentralization policies of the 1970s, the focus on capacity building grew through the 1990s. An analysis of the failure of technical support projects, particularly in Africa, identified several issues: a donor-centric, rigid blueprint for reform, poor pay and incentives for local actors, and pre-defined outputs rather than dynamic and adaptable ones. From then on, a focus on ownership and partnership, and capacity building at the level of 'the individual, the organisation and the broader environment' (Zamfir, 2017, p. 2) came to be cemented into development frameworks, agreements and funding models.

Capacity building was listed as a precondition in the 2005 Paris Declaration for Aid Effectiveness. The 2008 Accra Accord for Action shifted the responsibility for the success of capacity building from the donor to the developing nation. Rather than donors demanding that the nation built its capacity, the developing nations were now *required to demand* capacity building, and donors were to respond to this demand, incorporating local institutions and systems as far as possible in identifying needs and developing capacity.

This transfer of responsibility for capacity building to developing nations, and the location of capacity-building activities in local, existing institutions, promoted the notion that capacity building is a practical, supportive activity driven by developing nations, rather than a political enterprise driven top-down by donor nations or development partners. But capacity building is a deeply political exercise, since it strikes at the very culture of a nation's organizations:

> Development professionals tend to define capacity building exclusively in training terms. It's an important part of the process, but ... [it] is also about an organisation's dynamics, its structural profile, its role – and above all, culture.
>
> (Guy, 2016, n.p)

Studying capacity building provides an opportunity to more clearly understand the socio-technical nature of such exercises (Gorur & Dey, 2020) and thus adds to the literatures on education reform, policy borrowing, the travels of ideas, and global policy regimes. Much has already been written about the influence of PISA on participating nations (for example, Ertl, 2006; Breakspear 2012; Baird et al. 2016; Fischman et al., 2019). Studies have also examined how the media and policymakers react to PISA (Waldow et al., 2014; Waldow, 2017; Grey & Morris 2018). Most of these studies engage with the influence of PISA *results* (for an exception, see Grek, 2017). Many papers also locate PISA within the larger politics of neoliberalism and the practices of new public management, emphasizing the 'big P' politics (Maroy, 2012; Verger, 2014).

Our analysis focuses on the politics of mundane practices (Woolgar & Neyland, 2013): the ways in which 'capacity-building' practices can profoundly change the operations, functioning, relations, and the very identity of a nation. It focuses on how specific training programmes, technical meetings and protocols seek to configure participating nations in particular ways, creating new aspirations, demands and obligations.

The empirical material comes from the two authors' separate engagements with PISA-D over the course of several projects located in India, Cambodia, Paraguay and Ecuador, as well as the OECD. Collectively, our projects included interviews with key OECD officials; the National Project Manager and other officials in the team; those involved in training them; high-level policy actors; private contractors developing PISA-D; and observations of gatherings such as the launch of the PISA-D results in Cambodia and a PISA-D advisory board meeting. Our sources included the OECD website and other publicly accessible sites and several reports, including Cambodia's Capacity Needs Analysis (CNA) and Cambodia's Capacity Building Plan. We take a material-semiotic, practice-based approach, and the notion of 'the third translation' (Callon et al., 2009), to examine the ways in which 'capacity building' sought to transform Cambodia in significant and enduring ways.

Theoretical framing: The three stages of translation

For many scholars, including ourselves, PISA has been an object of research. But PISA is also, itself, a research exercise that measures and ranks the quality and equity of school systems, using sample-based survey instruments. It is a socio-technical exercise in the doing of science or the making of knowledge. It is an exemplar of a genre of scientific exercises in the contemporary 'regime of exactness' (Callon et al., 2009) characterized by science conducted in sites secluded from the 'real world', performed by a select elite of experts.

Doing science in the 'regime of exactness' involves three translations (with a small 't'), according to Callon et al. The first is the reduction of a complex, chaotic, disordered world or phenomenon into a simpler, more ordered set that can be transported back to the laboratory. A forest may be represented by samples of leaves, twigs and soil, a rat by a smear on a slide, or a large population by a representative sample, categorized by pre-determined criteria. In the second translation, specialist knowledge can be applied to the samples that are now in ordered formats. Manipulations can be done, chemicals added, microscopes employed, particles subjected to forces to reveal themselves.

At the end of the second translation, scientists are ready to state a truth, name a fact or produce an object or prototype. However, at this stage, claims about these facts and objects are only held in the specialized conditions of the laboratory, or in the epistemic spaces of a select group. If the world has been scaled down and made transportable in translation 1 to make a journey to the laboratory, in translation 3, it must prepare to make a return journey – from the safety of the controlled environment of the laboratory to the wild world. Unless what is produced in the laboratory survives in the 'wild' – the more complex world outside the laboratory – the work of the scientists would have been in vain.

To provide the best chance for the science to survive outside the laboratory, a third translation is required that bridges the gulf between the laboratory and the world. The key to success in this third translation – this perilous journey that requires a change of scale, a re-complication of models and the introduction of new variables – is laboratorization:

> For the world to behave as in the research laboratory … we simply have to transform the world so that at every strategic point a 'replica' of the laboratory, the site where we can control the phenomenon studied, is placed.
>
> (Callon et al., 2009, p. 65)

Callon et al. distinguish between these three translations, which they indicate with a lower case 't', and Translation, with a capital 'T', with which they denote the partial reconfiguration of the macrocosm. Success in the chain of translations results in Translation: a reconfigured world – a laboratorized world, that is similar in essential ways to the world made in the laboratory. In the sections that follow, we examine this process of laboratorization.

Capacity building in PISA-D and the third translation

Although the translations are numbered, they do not occur in sequence. While translation 2 must follow translation 1, translation 3 often starts even before translation 1. Even before PISA-D was fully conceptualized, strategies were being developed to ensure that PISA-D nations could not only conduct the tests to PISA's stringent technical standards, but would also utilize the exercise and the results to influence policy. Indeed, the idea was to entrench a culture of evidence-based policy driven by regular assessment and monitoring.

Identifying challenges: Establishing an accountability culture

As a first step in the development of PISA-D, the OECD commissioned a series of studies and papers to support its development. One significant input was the Lockheed Report (Lockheed, Prokic-Bruer & Shadrova, 2015), which examined the extent to which PISA was being used in middle-income nations which had participated in PISA, and the barriers which prevented more extensive use. The study identified three types of challenges, particularly in lower-middle-income nations: financial, technical and contextual. The 'contextual challenges' concerned 'the political, regulatory and cultural environment of the countries, which can affect ease of assessment implementation and use' (Lockheed et al., 2015, p. 15). Their first recommendation for PISA-D included 'encouraging greater discussion and reporting of the results' (Lockheed, Prokic-Bruer & Shadrova, 2015, p. 16).

Addressing these 'contextual challenges' was essential to the success of the third translation. Keeping in mind not only the technical training needed to carry out the tests, but also the financial and political support required to ensure that the data are analysed and used well, every participating country was required to undergo a 'capacity needs analysis' (CNA) and to develop a Capacity Building Plan (CBP). These instruments identified a range of issues to be addressed for the successful implementation and use of PISA-D, and it is to this we now turn – with a focus on Cambodia.

Enrolling allies, delegating needs

A key requirement for translation 3 to be successful is support from allies in the 'wild' – the world outside the laboratory:

> The return to the macrocosm raises, first, the problem of alliances the labora-tory has been able to form around its research subjects. In order to mobilize the resources and support without which it would quickly disappear, the research collective must interest other actors in its enterprise. It's not impor-tant who they are as long as they have influence or money!
>
> (Callon et al., 2009, p. 61)

To secure translation 3, participating nations would need to be entangled, from the outset, in a community of practice that included the OECD, development partners and other developing nations – actors who would continue to have expectations of PISA-D nations even after the OECD's PISA-D team has left the scene. For this reason, developing the nation's ability to carry on with such engage-ment became one of the five specified PISA-D programme outputs:

> Engagement with OECD, development partners and, *prospectively*, with other developing countries in order to identify peer-to-peer learning oppor-tunities regarding participation in PISA and its potential contribution to the UN-led discussions on the post-2015 framework.
>
> (OECD, 2016b, pp 7–8, our emphasis)

Supplementing ongoing relations with *external* actors (OECD, peer nations and the UN) that would encourage Cambodia to stay translated, there was a simulta-neous move to encourage a range of *internal* relations, enrolling local individuals and institutions into the PISA-D effort. To identify Cambodia's needs, a range of Cambodian actors were interviewed and surveyed. While PISA-D was a concern of the Ministry for Education, Youth and Sports (MoEYS), other ministries, such as Labour and Finance, were also consulted. Later, the Royal University of Phnom Penh (RUPP) was also drawn in to assist with analysis.

Next, the internal and external actors were thoroughly shuffled together. The findings of the CNA were presented to MoEYS and several development partners, including 'ADB, EU, JICA, UNICEF, UNESCO and the World Bank'[1] (OECD, 2016a, p.14), at a meeting chaired by the Minister from MoEYS. By requesting the Minister to chair the session, witnessed by a range of influential development partners, the 'ownership' of the project was decentred from the OECD and located more firmly in the Ministry.

By involving and embedding a range of individuals and actors internal to Cambodia, and by involving a number of development partners outside the government of Cambodia, the OECD prepared the ground, even before PISA-D was ready to be implemented, for the eventual announcement of PISA-D results. Through the high-visibility involvement of the minister, PISA-D's needs became Cambodia's needs, PISA-D's demands became Cambodia's demands. The processes of CNA ensured that Cambodia's commitment to a culture of assessment and accountability were recited before a range of audiences, in a number of settings, and across time, ensuring that it would be difficult for it to brush things under the carpet later, as India had done.

Enabling contexts

The CNA framework was comprehensive – with 112 'capacity elements' identified as required for 'successful implementation and stakeholder use of PISA for Development products' (OECD, 2016a, p. 9). The steadfast focus on enabling the local contexts to use 'PISA-D products' rather than just conducting PISA-D – i.e., the focus on the political and not just the technical, as well as a horizoning of the future, and not just the limited term of the one-off PISA-D exercise – is apparent throughout the CNA document. The focus was on 'programme sustainability and the social, cultural and economic climates that will be necessary for meaningful use of the PISA results' (OECD, 2016a, p. 11).

One example of this planning is reflected in the CNA recommendation that the National Centre collaborate with the Faculty of Education at the Royal University of Phnom Penh (RUPP) 'to properly utilise the PISA-D data and to address the informational needs of stakeholders'. With this, the PISA-D results were taken out of the immediate purview of MoEYS and made available outside the ministry. Drawing in RUPP was a strategic move – it distributed authority to another group of experts, further laboratorizing Cambodia. Other PISA-D countries developed similar partnerships to ensure the use of PISA-D data. For example, Paraguay developed a Master's programme for future education assessment analysts who would be ready to join the ministry of education and engage with global forms of assessment. Each PISA-D nation was also asked to develop Communication Strategies (i.e. PISA-D Facebook pages, etc.) to promote PISA's testing culture and to enrol allies among all education stakeholders in order to prevent or overcome resistance from school communities and the wider society.

Importantly, the CNA also highlighted many shortcomings which went to the core of the governance practices and structures, as well as the culture of Cambodian politics:

> [F]actors related to *the management of assessment activities* and *co-operation between stakeholders* in Cambodia currently limit the ability of Cambodia to utilise existing capacity to successfully meet all goals of PISA-D. Historically, the government department responsible for the National Assessment *did not operate with the transparency and autonomy* necessary for effective monitoring and reporting about the status of the education system. In addition, the development of human resources to sustain long-term operation of a large-scale assessment system has been *ad hoc*, through Development Partners, and has *not been supported by government initiatives*. Successful implementation of PISA-D, including capacity building activities, will require greater *commitment* from a variety of stakeholders to institutionalise assessment operations and utilise assessment results.
>
> (OECD, 2016a, p. 8, our emphases)

The CNA thus boldly demanded significant changes in the functioning of a nation that was ruled with an iron fist. If successful, this demand for commitment to a culture of assessment and accountability would have far ranging effects on a nation widely known to be opaque and corrupt.

As part of the capacity-building activities, the OECD organized peer-to-peer learning between PISA-D nations and middle-income countries which had successfully enrolled a broad network of actors in the dissemination and use of the PISA data. For example, the Vice Minister of Kosovo was invited to present to the PISA-D nations gathered in Paraguay for the PISA-D Advisory Group meeting in 2016:

> We've got the PISA team from Kosovo coming to join and they will be presenting [...] on Kosovo's experience. So Kosovo, new to PISA, so how did we prepare our population, what are the activities we have gone through to communicate with teachers, communicate with principals, communicate with other ministers and other bits of the government, how have we sensitized them to our participation in this programme? [...]
>
> (OECD, Interview extract)

A very important part of developing the 'enabling context' was bolstering the human resources available to PISA-D. The assessment wing of the MoEYS was rather sparsely resourced. To make matters worse, the few people with the required technical capacity were busy developing a national assessment, which was also a key priority in Cambodia's Sector Plan. Because of this, the PISA-D project, which aimed to establish a culture of assessment and evidence-based policy, was in competition with another project with a similar aim – the development of a strong *national* assessment regime. There were literally only two individuals – Ung Chinna, who was with the MoEYS's assessment centre, and Hang Kreng, who worked at RUPP. Both were involved in the national assessment scheme. Both came to be involved in the PISA-D project. The OECD worked in a very detailed way, identifying individuals, reworking contracts, and in the process, perhaps competing with – or translating – other national priorities, such as developing the national assessment.

The CNA document also recommended 'greater direct engagement of key stakeholders' (p. 20), via a Steering Committee, chaired by the Minister and including key bureaucrats from several government departments (including Labour and Finance). This mingling of departments was deliberately political, and focused on the realigning of priorities:

> At an operational level, the main challenge of the Steering Committee will be to exert sufficient pressure on the various departments within the MoEYS to commit to the success of the programme. The general operations of PISA-D clearly fall within the mandate of EQAD [Education Quality Assurance Department]. However, the programme will not be successful in meeting its goals without the collaboration of several departments, including Curriculum, Higher Education, and Secondary Education (Examinations). To unify many

of these departments, stakeholders will need to understand how PISA-D can inform national priorities such as the 'skills for life' curriculum focus. Clear direction from the Steering Committee will minimise issues related to inter-departmental authority and hierarchy.

(OECD, 2016a, p. 20)

In this way, the CNA went to the heart of the operations of the nation – rearranging relations between different government departments and committees, and creating structures which allowed pressure to be exerted on particular actors, to create an 'enabling context' in which the PISA results could survive and thrive. The CNA provided an organizational chart that would create a particular chain of command and arrange relations to produce the most conducive environment for the acceptance of PISA-D results.

Proliferating laboratories

The CNA was completed in 2014, and was followed by the Capacity Building Plan (CBP) for the four years of the implementation of PISA-D. These plans were extremely detailed. Each year has an overall objective, followed by a description of the activity, the 'deliverables', the country responsibilities, the administrative details, the relevant documentation, the international and in-country costs, and the expected additional funding. For example, the CBP for Year 3 includes this objective:

> Year 3 (2017–2018): Researchers will translate information needs of stakeholders into specific research questions, select an appropriate statistical method for the research question, and communicate the statistical results in a manner that is accessible to non-statistical audiences.

(OECD, 2016b. p. 24)

The 'Deliverables' for the workshops to be conducted as part of the CBP were described in specific detail. For example, one of the workshops had these instructions:

> The workshop should replicate and redistribute the material from the international workshop. The focus of the workshop should be learning-by-doing, with participants replicating research activities using data and software provided by the NC [National Centre – the unit in charge of PISA-D in Cambodia]. The NC should also distribute working versions of the necessary software used in the workshop.

In this way, the PISA laboratory was recreated and laboratory replicas proliferated within Cambodia and in several other sites where PISA-D workshops were held, and where the national team engaged in activities listed out by the PISA manuals and operationalized through the CBP. Key to the success of this proliferation of laboratories was specifying not only what should be done but how – the mundane details that included who would chair and what documents would be distributed and what ideas would be workshopped.

To further ensure PISA-D data would not be rejected, an analyst from each PISA-D country was invited to Paris for three months to write the PISA national report under the close supervision of the OECD. Here we see a minutely controlled preparation of PISA-D's entry into the wild world, the moment of greatest uncertainty.

> The purpose of the residency was to collaborate, build capacity, mentor, and produce national reports for the country. [...] So to get up with the analysis quicker, we prepared first an outline of the national report. [...] Using the templates meant that the analysts did not have to spend too much time drafting, they could focus their energy and time on the analysis of the data and then just adjust the text so that it suited their findings for their country.
>
> (OECD, interview extract)

Once the reports had been written by analysts in Paris, the OECD sought to enrol key actors who would defend the data and defeat adversaries from the former world. This is a moment in which specific resources and allies needed to be enrolled to ensure the freshly minted secluded knowledge survived in the wild:

> So we spent about three hours with each country reviewing particularly chapter 6, the policy implications, and suggested ways forward [...]. So in each case we were asking our teams, who owns this key policy message here, which bit of the ministry, which bit of the government is going to be responsible for taking this forward, we asked them to come up with a name, who is the head of the teacher department, head of the curriculum, head of administration, who owns this?
>
> (OECD, Interview extract)

This led to a fresh round of identifying potential resisters and translating them into allies. They would be enrolled into the problematization and in the search for a solution. Sharing confidential, embargoed information with potential resisters and getting their advice is one way of turning them into allies:

> And then having gone through each of the three or four key policy messages and identified who it is that is going to own it, we then worked with them about how they can develop a plan to go to that person and have some structured discussion about how to take this forward, firstly to inform them of the results, all of it in confidence as it in under embargo before the launch, and get the input of those individuals into chapter 6 of the report, so what is elaborated there, as a suggested way forward is something the owners of this, [...] whatever it is, that those who are responsible own it, they own it, they say yes, okay we agree with these findings, we agree with the implications, we agree with what you are saying is the way forward, we support this proposal. [...] The minister of education is presenting it, and then when it comes to the

policy implications, those bits of the Ministry or of the government which are responsible for each of those areas, are standing up and saying yes, absolutely, this is the way forward, this is what we must do, and that leads to a broad consensus in terms of how to move forward in terms of an evidence-based policy dialogue in education.

(OECD, Interview extract)

Having high-level ministerial actors standing up publicly and in many high-level meetings, and proclaiming their support of the data, the analysis, and the recommendation for next steps was a crucial step in the acceptance and invitation to accept the newly created worlds.

While the enrolment of high-level actors is crucial, successfully embedding the cultures of assessment and accountability and routinizing the laboratorization of Cambodia required that PISA-D-recommended practices were distributed widely and in related practices. A range of institutions needed to be involved and to be in sync with the PISA-D practices, over a period of time. 'A network of strongly interdependent interests' (Callon et al., 2009, p. 66) needed to be created within Cambodia. As more and more actors got drawn in, 'recalcitrant adversaries … [were] swept aside by the tidal wave' (Callon et al., 2009, p. 66).

A culture of accountability, assessment and monitoring was built into the capacity-building process itself – i.e., the progress on the CBP itself was to be evaluated and monitored systematically. To this end, the CBP presents a detailed table called 'Indicators for monitoring and evaluation based on the ultimate goals for each area of development' – and this lists seven areas, including 'Project utilisation and knowledge mobilisation' and 'Statistical analysis, data visualisation and reporting' (OECD, 2016b, pp. 31–32). In this way, continued fidelity to a world favoured by PISA-D was promoted.

Translation with a Capital T?

The PISA-D results were launched in December 2018. This was the moment the capacity building process had been preparing for since the beginning – even before translation 1. In Cambodia, OECD was represented by Michael Ward, who headed PISA-D. The launch was a high-profile event at Siem Reap, presided over by the Minister for Education, Youth and Sports, and attended by a range of development partners, government officials and academics. The press was invited and visibly present.

Overall, the OECD staff expressed satisfaction with the care with which these processes of remaking of PISA-D nations to fit the PISA world had been handled:

The actual implementation was not as challenging as we thought it was going to be. We put a lot of resources into preparation of the country; every country had a needs analysis, a plan, we got everybody up to speed in terms of what to expect, we gave them a lot of support, the contractors had additional resources to hold the hands of the countries, more international meetings than we usually have to do training [...].

(OECD, interview extract)

As far as the OECD was concerned, Translation – the one with the Capital T – had been achieved. The PISA-D nations had been laboratorized.

However, some of the PISA-D participants we interviewed from several PISA-D nations suggested that things were not quite as smooth in practice. National-level experts in assessment often had limited English and could not benefit fully from the capacity-building exercises. Many training sessions were carried out abroad – and the attraction of an expenses-paid foreign trip meant that sometimes these sessions were attended by friends of those in power, rather than the most appropriate experts. Frequent changes in government also resulted in new appointments and constant losses of newly acquired capacity in some countries. The often very small and under-resourced teams running PISA did not always result in broad capacity building. Moreover, capacity building was being rushed to meet the hard deadlines of international implementation, with all nations in sync. The success of capacity building was being measured by green ticks on Sharepoint software automatically assigned upon submission of tasks by national project managers, and these did not reflect the quality of the tasks or their consequences. Moreover, some of the development partners strongly felt that participation in PISA-D, which focused on 15-year-olds, was not appropriate for Cambodia, where a significant percentage of 15-year-olds were out of school and would be left out of the PISA-D survey.[2]

But the OECD had done well to develop 'a network of strongly interdependent interests' (Callon et al., 2009, p. 65), so that allies stayed together and kept their misgivings and dissatisfactions to themselves:

There are some recalcitrant adversaries but they are swept aside by the tidal wave. The laboratory has spread by reconfiguring all those who want to have it ready to hand. The difference between the world before translation 1 and the world after translations 2 and 3 is the sudden proliferation of laboratories along with the techniques and entities that they bring with them, and the interests and the projects they authorize.

(Callon et al., 2009, p. 66)

The pride that Cambodia was able to pull off the feat of implementing a complex international assessment to PISA standards was a more attractive national story than the complaints of a few individuals:

In terms of the country's performance – well, just look at the results – they have implemented PISA according to the PISA technical standards. So they are the same technical standard that UK and Sweden and Australia and Germany – and they all have to follow that.

(OECD, interview transcript)

Through PISA-D capacity building, Cambodia had been transformed into a world that had already come to resemble the PISA laboratory. PISA-D came to be embedded into Cambodia's National Education Sector Plan, which is supported by UNECO, UNICEF, GPE and other partners. It was listed under the banner of priority programs.

Most importantly, the Minister signed the contract to participate in PISA 2021, to ensure that the newly created world would not be swept aside as soon as the PISA-D results were launched, but, rather, that its effects would continue to proliferate. As Michael Ward said in his speech commending Cambodia for being brave enough to participate in PISA-D, Cambodia was part of a little family when it was participating in PISA-D. Now it was leaving this little family and setting out into the big world, on par with other nations globally that had the technical and political sophistication to particulate in PISA. Cambodia had been translated – laboratorized – so that the Minister (who, incidentally, is an erudite scholar with a PhD) – is himself able to act like the Director of the newly disseminated PISA-D laboratories, having chaired several workshops and meetings.

Politics by other means

Let us for a moment step back and consider the movement from Cambodia 'in the wild' (macrocosm 1) to the laboratorized Cambodia (macrocosm 2). Successful Translation replaces one set of options with another; it involves making a choice between two worlds. Herein lies the politics of capacity building – a great example of Latour's 'politics by other means'. Would Cambodia want to be seen among nations such as Germany and Australia, confidently participating in PISA, on a progressive path to reforming its education with powerful psychometrics and statistical analysis, or would it, like India, choose to dismiss the results and blame the tests as being inappropriate? As Callon et al. assert, 'The communities, and consequently the forms of common life, will differ according to the choices we make' (Callon et al., 2009, p. 69)

This choice is not a free choice – the options are restricted by the research collective. The translation of Cambodia is performed by a powerful and elite 'research collective' mustered up by the OECD. In the first instance, Cambodia's assessment experts – and even the Minister, his PhD notwithstanding – are cast as laypersons – unable to participate as more than mere informants and innocents who would learn more about themselves and their needs from the powerful experts of OECD and its allies. The whole choreography of the research collective is organized not as a political exercise but as a technical and practical one – laid out in a series of workshops, training sessions, technical protocols and so on. Indeed, it is this very appearance of scientific neutrality or economic logic that suppresses debate (Callon et al., 2009, p. 69)

While Callon et al. focus on the logic of markets which is usually presented as a measure of some sort of equalizer or neutrality, here, at first glance, the choice appears to be between 'science' and a kind of irrationality or ignorance: join PISA-D and become enlightened, like all the major nations of the world, and be counted on an international stage, says OECD. The alternative is to be left out – or, worse, left behind – in a world that has not been tamed. But a closer look alerts us to the idea that the choices before Cambodia are not between the 'science' of evidence and assessment promoted by OECD and the World Bank and a kind of irrationality or politics; rather, it is between different kinds of science-politics. Cambodia had the choice of repeating its participation in a regional assessment such as PASEC.[3] Or it could have stuck to the plan of focusing on improving its national assessment.

Insider stories of the machinations that preceded Cambodia's surprise decision to participate in PISA demonstrate that there is an alternative narrative to the one told by the OECD (Auld et al., 2018). They posit that the decision to include Cambodia in PISA-D was taken long before Cambodia showed any inclination to participate. In any case, the OECD's translations and the carefully choreographed and orchestrated series of presentations, workshops, meetings, training programs, and statistical processes systematically shut down other choices.

To bring our story full circle, India has now signed up to participate in PISA 2021. After a ten-year hiatus during which PISA results had been expunged from most records (Chakraborty et al., 2019), India is determined to do well, and is preparing special practice material for the tests. Overseas experts are training teachers and students for the tests. Changes to the curriculum have been made to prepare students better for PISA. OECD's Andreas Schleicher has visited India and presented in joint press conferences with the concerned minister. Whether the 'enabling contexts' have been sufficiently primed to withstand another dismal performance will only be known in due course.

PISA-D was a once-off pilot, but it is now being scaled up, becoming part of the PISA suite of offerings. The instruments developed for PISA-D and its capacity-building models will now be available to any participating country that chooses to use them and is able to pay for them. The capacity-building activities for countries new to PISA has been contracted to the Australian Council for Educational Research (ACER) and currently five nations have signed up for this option – El Salvador, India (Chandigarh), Mongolia, Panama and Uzbekistan. Translation through capacity building has now come to be firmly entrenched as part of successful assessment practice.

Acknowledgements

This chapter was made possible by a grant (DE170700460) from the Australian Research Council granted to the first author, and by a grant from the Fritz Thyssen Foundation to the second author (No grant number).

Notes

1 ADB: Asian Development Bank; JICA: Japan International Cooperation Agency.
2 Although PISA-D included a survey of out of school student's skills, not all countries participated in this survey.
3 Programme d'analyse des systèms éducatifs de la confemen (the Programme for Analysis of Education Systems in French-Speaking Countries)

References

Addey, C. (2017). Golden relics & historical standards: how the OECD is expanding global education governance through PISA for Development, *Critical Studies in Education*, 58(3), 311–325, DOI: 10.1080/17508487.2017.1352006

Addey, C., & R. Gorur. (2020). Translating PISA, Translating the World. *Comparative Education*. DOI: 10.1080/03050068.2020.1771873

Auld, E., J. Rappleye, & P. Morris. (2018). PISA for Development: how the OECD and World Bank shaped education governance post-2015, *Comparative Education*, 55(2), 197–219, DOI: 10.1080/03050068.2018.1538635

Baird, J.A., S. Johnson, T. N. Hopfenbeck, T. Isaacs, T. Sprague, G. Stobart, & Y. Guoxing. (2016). On the supranational spell of PISA in policy, *Educational Research*, 58(2), 121–138, DOI: 10.1080/00131881.2016.1165410

Breakspear, S. (2012). *The Policy Impact of PISA: An Exploration of the Normative Effects of International Benchmarking in School System Performance*. OECD Education Working Papers, No. 71. Paris: OECD Publishing.

Callon, M., P. Lascoumes, & Y. Barthe (2009). *Acting in an Uncertain World: An Essay on Technical Democracy*. Cambridge, MA: MIT Press.

Chakraborty, S. et al. (2019). The reception of large-scale assessments in China and India. In C. E. Molstad and D. Petterson (Eds.), *New Practices of Comparison, Quantification and Expertise in Education* (pp. 157–174). London/New York: Routledge

Constantinou, N. (2007). *Capacity Development in the World Bank Group: A Review of Nonlending Approaches*. Capacity Development Briefs, Washington, DC: World Bank Institute.

Ertl, H. (2006): Educational standards and the changing discourse on education: the reception and consequences of the PISA study in Germany, *Oxford Review of Education*, 32(5), 619–634

Fischman, G. E., A. M. Topper, I. Silova, J. Goebel, & J. L. Holloway. (2019). Examining the influence of international large-scale assessments on national education policies, *Journal of Education Policy*, 34(4), 470–499, DOI: 10.1080/02680939.2018.1460493

Gorur, R. & J. Dey. (2020). Making the user friendly: The ontological politics of digital data platforms. *Critical Studies in Education*. DOI: 10.1080/17508487.2020.1727544

Grek, S. (2017) Socialisation, learning and the OECD's Reviews of National Policies for Education: the case of Sweden, *Critical Studies in Education*, 58(3), 295–310, DOI: 10.1080/17508487.2017.1337586

Grey, S., & P. Morris. (2018). PISA: multiple 'truths' and mediatised global governance. *Comparative Education*, 54(2), 109–131, DOI: 10.1080/03050068.2018.1425243

Guy, D. (2016). Aid Workers Talk Endlessly about Capacity Building - But What Does it Really Mean? *The Guardian*, 10/11/2016, Available at: https://www.theguardian.com/global-development-professionals-network/2016/nov/10/what-does-capacity-building-mean (Accessed: 6 August 2020).

International Money Fund (IMF) (2010). *World Economic Outlook : A Survey of the International Monetary Fund*. Washington, DC: International Money Fund.

Lockheed, M., T. Prokic-Bruer, & A. Shadrova. (2015), The Experience of Middle-Income Countries Participating in PISA 2000-2015, PISA, World Bank, Washington, DC/OECD Publishing, Paris, DOI http://dx.doi.org/10.1787/9789264246195-en

Makuwira, J. (2015). The politics of community capacity-building: Contestations, contradictions, tensions and ambivalences in the discourse in indigenous communities in Australia. *The Australian Journal of Indigenous Education*, 36(S1), 129–136, DOI: 10.1017/S1326011100004804

Maroy, C. (2012). Towards post-bureaucratic modes of governance: A European perspective. In G. Steiner-Khamsi & F. Waldow (Eds.), *World Yearbook of Education 2012. Policy Borrowing and Lending in Education* (pp. 62–79). London & New York: Routledge.

OECD. (2013). *Beyond PISA 2015: A longer-term strategy for PISA*. Paris: OECD.

OECD. (2016a). *PISA-D Capacity Needs Analysis: Cambodia*. Paris: OECD.

OECD. (2016b). *PISA-D Capacity Building Plan: Cambodia*. Paris: OECD.

Rose, P. (2015). Is a global system of international largescale assessments necessary for tracking progress of a post-2015 learning target? *Compare: A Journal of Comparative and International Education*, 45(3), 486–490, DOI:10.1080/03057925.2015.1027514

UNESCO-UIS. (2016). *Laying the Foundation to Measure Sustainable Development Goal 4*. Montreal: UNESCO Institute for Statistics

Verger, A. (2014). Why do policy-makers adopt global education policies? Toward a research framework on the varying role of ideas in education reform. *Current Issues in Comparative Education* 16(2), 14–29.

Waldow, F., K. Takayama, & Y. Sung. (2014). Rethinking the pattern of external policy referencing: media discourses over the 'Asian Tigers' PISA success in Australia, Germany and South Korea. *Comparative Education*, 50(3), 302–321.

Waldow, F. (2017). Projecting images of the 'good' and the 'bad school': top scorers in educational large-scale assessments as reference societies, *Compare: A Journal of Comparative and International Education*, 47(5), 647–664, DOI: 10.1080/03057925.2016.1262245

Woolgar, S. & D. Neyland. (2013). *Mundane Governance: Ontology and Accountability*. Oxford: Oxford University Press.

Zamfir, I. (2017). Understanding capacity-building/ capacity development - A core concept of development policy. Members' Research Service. Brussels, European Parliamentary Research Service. PE599.411.

Zi, H. & O. Pizmony-Levy. (2020). Local meanings of international student assessments: An Analysis of Media Discourses of PISA in China, 2010–2016. *Compare: A Journal of Comparative and International Education*. DOI: 10.1080/03057925.2020.1775553

Part II

Global discourse and national translations of performance-based accountability policies

6 National testing and accountability in the Scandinavian welfare states: Education policy translations in Norway, Denmark and Sweden

*Guri Skedsmo, Linda Rönnberg
and Christian Ydesen*

Introduction

This chapter explores how global education policy and accountability trends are variously translated and adapted in three Scandinavian countries, focusing in particular on the links between national standardized testing and accountability. Norway, Denmark and Sweden are used as empirical cases to reflect on the importance of national trajectories and translations of global ideas and policy. While reference is often made to the 'universal Scandinavian welfare states' or the 'Nordic model' of education (Antikainen, 2010; Blossing et al., 2014; Telhaug et al., 2006), there are also many differences between the Nordic countries, as for instance in their diverging responses to neoliberal policy developments (Dovemark et al., 2018; Lundahl, 2016; Wiborg, 2013).

Our analysis investigates how national testing as an instrument of accountability is linked to translations and enactments in decentralized school systems – including re-centralization processes – under the auspices of a universal welfare state. In particular, we examine how global policy is translated and adapted to serve different purposes and functions within these distinct national contexts.

After briefly discussing the contested 'Nordic model' in education, we introduce the concept of 'instrument constituencies' and the empirical sources that inform our analysis and methodology. Turning to the key features of school governance in Norway, Denmark and Sweden, with particular reference to national testing, we analyse the trajectories and uses of this policy instrument and how these are linked to the (re)positioning of diverse key stakeholders. The concluding discussion explores these developments in the three case countries, highlighting similarities and differences in the uptake and use of national testing in the context of accountability reforms and the need to acknowledge the inherently political nature of instrument design and enactment.

Accountability in Nordic education:
Welfare legacies and policy instruments

Nordic societies are commonly said to be characterized by stable social structures, democratic decision-making, high levels of education and a capacity for cooperation and compromise (Telhaug et al., 2006). Balancing the interests of the state, the market and civil society, these liberal economies include a large public sector (Schubert & Martens, 2005). Shared general principles include the alignment of economic efficiency with equality, tax-financed welfare and universal distribution of benefits. Another common feature is the key role of local government in welfare delivery, including education (West Pedersen & Kuhnle, 2017).

However, many scholars have questioned the universality of this 'Nordic model' of society, economy, welfare and education, arguing that the so-called 'Nordic model' seems more like a model with five exceptions: Denmark, Finland, Iceland, Norway and Sweden (Hilson, 2008). With regard to education, the common features of the Nordic model are said to include a comprehensive approach with little streaming or tracking, in which all students can access education of equal quality, pedagogy is relatively pupil-centred and schools maintain close contact with the local community (cf. Eide, 1990). In their historical analysis of the Nordic model in politics and education, Telhaug et al. (2006) referred to principles of equal opportunity, community fellowship and inclusion.

More recently, the promotion and implementation of more instrumental goals and output-oriented management (Telhaug et al., 2006) aligns with global neoliberal education policies, which Nordic education systems may translate in different ways (Lundahl, 2016). For example, Uljens et al. (2013) described how the design and institutional set-up of accountabilities in education in the Nordic countries have developed over time, beginning from a centralized nation-state model in which schools were governed by detailed national curricula and regulations that emphasized legal accountability. With the rise of the welfare state, decentralized models and local interpretations of the national curricula were promoted, along with professional autonomy and accountability. The recent move towards globalized competition includes re-centralization and competency-based curricula linked to national testing and performative accountability. Beyond rules and regulations, the emphasis has shifted to a trust in the profession and results. In a critical assessment of this increasing trust in results and data, Ozga (2020) noted the role of political decisions in the use of data-generating tools that are '(…) applied without explicit reference to the choices they contain' (Ozga, 2020, p. 27). As a policy instrument, national testing reflects particular political choices, agendas and priorities. Here, we seek to unravel the political dimension of the enactment of national testing as an instrument of accountability in Norway, Denmark and Sweden.

Analytical focus, sources and methodology

In their analysis of accountability policies, Maroy and Pons (2019) insist that any such analysis requires an appropriate theoretical lens to decipher 'actor configurations, sets of tools, sensemaking, and the problematization of the policy by local and intermediate actors, their political struggles, and local logics of action' (p. 3). This applies equally to the analysis of policy translations and enactments in systems of accountability in education. For present purposes, we employ welfare regime theory (Kettunen & Petersen, 2011) and the concept of 'instrument constituencies' (Simons & Voß, 2018) to interpret the empirical data. Policy instruments are essentially the tools that governments use to implement policies. Exploring the social practices and agency that inform the design, testing, development and evaluation of these instruments serves to illuminate how they shape the policy process to their own logic (Lascoumes & Le Galès, 2007). Although choosing a policy instrument is often portrayed as a more or less technical decision, such choices are not neutral but inherently political (Lascoumes & Le Galès, 2007). Acknowledging the political and dynamic character of policy instruments, the concept of 'instrument constituencies' (Simons & Voß, 2018; cf. Béland & Howlett, 2016) foregrounds some important sociological features of public policy instrumentation. As Simons and Voß noted, policy instruments may develop a 'life of their own' through their constituencies:

> Policy instruments, it turns out, are not only 'active' or 'alive' because they contain scripts for reordering society (…) but also because they gather a constituency comprised of practices and actors oriented towards developing, maintaining and expanding a specific instrumental model of governing. Through such constituencies, policy instruments can develop a life of their own, partly determining preferences and actively enrolling allies. The concept thereby helps to explain the often-observed paradox that solutions sometimes chase – or even make – problems, although the former are meant to emerge as answers to the latter.
>
> (2018, p. 31)

Through the analytical lens of instrument constituencies, we can identify similarities and differences in the translation and enactment of accountability policies (and, by implication, in the 'Nordic model' of education) and how these instrument constituencies differently form and enable national testing in these countries.

The empirical material consists mainly of policy documents and research studies related to accountability and testing in the three case countries. These sources inform the analysis of the functions and uses of national testing, focusing in particular on recent policies and initiatives (occurring at different times in each country) (Table 6.1).

To situate national testing in its wider constituency and policy context, reading and analysis of national sources was informed by the concept of instrument constituencies. This analytical approach foregrounds the role of debate, political agendas and stakeholder interests when opening the 'black box' of accountability regimes (Ozga, 2020). In education, the diversity of stakeholders in such regimes – governments, local authorities, schools and headteachers, teachers, parents, students, international organizations, edu-businesses and employers – makes conflict inevitable (UNESCO, 2017). In brief, as Simons and Voß (2018) argue, 'the concept of instrument constituencies leads us to de-technicize and to re-politicize

Table 6.1 Document selection

	Key documents
Norway	Green Paper (NOU, 2003:16) on Improving Quality in Basic Education for All; White paper No. 30 Culture for Learning (2003–2004), introducing national testing and NQAS; White Paper No. 28 (2015-2016), a renewal of the latest reform, Knowledge Promotion, focusing on subject, deep learning and understanding; Green Paper (NOU, 2019:3) on gender differences in school performance and educational tracks and improving learning opportunities.
Denmark	Two green papers from the Danish Institute for Evaluation (2004), a government research institution; OECD-report on compulsory schooling in Denmark (2004); Northern Lights on PISA 2006 report; Country Background Report by Rambøll consultants for the OECD (2011); Report from the government's Agency for the Quality Development of the Public School (2011) (green paper); 2018 Inspection Report from the Ministry of Education.
Sweden	OECD report on Sweden (2015); Government committee directions 2015:36 to reform national testing; Committee report SOU 2016:25 (green paper): Equal, fair and efficient – a new national system for knowledge assessment; Government Bill 2017/18:14 (White paper); Protokoll 2017/18:31: parliamentary debate and decision on reforming and digitalizing national tests.

the making of governance knowledge and the design of instruments' (p. 29), highlighting the supply side of politics, including the mobilization and enrolment of organized interests and stakeholders.

Education governance and national testing in Norway, Denmark and Sweden

This section outlines some key features of education governance in each of the case countries. The subsequent analysis of accountability issues focuses on national testing and its evolving uses once enacted (cf. Verger, Fontdevila & Parcerisa, 2019). In each case, we discuss the formation and development of instrument constituencies and how different stakeholders are (re)positioned as national testing develops 'a life of its own'.

Norway

In the early 2000s, the Norwegian authorities introduced national standardized testing and a competency-based curriculum while promoting further devolution of responsibilities to schools and local education authorities (defined as 'school owners'). These policy initiatives were first discussed at formal committee level during the 1990s after an OECD report in 1988/89 questioned the lack of educational quality documentation at national level. During the 1990s, tasks were delegated to municipalities and schools, and new municipal regulations and a 'management by objectives' steering system were implemented (Møller & Skedsmo, 2013). The new national testing policies represented a disruptive transformation in educational institutions and school governance and were seen to be at odds with Norwegian values and traditions (Skedsmo 2009; Tveit, 2014). Interestingly, the instruments suggested in the 2003 Green Paper informed the later White Paper No. 30 (2003-2004). These echoed a 1997 report that was sidelined because its recommendations were considered controversial at that time (Skedsmo, 2009).

The first PISA results ranked Norway below the OECD average, prompting the reintroduction of national testing. This was implemented for the first time in 2004, followed by an improved version in 2007. A National Quality Assessment System (NQAS) was introduced in 2005. National testing has since become a key governance instrument, serving the dual functions of controlling and monitoring educational quality and improvement – although national education policy conceals the former (Skedsmo, 2011). White Paper No. 30, which defined the basis for the introduction of national testing and NQAS, noted that school governance was previously characterized by detailed regulation and control:

> The idea that the state can provide equitable education by detailed regulation
> is replaced by confidence that the teacher, the school leader and the munici-
> pality are capable of creating good learning opportunities within the frame-
> work of the national aims.
> (White Paper No. 30, 2003-2004, p. 25 [our translation])

Although Knowledge Promotion (K06), the latest reform, continued to stress professional autonomy, trust in education was now communicated by emphasizing national testing as a means of increasing transparency and monitoring students' performance for continuous improvement. The document identifies key stakeholders (students, teachers, parents, school leaders, municipalities, regional and national authorities) and notes that distribution of the new data will guide improvement. Schools were assigned responsibility for making productive use of the data while municipalities implemented local quality assessment systems for monitoring and control.

In many municipalities, national test data serve as the main indicator of education quality, and new organizational routines such as 'result meetings' have been established to discuss results and performance improvement (Mausethagen et al., 2018; Skedsmo, 2018). In this way, national testing has gathered a constituency by prompting new interactions and chains of accountability, as municipal educational leaders attend results meetings with principals, principals hold meetings with their leadership and/or teacher teams and teachers engage in 'development dialogues' with students and their parents twice a year. At each level, the focus is on reporting achievement, setting targets and agreeing improvements to achieve those targets by working harder or more effectively. However, municipalities differ widely in their use of national test results in performance management systems and accountability practices (Prøitz et al., 2019), and it remains questionable whether these new interactions have achieved more hierarchical school governance, at least in many of the larger municipalities.

Although all political parties agreed to national testing in 2003, there is ongoing debate around how tests are used. For example, the public availability of test results changes according to which coalition government is in power; while conservative/centre or conservative/right-wing coalitions publish the results, red/green coalitions prefer to avoid any negative consequences arising from public ranking of schools (Camphuijsen et al., 2020). Publication of aggregated test results on the government's online 'School Portal' follows a benchmarking logic similar to PISA, comparing schools with each other or against national, regional or municipal averages as quality thresholds for teachers and school leaders (Skedsmo, 2018). Political interests determine the level of transparency, and even where schools suffer no sanctions, teachers and school leaders are concerned about their school's reputation in the local community.

At national level, testing and benchmarking can create their own dynamic by prompting new reforms that in turn require further testing and assessment to determine their effects (cf. Baker & Le Tendre, 2005). At local level, educators must constantly strive to improve student outcomes, creating a market for private companies offering digital systems and tools that synthesize and monitor results and programmes. The potential for improvement ultimately depends on professional reflection and discussion among teachers and principals regarding national test results (Gunnulfsen, 2017; Mausethagen et al., 2018). While the use of test results is intended to ensure a basic standard of education for everyone, it also represents a drive for individualization to equalize disadvantage (Møller & Skedsmo, 2013).

National testing is positioned as a key instrument that facilitates monitoring of individuals and groups of students at different points throughout their primary and lower secondary education. A 2019 Green Paper reflected growing concern that females are performing better than males in terms of grades, examination results and entry to higher education and high-prestige professions. To enhance knowledge of this problem and how to address it through early intervention, the committee suggested that a similar monitoring system should be introduced in kindergarten as part of an overall 'knowledge based' steering system (NOU, 2019, p. 4). The document also suggests the development of indicators to assess teachers' contributions to student learning. It remains to be seen whether this proposal will be developed further, as it raises questions about the accountability of individual teachers. Until now, the instrument has been used primarily to hold schools and school principals to account and to promote a collective responsibility to improve (Skedsmo & Mausethagen, 2016). While accountability for results is one element of performance appraisal for school leaders and teachers, based on documented development goals, such indicators are likely to increase pressure on the individual. White Paper 28 (2015-2016), which introduced the new curriculum to be implemented from 2020/21, focuses on subject renewal and deep learning. This follows the trends described above, emphasizing the need to prioritize core knowledge, to specify competency aims, to use nationally developed tests to support student learning within NQAS and to develop learning standards to assess student goal attainment.

In comparison to many other countries, Norway has been slow to introduce global policies for monitoring student performance and the accompanying accountability of school actors, including parents, to boost improvement. In particular, school leaders are under pressure to improve student outcomes, which does not always align with other pressing local priorities or the diverse needs of students and student welfare (Skedsmo & Møller, 2016; Mausethagen et al., 2020). In recent years, parents have also reacted publicly against the increasing pressures on students, as on the Facebook site 'parents' protest in Oslo', and research shows that the use of test results does not necessarily foster professional dialogue on improving teaching and learning in diverse classroom contexts with specific student challenges (Skedsmo & Møller, 2016).

Denmark

Accountability structures are a long-standing feature of the Danish public school system (Ydesen & Andreasen, 2014). In the 1990s, the jurisdiction of school boards was expanded, and parental majorities were instituted. At the same time, school leaders acquired greater powers in respect of daily operations. These developments attest to the decentralized nature of the Danish public education system.

In the 2000s, Danish education policymaking looked increasingly to transnational trends and the international community for inspiration following poor results in large-scale international assessments such as PISA (Moos, 2019). Against this backdrop, a number of new accountability measures were introduced to render the '(…) knowledge and skills of Danish students comparable to the best in the world' (Rambøll, 2011, p. 10). According to a 2011 report by *Styrelsen for Evaluering og Kvalitetsudvikling af Grundskolen* [the Agency for the Quality Development of Public Schools], quality assurance, evaluation and accountability in the public school system rest on four pillars:

- the school leaving examination after grade 9 (instituted in 1964, mandatory from 2006);
- the national tests (instituted in 2006 and launched effectively in 2010);
- individual student plans and municipal quality reports (instituted in 2006); and
- user satisfaction surveys (effectively launched in 2010).

The introduction of new policy instruments in the 2000s brought major changes in education governance. While the key stakeholders remain the same, power positions among them shifted significantly. Local authorities were strengthened during the 1990s, but the 2000s brought a clear commitment to centralization (Nordic Council of Ministers, 2009). From 2001, changes in education governance provisions followed an electoral shift to the right (Gustafsson, 2012). In 2003, Prime Minister Anders Fogh Rasmussen signalled a break with the progressive approach that had prevailed in Denmark since the interwar years (Nørgaard, 1977). In his opening speech to parliament, he observed:

'It is as if learning of academic skills has been sidelined in favour of sitting in a circle on the floor and asking: "What do you think?"' (cited in Gustafsson, 2012, p. 185). Playing into this right-wing agenda of strengthening learning outcomes and subject knowledge, three reports published in 2004 – one from the OECD (Ekholm, 2004) and two from the Danish Institute for Evaluation (EVA) (2004a, 2004b) – called for an 'evaluation culture' in the Danish public school system.

Testing in various forms has been a key component of Danish public education since the interwar years (Ydesen, 2011) as a means of distinguishing between normality and deviance in the emerging universal education system. Interestingly in the present context, randomized ministry tests to monitor students' academic level on leaving the public school system (between 1914 and 1954) were abandoned because some stakeholders made use of these data for unintended purposes – for instance, some school leaders used test results to hold individual teachers to account (Ydesen, 2013).

As a policy instrument, the new national tests were introduced to achieve the political goals referred to above. Their advanced IT-based design promised to make every child testable, and it was claimed that their introduction would support the formative development of the individual student. This was an appealing argument in the prevailing culture (Kelly et al., 2018; Kousholt & Hamre, 2016), not least because it meant that a change of government would not lead to the publication of school league tables based on national test results. The tests also linked teaching to national curriculum standards and served as a key indicator in municipal reports on education quality. The availability of these data prompted the libertarian think-tank CEPOS to publish school league tables in the national media. In other words, while the OECD and EVA reports served as instruments of diagnosis in line with ideological priorities, the national tests package was introduced as a remedy for problems in the education system.

Through the lens of instrument constituency, the national tests can be seen as an expensive and high-profile prestige-building Ministry of Education project that was largely a preordained success, remaining immune to criticism for several years.[1] Nevertheless, the national tests quickly polarized stakeholder groups at all levels of the education system – teachers, politicians, economists, think-tanks, researchers, parents, students, interest groups, professional organizations and most recently edu-businesses – all of whom engage in the ongoing debate about education policy, including the national tests (e.g. Norling, 2016).

The sampled policy documents serve to illuminate how the national tests have changed education governance in general and accountability practices in particular. In what is essentially a decentralized system, municipalities are responsible for the supervision and monitoring of schools. However, as we have seen, the increasing incursion of state-level policy instruments sought '(…) to ensure that evaluation and assessment of school practice were comprehensive, efficient and timely' (Rambøll, 2011, p. 13). This has created a centralization/decentralization tension in Danish education governance. As in Norway, contemporary Danish education is characterized by clear top-down accountability chains while bottom-up accountability is much weaker. At a theoretical level, this tension can be described as a case of policy instruments from the curriculum tradition being rolled out in a historically *didaktik*-oriented system (Westbury, 1998).

Since 2007, the Ministry of Education has worked to install a unified system of accountability based on so-called 'data-based risk assessment indicators' associated with the four pillars referred to above (Ministry of Education, 2018). This system makes it easier for the Ministry to identify at-risk schools and municipal authorities, which can ultimately be placed under administration. The national tests play a pivotal role in this respect. Viewed as a policy instrument, however, the national tests embody a number of problems, all with significant implications for education governance. As noted above, the national tests were introduced as a formative assessment tool, but have gradually come to play a broader role in the accountability system, calling into question their initial framing as low-stakes measures. In fact, there is evidence that students, teachers and school leaders experience the tests as high-stakes, which impacts negatively on their practices (Kousholt and Hamre, 2016; McNess et al., 2015). As in Norway, there is a somewhat naïve expectation that test results will automatically generate improvements in stakeholder practices. However, the evidence suggests that teachers commonly misunderstand the test results and draw wrong conclusions from them (Bundsgaard & Puck, 2016).

In the spring of 2019, the national tests attracted fierce criticism, which was aired in the national media. Based on an extensive review, professors Jeppe Bundsgaard and Svend Kreiner (2019) found the national tests to be fundamentally flawed and inaccurate in both design and implementation, and they recommended that the tests should be terminated as soon as possible. In the heated debate that followed, it became apparent that the inaccuracies of the national tests had already been communicated to parliament at a hearing in 2016, but no-one had taken action. In June 2019, the new Social Democratic government (supported by social liberal and left-wing parties) announced the suspension of national tests in the school year 2019/20, and the Ministry of Education has commenced the process of rethinking provisions for assessment and accountability.

The Danish case clearly illustrates the politics of policy, as outlined above. It seems clear that political interests and priorities have influenced the environment in which PISA results are processed, as well as the ensuing political reforms. They were driven by the collision between a cross-stakeholder constituency and a counter-constituency, highlighting the role of incommensurable results and priorities in implementing new policy instruments such as the national tests.

Sweden

In Sweden, the 1990s have been characterized as a 'breaking point' in education governance (OECD, 2015, p. 49), as a relatively centralized system was restructured to almost its opposite, and governance by objectives and results replaced strong state governance. The 290 municipalities assumed full employer responsibility for all teachers, principals and other staff, with extensive local autonomy and freedom in pursuing national goals. Reforms in the early 1990s also included school choice, with tax-funded vouchers and liberal provisions for public funding of private schools. These reforms were accompanied by measures to retain state power in education, and different forms of state control and accountability have been introduced or expanded. For example, the implementation of an intensified school inspection scheme and more frequent testing of student performance in the first decade of the 2000s meant that, despite extensive local autonomy and decentralization, some instruments remained firmly centralized in the hands of the state (Rönnberg et al., 2019).

As a long-standing feature of the Swedish education system (since the 1940s), national testing was embedded mainly in the American tradition of psychometric assessment, adapted to serve meritocratic functions and to support grading and assessment (Lundahl & Tveit, 2014). Over time, the tests have served different purposes and aims. In the 1990s, national testing was decentralized to support (though not to determine) teacher grading (Lundahl, 2017). More recently, the centre-right coalition that held office from 2006 implemented several reforms that intensified accountability mechanisms and state control. The coalition's far-reaching education reform agenda prioritized the intensification and expansion of standardized national testing. The political motives included a desire to ensure equal grading and early identification of pupils in need of special support. As a result, the tests now cover more subjects and are introduced earlier than before. National testing of all pupils is now mandatory in grades 3, 6 and 9 in compulsory school and includes a number of subjects, with an emphasis on Swedish, Mathematics and English (Jarl & Rönnberg, 2019). Test results for each school are published and are used by parents and students to guide their choice of school.

In the wake of Sweden's poor PISA performance in 2013, the OECD (2015) policy advice to the Swedish Government emphasized the need to reform accountability arrangements and to address the issue of 'unreliable national student achievement data' (OECD, 2015, p. 143). This was seen to cast doubt on the perceived 'fairness' of national test grading and results, in that the 'credibility of the results is heavily dependent on the integrity of local marking' (p. 168). The national tests reappeared on the policy agenda and underwent further reform (cf. Committee directions 2015:36, 2015; SOU 2016:25, 2016; Government Bill 2017/18:14, 2017), prioritizing the issue of variations in grading and the tendency to overstate student performance. A central point in this debate was that teachers assessed their own pupils; in combination with a criterion reference grading system and the increased competition between schools to attract pupils following the school choice reforms mentioned above, this spurred a discussion of so-called 'grade inflation'. In brief, the argument was that teachers might award higher grades than student (test) performance warranted in order to satisfy 'education consumers' (i.e. parents and pupils), as well as school management (cf. Tyrefors Hinnerich & Vlachos, 2016).

As a partial solution, implemented before the most recent revision of national testing, the National Schools Inspectorate was assigned to re-assess samples of teachers' grading on national tests. According to Novak and Carlbaum (2017, p. 685), this move has added to national 'mistrust in the teaching profession' by facilitating 'a game of naming and shaming'. The most recent decision (Protokoll 2017/18:31, 2017) assigned a more significant and decisive role to the tests for grading – not as 'advisory' for teachers but as 'strong evidence' of the subject grade. It is increasingly recognised that, although largely developed with the support of the teaching profession (Lundahl & Tveit, 2014), the tests take up too much time and cause great stress for teachers and students (Lundahl, 2017). Prior to the parliament decision of 2017, one teacher union had argued against assigning national tests a more decisive role in teacher grading (Lärarförbundet, 2017). Nevertheless, parliament decided to implement the new regulations, and there were no significant party political struggles (Protokoll 2017/18:31, 2017). In an attempt to address workload concerns, some of the tests are now voluntary in light of the time needed for administration and assessment. As another partial solution, it is hoped that digitalization of the tests may enhance the efficiency of administration, distribution and assessment (Government Bill 2017/18:14, 2017).

As in the Danish case, one central recurring issue is how best to merge the tests' multiple purposes – identification of each child's needs and formative assessment to improve classroom teaching, as well as the promotion of 'equal' grading practices to assess school and school system quality. In addition, teacher quality is indirectly assessed by the tests; for instance, test results may influence performance-related pay negotiations, as headteachers are authorized to decide teacher salaries (UNESCO, 2017). Overall, it should be noted that there is no extensive public opposition to national tests, and stakeholders with diverging interests are drawn together in support of this approach. Rather, the Swedish case demonstrates that as an accountability instrument that is continuously reformed and redesigned, national testing has successfully created and adapted to 'new' circumstances. As new elements, goals and uses are layered into previous test policies and practices (Mahoney & Thelen, 2010), testing comes to life as an enduring and expanding practice.

Returning to the issue of instrument constituency and how the national testing instrument is applied, the intensification of national testing has indeed brought stakeholders who rely on the tests closer together. Test developers are commissioned by the state and placed in universities, where the tests provide funding and opportunities for individual careers. Parents are, on the one hand, positioned as needing information to guide their choice of school, but also needing early and reliable information about their children's performance. The tests hold teachers to account in relation to parents and employers alike, creating particular forms of dependencies and loyalties, not the least in the context of school choice and the intense competition between schools in many urban areas. At the same time, the tests also guide teachers in adjusting their teaching to target each student's individual needs (at the cost of some additional workload). This remains a concern for the teacher unions, which have historically been supportive of testing.

For national politicians, the tests signal a policy commitment to improving academic achievement, both as a response to declining PISA results and also to provide a sense of assurance that the system is closely monitored and 'under control'. As a policy instrument, testing is also used to monitor performance at various levels for different school owners, both public and private. Despite their far-reaching autonomy in other respects, municipalities are positioned as test administrators and must use the results to develop and improve schools and academic achievement. The tests also afford opportunities to further intensify and legitimize the school inspection regime positioned as a problem solver both as a re-assessor of the test results and as a watchdog, guarding against potential grade inflation. Finally, national tests are implemented in a marketized and commercialized education sector that includes some new stakeholders. The forthcoming implementation of digital national tests will provide further business opportunities for software and hardware developers, further expanding the constituency and helping to build alliances that enable and sustain, rather than challenge, the many roles of national testing in Swedish education policy.

Concluding discussion

Across the three cases, our analysis identifies similar development trends during the 1990s in the decentralization of tasks and responsibilities to local authorities and schools. The release of the first PISA results in 2001 added another layer of globalization and competition that was translated into national education governance provisions. These developments paved the way for the reform of national testing and accountability arrangements, although these differed somewhat in nature and pace across the three countries. During the 2000s, along with other types of evaluation such as school inspection, the introduction or intensification of national testing was an important policy instrument for documenting and monitoring educational quality, strengthening state control of schools through performative accountability.

In Norway and Denmark, national testing instruments used comparison and benchmarking at various levels in line with global discourses demanding increased transparency and accountability to justify public spending, and constituencies were assembled and formed accordingly. These elements are also discernible in Sweden, but the country has followed its own path in combining high-stakes national testing and school inspection with a strong market orientation and privatization. The explicit intention is to ensure 'equal' grading practices by and through national testing. Teachers' overall responsibility for assessing their own students' test performance is also worthy of mention in the context of policy instruments.

In all three cases, instrument constituencies include and enrol market actors that develop and apply technologies for synthesizing results and developing relevant skills (e.g. data literacy). It is also clear that new patterns of interaction have emerged at stakeholder and organizational levels, and that power relationships continue to develop and change over time. Although tasks and responsibilities have been decentralized in all three countries, national authorities have visibly engaged in re-centralization by setting the agenda by and through testing, and by holding local actors to account. In this context, accountability arrangements that build hierarchies seem to promote increasingly centralized governing structures. This challenges a key characteristic commonly attributed to the 'Nordic' or 'Scandinavian' welfare state, where municipal autonomy and local governance prevail.

Nevertheless, the welfarist legacy remains strong in the Nordic model. Emphasizing education for the public good, policy discourse frames national testing and performative accountability as a means of providing universal access to education of equal quality, prioritizing the need to identify and support low-performing students. However, the conflicting rationales that accompany the roll-out of neo-liberal reforms, competency-based curricula and/or technical-economic rationality have gained ground in some Scandinavian contexts more than others, as in the far-reaching Swedish transformation mentioned above. Despite their somewhat different approaches to neo-liberalism, all three countries invite one general question: whether trust in results trumps trust in the professions (cf. Uljens et al., 2013). In particular, it will be interesting to follow Denmark's suspension of national testing and its plans to rethink assessment and acceptance criteria and admission practices across education levels. One main source of tension is the conflict between discourses rooted in traditional social democratic ideologies linked to notions of equity, participation and comprehensive education, and the discourses of accountability and competition that underpin managerial forms of school governance.

In exploring how Norway, Denmark and Sweden have accommodated global trends in education, we argue for the importance of acknowledging different national legacies and policy histories. In responding to new global accountability trends, the Scandinavian welfare states have made policy choices that influence the design and enactment of national testing and accountability regimes. The analysis also illustrates how testing develops a life of its own, shaped by the particular circumstances and policy context from which they emerge. Drawing on Simon and Voß (2018), we conclude that national testing is more than a solution to known problems. Nurtured by their growing constituencies, testing 'comes to life', expanding its application to policy problems. In this way, tests become adaptable and agile instruments for targeting new and/or redefined problems and value dilemmas, such as gender performance gaps in Norway or grade inflation in Sweden. In all cases, the knowledge produced by test data impacts on education policy and the political agenda, demonstrating its potency as a policy instrument.

As illustrated here, the concept of instrument constituencies serves as a lens for exploring the evolving uses, functions and challenges of the politics of public policy instrumentation in national testing. For scholarship and democracy alike, it is important to acknowledge the inherently political dimension of instrument selection in policymaking.

Note

1 The Government Auditor has estimated the cost of developing the national tests (between 2005 and 2010) at about US$16.5 million.

References

Antikainen, A. (2010). The capitalist state and education: The case of restructuring the Nordic model. *Current Sociology, 58*(4), 530–550.

Baker, D. P., & Le Tendre, G. K. (2005). *National differences, global similiarities. World culture and the future of schooling.* Palo Alto: Stanford University Press, 21 January 2020.

Béland, D., & Howlett, M. (2016). How solutions chase problems: Instrument constituencies in the policy process. *Governance, 29*(3), 393–409.

Blossing, U., Imsen, G., and Moos, L. (2014). *The Nordic Education Model: 'A school for all'* *Encounters Neo-Liberal Policy*. New York, Berlin and Heidelberg: Springer.

Bundsgaard, J., & Kreiner, S. (2019). *Undersøgelse af De Nationale Tests måleegenskaber*. Aarhus Universitet, DPU.

Bundsgaard, J., & Puck, M. R. (2016). *Nationale test: Danske lærere og skolelederes brug, holdninger og viden*. DPU, Aarhus Universitet: Center for Anvendt Skoleforskning ved University College Lillebælt.

Camphuijsen, M., Møller, J., & Skedsmo, G. (2020). Test-based accountability in the Norwegian context: Exploring drivers, expectations and strategies. *Journal of Education Policy* Published online 11 March. https://doi.org/10.1080/02680939.2020.1739337

Committee directions 2015:36. (2015). *Kommittédirektivet Översyn av de nationella proven för grund och gymnasieskolan*. Stockholm: Utbildningsdepartementet.

Dovemark, M., Kosunen, S., Kauko, J., Magnúsdóttir, B., Hansen, P., & Rasmussen, P. (2018). Deregulation, privatisation and marketisation of Nordic comprehensive education: Social changes reflected in schooling. *Education Inquiry, 9*(1), 122–141.

Eide, K. (1990). 30 years of educational collaboration in the OECD. *International Congress 'Planning and Management of Educational Development'*, Mexico, 26–30 March 1990. Available at http://unesdoc.unesco.org/images/0008/000857/085725eo.pdf

Ekholm, M. (2004). *OECD-rapport om grundskolen i Danmark - 2004*. Copenhagen: Uddannelsesstyrelsen.

EVA. (2004a). *Undervisningsdifferentiering i folkeskolen*. Copenhagen: Danmarks Evalueringsinstitut.

EVA. (2004b). *Løbende evaluering af elevernes udbytte af undervisningen på hhx, htx og stx*. Copenhagen: Danmarks Evalueringsinstitut.

Government Bill 2017/18:14. 2017. *Nationella prov – rättvisa, likvärdiga, digitala*. Stockholm: Utbildningsdepartementet.

Green Paper (NOU 2003:16). (2003). I første rekke. Forsterket kvalitet i en grunnopplæring for alle. Ministry of Education and Research. https://www.regjeringen.no/cont entassets/37a02a7bd6d94f5aacd8b477a3a95

Green Paper (NOU 2019:3). (2019). Nye sjanser – bedre læring — Kjønnsforskjeller i skoleprestasjoner og utdanningsløp. Ministry of Education and Research. https://www. regjeringen.no/contentassets/8b06e9565c9e403497cc79b9fdf5e177/no/pdfs/ nou201920190003000dddpdfs.pdf

Gunnulfsen, A. E. (2017). School leaders' and teachers' work with national test results: Lost in translation? *Journal of Educational Change, 18*(4), 495–519.

Gustafsson, L. R. (2012). What did you learn in school today? How ideas mattered for policy changes in Danish and Swedish schools 1990–2011 (PhD dissertation). Aarhus: Aarhus University.

Hilson, M. (2008). *The Nordic model: Scandinavia since 1945*. London: Reaktion Books.

Jarl, M., & Rönnberg, L. (2019). *Skolpolitik. Från riksdagshus till klassrum*. Stockholm: Liber.

Kettunen, P., & Petersen, K. (2011). Introduction: Rethinking welfare state model. In Kettunen, P & Petersen, K (Eds.), *Beyond welfare state models – Transnational historical perspectives on social policy* (1–15). Cheltenham/Northampton: Edward Elgar.

Kelly, P., Andreasen, K. E., Kousholt, K., McNess, E., & Ydesen, C. (2018). Education governance and standardised tests in Denmark and England. *Journal of Education Policy, 33*(6), 739–758. https://doi.org/10.1080/02680939.2017.1360518

Kousholt, K., & Hamre, B. (2016). Testing and school reform in Danish education: An analysis informed by the use of 'the dispositive'. In: W. C. Smith (Ed.), *The global testing culture: Shaping education policy, perceptions, and practice* (231–247). Oxford: Symposium Books.

Lärarförbundet. (2017). Nationella provens roll för betygen – kampen går vidare! https://www.lararforbundet.se/bloggar/ordforandebloggen-johanna-jaara-aastrand/nationella-provens-roll-for-betygen-kampen-gaar-vidare (accessed 21 January 2020).

Lascoumes, P., & Le Galès, P. (2007). Introduction: Understanding public policy through its instruments—from the nature of instruments to the sociology of public policy instrumentation. *Governance, 20*(1), 1–21.

Lundahl, C., & Tveit, S. (2014). Att legitimera nationella prov i Sverige och i Norge – en fråga om profession och tradition. *Pedagogisk Forskning i Sverige, 19*(4–5), 297–323.

Lundahl, C. (2017). Tema: Perspektiv på nationella prov. *Utbildning & Demokrati, 26*(2), 5–20.

Lundahl, L. (2016). Equality, inclusion and marketization of Nordic education: Introductory notes. *Research in Comparative and International Education, 11*(1), 3–12.

Mahoney, J., & Thelen, K. (2010). A theory of gradual institutional change. In J. Mahoney & K. Thelen (Eds.), *Explaining institutional change: Ambiguity, agency, and power* (pp. 1–36). Cambridge: Cambridge University Press.

Maroy, C., & Pons, X. (Eds.). (2019). *Accountability policies in education: A comparative and multilevel analysis in France and Quebec.* Dordrecht: Springer.

Mausethagen, S., Prøitz, T.S. & Skedsmo, G. (2020): Redefining public values: Data use and value dilemmas in education. *Education Inquiry.* Published online 2 March. https://doi.org/10.1080/20004508.2020.1733744

Mausethagen, S., Prøitz, T. S., & Skedsmo, G. (2018). Teachers' use of knowledge sources in 'result meetings': Thin data and thick data use. *Teachers and Teaching: Theory and Practice, 43*(6), 37–49.

McNess, E., Kelly, P., Kousholt, K., Andreasen, K. E., & Ydesen, C. (2015). Standardised testing in compulsory schooling in England and Denmark: A comparative study and analysis. *Bildung und Erziehung, 68*(3), 329–348.

Ministry of Education. (2018). *Tilsynsberetning 2018.* Copenhagen: Undervisningsministeriet

Moos, L. (2019) Fra en dannelsesdiskurs mod en læringsmålstyret diskurs. In Moos, L. (Ed.), *Glidninger: 'usynlige' forandringer inden for pædagogik og uddannelser* (pp. 40–65). DPU: Aarhus Universitet.

Møller, J., & Skedsmo, G. (2013). Modernizing education—NPM reform in the Norwegian education system. *Journal of Educational Administration and History, 45*(4), 336–355.

Nordic Council of Ministers. (2009). Northern Lights on PISA 2006. In Matti, T. (Ed.), *TemaNord 2009:547.* Copenhagen: Nordic Council of Ministers.

Nørgaard, E. (1977). *Lille barn, hvis er du?: En skolehistorisk undersøgelse over reformbestræbelser inden for den danske folkeskole i mellemkrigstiden.* Copenhagen: Gyldendal.

Norling, M. (2016) De nationale test 2016 - hvor galt står det til? *Folkeskolen.* Retrieved 13 March, 2020. https://www.folkeskolen.dk/586828/de-nationale-test-2016—hvor-galt-staar-det-til-1

Novak, J., & Carlbaum, S. (2017). Juridification of examination systems: Extending state level authority over teacher assessments through regrading of national tests. *Journal of Education Policy, 32*(5), 673–693.

OECD. (2015). *Improving schools in Sweden.* Paris: OECD.

Ozga, J. (2020). The politics of accountability. *Journal of Educational Change, 21*, 19–35.

Protokoll 2017/18:31. (2017). *Riksdagens protokoll den 15 November.* Stockholm: Riksdagen.

Prøitz, T., Mausethagen, S., & Skedsmo, G. (2019). District administrators' governing styles in the enactment of data use practices. *International Journal of Leadership in Education.* Published online 28 January. https://doi.org/10.1080/13603124.2018.1562097

Rambøll. (2011). *Country background report (CBR) for Denmark in relation to the OECD Review on Evaluation and Assessment Frameworks for Improving School Outcomes.* Aarhus: Rambøll.

Rönnberg, L., Lindgren, J., & Lundahl, L. (2019). Education governance in times of marketization: The quiet Swedish revolution. In R. Langer & T. Brüsemeister (Eds.), *Handbuch educational governance Theorien* (pp. 711–728). Dordrecht: Springer.

Schubert, C. B., & Martens, H. (2005). The Nordic Model: A Recipe for European Success? *European Policy Centre Working Paper*, No. 20.

Simons, A., & Voß, J.-P. (2018). The concept of instrument constituencies: Accounting for dynamics and practices of knowing governance. *Policy and Society*, *37*(1), 14–35.

Skedsmo, G. (2009). School Governing in Transition? Perspectives, Purposes and Perceptions of Evaluation Policy. (PhD), University of Oslo.

Skedsmo, G. (2011). Formulation and realisation of evaluation policy: Inconsistencies and problematic issues. *Educational Assessment, Evaluation and Accountability*, *23*(1), 5–20.

Skedsmo, G. (2018). Comparison and benchmarking as governing processes in Norwegian schools. In L. M. Carvalho, L. Levasseur, M. Liu, R. Normand, & D. A. Oliveira (Eds.), *Education policies and the restructuring of the educational profession* (pp. 137–158). Singapore: Springer.

Skedsmo, G., & Møller, J. (2016): Governing by new performance expectations in Norwegian schools. In H. Gunter, D. Hall, R Serpieri, & E. Grimaldi (Eds.), *New public management and the reform of education: European lessons for policy and practice* (pp. 53–65). London: Routledge.

Skedsmo, G., & Mausethagen, S. (2016). Accountability policies and educational leadership—A Norwegian perspective. In J. Easley, & Tulowitzki, P. (Eds.), *Accountability and educational leadership—Country perspective* (pp. 205–223). London. Routledge.

SOU 2016:25. (2016). *Likvärdigt, rättssäkert och effektivt: Ett nytt nationellt system för kunskapsbedömning*. Stockholm: Wolters Kluwer.

Styrelsen for Evaluering og Kvalitetsudvikling af Grundskolen. (2011). *Beretning om evaluering og kvalitetsudvikling af folkeskolen*. Kbh.: Styrelsen for Evaluering og Kvalitetsudvikling af Grundskolen.

Telhaug, A., Mediås, O., & Aasen, P. (2006). The Nordic model in education: Education as part of the political system in the last 50 years. *Scandinavian Journal of Educational Research*, *50*(3), 245–283.

Tveit, S. (2014). Educational assessment in Norway. *Assessment in Education: Principles, Policy and Practice*, *21*(2), 221–237.

Tylefors Hinnerich, B., & Vlachos, J. (2016). Skillnader i resultat mellan gymnasieelever i fristående och kommunala skolor. *IFAU rapport 2016:10*. Stockholm: IFAU.

Uljens, M., Møller, J., Ärlestig, H., & Frederiksen, L. F. (2013). The professionalisation of Nordic school leadership. In L. Moos (Ed.), *Transnational influences on values and practices in Nordic Educational Leadership. Is there a Nordic Model?* (pp. 33–158). Dordrecht: Springer.

UNESCO. (2017). *Global education monitoring report: Accountability in education*. Paris: UNESCO.

Verger, A., Fontdevila, C., & Parcerisa, L. (2019). Reforming governance through policy instruments: How and to what extent standards, tests and accountability in education spread worldwide. *Discourse: Studies in the Cultural Politics of Education*, *40*(2), 248–270.

West Pedersen, A., & Kuhnle, S. (2017). The Nordic welfare state model. In O. P. Knutsen (Ed.), *The Nordic models in political science: Challenged, but still viable?* (pp. 249–272). Bergen: Fagbokforlaget

Westbury, I. D. (1998). Didaktik and curriculum studies. In B. B. Gundem & S. Hopmann (Eds.), *Didaktik and/or Curriculum: An International Dialogue* (pp. 47–78). New York: Peter Lang.

White Paper No. 30. (2003-2004). *Kultur for læring*. Oslo: The Royal Ministry of Education and Research.

White Paper No. 28. (2015-2016). *Fag – Fordypning – Forståelse. En fornyelse av Kunnskapsløftet*. Oslo: The Royal Ministry of Education and Research.

Wiborg, S. (2013). Neo-liberalism and universal state education: The cases of Denmark, Norway and Sweden 1980–2011. *Comparative Education*, 49(4), 407–423.

Ydesen, C. (2011). *The rise of high-stakes educational testing in Denmark, 1920–1970*. New York/Berlin: Peter Lang.

Ydesen, C. (2013). Educational testing as an accountability measure: Drawing on twentieth-century Danish history of education experiences. *Paedagogica Historica*, 49(5), 716–733.

Ydesen, C., & Andreasen, K. E. (2014). Accountability practices in the history of Danish primary public education from the 1660s to the present. *Education Policy Analysis Archives*, 22(120), 1–31.

7 Accountability and datafication in francophone contexts: A reinforcing cognitive state still challenged by local actors

Christian Maroy, Vincent Dupriez and Xavier Pons

Introduction

This chapter compares the implementation of performance-based accountability policies in three French-speaking school systems (Belgium, France and Quebec) on the basis of a synthesis of our own research and the main existing studies in the different areas. Comparing these three systems has at least two major interests beyond improving the empirical coverage of international research on the subject, which tends to focus on policies applied in English-speaking systems, as the literature review prepared by Verger and Parcerisa (2017) demonstrates.

First, the accountability and datafication policies implemented in these systems, which have sometimes been described as soft or reflective (Maroy, 2015; Mons & Dupriez, 2010), enrich the main interpretations proposed on the development of these accountability policies. These examples do not necessarily correspond to an alignment with an international or transnational norm such as neo-liberalism (Ambrosio, 2013) or a global testing culture, for example (Smith, 2016). They are not only a euphemized version of the dominant model of hard accountability that would inevitably be the default definition of an accountability policy in education. They show a wide variety of forms of hybridization and vernacularization (Lingard, 2006) at work in the accountability policies implemented.

Secondly, the many differences that characterize these three school systems make it possible to envisage a particularly productive strategy of comparison by the most different cases, except their francophone character. Indeed, despite major differences in terms of political systems, the structure of school systems, the degree of exposure to international influences, or the implementation of accountability policies themselves, in all three cases, these policies are characterized by long-term trajectories that tend to strengthen state power, even if there is a contrast in the empirical forms of these 'neostatist trajectories' (Clark, 2002). At the same time, the local implementation of the accountability tools in schools leads, in each context, to contrasted effects, related to local context and actors.

After a short presentation of our main concepts, we will present the specific trajectory of the accountability policy in each system, emphasizing how historical dependence on institutions, bricolage and translation lead to specific features of this policy. For each jurisdiction, we also analyze the effects of these policies, at two levels: on the governance of the education systems as a whole; and, at the microlevel, on the functioning of schools and their actors. We conclude with a discussion of the main findings of our comparison.

Theoretical framework and comparison methodology

Our comparison is based on a re-reading of our previous work with a theoretical framework derived from the comparative research NewAGE (Maroy & Pons, 2019) extended to the Belgian case.

The vernacularization at work in each context is studied through the specific trajectories (Ball, 1993) of these accountability policies, which makes it necessary to take into account their implementation over the long term, and to consider the institutional, ideological and political context within which this trajectory is developed and transformed. Three intertwined processes are at work in the formation of this trajectory of politics: dependence on existing institutions, bricolage and translation.

The trajectory is first conditioned by existing institutions in the broad sense (composed of formal rules, shared norms, but also cognitive categories). Path-dependency mechanisms constitute 'normative' or 'regulatory locks' that prevent or slow down change, not only because of the viscosity of institutions, but also because of coalitions of actors that can defend them. This institutional viscosity can therefore foster processes of gradual change, for example, through the sedimentation of different institutional arrangements, which result from the impossibility of removing some existing institutions (Streeck & Thelen, 2005).

However, institutional, political or cognitive bricolage (Campbell, 2004) is also at work. Policy is the result of a dynamic assemblage of various heterogeneous elements: institutional change promoted by political or administrative entrepreneurs; existing institutional arrangements; new managerial tools; and discursive formalizations. This composite construction derives from struggles, negotiations, compromises within various forums in which either the 'problems' that policy is supposed to face, or the 'solutions' or theories of change or action that it should follow, or their operationalization in effective political instruments, are defined. This bricolage could lead to a form of hybridization of transnational models with existing political priorities or public problems as well as the idiosyncratic design of accountability tools.

Finally, in an increasingly transnationalized context, a process of translation of transnational political elements (ideas, frames of reference, political goals, tools, etc.) leads to their redefinition or to their composition with already institutionalized rules, values, conventions or practices. Imported elements are therefore not simply 'diffused', but are translated (Callon, 1986).

Policies' trajectories: A neo-statist convergence with contrasted effects

In this section, we develop an analysis of the trajectories of these policies, which belong to very different structural and institutional contexts. First of all, the temporalities differ, and the international influences come from different sources (PISA in Belgium, the Lisbon process in France, 'pan-Canadian' influence and the proximity of neo-liberal provinces in Quebec). Moreover, the political forces conducive to the accountability policy are various depending on the context and the stage of the trajectory. Finally, the path dependence, bricolage and translation processes are leading to different institutional arrangements and tools constitutive of each accountability system.

Besides, these accountability policy trajectories have contrasting effects on the school system. As far as the type of governance is concerned, there is an ongoing reinforcement of the state in each context, either through the development of cognitive instruments of surveillance and monitoring of local schools and authorities or through more classical hierarchical mechanisms. We could speak of a neo-statist translation of the New Public Management doctrine, different from a neo-liberal one leading to the state withdrawal or a simple privatization or marketization, which is often reported as central in many Anglo-Saxon jurisdictions (Clark, 2002).

On the other hand, there is a strong contrast between the countries concerning the responses of schools and teachers to the policies: symbolic measures variable depending on the school composition in Belgium, complete dilution of the measures in France, while in Quebec, the accountability system favor the rise of a local management of pedagogical practices.

French-speaking Belgium: Accountability as a composite construction in a consociational context

The singularity of the accountability policies developed in French-speaking Belgium can only be understood in the light of the history of the education system and the political context of this country. In fact, the translation of these policies, largely based on New Public Management, has taken place within the framework of the Belgian consociational regime (Lijphart, 1999), which has organized the cohabitation between the secular and Catholic worlds since the 19th century.

This consociational regime is at the origin of an institutional structure in the field of education in which three educational networks coexist: schools under the aegis either of the central public authority, or of the local public authorities (in particular, the municipalities) or of the Catholic institutions. Historically, each municipality and each Catholic school has enjoyed a wide autonomy, setting its own curricula, appointing its teachers, defining its pedagogic mission, and being responsible for evaluating its pupils. Since the School Pact of 1958, all schools have been financed by the State according to their enrollment. Schools thus objectively compete to attract pupils in a context that has been described as a quasi-market system (Vandenberghe, 1999).

Since 1989, education has no longer been the responsibility of the Belgian state, but has been entrusted to the three linguistic and cultural communities of the country. In the southern part of the country, the government of the French community, most often based on a centre-left majority, has progressively introduced new modes of governance. In the 1990s, this process started with a stage of harmonization of the school system by laying down common regulations for all networks and all schools (Dupriez & Maroy, 2003). These norms firstly concerned the key competences to be attained by all pupils (setting standards), teachers' statuses, and school management procedures.

The second stage saw the introduction of the external testing of pupils. Until the end of the 20th century, there was no systematic external testing of all pupils at the same school level. This situation was progressively called into question under the influence of a twofold phenomenon (Maroy & Mangez, 2011). On the one hand, an awareness of the poor results of French community pupils in international evaluations spread from the governing elites to the general public (following the publication of the first PISA results in 2001); on the other hand, from the 1990s, a network of promoters of political change (bringing together experts, political decision-makers and administrators from the different educational networks) supported several recommendations of the international organizations (OECD, 1993). In particular, it translated into the Belgian context the need to better know and evaluate the system, and to develop curriculum and evaluation standards beyond the philosophical and pedagogical differences among the networks.

After the creation of a 'Education Steering Commission' for the system in 2002 (mandated to set up external evaluations and statistical monitoring of pupils, and to deliver opinions on the state of the education system) and several years of various experiments with optional external tests, compulsory certifying external tests were created. In 2009, the end of primary school examination leading to the Certificate of Basic Education became obligatory for all schools; in 2013, the same was done with the examination leading to the Certificate for the First Level of Secondary Education.

Beyond international pressures and a process of imitation which led the actors, in the traditional way, to justify these policies in terms of the improvement of the quality of schools, these provisions were also justified in terms of a struggle against inequalities in the school system and the need for data on the state of the system (Mangez, 2011). Moreover, the governing coalitions and the main stakeholders in the system were becoming increasingly aware of the negative effects of the 'educational quasi-market' and rejecting a liberal conception of steering by results, based on competition among schools (Mangez, 2011). The decrees on external evaluation therefore forbid any form of communication of a school's results, which also makes it possible to respect the traditional discretion of the Belgian system, characteristic of a consociational regime. This dependence to the historical context considerably attenuates the 'transparency' at the heart of the discourse of New Public Management. Belgian institutional specificities encourage a particular translation of transnational influences and the creation of hybrid schemes which combine – sometimes in tension – Belgian institutional arrangements and the transnational doctrine (Mangez & Cattonar, 2009).

These external tests are also accompanied by a range of 'reflective instruments': teaching recommendations for teachers, indications making it possible to compare a school's results with the mean scores of similar schools, or access to previous years' tests (Barbana, 2018). So devices encouraging reflexivity, rather than rewards and sanctions linked to schools' performances, have so far been mobilized.

It should be noted, however, that since 2019, schools have been invited to draw up a 'steering plan' which, after approval by the public authority, becomes an 'objectives contract' between the school and the authority (Cattonar & Dupriez, 2019). So there is a slippage towards a real system of contractualization with schools, which can lead to pressures being applied to schools with 'performance shortfalls' and financial sanctions for schools manifesting a clear lack of will to improve.

What are now the effects of this accountability policy? In terms of governance, it is important to stress that the launching of these new policies could only be done through a progressive transformation of the relations among actors in the school field. The educational system of French-speaking Belgium remains a decentralized one, with, on the one hand, a significant autonomy of each school and, on the other hand, the cohabitation of three networks of schools. But, much more than twenty years ago, these entities have to operate within a wider school system with standards defining the objectives to be attained by all pupils, external evaluation tests for all pupils, steering plans to be drawn up by each school, and, finally, objectives contracts in which these schools commit themselves to achieve specific targets.

This evolution, while leading to a clear strengthening of the public authorities and the central educational administration, is based on a long dialogue with the actors of the school field and, in particular, with the representatives of the school networks, who, in exchange for these new constraints, secured the deployment of mechanisms for a 'negotiated steering' of the educational system. Thus, the 'Missions' decree of 1997, which initiated these profound changes, consolidated the place of the school federations as entities speaking for each of the networks and gave key positions to the networks' representatives in a series of consultative bodies associated with the steering of education. In this way, the consociational tradition was in a sense embedded in the new steering arrangements.

At the level of schools and their actors, some research has been done on the reception and impact of the instruments for 'reflective accountability' deployed in recent years (Barbana, Dumay & Dupriez, 2020; Cattonar, Dumay & Maroy, 2013; Mangez, 2011). In primary schools, in particular, the legitimacy of these policies is little questioned. The teachers and principals interviewed see external evaluation and the rhetoric of actor accountability relayed by the political authority as legitimate. However, Yerly and Maroy (2017) highlight teachers' ambivalences: they tend to agree with the aims of these policies, have reservations about their cognitive tools, and are critical of their impact on their work. In secondary schools, while the principle of external tests is more or less accepted, there are recurring doubts about the capacity of testing to represent the quality of a teacher's or an educational team's work. Many school heads emphasize that in the context of strong school segregation, regardless of the precautions taken in interpreting the results, test results say much more about the characteristics of the pupils attending a school than the quality of its teaching.

In both primary and secondary schools, one should also note the low use of what Barbana et al. (2020) call reflective instruments (teaching recommendations, comparison of results with similar schools, previous years' tests, etc.). Although differences appear depending on the schools and the contexts, most schools' teaching teams do not carry out a systematic analysis of their results and make only moderate use of the tools available. These studies were obviously made very soon after the deployment of the policies, but they seem to indicate at this stage that the reflective ambition of the policy has had only a limited impact on schools and teachers.

Barbana et al. (2020) also describe a threefold case study carried out in secondary schools with contrasting profiles with a view to analyzing how they perceive and adapt to these new policies and to the deployment of instruments for 'soft responsibilization'. The authors emphasize that these tools are indeed present in the schools: the tests are organized systematically and rigorously, the teaching recommendations and other aids are communicated to the teachers by the school management, but all this seems to be perceived as a relatively marginal phenomenon which barely 'disturbs' the schools' project and identity, without deeply affecting the actors' cognitive schemas and practices. Ultimately, between the (quasi-)market and the state as modes of regulation of practices, it is indeed the market that seems more powerful. Thus, the schools' projects seem more indexed on their position in a local market and on their historical identity than on adjustment to new policies of homogenization of practices and an invitation to reflexivity.

France: The cognitive effects of a contested policy

In France, the very legitimacy of accountability policies is still strongly questioned. This aspect is visible at the national level in the regular debate on the 'performance obligation' (*obligation de résultats*), which has divided the policy community since the mid-1990s. On one side has been a reforming cluster promoting the development of such an obligation, made up of right-wing politicians, think-tanks politically close to them, parents' associations, high-level committees variously named at different times, international or transnational actors (essentially the OECD and the European Commission), and also some researchers; on the other, a range of opponents made up of trade unions (mainly the teachers' unions), university academies and pedagogical associations (Maroy & Pons, 2019).

Beyond the national political level, this debate has also been visible in the regional education authorities, as, for example, in the *Académie*[1] of Lille who introduces regular, codified evaluation of schools (Demailly, 2001). Researchers point to the existence of different ideal-typical positions regarding the development of a culture of evaluation which transcend the different professional groups present. A more recent study in three *Académies* brings to light the critical distance taken by some officials from a 'steering by results' of schools, at the very moment when they are supposed to implement it (Maroy & Pons, 2019).

This challenge to legitimacy, itself resulting from a convergence of factors, has given rise to particularly strong mobilizations of actors and long-lasting controversies in public debate, such as those concerning the implementation of new evaluations of pupils' attainments in primary schooling between October 2008 and May 2011 (Dutercq & Lanéelle, 2013).

The upsurge of these protest movements and the long-standing and repeated opposition of a proportion of the actors of education, who see accountability and datafication as forms of a liberalization unacceptable in the 'republican school' and as its subjection to the social norm of capitalism (Laval et al., 2011), have clearly been internalized by the successive reformers. They have thus oscillated between three different political strategies to cope with them, deployed successively or in combination. The first refuses any strong codification of the accountability policy which might provoke too much opposition, by, for example, linking some institutional sanctions to it, and prefers an 'institutionalization of vagueness' which consists in producing ever more official texts framing this policy and instructing the actors to implement it, without a clear statement in these texts of the purposes, procedures and consequences of this accountability (Pons, 2010). The second strategy consists in developing new instruments of regulation (projects, contracts, evaluations, performance indicators, digital architectures) in response to functional needs arising from the structural transformations of the school system, without these instruments being either formally or actually linked together in a new model for the governance of education. Depending on the circumstances, schools' 'objectives contracts', for example, are not always based on projects and are not always evaluated (Buisson-Fenet & Pons, 2014). The third strategy, more especially used by right-wing governments, has been to legitimize the accountability reforms with the need to take account of parents' views and those of civil society, and of international comparisons, so as to find a way round the expected resistance of the traditional policy community and extend the debate beyond the institutional boundaries of the education sector (the desectorization process).

Because of this challenge to legitimacy and its internalization by the successive reformers, the trajectory of French accountability policy develops essentially through a discreet logic and it can be regarded as the outcome of three main processes of translation of international issues, bricolage (political, institutional and cognitive) and ad hoc institutional changes with contrasting effects (Maroy & Pons, 2019).

If no political period (for the moment at least) has been marked by the announcement and application of an accountability policy presented and explicitly formulated in those terms, the mid-2000s nonetheless represent an important stage in which 'steering by results' was explicitly formulated, both in regulatory texts and in interface journals, as a nexus for projects, objectives contracts and evaluation. This period corresponds to the time when the Lisbon Strategy was explicitly translated and integrated into ministry policy, when politicians referred much more than in the past to international studies to legitimize their reforms and when a reform of the budgetary framework of the state, making parliamentary approval of the budget subject to meeting target figures, was introduced.

This trajectory then takes the form of a succession of critical conjunctures and periods of stabilization, which itself leads to a sedimentation of the public policy instruments used and more especially promoted from the 1970s: the policy of education minister Blanquer from May 2017 emphasized school evaluations and the production of results indicators; those of his left-wing predecessors had sidelined these instruments in favour of a discrete meta-reflection on the transformations of public administrations as a whole; the policy of education minister Chatel (2009–2012) was based on contractualization at all levels, etc.

In this context, the administrative elites play an important role of retrospective rationalization of governmental initiatives, aimed both at ensuring their temporal coherence, making their meaning and potential uses more explicit, and interlinking them in accordance with nonetheless varying logics. In addition to this cognitive bricolage, there is also an institutional and political bricolage within the *Académies* who, especially within a growing deconcentrated education system, can implement various accountability policies depending both on the political conjunctures and on the regional policy configurations (Buisson-Fenet & Pons, 2014; Maroy & Pons, 2019).

Unsurprisingly, the implementation of this policy does not have the effect of introducing a path breakpoint that would see France swing into a post-bureaucratic mode of regulation (Maroy, 2012). The sedimentation of the successive reform projects and of the favoured policy instruments action are accompanied by great instability of the procedures and data available, especially in primary education. This instability makes it difficult to assess the impact of the accountability procedures in reorienting educational policies and the actors' professional practices. Significantly, in contrast to some English-speaking educational systems, there has been no tradition of analysis based on the impact of inspections or tests, for example.

However, the specifically cognitive effects of this accountability policy remain numerous. First, it has led the state, at all levels, to improve the datafication of the policy process (in the allocation of finance, for example) and adopt a more dialogical approach to the policies carried out on the ground with the authorities of the *Académies* and with schools. The case of contractualization between the central administration and the *Académies* is emblematic of this process (Maroy & Pons, 2019).

The production of these new indicators, tools and mechanisms also exposes the French administrative elites to various international influences which lead them to modify the models they refer to in constructing their tools. The production of added-value indicators for secondary schools in the 1990s, for example, aims at a compromise between taking account of the imperatives of democratization of education and the reduction of educational inequalities characteristic of the model of social justice of the previous decades, and taking account of the work on school effectiveness and human capital (Normand, 2011).

More generally, this policy has also had the effect of redistributing politically legitimate expertise. In the field of evaluation, the effect has been to diversify the agencies of evaluation and increase competition among them: new evaluators such as international experts, private consultancies, think-tanks or researchers specializing in conducting randomized experiments have joined, and sometimes replaced, the traditional official evaluators of the school system, namely the general inspectorates and statisticians of the Ministry (Pons, 2010). In the field of research, some studies argue that this type of policy has had the effect of confirming the domination symbolic of evaluation-oriented research in French educational research at the expense of other currents (Lapostolle, 2019; Poupeau, 2003).

At the level of schools, French accountability policy is marked by a strong instability of the prescriptions given to local actors. In a context marked by the sedimentation of instruments of regulation and the absence of systematization of their use, the institutional pressures for change exerted at school level are found to be very different depending on the configurations in the *Académie* and the logics of mediation of national policy at work at *Académie* level (Maroy & Pons, 2019).

This movement for reform is, however, sufficiently strong and regular to incite the actors concerned to modify their professional approach. This is true of the evaluators themselves, but also of the actors in schools. But in their case, the studies of the last twenty years converge strongly to highlight a great difference between school principals and teachers. The former remain the major targets of the ministry's accountability policy inasmuch as, being required to implement the main instruments of this policy, they are clearly incited to give an account of their school policy to the authorities of the *Académie*, especially in phases of budget discussion (Buisson-Fenet & Pons, 2014; Maroy & Pons, 2019). Despite everything, while they sometimes make a targeted use of evaluations when seeking to establish the reputation of their school or their legitimacy as managers (Barrère, 2006), use of these instruments within the school itself with a view to steering it proves to be very limited, for reasons linked to their weak legitimacy among teachers and the tensions they could induce by confronting the actors in real time with a synthetic, quantified image of their activity which they do not always regard as fair (Barrère, 2010; Verdière, 2001).

The teachers in this context remain little exposed to the accountability policy, except when it takes the form of standardized evaluations of pupils' attainments which penetrate directly into the world of the classroom. In this case, however, the studies highlight the limited use made of these evaluations, which are carried out discontinuously, are poorly integrated into the temporality of classroom life and which teachers see as methodologically, professionally and ethically questionable (Derouet & Normand, 2003; Demailly, 2003; Dutercq & Cuculou, 2013).

However, rather than a decoupling between the classroom and the institutional environment as regards accountability, we are seeing a recomposition of the models of responsibilization at work in schools, depending on the local educational orders that characterize them, with teachers being more or less inclined to be accountable for the results of their work depending on the steering tools instruments favoured by the school management, the system of staff relations that characterizes the school, and the school's trajectory within the institution (Buisson-Fenet & Pons, 2019).

Quebec (Canada): Accountability as institutional reform

In the Quebec educational system, accountability has developed through the passing of successive laws between 2000 and 2016, in the form of a policy of 'results-based management' (RBM). Act 82[2] (2000) first introduced it for the whole of public administration. In 2002, Act 124 extended it to the public school network, requiring the school boards (SB[3]) to carry out strategic planning and schools to define 'plans for success'. Act 88 (2008) further prescribed contractualization by each level with the one above and submission of results. Consequently, in sequence the SB and the schools must set out in 'conventions' their performance objectives, aligned on those of the ministry. They must also publish these conventions to parents and local communities. However, the implications of this accountability for the SB and the schools remain limited since staff salaries and jobs are not directly affected. Nonetheless, some sanctions on the SB are possible under the ministerial oversight. Moreover, the results are published and compared (in particular with those of private schools); this can have significant consequences for the external image of the schools, given that since 1996 parents have had greater choice among the public schools.

The genesis of these laws lies in convergence of a dynamic of political debates in Quebec and the carrying-over of pan-Canadian models and discourses. The RBM model was actively imported in a context of 'crisis' of public finances and the neo-liberal challenge to the 'Quebec model' in the 1980s and 1990s (zero deficit policy, staff cuts in the public services) (Fortier, 2010). The *Treasury Board* drew up a planned reform of the Quebec administration which led to Act 82. His 'policy statement' on RBM is drawing on administration reforms made in other countries (the USA, Australia and the UK) or elsewhere in Canada (Alberta, Ontario, Manitoba). RBM was also favoured by the Council of Ministers of Education of Canada who translates the transnational discourse on 'education quality' favouring the construction of pan-Canadian indicators and promoting performance-based accountability. (Lessard, 2006). These transnational ideas underwent a number of bricolages and inflections in response to the interaction of political dynamics internal to Quebec society and brakes or opportunities offered by the institutional arrangements of the education system.

The discourse justifying RBM was introduced based on cognitive bricolages of two types. On the one hand, it attached RBM to key objectives of the Quebec education system and problems that actors regarded as central, such as reducing drop-out and 'success for all'. Through transparency regarding results, and accountability to parents and elected politicians, RBM was also expected to improve the functioning of an educational democracy regarded as 'ailing' (low participation in school elections, financial cost).

In a second cognitive bricolage, the tools of RBM were sedimented on earlier tools without dismantling them. Through Act 124, the tools of planning were grafted onto the pre-existing 'educational project' stemmed from a participatory reflection by professionals, parents and partner institutions. The 'plan for success' initially aimed to operationalize the educational project (by specifying its means and its results indicators) and to articulate it with the plans of the hierarchically higher levels. Then, with Act 88, came the conventions. One thus sees a sedimentation of a device (the educational project), typical of community-based, horizontal regulation with tools of a vertical regulation by results which progressively changed its meaning and equilibrium. The bricolage was to continue with Act 105 which 'simplified' the different tools in the form of the 'school project', which effaced the formally contractual dimension of the conventions, and returned to the participatory term 'project', but imposed on it a content which again took up the ingredients of vertical regulation through results (targets, priority measures, evaluation, and accountability).

These bricolages are clearly not independent of the power relations among the actors and stakeholders of Quebec education policy. Between 2002 and 2014, a partial consensus was established around a public policy narrative which, in the name of a better alignment of all components of the system, privileged a governance that combined cognitive tools of regulation by results with increased assertion of hierarchical control in the framework of the existing structures. It managed to minoritize a narrative promoted by one opposition party (nationalist right) and associations of school principals, who argued for more radical change in the system: conversion of the SB into 'service centers', development of school autonomy and parental choice (Maroy & Pons, 2019). However, from 2015, the latter discourse grew stronger as a result of the changing power relations among the parties. The party Coalition Avenir Québec, based on the opposition party, won the provincial elections of 2018. Its majority government aims to abolish school elections and the SB in their present form and increase school autonomy, without removing RBM. To this end, he has proposed the Bill 40, which became law in winter 2020.

The trajectory of RBM is developed further through incremental changes in the existing institutions. The SB, while being maintained until 2019 (and beyond for anglophone community) because of constitutional and political safeguards (Maroy & Pons, 2019), are also undergoing a process of conversion of their missions and functions (Streeck & Thelen, 2005). While they have until recently retained their old function of 'community representation' (via the school elections), this is increasingly dominated by a role of efficient manager of educational resources (support for schools), but also of relay and vector of the objectives of the central ministry, through its pivotal role in the vertical logic of RBM, a conversion which began in the 1990s (Brassard, 2014). The recent passing of Bill 40 has achieved this process.

The sedimentation of tools also contributes to this incremental change: the successive governments more easily introduce and legitimize tools for vertical regulation by results, while claiming to preserve earlier tools such as 'educational projects' that are symbolic of a more horizontal and community-based school governance.

Concerning the effects at the level of the overall governance of the Quebec school system, the trajectory of RBM has developed around the neo-statist translation of New Public Management (NPM) (Clark, 2002). Indeed, there has been a hybridization of the principles of NPM with a strengthening of the state and a model of bureaucratic regulation that remains influential. The three-tier structure of the Quebec system has been maintained, but the 'vertical' mechanisms (both regulatory and cognitive) of regulation and governance and the higher levels' capacities for control and surveillance of the lower levels have been strengthened. The more 'horizontal' regulations (by parents or local communities) have not disappeared, and are even strengthened for parents, but have been increasingly concentrated solely on issues of educational effectiveness (Maroy & Pons, 2019).

However, with the recent coming to power of the nationalist right, this neo-statist version could be combined with more neo-liberal measures, through a shrinkage of the political autonomy of the intermediate regulatory level, enhanced autonomy for schools, and a *laissez-faire* approach to the growth of competition among schools and between the public and private sectors.

As regards the Belgian and French cases, one should stress the effectiveness of the implementation of RBM in the organizations, at least at the level of formal tools. By 2004, 75% of the SB had published a first strategic plan in response to Act 124 (Lapointe et al. 2012) and, since the passing of Act 88, partnership conventions have generally been implemented in accordance with ministerial aims and prescriptions (Savard et al. 2012). This effectiveness can be seen in relation to a context favourable to the reception of these tools. On the one hand, school and SB managers have long experience of an institutionalization of their training in the universities, where discourses and research on 'effective schools' or the necessary role of 'instructional leadership' by management are highlighted (D'Arrisso, 2013). This cognitive and normative congruence has favoured a very largely positive reception of RBM by administrators and school managers (Faye, 2017). On the other hand, the ministry has monitored the implementation fairly closely and the SB have adhered to it, seeing it as a way of improving their monitoring of and even their hold over the schools that they organize. Finally, various experts or conferences of school administrators have assisted the dissemination of RBM tools in the SB. Moreover, a body linked to the SB has developed and promoted a digital platform allowing management of the statistical data of RBM, and it is widely used on the ground (Maroy & Pons, 2019).

The situation is more complex as regards the impact on teachers' pedagogical practices or their representations. First, teachers have a negative view of the tools and effects of RBM, even if they endorse its aims of improved success (Faye, 2017). Moreover, Lapointe and Brassard (2017) emphasize that teachers are not very aware of the content of the plans and conventions, which they associate with the work of the school management. However, beyond the level of opinion, Maroy and Vaillancourt (2019) find that these 'contractual' mechanisms tend to institutionalize the cognitive and normative framework on the basis of which a discourse can be acceptable and legitimate in the school. They also stress the need to consider a wider range of tools to gain a clear view of their effects on the implementation of RBM on pedagogical practices. Beyond plans and conventions, it is mainly the statistical platforms (data on teachers' results and practices), combined with their uses in pedagogical monitoring (definition of problems, advice, support, monitoring) by school management and pedagogical advisors, that have an impact – partial but effective – on teachers' practices. The teacher's reflexivity is directed towards improving his or her effectiveness, and control is accentuated on coverage of the prescribed curriculum (which is evaluated by the ministerial examinations) and his/her evaluation practices. Classroom pedagogical choices remain discretionary (Maroy et al., 2017).

We thus see an erosion of professional autonomy and a tendency towards redefinition of the teacher's professionalism, which becomes more organizational than vocational (Evetts, 2009). Thus RBM produces its effects by setting up social relations of management within schools, whose object is increasingly at the heart of teachers' professional practices, where power moves towards school managers, and knowledge tends to be redistributed in favour of the various specialists in pedagogy (pedagogical advisors, 'educational services' of the SB responsible for disseminating 'good practices' and knowledge derived from research).

Conclusion: The strength of weak cases

Finally, the choice we have made to focus on French-speaking Belgium, France and Quebec enables us to highlight two conclusions that are particularly important in our view.

The first refers to the homogeneous vision that is sometimes given of these accountability policies. This vision, which we believe to be false, is maintained by the fact that these policies are based on similar regulatory instruments in a large number of countries (projects, contracts, evaluations, performance indicators, datafication), but also by the discourses of the promoters of these policies, which, in the name of the so-called generic nature of these instruments, are supposed to able to 'travel' easily from one context to another. The comparison of the three school systems studied shows clearly that the long-term trajectory of these policies, and also their effects, can be quite different depending on the political, institutional and professional contexts involved. In each context, there is a selection and translation of transnational accountability tools coming from the NPM repertory (projects, contracts, tests, reflexivity on results and practices) whose configuration is evolving. In the design of the policy, there is also a bricolage of these tools and models, related to existing institutional constraints, or the balance of the political forces. In the same time, hybridization of those tools with the existing one and a sedimentation of new institutions, tools or ideas on those that already existed could occur.

Moreover, our comparison underlines the various effects and usages of accountability tools in the everyday life of the schools of each system. There is a strong contrast between the diffusion of a pedagogical management led by school administrators in Quebec, the active resistance of the teaching profession and defence of its autonomy in France, and, finally, the variations of the pedagogical usages of the tools depending on the context and place of the school in the local market in Belgium.

Consequently, it is not enough to identify in a school system the presence of instruments or imperatives observed in more liberal systems with a strong tradition of hard accountability for the researcher to conclude that this system is neo-liberalizing or that a new global culture is being implemented.

The second conclusion, directly related to the first, refers to our comparison strategy. Despite the great diversity of the three cases studied, in all of them the development of an accountability policy in education has led to the strengthening or consolidation (to varying degrees and through varying mechanisms) of the state in school governance. Although these systems are partly decentralized (more or less recently and to different degrees), either through the process of datafication and accountability of decentralized institutional entities as in French-speaking Belgium and Quebec, or in France through the production of new indicators, the state is reinforcing knowledge instruments and categories of analysis that increase its monitoring power over the actors of education and enable it to learn more about its own activity. Moreover, in Belgium and Quebec, the central power of the state is also reinforced through classical hierarchical mechanisms. In this sense, in all three cases studied, we are witnessing neo-statist reform trajectories (Clark, 2002). The state regulation is renewed and reinforced through cognitive and classical tools, even if at the same time it is combined with other pre-existing sources of local actors' regulation, such as quasi-markets or parental power. We are thus here far away from a pure 'neo-liberal' trend leading to state withdrawal; at the contrary, marketization could cohabit or even be fuelled with the cognitive regulation tools of local schools, related to accountability policies (Ozga, 2013). And, as shown elsewhere, these trajectories can be understood as the outcome of the combination of three processes, often intertwined empirically: translation by certain national actors of policy ideas and instruments circulating at a transnational level; various forms of policy bricolage; and various forms of long-run institutional change (Maroy & Pons, 2019).

Notes

1 In the French education system, the *Académies* are administrative divisions of the national Ministry of Education. The term designates both territories and the state administrative authorities which run them, under the authority of a rector.
2 For simplicity, we refer to each act by the number of the bill passed by the Quebec National Assembly.
3 The SB are public institutions for the intermediate regulation of the system. They organize schools in a territory, appoint staff, manage the buildings and provide support services for schools. They are run by elected *commissioners* and can levy school taxes, but at the same time are subject to monitoring by the provincial administration, which provides 75% of their funding.

References

Ambrosio, J. (2013). Changing the subject: Neoliberalism and accountability in public education. *Educational Studies, 49*(4), 316–333. doi:10.1080/00131946.2013.783835
Ball, S. J. (1993). What is policy? Texts, trajectories and toolboxes. *Discourse, 13*(2), 10–17.
Barbana, S. (2018). *Les tests en Belgique francophone. Une tentative politique de gouverner l'école? Pour quels effets?* PhD Thesis, Université catholique de Louvain.
Barbana, S., Dumay, X., & Dupriez, V. (2020). Local implementation of accountability instruments in the French-speaking community of Belgium. *European Educational Research Journal, 19*(2), 94–108. Advance online publication: https://doi.org/10.1177/1474904119850964.

Barrère, A. (2006). *Sociologie des chefs d'établissement*. Paris: PUF.

Barrère, A. (2010). Ce que fait l'évaluation aux établissements scolaires. Une année dans un collège d'"éducation prioritaire'. *Ethnologie française, 40*(1), 141–149.

Brassard, A. (2014). La commission scolaire comme lieu de gouvernance autonome (1959 à 2013)? *Télescope, 20*(2), 17–34.

Buisson-Fenet, H., & Pons, X. (2014). *School evaluation policies and educating states: Trends in four European countries*. Berne, Switzerland: Peter Lang.

Buisson-Fenet, H., & Pons, X. (2019). Responsable, mais pas redevable? Gouvernance par les resultats et relations d'accountability' dans les établissements scolaires en France. *Éducation et sociétés, 43*(1), 41–56.

Callon, M. (1986). Some elements of a sociology of translation: domestication of the scallops and the fisherman in St Brieuc Bay. In K. Knorr-Cetina & A. V. Cicourel (Eds.), *Advances in social theory and methodology: Toward an integration of micro and macro-sociologies* (pp. 196–223). Boston, MA: Routledge & Kegan Paul.

Campbell, J. L. (2004). *Institutional change and globalization*. Princeton, NJ: Princeton University Press.

Cattonar, B., Dumay, X., & Maroy, C. (2013). Politique d'évaluation externe et recomposition des professionnalités dans l'enseignement primaire: un cas de responsabilisation (accountability) douce. *Education et sociétés, 2*, 35–51.

Cattonar, B. and Dupriez, V. (2019). Recomposition des professionnalités et de la division du travail enseignant en contexte d'accountability réflexive. Le cas des professionnels de l'éducation en Belgique francophone. *Education et Sociétés, 43*, 25–39.

Clark, D. (2002). Neoliberalism and public service reform: Canada in comparative perspective. *Canadian Journal of Political Science/Revue canadienne de science politique, 35*(04), 771–793.

D'Arrisso, D. (2013). *Pressions et stratégies dans la formation professionnelle universitaire: le cas de la formation des directions d'établissement scolaire du Québec (1988-1989 à 2008-2009)*. (Thèse de doctorat en sciences de l'éducation). Université de Montréal, Montréal. Retrieved from http://hdl.handle.net/1866/10219

Demailly, L. (Ed.) (2001). *Évaluer les politiques éducatives. Sens, enjeux, pratiques*. Louvain-la-Neuve: De Boeck Université.

Demailly, L. (2003). L'évaluation de l'action éducative comme apprentissage et négociation. *Revue française de pédagogie, 142*, 114–127.

Derouet, J-L., & Normand, R. (2003). *Le Développement d'une culture de l'évaluation dans l'Éducation nationale: comment les enseignants utilisent-ils les résultats des évaluations nationales?* Lyon: INRP.

Dupriez, V., & Maroy, C. (2003). Regulation in school systems: a theoretical analysis of the structural framework of the school system in French-speaking Belgium. *Journal of Education Policy, 18* (4), 375–393.

Dutercq, Y., & Lanéelle, X. (2013). La dispute autour des évaluations des élèves dans l'enseignement français du premier degré. *Sociologie, 4*(1), 43–62.

Dutercq, Y., & Cuculou, S. (2013). La performance comme outil de gouvernance: quelles conséquences sur le travail des enseignants de l'école primaire? In C. Maroy (Ed.), *L'école à l'épreuve de la performance* (pp. 195–210). Brussels: De Boeck.

Evetts, J. (2009). The management of professionalism: A contemporary paradox. In S. Gewirtz, P. Mahony, I. Hextall, & A. Cribb (Eds.), *Changing teacher professionalism. International trends, challenges and ways forward* (pp. 17–30). New York: Taylor & Francis.

Faye, P. W. (2017). *Analyse des opinions et des perceptions des enseignants et des directeurs d'établissement sur l'implantation de la gestion axée sur les résultats dans les établissements scolaires québécois.* PhD. Université Laval, Retrieved from https://corpus.ulaval.ca/jspui/handle/20.500.11794/28175

Fortier, I. (2010). La 'réingénierie de l'État', réforme québécoise inspirée du managérialisme. *Revue française d'administration publique 4*, 803–820.

Lapointe, P., Garon, R., Dembélé, M., & Tessier, C. (2012). Les plans stratégiques des commissions scolaires du Québec: regard sur la mise en application d'un dispositif de régulation intermédiaire dans un système éducatif. *Mesure et évaluation en éducation, 35*(1), 1–26.

Lapointe, P., & Brassard, A. (2017). L'appropriation de la gestion axée sur les résultats par les enseignants du primaire et secondaire au Québec. In Y. Dutercq & C. Maroy (Eds.), *Professionnalisme et politiques de responsabilisation* (pp. 55–72). Brussels De Boeck.

Lapostolle, G. (2019). *Les experts contre les intellectuels.* Nancy: Presses universitaires de Lorraine.

Laval, C., Vergne, F., Clément, P., Dreux, G. (2011). *La nouvelle école capitaliste.* Paris: La Découverte.

Lessard, C. (2006). La 'gouvernance' de l'éducation au Canada: tendances et significations. *Education et sociétés, 18*(2), 181–200. doi:10.3917/es.018.0181

Lijphart, L. (1999). *Patterns of democracy: Government forms and performance in thirty-six countries,* New Haven, CT: Yale University Press.

Lingard, B. (2006). Globalisation, the research imagination and deparochialising the study of education. *Globalisation, Societies and Education, 4*(2), 287–302.

Mangez, C. (2011). Evaluer et piloter l'enseignement: analyse d'instruments de la politique scolaire en Belgique francophone. PhD Thesis, Université catholique de Louvain.

Mangez, E., & Cattonar, B. (2009). The status of PISA in the relationship between civil society and the educational sector in French-speaking Belgium, *Sísifo, 10*, 15–26.

Maroy, C. (2012). Towards post-bureaucratic modes of governance: a European perspective. In G. Steiner-Khamsi & F. Waldow (Eds.), *Policy borrowing and lending in education* (pp. 62–79). London: Routledge.

Maroy, C. (2015). Comparing accountability tools and rationales: Various ways, various effects. In H.-G. Kotthof & E. Klerides (Eds.), *Governing educational spaces. Knowledge, teaching and learning in transition* (pp. 35–58). Rotterdam: Sense Publisher.

Maroy, C., & Mangez, C. (2011). Les construction des politiques d'évaluation et de pilotage du système scolaire en Belgique francophone: nouveau paradigme politique et médiation des experts. In G. Felouzis & S. Hanhart (Ed.), *Gouverner l'éducation par les nombres? Usages, débats et controverses (Raisons éducatives)* (pp. 53–75). Brussels: De Boeck.

Maroy, C., Mathou, C., & Vaillancourt, S. (2017). Les enseignants québécois à l'épreuve de la 'gestion axée sur les résultats'. Une étude qualitative dans quatre établissements secondaires. *Revista de Sociología de la Educación (RASE), 11*(4), 539-557. http://dx.doi.org/10.7203/RASE.10.9906

Maroy, C., & Vaillancourt, S. (2019). L'instrumentation de la nouvelle gestion publique dans les écoles québécoises: dispositifs et travail de changement institutionnel. *SociologieS [En ligne],* 1–17. Retrieved from https://journals.openedition.org/sociologies/10075

Maroy, C., & Pons, X. (Eds.). (2019). *Accountability policies in education: A comparative and multilevel analysis in France and Quebec.* Basel: Springer.

Mons, N., & Dupriez, V. (2010). Les politiques d'accountability. *Recherche et formation, 65*, 45–59.

Normand, R. (2011). *Gouverner la réussite scolaire: Une arithmétique politique des inégalités.* Berne: Peter Lang.

OECD. (1993). *Reviews of national policies for education: Belgium.* Paris: OECD.

Ozga, J. (2013). Accountability as a policy technology: Accounting for education performance in Europe. *International Review of Administrative Sciences, 79*(2), 292–309.

Pons, X. (2010). *Évaluer l'action éducative. Des professionnels en concurrence.* Paris: PUF.

Poupeau, F. (2003). *Une sociologie d'État. L'école et ses experts en France.* Paris: Raisons d'agir.

Savard, D., Larouche, C., Laferrière, T., Lapointe, C., & Viau-Guay, A. (2012). *Rapport de recherche -- Les Conventions de partenariat dans le système d'éducation québécois: une évaluation pansystémique de l'implantation et des effets.* Retrieved from Sainte-Foy: https://pdfs.semanticscholar.org/bfa5/730727e1a2c8ed57c92b23c65c070d0b45a6.pdf

Smith, W. C. (Ed.) (2016). *The global testing culture: Shaping education policy, perceptions, and practice.* Oxford: Symposium Books.

Streeck, W., & Thelen, K. (2005). *Beyond continuity: Institutional change in advanced political economies.* Oxford, Oxford University Press.

Vandenberghe, V. (1999). Combining market and bureaucratic control in education: An answer to market and bureaucratic failure? *Comparative Education, 35*(3), 271–282.

Verdière, J. (2001). *Les pratiques d'évaluation du travail d'enseignement.* PhD in sociology, Université Lille I.

Verger, A., & Parcerisa, L. (2017). *Monitoring and accountability in education – Opportunities, risks and innovations in the post-2015 period. Think piece on accountability policies for the Global Education Monitoring Report.* Paris: Unesco.

Yerly, G., & Maroy, C. (2017). La gouvernance par les résultats est-elle un mode de régulation de l'école légitime aux yeux des enseignants? Une enquête qualitative dans 4 systèmes scolaires. *Revue Française de Pédagogie, 198*, 93–108.

8 National standardized assessments in South Africa: Policy and power play

*Thokozani Chilenga-Butao, Melanie Ehren
and Nomancotsho Pakade*

Introduction

Education governance across the globe has come to rely increasingly on intense data collection and data-driven policy instruments. Sub-Saharan Africa has followed this trend. Introduced in the 1990s, funded by the World Bank and other international NGOs (Bashir, Lockheed, Ninan, & Tan, 2018), assessments aim to provide information on outcomes and inform policy decision-making. The World Conference on Education for All hosted in Thailand in March 1990, along with its ten-year follow-up, the Dakar Framework Action in 2000, reinforced the importance of accurate assessment of learning outcomes. South Africa was among other developing countries in the 1990s that sought to incorporate assessments in their policymaking, although the introduction and use of assessments have not gone unchallenged.

This chapter reflects on these challenges and situates these in the wider educational policy arena. We provide a synthesized timeline of some of South Africa's most important education policies and their outcomes, particularly where these included national assessments or had implications for assessments, such as when a national curriculum is introduced or reformed. The synthesis was informed by a document analysis of sources of the Education Programme at the Public Affairs Research Institute (PARI) in South Africa. The Programme includes a bank of policies and academic papers from the leading education experts in South Africa who wrote about the policymaking process during the early years of democracy in South Africa. These experts were involved in the policies discussed here, such as the initial curriculum review in 1994 and discussions of the outcomes-based curriculum. Documents were analysed for major policy changes where a timeline was constructed by triangulating the evidence from both policy documents and academic papers.

In setting out a timeline of changes, the chapter will initially demonstrate that most changes in curriculum and assessment policies in South Africa have been short-lived and often abandoned before any sustainable improvement could materialize. And second, how this trajectory of constant reform and overhaul of policy can be explained by the lack of collaborative capacity in the system. We illustrate this in detail for the most recent introduction and collapse of the Annual National Assessments in primary education (ANA). We conclude that, as policy implementation literature would predict (see for instance Honig, 2006), assessments can only inform curriculum implementation, high-quality teaching and contribute to the improvement of learning outcomes when the main stakeholders in the system (for example, policymakers/politicians, teacher unions) have

1) a set of shared values and understanding of the purpose and use of standardized assessments;
2) have a collaborative relationship of high trust to negotiate differences and remedy potential technical faults; and
3) jointly develop the support for teachers and schools to use assessment outcomes for the benefit of teaching and learning.

Only when these conditions are met can national assessments effectively inform the work of teachers and school principals and inform system-wide improvement, particularly where there is high inequality and large performance gaps between schools across the country, such as in South Africa.

A timeline of change: Education policymaking in South Africa (after 1994)

After the abolition of the Apartheid regime in 1994 and the constitution of the Republic of South Africa in 1996, the schooling system was considered to be one of the key reform areas and one of the main building blocks towards achieving a well-functioning democracy. The South African Schools Act of 1996, for example, aimed to establish one new national system for schools to redress past injustices; a national curriculum and set of assessments for all schools was one of the key reforms to address the deep historical inequalities.[1] Curriculum policy in the new democratic state aimed to set out the subjects, the knowledge content and the methodology of teaching and learning, thereby ensuring an equal knowledge base and cultural canon shared by all learners. A national curriculum was expected to structure the expectations and demand of teachers and as such contribute to a more equal system for all learners.

Between 1994 and the present day, the national curriculum and related assessments have undergone several changes. Here we discuss the four major curriculum changes and two assessment reforms. Through these changes, we identify how trends in education policy in South Africa shaped the current Annual National Assessment (ANA) policy, its implementation and its collapse. The changes in curriculum and assessment policy we discuss are: the review of the Apartheid curriculum (1994), the national assessment surveys (1996), Curriculum 2005 and Outcomes-Based Education (1997), the National Curriculum Statement

(NCS, 2000; including the Revised National Curriculum Statement of 2002), and the Curriculum Assessment Policy Statements (CAPS, 2011). We first outline the changes in curriculum policy before we describe the introduction of, and changes in, national assessments.

Curriculum policy

Review of the Apartheid curriculum (1994)

One of the first reforms under the democratic government in 1994 was to review the Apartheid curriculum (1994) to rid it of racism and segregationist teaching practices such as Bantu Education, as well as unifying segregated education systems in a single and comprehensive basic education system. Thus, the then Ministry of Education embarked on a process to reform the school curriculum syllabus in order to align it with the aims of an inclusive education system in a democratic state. The problem with this review, however, was that the new government needed quick results and only allowed for a three-month transition period at the end of 1994, requiring it to inform a new curriculum to be ready for the start of the 1995 school year (Jansen, 1998). This was a 'swift review of more than 100 Apartheid syllabuses', the result of which was that 'most [Apartheid syllabuses] remained unchanged and not a single intervention was made to support or enable these minor changes to be realised in the classroom' (Jansen, 1998: 56). There are many reasons for this poor curriculum review, including political pressure from forces resistant to change, political expediency for an incoming democratic government, attempting to keep all stakeholders on board – both education policy conservatives from the Apartheid era and new education reformers (Chisholm & Fuller, 1996; Jansen, 1999).

The second notable issue in this curriculum review process is that teachers were ill-equipped to participate in the changes that were going to take place and that they also did not have time to attend the review process because they were teaching (Jansen, 1999). Furthermore, at the time the country's largest teacher union (SADTU: the South African Democratic Teachers' Union) commented that the education ministry had not created ways to ensure that the curriculum changes were communicated to educators who were expected to teach the reviewed curriculum (Jansen, 1999). Finally, minimal effort was invested in 'reforming teaching methods that might advance the adjusted curriculum, or to further participatory social relations inside classrooms' (Chisholm & Fuller, 1996: 706).

Curriculum 2005 and outcomes-based education (1997)

Following the 1994 review and limited impact in the classroom, a major reform, called C2005, was introduced in 1997 to create a more equal and homogenous education system. Curriculum 2005 (hereafter C2005) was an education policy that involved an extensive curriculum overhaul, which began in 1997 and was planned to be completely phased into South Africa's basic education system by 2005.

The curriculum overhaul of C2005 was based on global trends in outcomes-based education (Chisholm, 2005: 193) and it was a better attempt at reforming the South African school curriculum more substantively, particularly to ensure more equal outcomes across the system and remove the racist content identified in the earlier review. Outcomes-based education focused less on a content-heavy curriculum that would be dictated to educators, and more on what the curriculum wanted learners to achieve as an outcome of a learning area, regardless of how this was taught by educators. Thus, the focus of the curriculum was the outcome or learning objective, as opposed to hierarchically determined content (Mncube & Madikizela-Madiya in Harber ed., 2013). A focus on outcomes would also allow teachers to offer a more personalized learning trajectory, taking into account the vast disparities in achievement across the country.

However, outcomes-based education was a form of 'policy borrowing' (Spreen, 2004: 101), whereby policymakers embrace international trends during educational reform. Once the policy is borrowed and co-opted, and amidst domestic resistance to the policy, the origins of the education policy must be 'concealed' (Spreen in Steiner-Khamsi, 2004: 101) in order to be legitimized in the domestic context. Although C2005 was 'highly sophisticated', it was also 'based on first-world assumptions about well-resourced classrooms and highly qualified teachers' (Jansen, 1998: 56). Knowledge and skills they did not have, particularly those teachers who were trained under the Apartheid regime to teach a very impoverished curriculum (Jansen, 1998: 56). In addition to this, policy borrowing led to there being multiple interpretations of the meaning of outcomes-based education. This led to 'loosely constructed outcomes' (Spreen, 2004: 104), as opposed to a more definitive path for what South African education and curriculum should look like following Apartheid. Policy borrowing was also used as a way to remove the 'vocational aspects of OBE' which were important to education policy stakeholders such as organized labour unions (Spreen, 2004: 110). Once again, the practicalities of teaching a new curriculum were ignored, and policy-making was centralized to suit a legitimation agenda instead of a steady education policy agenda.

National Curriculum Statement (NCS, 2000)

Over time, various reviews (DoE, 1997; OECD, 2008) highlighted the problematic implementation of C2005, pointing to a lack of adequate resourcing, reportedly unmanageable timeframes for implementation and poor monitoring and review. An OECD report (2008) criticized C2005 for being too elaborate, involving new and unnecessarily complex terminology and depending for its implementation on poorly trained and already overworked educators. The intended strategies to transform teachers' instructional practices from a traditional teacher-centred to a more learner-centred approach, proved much more difficult than assumed and led the Education Department to 'simplify' and further regulate the curriculum, first by introducing the National Curriculum Statement (NCS) in 2000, revising these again in 2002 and then again by revising the NCS into even more detailed Curriculum and Assessment Policy Statements (CAPS).

As Motala et al. (2007: 22) explain, the NCS was a revised version of C2005 which was 'written in plain language, gives more emphasis to basic skills, content knowledge and a logical progression from one grade to the next ... [and] combines a learner-centred curriculum requiring critical thought and emphasising democratic values embedded in the Constitution, with an appreciation of the importance of content and support for educators' (Motala et al., 2007: 22). Furthermore, and in contrast to C2005, this curriculum aimed 'to ensure that children acquire and apply knowledge and skills in ways that are meaningful to their own lives ... promotes knowledge in local contexts, while being sensitive to global imperatives' (DBE, 2019: online).

The NCS reflected a policy revision of C2005 following teacher union and public consultations (Chisholm, 2005: 193), and also following the recommendations of the report of the Review Committee provided on 31 May 2000 to 'streamline and strengthen Curriculum 2005' (Policy Overview, 2006: 2). The Review Committee particularly recommended that 'implementation needed to be strengthened by improving teacher orientation and training, learning support materials' and more support from provincial education departments (Policy Overview, 2006: 5), whose role includes decentralized implementation of national education policies.

One of the key observations about the policy revisions that took place between C2005 and the revised NCS are the changes in the stakeholders within the education policy environment. In the curriculum review process that occurred in 1994, education policy was determined by a number of political and economic stakeholders, such as the tripartite alliance between the African National Congress (ANC), the Congress of South African Trade Unions (COSATU) and the South African Communist Party (SACP). By the time C2005 was being considered by the Department for Basic Education, there were vocational, environmental, history and conservative Christian lobbies who all advocated for specific curriculum changes that aligned with their interests (Chisholm, 2005). These included the History/Archaeology Panel, the Pestalozzi Trust, Frontline Fellowship, the African Christian Party and the New National Party (Chisholm, 2005). Other stakeholders also included universities and NGOs trying to align the school curriculum with the broader post-school education system (Chisholm, 2005).

As mentioned earlier, one of the key stakeholder groups were the three teacher unions: SADTU, the National Association of Professional Teachers Organisations of South Africa (NAPTOSA), and the Suid Afrikaanse Onderwysers Unie (SAOU). The reactions of NAPTOSA and SAOU to the introduction of C2005 and outcomes-based education was 'sympathetic' (Chisholm, 2005: 202). SADTU, however, had 'curricular objections [that] were mainly focused on an apparent divergence from the official outcomes-based education policy' under C2005 (Chisholm, 2005: 202), which allowed greater autonomy for teachers to make curricular choices. This objection is said to be based on SADTU's 'strong sense of ownership' (Chisholm, 2005: 202) of the outcomes-based education policy under C2005, because it was 'heavily involved in [C2005's] development and implementation' (Chisholm, 2005: 202).

Another key change was the explicit attention to capacity of teachers and schools to implement curriculum changes. The lack of overall capacity in the system to mobilize such support, however, meant that the NCS also failed to deliver on its promise of improving learning outcomes and reducing performance gaps across the country, leading to the introduction of the Curriculum Assessment Policy Statements (CAPS) in 2011, which offered teachers with detailed scripts to enable them (and particularly those with limited knowledge and skills), to implement the curriculum and related assessments.

Curriculum Assessment Policy Statements (CAPS, 2011)

'Curriculum and Assessment Policy Statements' (or CAPS) were first introduced by the Department of Education in 2011 (Mncube & Madikizela-Madiya in Harber ed., 2013: 173). CAPS aimed to provide a 'single, comprehensive, and concise policy document, which contains detailed guidelines for teaching all subject areas that are listed in the NCS' (DBE, 2019: online). Therefore, each subject in the curriculum has one document that details the content for teaching in that subject area (Mncube & Madikizela-Madiya in Harber ed., 2013: 174). CAPS reversed the aims of C2005 outcomes-based education by 'going back to terminology that was used in education in South Africa before outcome-based education was introduced' (Mncube & Madikizela-Madiya in Harber ed., 2013: 174). The detailed instructions in CAPS aimed to reduce the time and administrative load on teachers; the clear guidance and expected consistency in instruction across schools was expected to result in higher learning outcomes across the country.

Assessment policy

The changes in assessment policy in basic education follow a somewhat different timeline where, only with the introduction of CAPS in 2011, a clear connection was established with the underlying curriculum. Over time, the goals of assessments also changed from preparing learners for exit exams in secondary education to becoming standalone assessments for student progression, school improvement and/or teacher learning and accountability.

Up until 1996, the only standardized testing that existed in the country was the National Senior Certificate (NSC). The NSC tested learners in their final grade of secondary education, grade 12. These matriculation exams, also known as 'matric', were (and are still) used as indicators for learner performance, the entry of learners into higher and further education and the general condition of the South African basic education system. Due to the intense resource concentration and public obsession on grade 12 matric results there initially was little scope to determine the performance of primary schools, hold schools accountable for learning performance, or provide support to schools where it was needed most (Van Wyk, 2015).

The national assessment surveys (1996), administered in 2001–2007

In 1996, the Department of Basic Education (DBE) introduced standardized testing for learners in grades 3, 6 and 9 in 1996 as part of the 'Systemic Evaluation Programme' (Kanjee & Moloi, 2014). At that point, the rationale for assessment in primary education was only to improve learner performance on the matric in grade 12 by more systematically monitoring the performance of learners in earlier grades in order to identify learning and teaching gaps sooner. These assessments were to be conducted annually with the main objective of benchmarking performance and tracking progress towards achieving the set targets and the goal of education transformation process (see section 48 of the Department of Education's 1998 *Assessment Policy for General Education and Training;* and the Systemic Evaluation Report, 2003). The programme was developed over a long period of time and only administered in 2001, 2004, and 2007 in one grade with a sample covering between 35,000 and 55,000 learners (DBE, 2011).

According to the 2003 Systemic Report by DBE, as early as 1998 the department identified a set of indicators of quality education deemed appropriate for measuring performance of the education system. It was this process that led to the development and subsequent piloting of the evaluation instruments in 2000 with the main Systemic Evaluation study at the Foundation Phase conducted in 2001/2. The then Minister of Education, Kader Asmal, noted that the South African Qualification Framework sets the broader context for education transformation which identified the need to measure educational outcomes against predetermined standards (DBE System Evaluation Report, 2003). Two of the primary Acts that govern the basic education namely; the National Education Policy Act (NEPA 27 of 1996) and SASA (Act 94 of 1996) were both amended between 1997 and 2011. These amendments included specific changes pertaining to the curriculum and assessments which would explain the incremental approach of assessments and their implementation. Van der Berg and Gustafsson (2017) provide an outline of the subsequent changes of NEPA and SASA; more specifically, it was in 2011, 2012 and 2016 that much alignment of national processes and procedures for learner assessments with the national curriculum was adjusted.

The data sampled through the Systemic Evaluation Programme identified some areas of weakness and informed subsequent policy changes, such as the Annual National Assessments (ANA), which were introduced in 2011. ANA is a large-scale adaptation of the sample-based Systemic Evaluation programme (Basic Education Portfolio Committee Presentation, 2011). The ANA trials were conducted in 2008 and 2009 with an emphasis on: (i) exposing teachers to better assessment practices; (ii) easy identification of poor-performing schools that require more assistance and those that could serve as examples of best practices; and (iii) learning in the area of standardized assessments (DBE ANA, 2011).

ANA (2011–2015)

One of the fundamental aspects of the last curriculum reforms, introduced in the previous section – CAPS,– was that it was positioned to introduce 'Annual National testing to be fully implemented by the end of 2011' (Mncube & Madikizela-Madiya in Harber ed., 2013: 174). These standardized national assessments test learner achievement in languages and mathematics in the intermediate phase (grades 4–6) and in literacy and numeracy for the foundation phase (grades 1–3). The ANA was introduced with a clear admission from the

DBE that education outcomes in schools in South Africa were low and that these outcomes needed to be improved by using standardized testing at crucial stages of the school career, to indicate where learners were struggling with specific subjects, such as maths and languages (Thulare, 2018). As Thulare states, 'accepting the failures of primary schooling, the Minister of Education declared the assessment policy an important step not only in evaluating the latest move to standardise workbooks in grades 1–6 but also ensuing that the ministry reaches its [pass] targets ... in maths and languages at secondary school level as set by the National Development Plan' (Thulare, 2018: 83). As such, the ANA sought to annually monitor the extent to which these outcomes would be achieved, with an emphasis to strengthen the foundational skills of literacy and numeracy of learners (DBE, 2011).

The ANA drew from experiences in several international assessment programmes in which South Africa participated. These included the regional Southern and East Africa Consortium for Monitoring Education Quality (SACMEQ) programme and the global Progress in International Reading Literacy Study (PIRLS) and Trends in International Mathematics, and Science Studies (TIMSS) programmes. After participating in these cross-national assessments, the decision was to focus nationally (Thulare, 2018) and have a large-scale diagnostic tool that would provide a better understanding of the performance-related problems within schools.

The outcome of ANA was for the information gathered from this standardized assessment to serve as a diagnostic tool identifying areas of strength and weakness in teaching and learning by exposing teachers to better assessment practices, providing districts with information to target schools in need of assistance, encouraging schools to celebrate outstanding performance – those that could serve as examples of best practices and learning in the area of standardized assessments and empowering parents by providing them information about the education of their children (DBE ANA, 2011).

Moreover, the ANA sought to measure progress on learner achievements towards the set targets in *Action Plan to 2014: Towards the Realisation of Schooling 2025* (DBE, 2014). These targets were part of the government's long-term education commitments outlined in the *National Development Plan for 2030* that prioritizes the improvement of learner outcomes. One of the commitments is in improving the country's average score in international comparative studies, more specifically the envisaged 105 increase (from 495 to 600) on SAQMEQ by 2022 and for TIMSS the expected increased performance score of 156 (264–420) by 2023. While for the national scores, the aims are for 90% of learners in grades 3, 6 and 9, respectively to achieve 50% or more in the annual national assessments in language in numeracy.

The 2011 ANA process involved both 'universal ANA' and 'verification ANA'. The universal ANA was administered by teachers who tested all learners in Grades 2 to 7 in both languages and mathematics. By contrast, independent service providers administer the Verification-ANAs, but only to Grade 3 and 6 learners in a selected sample of schools in order to verify the credibility of the Universal ANA results. For 2011, the Human Science Research Council (HSRC) was the independent provider[2] responsible for the verification process. Verification ANA involved applying rigorous procedures to a sample of around 1,800 schools offering Grades 3 or 6 in order to verify results emerging from universal ANA. It must be noted that in 2011, the department, through the HSRC, sampled 450 schools targeting Grade 9 and Grade 10 for the pilot of the ANA; Grade 9 tests were included since 2012 (DBE ANA, 2011; see RSE DBE, 2012b, for the findings). Expressly, in order to verify ANA, external controls in the test administration process were set up to test scripts from each school were re-marked after the initial marking by teachers (DBE ANA, 2011). In addition to testing learners, a learner background questionnaire, an educator questionnaire and a principal questionnaire were part of the 2013 Verification-ANA process (Wills, 2016). Despite the aims of the ANA to inform school and system-wide improvements, the assessments were discontinued after 2005 following widespread and increasing opposition. Below we first explain the systemic constraints that affected the ANA process, administration and validity before arguing that the confusion and contestation over the purpose of the ANAs and an increasing deficiency of trust between the unions and the department were important reasons for its suspension.

Flawed assessments: The ANA (2011–2015)

The ANA ended abruptly in 2015 after disagreements between the DBE and teacher unions about its implementation. Disagreements centred on how to best deal with the many flaws in the assessments where the DBE, in its 25 Year Review of Basic Education (2019), explained that they favoured gradual design improvements without suspending the programme. However, teacher unions argued for suspending the programme until the redesign had been completed as there were too many flaws in the design and their strong opposition resulted in the termination of ANA in 2015. The critiques of the short-lived ANA policy were summarized in the 2011 DBE ANA report and a subsequent report from the Public Servants Association of South Africa (PSA, 2016).

Weak assessment system

The DBE ANA report (2011) invigorated discussions and criticisms which had already started after the analysis of the first batch of the ANA data. One of these criticisms was the fact that the South African education system is too weak to implement standardized testing. Van der Berg et al. (2011) point to the vulnerability of the assessment system due to various forms of cheating and lenient marking, given that the ANA is administered and marked by local schools. Frempong et al. (2013) refer to this as 'limited credibility' (see also Van Wyk, 2015). A similar point is made by Van Wyk (2015), who describes how the DBE supplied the question papers and marking memoranda, but schools conducted the tests and managed the marking and internal moderation themselves. Therefore, the quality of the ANA data can be compromised if there is no proper oversight. Moreover, the verification of ANA is based on a sample of schools and, as such, the results emerging from samples must always be interpreted with a margin of error, according to Spaull (2012).

Weaknesses also refers to the fact that the ANAs did not offer guidance on the level of understanding of learners, but instead focused on broad trends in the right/ wrong answers (PSA, 2016). Although the ANA potentially offered reliable data as the tests are standardized, it was unclear what new lessons emerged from it that the department was not aware of given that many of the same schools and districts that struggle with the curriculum, would also struggle with doing well on the ANAs.

As such, broader areas for improvement in the administration and use of the ANA included the need to develop better logistics in the distribution of the ANA material to schools, more rigorous quality assurance measures in the verification of the ANA, more standardization with universal ANA, better data collection procedures and improvement in the design of the tests, the alignment of the tests with the curriculum, and giving parents better information on the education of their children (DBE, 2011). For teachers, the inability to translate or interpret the ANA assessment as a form of care for learners in lower grades also led to questioning the fairness and accessibility of the tests (Long et al., 2017).

Teacher testing, not standardized testing

A second criticism that arose from the ANA testing is that there was no programme of support to ensure teachers and the capacity to teach the tested content and that ANA actually tested teachers and their skills as opposed to finding the challenges in the curriculum and addressing them appropriately. Thus, the ANA came to be seen as a punitive measure against teachers rather than a standardized assessment of the curriculum at critical stages in the basic education system. This point was raised in the SADTU 2014 Perspective document, in which SADTU called out the unfairness of the ANA increasingly being used, as we detail below, to hold teachers accountable; a purpose for which the assessments were not designed originally. The union affirmed the relevance of a systemic evaluation but proposed that the ANA should be administered triennially instead of annually as this would allow more time to capacitate teachers. The union also identified that capacitating teachers required support and assessment training, adequate resources, the development and administration of more informative assessments of learners' content knowledge and multiple forms of understanding. SADTU also recommended the discontinuation of ANA at Grades 1 and 3, as the union argued that learners had insufficient opportunities to acquire the skills on which they were tested (SADTU, 2014). Van der Berg et al. (2011) make a similar case but instead of discontinuation of the ANA, they advocate moving the testing from the beginning to the end of the year. Further noting that it may be unclear whether learning deficits may already have existed in the earliest grades, or if it snowballs in these early grades. More reflections of the ANA cautioned against how the ANA was leading to widespread 'teaching to test' and a narrowing of the curriculum, caused by the increased workload of teachers in administering the test instead of using their time to teach a broad curriculum (Frempong et al., 2013).

Non-comparability of the assessments

Non-comparability is an issue raised by both unions, the Public Servants Association (PSA) and (academic and policy) researchers. This refers to the fact that there is neither a baseline from which to compare ANA results as they are released nor is there any ability to compare the ANA results over time. The PSA (2016), for example, points out that the testing structure changed almost every year since it was introduced. As a result, there is a lack of inter-temporal and inter-grade comparability and this limits the usefulness of learning gains as well as the standardization of scores; ANA was not designed to be compared over time (Taylor, 2013). Moreover, the PSA specifically highlighted that often areas with very low marks would get easier tests the following year, creating a misleading picture of the actual changes in the education system. This critique focused on the lack of reflexive interventions and adequate responses to the generated data for low-performing schools. SADTU, for instance, proposed using ANA for constructive feedback to teachers, learners and parents, i.e. marked scripts to be returned learners and teachers for further reflection, and less focus on the results, but more on what areas could be improved in both teaching and learning. SADTU further advocated for multiple intelligence testing that takes account of learners with learning disabilities. These were, however, not taken on board.

ANA: A contested policy arena

Firstly, discussions about the value and technical aspects of the ANA invigorated a power struggle over education and educational improvement, particularly between the DBE and the teacher unions. Teacher unions contested the introduction of ANA from the start, sharing their frustration with the department on the use and administration of the assessments on various occasions (Cereseto & Joseph, 2015).

Despite the unions' reluctance to the assessments, they participated in discussions to try and improve the implementation of the ANAs. For instance, SADTU (2011) initially proposed a model to disaggregate learning outcomes in a way that would take into account the factors which have a negative impact on the quality of learning and teaching in schools – taking into account factors such as lack of parental involvement, teachers' professional development, school leadership and management, socio-economic status and resources necessary in addressing challenges identifiable through the ANA data.

These concerns were, however, not sufficiently taken into account, according to the unions who, as a result, called into question the motivations of the department to issue the ANAs, critiquing the initiative aims to use these assessments to improve learning outcomes. For example, the 2014 SADTU Congress document critiqued how the poor performance on ANA test scores was used to assign blamed on teachers and schools, further highlighting the (in)capacity of the School Management Team to analyse the results and plan for interventions and the lack of support from the department to equip them with the necessary skills and capacity.

The unions released a joint statement on 21 September 2015, titled *The Annual National Assessment (ANA) Adds No Value To The South African Learner*, to clarify their positions on the proposed discontinuation of the ANAs in 2015. The unions opposed the administering of the ANA in its then formation advocating the establishment of a task team consisting of unions and DBE officials that would develop a remodelled, systematic and diagnostic tool. The unions committed to participate in the process. What was received as a unilateral decision by DBE to continue with the 2015 ANA implementation scheduled for 1–4 December 2015, organized labour mobilized against it while encouraging year-end examination of learners to be supported. In what appeared to be a last-minute move, on 28 November 2015, just 48 hours before the scheduled ANA administration, the DBE announced the postponement of the ANA to February 2016 – there was no consensus on this date, especially from the unions. The ANA was eventually discontinued in 2015.

Glaser (2016) situates the reluctance towards national assessments in the broader opposition of the unions towards monitoring and evaluation of schools and teachers, originating from South Africa's Apartheid legacy and the surveillance of teachers under the system of Bantu Education at the time. Chetty et al.'s (1993) study on the Apartheid era evaluation systems, for example, shows how the nature and purpose of the evaluations were fiercely debated by teachers, illustrating the distrust and suspicion towards the unfair and bias appraisal systems at the service of state control. Pillay (2018) makes the case that teacher evaluations under the Apartheid regime education's inspectorate prioritized the management function through the evaluation for accountability and less on professional development. The emphasis was on the monitoring and surveillance of Black teachers, with no autonomy and limited programmes on teacher development. Assessments thus had a history of being used to penalize teachers and it is no wonder that the ANA was approached by the unions, mainly SADTU, in a similar manner, particularly when there is a lack of balance between standardized testing, which can pinpoint the weaknesses in the education system, and teaching skills, which need to be improved and assessed in an enabling educational environment.

Post-ANA: A new National Assessment Programme (NAP)

The story does not end here, however, as the ANA evolved into what is now known as the National Assessment Programme (NAP) – previously referred to as the National Integrated Assessment Framework (NIAF). The NIAF was introduced in 2018, and was scheduled to be implemented in 2019 over three-year cycles (DBE, 2017). The NAP aims to remedy some of the technical flaws in ANA by introducing three tiers into the assessment:

(i) *The Systemic Assessment*, which will be sample-based, and administered in Grades 3, 6 and 9, once every three years – this will provide the Basic Education Sector, especially those involved in planning and evaluation, with valuable data on the health of the system and trends in learner performance;

(ii) *The Diagnostic Assessment*, which will be administered by teachers in the classroom to identify learning gaps, and to plan remedial measures early in the learning process, so as to avoid learning deficits; and

(iii) *The Summative Assessment*, which will be a national examination, administered in selected grades (with an emphasis on Grade 9) and subjects to provide parents and teachers with a national benchmark to measure the performance of their children. (Department of Basic Education, 2016)

These proposals mark a unique point in South Africa's policy history as this system of assessments was initially developed by a Task Team, comprised of representatives of the Department of Basic Education and the unions who remodelled ANA into this new system. They undertook a comprehensive review of the strengths and weaknesses of the ANAs, drawing on inputs from various education stakeholders. The review resulted in a concept document, and a proposal for a universal and systemic assessment system which has, thus far, been welcomed as a foundational step in the re-design process. A second Inter-Ministerial Committee (IMC) further informed a more collaborative approach by attending to the broader issues of dispute presented by the five unions, as mentioned earlier; thereby allowing for a process of reconciliation and trust-building which should support further implementation of the new assessment system.

The process was also unique in the collaboration between unions who tend to take very different positions in the debate. As the Public Servants Association (2016) stated

> The unified stance on the ANAs is extremely rare, and indicative that differences run deeper. Unions have, in this case, supported evaluation, and pledged to work towards revising the system of ANAs, a rare of the show of support for monitoring and evaluation systems.
>
> (PSA, 2016: 4)

Given the broad consultation and the attempt to address weaknesses of the ANA, NAP appears to have incorporated inputs from education stakeholders. Hopefully, the consensus on the usefulness of national assessments, and acknowledgement that the impact of assessments requires time, will allow the new NAP to offer a more positive contribution to the improvement of learning outcomes in South Africa.

Conclusion and discussion

This chapter presented a structured timeline of changes in curriculum and assessment policy in South Africa, demonstrating how these reforms have been short-lived and often abandoned before any sustainable improvement could materialize. Our policy reconstruction shows how a resistance to teacher accountability and change in general, particularly by the teacher unions, political expediency for quick improvements, and the lack of collaborative capacity in the system, led to a trajectory of constant reform and overhaul of policy. Instead of embarking on a more substantive programme of support across the country when curriculum and assessment implementation failed, the response of the Department for Basic Education seems generally have been to introduce new policy. We illustrated this in detail for the most recent introduction and collapse of the Annual National Assessments in primary education (ANA).

The collapse of these Annual National Assessments highlights how policy is a negotiated process where place and people interact to make meaning of suggested curriculum standards, assessment targets and related support and consequences of the policies. These findings speak to the wider policy implementation literature, which highlights how policies in general are highly situated and context-specific. The beliefs, knowledge and orientations toward policy demands of those involved in the curriculum reviews and assessments in South Africa all shaped these reforms and particularly why they failed to sustain over time. Particularly relevant here is South Africa's Apartheid history which explains the mind-set of some of the teacher unions and teachers and how they interpret assessment and account-ability as tools for oppression, rather than ways in which support for improve-ment could be organized. Given this context, the development of assessment and accountability can only inform improvement when accompanied by a policy implementation approach which is collaborative in nature, builds a set of shared values on the purpose of assessments and organizes support for teachers to use assessment outcomes to improve student outcomes.

Recent events in the establishment of a joint task force of unions and the department to develop the National Assessment Programme (NAP) offers a more collaborative alternative with, hopefully, a more productive role of assess-ments in improving learning outcomes. When implemented and used well, these national assessments can supplement information on inputs in the education system and its processes. They can provide evidence on the achievements of learners and constraints in schools and in the system to progress learning, all of which should provide the basis for proposals for remedial action. Outcomes of assessments, when used for evaluation and improvement purposes, can explore differences between schools and better allocate resources and address teachers' professional needs. They do so when, for example, identifying gaps in the knowl-edge of teachers about school subjects and allow for a more coordinated effort to build teacher capacity across the system (Postlethwaite & Kellaghan, 2008). Despite the proliferation of teacher development programmes, offered by the department, unions and other education-oriented institutions in post 1994-South Africa, ANA data consistently indicated poor teacher content knowledge, and this continues to be a challenge.

Teacher accountability and subsequent learning as such remains underdevel-oped within the South African education system. The struggle over the ANA pur-pose and its usage of the information for remedial work clearly negated teacher accountability as well as their professional development. Indeed, in numerous country contexts, national learning assessments such as ANA are controversial policy instruments that generate multiple disputes regarding their purpose and meaning (Maroy & Pons, 2019; Verger, Fontdevila, & Parcerisa, 2019) Although the continuous changes of learner assessments and performance-based

accountability reforms seek to improve quality teaching and learning, the conditions for educational improvement to happen are not always met. Skedsmo and
Huber (2019a) make the case that the meta-data from teacher observations has
potential if the data collection considers (innovative) classroom teaching practices and teacher's knowledge base in the assessment of decision-making processes concerning professional accountability. These authors advocate for a school
governance bottom-up approach through which the feedback from large-scale
testing can be used more meaningfully (2019b).

Nonetheless, the recent concerted effort in South Africa to make the objectives
of national assessments clearer along with the intended use of the generated data
is hoped to set a more collaborative environment for the implementation of these
assessments. Our analysis indicate that contestation over curriculum and assessment policy offer little ground to negotiate differences and remedy potential technical faults in assessments, or jointly develop the support for teachers and schools
to use assessment outcomes for the benefit of teaching and learning. Only when
these conditions are met can national assessments effectively inform the work of
teachers and school principals and inform system-wide improvement, particularly where there is high inequality and large performance gaps between schools
across the country, such as in South Africa.

Notes

1 https://ossafrica.com/esst/index.php?title=Summary_of_the_South_African_
  Schools_Act%2C_no._84_of_1996
2 Spaull (2015) lists the independent service providers as HSRC (2011) and Deloitte
  (2013). There was no verification process in 2012 because the tender for service providers went out too late while in the 2014 ANA Report 'verification' only appears once in
  the introduction under methods https://www.umalusi.org.za/docs/presentations/2015/
  nspaull.pdf

References

Bashir, S., Lockheed, M., Ninan, E., & Tan, J. 2018. *Facing forward: Schooling for learning in
  Africa*. Washington, DC: World Bank.
Chisholm, L. 2005. 'The making of South Africa's national curriculum statement'. *Journal of
  Curriculum Studies*, 37(2), 193–208. Accessed: 8 November 2019.
Chisholm, L., & Fuller, B. 1996. 'Remember people's education? Shifting alliances, state-
  building and South Africa's narrowing policy agenda'. *Journal of Education Policy*, 11(6),
  693–716. Accessed: 9 November 2019.
Department of Basic Education (DBE), Republic of South Africa. 2011. 'Report on the
  annual national assessment of 2011: Grades 1 to 6 & 9'. Pretoria: DBE.
Department of Basic Education (DBE), Republic of South Africa, 2014. 'Report on the
  annual national assessment of 2014: Grades 1 to 6 & 9'. Pretoria: DBE.
Department of Basic Education (DBE). 2016. *The development of a national integrated
  assessment framework for 2016 and beyond*. Pretoria: DBE.
Glaser, C. 2016. *Champions of the poor or 'militant fighters for a better pay cheque?' Teacher
  unionism in Mexico and South Africa, 1979–2013*. University of the Witwatersrand,
  Johannesburg.

Government of South Africa, Department of Basic Education (DBE). 2006. 'Policy overview: Revised national curriculum statement grades R-9'. Available at: https://www.education.gov.za/Portals/0/CD/GET/doc/overview.pdf?ver=2006-11-21-100143-000. Accessed: 11 February 2020.

Government of South Africa, Department of Basic Education (DBE). 2019. 'Curriculum assessment policy statements (CAPS)'. Available at: https://www.education.gov.za/Curriculum/CurriculumAssessmentPolicyStatements(CAPS).aspx.   Accessed: 11 February 2020.

Harber, C. (ed.). 2013. *Education in Southern Africa*. London: Bllomsbury. Availiable at: http://www.education.gov.za/Examinations/AnnualNationalAssessmentsANA/tabid/569/

Honig, M. (2006). 'Chapter 1. Complexity and policy implementation'. In Honig, M. (ed.), *New directions in education policy implementation: Confronting complexity*. Albany: SUNY Press, pp. 1–25.

Jansen, J. D. 1998. 'Why education policies fail'. *Journal of Curriculum Studies*, 15(1), 56–58. Accessed: 12 November 2019.

Jansen, J. D. 1999. 'The school curriculum since apartheid: Intersections of politics and policy in the South African transition'. *Journal of Curriculum Studies*, 31(1), 57–67. Accessed: 12 November 2019.

Kanjee, A., & Sayed, Y. 2013. 'Assessment policy in post-apartheid South Africa: Challenges for improving education quality and learning'. *Assessment in Education: Principles, Policy and Practice*, 20(4), 442–469.

Kanjee, A., & Moloi, Q. 2014. 'South African teacher's use of national assessment data'. *South Africa Journal of Childhood Education*, 4(2), 90–113.

Long, C., Graven, M., Sayed. Y., & Lampen, E. 2017. 'Constraining conditions of professional teacher agency: The South African context'. *Contemporary Education Dialogue*, 14(1), 5–21. doi:10.1177/0973184916678681

Maroy, C., & Pons, X. (2019). *Accountability policies in education: A comparative and multilevel analysis in France and Quebec*. Cham, Switzerland: Springer.

Motala, S., Dieltiens, V., Carrim, N., Kgobe, P., Moyo, G., & Rembe, S. August 2007. *South Africa country analytic review: Educational access in South Africa*. Consortium for Research and Educational Access, Transitions and Equity (CREATE). Available at: http://www.create-rpc.org/pdf_documents/South_Africa_CAR.pdf.   Accessed: 11 February 2020.

Public Servants Association of South Africa (PSA). 2016. *Annual national assessments (ANA): What is at stake?* Pretoria: PSA.

RSA DBE. 2012a. *Action plan to 2014: Towards the realisation of schooling*. Pretoria: Department of Basic Education.

RSA DBE. 2012b. 'Annual National Assessment 2012: Report on the ANA of 2012'. Pretoria: Department of Basic Education, December 2012. Available at: http://www.education.gov.za/Examinations/AnnualNationalAssessmentsANA/tabid/569/

RSA DBE. 2013. 'Annual National Assessment 2013: Report on the ANA of 2013'. Pretoria: Department of Basic Education, December 2013. Available at: http://www.education.gov.za/Examinations/AnnualNationalAssessmentsANA/tabid/569/

RSA DBE. 2014. 'Annual National Assessment 2014: Report on the ANA of 2014'. Pretoria: Department of Basic Education, December 2014. Available at: http://www.education.gov.za/Examinations/AnnualNationalAssessmentsANA/tabid/569/ Default.aspx

SADTU. 2011. *Discussion document in response to ANA report*. Kempton Park.

SADTU. 2014. *Annual national assessment (ANA): A SADTU perspective*. Kempton Park.

Skedsmo, G., & Huber, S. G. 2019a. 'Forms and practices of accountability in education'. *Educational Assessment, Evaluation and Accountability*, 31, 251–255.

Skedsmo, G., & Huber, S. G. 2019b. 'Top-down and bottom-up approaches to improve educational quality: Their intended and unintended consequences'. *Educational Assessment, Evaluation and Accountability*, 31, 1–4.

Spreen, C. A. (2004). 'Appropriating borrowed policies: Outcomes-based education'. In Steiner-Khamsi, G. (ed.), *The global politics of educational borrowing and lending*, New York: Teachers College Press, pp. 101–113.

Taylor, N. 2013. *NEEDU national report 2012: The state of literacy teaching and learning in the foundation phase*. Pretoria: National Education Evaluation and Development Unit.

Thulare, T. D. 15 June 2018. 'A policy analysis of the annual national assessments in South Africa'. In Wiseman, A. W. & Davidson, P. M. (eds.), *Cross-nationally comparative, evidence-based educational policymaking and reform*. Bingley: Emerald Publishing Limited.

Van der Berg, S., Taylor, S., Gustafsson, M., Spaull, N., & Armstrong, P. 2011. *Improving education quality in South Africa*. Report for the National Planning Commission. Department of Economics, University of Stellenbosch.

Van der Berg, S., & Martin Gustafsson, M. 2017. *Quality of basic education: A report to working group 1 of the high level panel on the assessment of key legislation*. Research on Socio-Economic Policy Report. Department of Economics, University of Stellenbosch.

Van der Berg, S., Taylor, S., Gustafsson, M., Spaull, N., & Armstrong, P. (2011). Improving education quality in South Africa. *Report for the National Planning Commission*, 2, 1–23.

Verger, A., Fontdevila, C., & Parcerisa, L. (2019). 'Reforming governance through policy instruments: How and to what extent standards, tests and accountability in education spread worldwide'. *Discourse: Studies in the Cultural Politics of Education*, 40(2), 248–270.

Wills, G. 2016. *An economic perspective on school leadership and teachers' unions in South Africa*. PhD thesis. Department of Economic and Management Sciences, University of Stellenbosch.

9 Accountability policies in Chinese basic education: The Long March towards quality and evidence

Xingguo Zhou and Romuald Normand

Introduction

The development of accountability in Chinese education has been boosted by the circulation of educational reforms around the world; this has been achieved primarily through the introduction of national tests and assessments. OECD recommendations and international surveys have been used for comparison and benchmarking in China (Sellar & Lingard, 2013). Following the example of Shanghai, several Chinese cities, including Beijing, have joined the PISA club, and have achieved consecutive yearly high rankings in PISA scores. Centralized educational planning is supported by an unprecedented effort to systematically gather data and develop assessments within the educational system. However, the implementation of quality assurance and evaluation has to tackle significant disparities between regions as well as different governing levels. As such, accountability in Chinese basic education lies between top-down bureaucracy and Western-style governance, as a component of its political system institutionalizes a regime of surveillance and control. These mechanisms include policy negotiation, adaption and localization, and even innovation with some moral dimensions.

This chapter attempts to sketch out institutional and political reforms in educational supervision, assessment, evaluation, and examination, and curriculum by which the Chinese government attempts to strengthen its educational accountability. However, these reforms are hardly irrelevant to the ongoing political struggles, where administrative accountability power remains high and the fight against corruption is at stake.

The chapter is arranged into three sections: the first section investigates the institutionalization of hard control aiming to increase accountability; the second describes the efforts of the Chinese authorities to increase accountability; finally, the third provides additional perspectives, especially at school level, on how updating the curriculum and embodying moral education contribute to enhancing accountability mechanisms.

The institutionalization of accountability in China: Between bureaucracy and modernization

Although China's participation in the international PISA survey is challenging, Chinese policymakers adhere strongly to international rankings as a prestige brand and recognition within the international community (Ji, 2018). This explains why Shanghai's success in the PISA ranking – where it outperforms even Singapore – has a strong symbolic and political connotation (Tan, 2017). Indeed, significant effort has been made by the Chinese central government and local authorities to restructure schools and maximize performativity with the support of the OECD. The ambition of the Chinese government is to improve the quality of education while making education equitable to meet international standards. The development of basic education, particularly in rural areas and western regions, is considered as a priority. The long-institutionalized practices of school inspection and supervision (*jiàoyù dūd˘ao*) are also tools to enhance the governmental surveillance of education in order to reduce power manipulation or corruption.

Updating accountability systems: Coupling monitoring and assessments

The Ministry of Education (MoE) aims to expand the monitoring of education policies based on data and in-depth tests to assess the quality of learning and teaching in all provinces. In 2010, the Communist Party Secretary-General, Hu Jintao, proclaimed at the National Conference on Education the great importance of improving education equality to build a strong human capital (Chen, 2010). Prior to that (2005–2009), several national reports justified the development of accountability at all levels with educational data related to subjects such as the Chinese language and mathematics, and it was later extended not only to sciences, but also to the mental health of students, as well as their social and emotional skills (Zhang, 2012). Since then, some local academies have set up systems for assessing student performance and reducing achievement gaps between schools, as well as warning mechanisms. Some studies claim that Chinese basic education quality assessments are inspired by the OECD and the global accountability reform movement (Kauko et al., 2018; Zhou, Kallo, et al., 2018).

The 'National Long-Term Development Reform and Planning Plan 2010–2020' states that quality improvement should be a fundamental task for developing Chinese education from a scientific perspective. A national programme for monitoring compulsory education quality in provinces, cities, and districts has been implemented to improve regional governance. All 26 provinces have set up education quality monitoring systems. However, more resources are needed according to the Chinese government to make the system function both more scientifically as well as more professionally. Shanghai's entrance into PISA 2009, and its outstanding performance across reading, mathematics, and science, has drawn the attention of the Chinese government (Deng & Gopinathan, 2016). Following Shanghai's example, the MOE has created the NAEQ, the National Assessment

Centre of Education Quality,[1] at Beijing Normal University (Zhou, Kallo, et al., 2018). This monitoring of basic education is conceived as a multi-level mode of governance from the central state down to provinces, municipalities, and counties, including training in accountability for all teachers and officials.

A significant effort has been made in the development of sampling and data analysis by the NAEQ as well as in testing students' skills, including social and psychological skills (Shen, 2010). Sampling systems have been implemented within provinces and counties to monitor student outcomes over time. At present, the national quality assessment of compulsory education focuses on students in Grades 4 and 8, in monitoring their achievement in Chinese, mathematics, science, art, moral education, and physical health. Each year two of the six domains are assessed, and the first whole period of all six domains was completed from 2015 to 2017 (Zhou, Kallo, et al., 2018). Many reports are regularly produced by the NAEQ according to different topics and classifications; these serve to establish the state of the Chinese education system based on evidence. Provinces and counties are responsible for ensuring good coordination with the NAEQ services, in order to ensure that data sampling and monitoring is carried out systematically. Some are exploring how to use school evaluation and monitoring outcomes for better coordinative actions between schools.

While the MOE is trying to strengthen the scientific dimension of these assessments, considering that these must be supported by evidence, many regions, particularly in the western parts of the country, still lack resources, training, tools and technologies to conduct rigorous assessments as well as to get expertise in identifying problems and developing appropriate assessment-based strategies. Many aspects are underdeveloped: designing indicators, information systems, sampling techniques, data collection and compiling reports. The practice of traditional examinations remains central to the promotion of students and evaluation of school performance. Local policymakers have to be convinced that education can be improved by solving problems identified by the evaluation process.

Holding people responsible, or making them accountable: China's model of school inspection and supervision

Chinese schools fall largely within the scope of direct control and surveillance under the umbrella of school management. Control and surveillance are implemented via various means e.g., daily school routines, finances, teaching, student enrolment and graduation, assessments, and so on. Public schools face more rigorous regulations than non-public schools (for example, private or *mínbàn*[2] schools). Although the latter are subject to the same regulation and controls, non-public schools have more autonomy in managing staff, student recruitment, and tuition fees. Prior to joining PISA, China's education governance struggled with the question of holding education units responsible. For a long time, China only had the concept of 'holding-for-responsibility' (*wèn zé*). This is a locally rooted in the mind-set 'whose fault is it?' or 'who is to blame?', which is very different from the western meaning of 'accountability'. This requires the person in charge to take the blame and associated consequences for any misconduct. Indeed, this partly explains why so many governmental inspections and regulations remain: they are essentially eyes on others to check whether schools and localities have properly implemented the State policies (MoE, 1991).

For this reason, Chinese teachers are weary of governmental inspections. Schools are fearful of being found to have made wrong decisions. Therefore, much effort is made to appear to be fulfilling all criteria during the inspection. This is a common phenomenon that has been witnessed in many countries (Ehren et al., 2013). This behaviour is exacerbated, as failure to pass the inspection incurs penalties such as suspension or disqualified as candidates for other rewards. In China, such high stakes mean that inspectors wield enormous power. Ironically, inspections were introduced to control misconduct, yet the system itself facilitates the manipulation of results. In order to limit manipulation during inspection, more tools, such as large-scale assessment, were introduced by the central government. However, they place an even heavier burden on schools whose focus shifts primarily to appearing responsible and compliant with regulations, rather than improving the quality of education. This is summed up by the phrase, 'shàng yǒu zhèng cè, xià yǒu duì cè', which translates roughly as 'those in power have policies, while those below have countermeasures'.

A recent political message indicates that the Chinese government realized the problem of 'holding schools responsible', and intentionally shifted the focus of inspection and education governance towards accountability (e.g., see MoE, 2016). Such reflections impact on the internal and administrative monitoring systems which become more reactive to daily school routines. Chinese policymakers believe that promoting professionalism is the key to enhancing accountability. Thus, when local authorities appoint heads of schools, they emphasize their skills in this area. In China, schools usually include two heads: one represents the Party Secretary, while the other deals with school management. In theory, the latter is primarily responsible for accountability issues (xiàozhǎng fùzé zhì). In practice, however, the sharing depends on several micro-level features (e.g., social and educational background, personal connections e.g., guān xi) as well as on macro-political ones. Professionalism remains an extra criterion despite the fact that policy documents emphasize professionalization in leadership for principals and teachers alike (State Council, 2010).

Professionalism on the side of inspectors has also been emphasized (State Council, 2012). Previously, inspections were carried out mainly by retired teachers or experts as part-time inspectors (Yang, 2001). However, the need to maintain a highly professionalized team of inspectors was recognised by the government. It therefore increased the number of full-time positions in the inspectorate and put several training programmes in place (Yang, 2001). Moreover, a more eye-catching reform of inspection is stated in the Inspector's Zone of Responsibility requirements (National Superintendent Committee, 2013). It corresponds to the Chinese government's attempt to shift its surveillance system towards accountability in better matching inspectors with schools. For example, each inspector is assigned to five schools; the identity of both schools and inspectors is published online and can be monitored by the public. Even though problems with this policy have been highlighted (Su, 2020), the Chinese government has scaled it up to the whole country. Thus, it appears that making the bottom-level inspection more accountable is a high priority.

Datafication: The vision of big data and evidence-based education

The efforts described above to update the chain of accountability represent a strong conviction on the side of policymakers for underpinning policies on big data and concrete evidence. Along with the implementation of NAEQ's large-scale assessments, China has amplified the datafication of accountability to cover territories and schools. Some observers suggest that evidence-based policymaking is fundamentally changing Chinese educational governance and decision-making (Xin, 2019). Supported by experimentalism at the local policy level (Heilmann, 2008), evidence-based policymaking and big data management bring more confidence and strengthen accountability policies. Policymakers welcome big data, arguing that they are more in touch with real problems, and are able to make decisions based on evidence. However, some argue that in a fragmented, top-down and authoritarian education system, policymakers are not really familiar with local situations and are vulnerable to being misinformed by manipulated bottom-up information (Lieberthal & Lampton, 2018).

NAEQ illustrates how big data could further develop accountability policies in China. First, big data connect the bottom layers of government with the top decision-making authorities. First-hand educational data collected by NAEQ headquarters are delivered directly to the MOE. These data enter a large national databank that contains measures of overall student academic performance, learning and teaching practices, school and family cooperation as well as physical, moral and mental health achievements. The aim is to inform policymaking using large datasets. Thus, more accurate solutions for specific problems in schools can be found, and more realistic plans are aligned to national goals. Secondly, big data provides a channel for communicating between different governing levels. Crucially, the MOE does not hold local authorities and schools solely responsible for performing badly in large-scale assessments. Instead, it promotes the idea that big data can help to identify problems which can be tackled together. This represents a major shift in the central government attitude from holding people at lower levels responsible, to making them accountable. Consequently, local policymakers provide training for their staff to develop their skills on interpreting data and compiling reports from large-scale assessments (Hu, 2019; Qin, 2019) and to them to adjust local plans. There are convergent efforts from researchers, teachers and headmasters to work together to improve accountability in education (Rasmussen & Zou, 2014).

As an example, the Chongqing Educational Evaluation Institute[3] has been built to develop detailed, scientific, complete, and objective evaluation based on big data (He et al., 2017). Since its creation in 2009, this Institute, under the supervision of the NAEQ, has sought to find modern quality assessment digital technologies for modernizing the Chongqing education system. These efforts represent the typically Chinese reforming rationale that combines the old practice of inspection with new assessments to develop educational services (Zhou, 2019). The institute has developed a data management platform equipped with powerful software and various testing tools and questionnaires for students and their families. This data processing is combined with the measurement of social participation indicators for students and teachers through tests and the collection of real-time data on WeChat. This information, on behaviour, performance, and communication, is then classified and refined according to artificial intelligence programmes and other identification technologies that handle responses to questions and tests (Chongqing Education Commission, 2015).

The dissemination of evidence-based education in China owes a great deal to global influences and policy borrowing (Normand, 2016). Chinese NAEQ, for instance, is an example of how global agendas (for example, OECD's educational agenda) influence local agendas (Kauko et al., 2018; Normand et al., 2018; Zhou, Kallo, et al., 2018). While the global movement of standardized large-scale assessments is gaining momentum, China has tapped into the potential of big data for devising improved accountability mechanisms and transferred them to the local level.

The tensions of policy accountability and quality issues

The implementation of Chinese accountability policies in education exhibits different cultural, institutional and political configurations, with a tension between centralized and hierarchical governance as opposed to heterogeneous regional and local realities. While improving performance is at stake for policymakers concerned with China's economic development and global influence, the country faces major challenges in allocating resources between eastern and western regions. In western China, underdevelopment (for example, lack of buildings, unqualified teachers, scarce public funding) impacts upon accountability requirements in counties or cities where illiterate young children face major social and health problems (Wang & Lewin, 2016). Top-down government monitoring is also thwarted by the extent of the education market which, despite regulative attempts, creates an alternative form of bottom-up accountability. Competition is exacerbated between families and between schools, regarding the success in *gāokǎo* (college entrance examination) – the ruler of educational quality in the Chinese mind-set. Therefore, tensions are perceptible between positivist demands from the central government which, by strengthening accountability, wants to increase its controlling power in coupling evidence-based technologies and decentralization.

Policy accountability: More responses to regional disparities and school choice

Due to its openness policy, the Chinese government attempted rounds of reforms from decentralization, re-centralization and re-decentralization (Hawkins, 2000) in order to find the right balance between central control and local autonomy. Many have argued that the Chinese political power structure could be described as consultative-authoritarian because policy framing has changed to include various experts, think-tank consultants from transnational organizations, and domestic research institutions (He & Thøgersen, 2010; Teets, 2013). These changes are part of the Chinese government's efforts to make policies more accountable from the bottom up. In the case of education, extra confidence is anchored in the development of big data and assessment technologies. The long-overlooked topics of educational equality and equity are also prioritized within the central government's agenda (Zhou, Risto, et al., 2018).

Balancing the management and allocation of resources between rich and poor regions is an arduous task. By the early 2000s, though the authority announced its big success in universalizing compulsory education (Rasmussen & Zou, 2014), western and rural China were still significantly lagging in primary and secondary education with high illiteracy and drop-out rates. Educational policies as well as laws gave scant room for addressing issues related to equality and fairness. However, prior to the 2000s, there were changes in education accountability reforms, as assessment datasets showed regional disparities in educational development levels. From 2005 to 2006, a new funding mechanism and share of responsibilities between the central government and provincial governments was set up based on the idea of extending accountability at different levels and ensuring financial security for compulsory rural education (Wang & Lewin, 2016). Rural students were exempted from tuition and textbook fees, while the poorest families received allowances to place their children in boarding schools. The level of funding was guaranteed by quotas according to benchmarks for primary and secondary schools. Teachers' salaries were consolidated and raised up, while a supervisory and inspection system was set up.

Consequently, the situation of rural schools has improved significantly, even though the level of public funding still varies from one region to another, as it is highly dependent on negotiations between the state and the local authorities, as well as on their discretionary power in the transfer and allocation of central government resources. Salaries and working conditions, with often poorly qualified teachers, are also prevalent. Nevertheless, in general, schools benefit more from state investment. Resolving arduous problems would require the renegotiation of a new political balance between different parties. For instance, in order to implement educational policies ensuring equal access to schools, the government would need to cancel access to schools based on the household registration scheme (*hùkǒu* system), or at least make it fairer. The *hùkǒu* system is a heritage from the Mao era whereby the registration of people was mandatory in exchange for an official identity and access to work and education, and other social services (Cheng & Selden, 1994). Since that time, as the result of processes of urbanization and industrialization, which led to a large proportion of the Chinese workforce – both skilled and unskilled – migrating to other parts of the country, the *hùkǒu* system created institutional barriers for those migrant students who wanted to study where they lived. Among them, only elites and small numbers of highly skilled migrants might benefit from the *hùkǒu* system. Efforts have been made by some public authorities to reduce this barrier (Hu & West, 2015), but there is still a long way to achieve equal access to schools.

Equal access raises the issue of school choice in China. The latter is conditioned by a set of economic, political, social and cultural factors (Dong & Li, 2019).

It is not a government-imposed system, but a local competitive process by which parents seek access to the best schools for their children through various means, for example, tuition fees, power relationships, use of *guānxi* or interpersonal ties, promotion by prizes or rewards. Against this, governmental regulations seek to prohibit and limit school choice while simultaneously turning a blind eye to many aspects of it (National People's Congress, 2006). Since the 1990s, some policy measures to limit tuition fees have been taken by the State Council Office and the MOE. The law also required families to enrol their children in nearby schools to limit the strategic use of key schools. The government also created other measures such as sharing resources, supporting the poorest-performing schools, and forcing the transfer of teacher and principal teams. The aim is to shrink the quality gap between different schools while diminishing the attractiveness of those schools with a good reputation. Despite some improvements, those measures have not been sufficient to curb the trend.

Due to the government's previous elitist policies in prioritizing resources to key schools (Hua, 2015), the quality gap between key schools and non-key school has widened. Even worse, elitist policies combined with marketization has strengthened school competition and opportunistic strategies among educators, schools and parents. In this competitive environment, the less privileged families become worse off, while middle- and upper-class families take advantage of these opportunities. This situation has generated a huge private tutoring market that it is difficult for the central government to regulate (Liu, 2018). This market includes a myriad of individual providers (students, teachers or retired teachers, tutors) and collective ones (small and large companies, internet portals and services). Chinese parents are using these services in part to strengthen their children's skills, to get psychological support, but also to care for them during their busy working days. Even though these institutions are under governmental pressure to regulate safety, qualification levels, class sizes, and curricula, and risk severe penalties otherwise, this private provision is nevertheless significantly developed (Zhang, 2019). Providers tend to ignore regulations or try to evade them while regulatory texts are relatively ambiguous and unable to cover all types of activities. In summary, accountability and quality assurance are therefore highly dependent on this overall consumerist pressure despite regulative efforts from the government.

Selective accountability: Balancing between fairness and sorting

Over the past four decades, the Chinese government has adjusted its methods for selecting students in balancing fairness and streaming, using selective accountability mechanisms the meanings of which have changed in parallel to the political aims. For instance, in the past, accountability was used to sort the best students. Today, national policymakers seek ways of sorting students while ensuring equal access to schools. This section describes one of the most important 'sorting tools'– the *gāokǎo* – as a means of finding a balanced, yet accountable method. *Gāokǎo* is the Chinese matriculation examination. The political discussion in China about ensuring both selectiveness and equal opportunities essentially comes down to choosing between a national standardized *gāokǎo*, or diversified local examinations.

This is a recurrent debate in Chinese education policy. The standardized *gāokǎo* would be easier for the Chinese people to accept, since they share the simple egalitarian idea that fairness consists of each student taking the same exam. However, given the unequal quality in educational provision and resources at the regional level, using this kind of standardized examination would be unfair for the less developed and poorer western districts. In 2014, the government announced new goals for educational reforms to set up a quality-oriented and diversified national examination system (i.e., a new *gāokǎo*) which would ensure a fairer selection in preparing students for the new challenges of the knowledge-based economy (State Council, 2014). Indeed, small pilot projects were carried out by different research institutions. For example, Peking University started a try-out practice called University Selection through the Principal's Recommendations. Following its lead, many key Chinese universities began to use a similar method to enrol students recommended by respected high school principals (Ou, 2012). MOE officially proclaimed the Principal's Recommendation as a countermeasure to the standardized *gāokǎo* for selecting talented students (Zhang, 2010). Compared to the traditional *gāokǎo*, such a method of selecting and enrolling students challenges the Chinese egalitarian idea on equal selection. It was no surprise, therefore, that these new accountability methods, as well as their objectivity and fairness, have been questioned by students and parents (Ou, 2012). These try-out practices concerned only a small fraction of students. In 2019, less than 370,000 students were enrolled via those programmes, compared with the 10 million students who took the standardized *gāokǎo*. From 2020, according to official announcements, such alternative recruitment methods would no longer be allowed.

The current status quo is that the Chinese government endeavours to maintain a balance between selectiveness and equality in maintaining a standardized national curriculum via the *gāokǎo*, which means the same examination for all provinces. On the other hand, the student curriculum allows for a personalized and flexible combination between three major subjects (Chinese, mathematics and English), and five optional subjects (history, physics, politics, geography, biology and chemistry), which is named as the new *gāokǎo* (State Council, 2014). The tests are thus aligned with people's expectations of equality and fairness in the selection process, while the new curriculum can be adapted to individual student interests. However, this new *gāokǎo* greatly challenges teachers because they have to guide students in choosing the necessary optional subjects to ensure eligibility for entrance into their desired degree pathways at the university level. Indeed, this personalized curriculum causes students to hesitate in their selection of subjects as their choice will necessarily impact the *gāokǎo* outcome, and may well have consequences for their future career choice. This places huge responsibility on teachers who feel under pressure to adapt to all those new changes.

Accountability in Chinese schools: A holistic and moral vision

The holistic vision of skills set out by the Chinese government is to prepare Chinese students for twenty-first-century challenges (*sù yǎng*) and a knowledge-based society. This section illustrates the curriculum reforms linked to the development of student assessments and accountability policies. However, being accountable in China means not only meeting accountability requirements, in terms of control, supervision or instrumentalization related to QAE tools. Rather, moral accountability is also deeply rooted in Chinese culture and practices, as expressed in the Chinese word *guānxi* (Ruan, 2016).

Student assessment: A holistic vision of skills

In 2014, the government started research projects that focused on developing a holistic version of core skills for Chinese students. Like many other countries, China updated its school curriculum to structure contents focused on lifelong learning and core skills at different stages to fit to the high speed of social development. Then, the MOE trusted Beijing Normal University to develop Chinese students' core competencies. Inspired by the OECD's Definition and Selection of Competencies (DeSeCo) as well as key skills scales from other countries (Xin et al., 2016), the research team proposed twenty-first century core competencies for Chinese students that include culture competency, self-development competencies, and social participation competency. Each of these categories contains multiple sub-categories of explicit explanations and instructions. These twenty-first-century core competencies and values holding by students were later accepted by the Chinese government as the official version. Looking into the detailed report (Lin, 2017), cultural competence means students should be equipped with cultural knowledge of Chinese history, cultural heritage, aesthetic taste, human-centric attitude and responsibility as a world citizen, as well as critical and rational thinking; the self-development competencies include learning how to learn, learning about healthy life and life management skills; the social participation competency contains cultivating students' social responsibility, innovative thinking, and the ability to apply learning, i.e., putting knowledge and theories into practice.

This holistic vision of education is matched with Quality Education Goals (*sùzhì jiàoyù*) to develop well-rounded students with future-oriented talents. A change happening at the local level is the promotion of studies outside the school environment. In November 2016, 11 national departments, including the MOE, the National Development and Reform Commission, and the former Ministry of Culture, jointly issued the Opinions on Promoting Study Trips for Primary and Middle School Students (MoE, 2016). It recommended the inclusion of study trips in primary and secondary educational plans and curricula. For the first time in the history of Chinese education, study tours and trips were integrated into the school curriculum. A growing number of Chinese students now travel abroad. This is not only because of they have the means to do so, but also because internationalization for learning is highly valued by the government and parents. International student study trips are an emerging market, and there are few specific governmental policies and regulations for travel companies and related organizations. However, this has recently been put on the policy agenda on behalf of quality assurance.

The moral dimension of accountability: Ethics, honour, and loyalty

The moral dimension in education is part of the Chinese society's structure with strong social relationships and the understanding of being accountable as a human being. Schools emphasize this high morality as daily life is governed by a set of common ethical principles related to the Confucian heritage. Even in ancient China, learning has always been associated with the cultivation of personal morality and the future of the country (Gu, 2006). Many studies have shown that *guānxi*, which can be roughly translated as 'a personal connection, a relationship, or a network', is a central feature of Chinese society. It has multiple ethical and relational components. People living in such a society face reciprocal obligations and can be benefited from, or burdened with, complicated social relationships. For instance, *rénqíng* corresponds to social norms and a moral obligation that leads the Chinese to engage in gift giving and reciprocity relationships with others: in short, they are accountable to others. This request for reciprocity is part of moral assessment that can be considered as asymmetrical favour exchanges. The quality of favour exchanges and their degree of reciprocity determines the strength of the relationship. *Rénqíng*, therefore, symbolizes a rational calculation, a moral obligation, and an emotional attachment.

From this notion, it is understandable how *guānxi* strongly determines relationships between parents, teachers and principals regarding school choice. Parents can intervene with a person in a position of authority to get their children accepted into a given school, which places strong pressure on the principal. The family network is also mobilized to exert influence and parents seek to get favours from teachers throughout the year. School principals likewise seek to develop good relationships with parents and the local community, but also with teachers. The school is considered as a large family, with its system of reciprocal duties and obligations, while maintaining a concern for balance and harmony, self-discipline and modesty, at the foundation of Confucian values and social relations between school principals and teachers (Ji, 2017).

These moral requirements also apply to students. Indeed, in addition to regular competitions in which students must participate, they are expected to have a sense of honour and demonstrate loyalty to the school (Gu et al., 2017). Classrooms are successively responsible for discipline in the school and must ensure that rules are respected. Social relationships within the school are collectively constructed with a sense of belonging and community. Expectations from both students and teachers are expressed through mottos such as 'self-discipline', 'moral integrity', and also 'effort', 'perseverance' in work. Mottos are placed on school walls or even in the entrance hall of the building as a reminder to students. Each school has its own song that contributes to its image and reputation. This song is particularly valued during ceremonies. Another example is wearing uniforms. Many schools require students to wear a uniform for at least three reasons: to remind them of their studying duties, to reinforce good student behaviour because everyone can be easily identified by their school uniform, and to give a sense of community and common belonging. This common sense of unity is also maintained by flag-raising ceremonies. Additionally, official instructions prescribe regular meetings within schools and classes to discuss issues related to school life. The topic of moral education appears as one of the regular topics discussed by students to construct shared moral values in each class and school.

Conclusion

To summarize, this chapter has introduced the accountability system in Chinese basic education. In the name of quality assurance, the Chinese basic education system does not only develop formal and institutionalized accountability systems such as inspection and surveillance, but also informal accountability, following principles of tradition and morality. The Chinese government seems to realize that too many direct regulations and control over schools do not necessarily lead to accountability in education. The path of current reforms is two-pronged: first, it aims to reduce direct control over schools in relation to adjusting and updating the rationale of education assessments and evaluation. As we have seen, this aim is achieved through extending the network of people involved (mainly inspectors and local policymakers) and developing evidence-based information systems and big data. The second aim is to enhance control over the inspection process in order to increase accountability in terms of professionalism and the allocation of clear responsibilities. In addition to these reforms, other regulations related to the quality of education are directed to the national curriculum, student selection and enrolment as well as the development of core skills at local level. Finally, alongside these more formal processes, a softer accountability also exists; this is perhaps the main reason why Chinese students, teachers, and schools still maintain the underlying value of Chinese accountability in education.

Notes

1 National Assessment Centre of Education Quality is *jiāoyùbù jīchǎ jiāoyù zhìliàng jiāncè zhōngxīn* in Chinese.
2 *Mínbàn* schools are non-public schools that complement the insufficient supply of public schools run by the non-governmental sector. *Mínbàn* schools are important education providers, especially to those migrant families that live in areas without local household registration. This is in spite of the government's efforts to provide free compulsory education.
3 Official webpage of this institute: http://www.cee.gov.cn.

References

Chen, X. (2010). The Chinese practice: New attempt of basic educational monitoring (中国的实践: 基础教育监测的新尝试). *Educational Research*, 4(363), 3–4.
Cheng, T., & Selden, M. (1994). The origins and social consequences of China's hukou system. *The China Quarterly*, 139, 644–668.
Chongqing Education Commission. (2015). *The Education Commission of Chongqing municipality forwarded the decision of the Ministry of Education on strengthening family education* (Original in Chinese). Retrieved from: http://cq.ggw.edu.cn/cq/ggzx/tztg/20151123-5179.shtml

Deng, Z., & Gopinathan, S. (2016). PISA and high-performing education systems: Explaining Singapore's education success. *Comparative Education*, 52(4), 449–472. doi:10.1080/03050068.2016.1219535

Dong, H., & Li, L. (2019). School choice in China: Past, present, and future, *ECNU Review of Education*, 2(1), 95–103. doi:10.1177/2096531119840854

Ehren, M. C., Altrichter, H., McNamara, G., & O'Hara, J. (2013). Impact of school inspections on improvement of schools – Describing assumptions on causal mechanisms in six European countries. *Educational Assessment, Evaluation and Accountability*, 25(1), 3–43.

Gu, M. (2006). An analysis of the impact of traditional Chinese culture on Chinese education. *Frontiers of Education in China*, 1(2), 169–190.

Gu, M., Ma, J., & Teng, J. (2017). *Portraits of Chinese schools*. Singapore: Springer.

Hawkins, J. (2000). Centralization, decentralization, recentralization – Educational reform in China. *Journal of Educational Administration*, 38(5), 442–455. doi:10.1108/09578230010378340

He, B., & Thøgersen, S. (2010). Giving the people a voice? Experiments with consultative authoritarian institutions in China. *Journal of Contemporary China*, 19(66), 675–692.

He, W., Yu, C., Lu, J., Tian, H., & Feng, Y. (2017). Let the data speak: Chongqing experience of educational quality evaluation (让数据说话: 教育质量评价的重庆经验). *Profession*, 100, 100–102.

Heilmann, S. (2008). From local experiments to national policy: The origins of China's distinctive policy process. *The China Journal*, (59), 1–30.

Hu, B., & West, A. (2015). Exam-oriented education and implementation of education policy for migrant children in urban China. *Educational Studies*, 41(3), 249–267. doi:10.1080/03055698.2014.977780

Hu, Y. (2019). Thoughts on the development of compulsory education in Guizhou based on the quality monitoring of compulsory education (基于义务教育质量监测对贵州义务教育发展的思考). *Guizhou Education*, 21, 9–10.

Hua, Y. (2015). Key-point schools and entry into tertiary education in China. *Chinese Sociological Review*, 47(2), 128–153. doi:10.1080/21620555.2014.990321

Ji, L. (2018). Government, media, and citizens: Understanding engagement with PISA in China (2009–2015). *Oxford Review of Education*, 45(3), 315–332, doi:10.1080/03054985.2018.1518832

Ji, R. (2017). *Guanxi, social capital and school choice in China: The rise of ritual capital*. London: Palgrave Macmillan.

Kauko, J., Rinne, R., & Takala, T. (Eds.). (2018). *Politics of quality in education: A comparative study of Brazil, China, and Russia*. London: Routledge.

Lieberthal, K. G., & Lampton, D. M. (Eds.). (2018). *Bureaucracy, politics, and decision making in post-Mao China* (Vol. 14). Berkeley, CA: University of California Press.

Lin, C. (2017). To construct sinicized core competencies and values for student development (构建中国化的学生发展核心素养). *Journal of Beijing Normal University (Social Sciences)*, 1, 66–73.

Liu, J. (2018). Review of regulatory policies on private supplementary tutoring in China. *ECNU Review of Education*, 1(3) 143–153. doi:10.30926/ecnuroe 2018010307

Ministry of Education. (1991). *(Interim) regulation of education supervision* (Original in Chinese). Retrieved from http://www.moe.gov.cn/s78/A02/zfs_left/s5911/moe_621/tnull_3459.html

Ministry of Education. (2016). *Collective decisions on middle school students' study trip from 11 departments including the Ministry of Education on promoting elementary* (Original in Chinese). Retrieved from http://www.moe.gov.cn/srcsite/A06/s3325/201612/t20161219_292354.htm

Ministry of Education. (2018). *China's first 'China compulsory education quality monitoring report' released* (Original in Chinese). Retrieved from http://www.moe.gov.cn/jyb_xwfb/gzdt_gzdt/s5987/201807/t20180724_343663.html

National People's Congress. (2006). *Amended law on compulsory education* (Original in Chinese). Retrieved from http://www.npc.gov.cn/wxzl/gongbao/2015-07/03/content_1942840.htm

National Superintendent Committee. (2013). Decisions on the inspector's zone of responsibility to all primary and secondary schools (Original in Chinese). Retrieved from http://www.moe.gov.cn/publicfiles/business/htmlfiles/moe/moe_1789/201309/157629.html

Normand, R. (2016). 'What works?': From health to education, the shaping of the European policy of evidence. In K. Trimmer (Ed.), *Political pressures on educational and social research* (pp. 25–40). London: Routledge.

Normand, R., Liu, M., Carvalho, L. M., Oliveira, D. A., & LeVasseur, L. (Eds.). (2018). *Education policies and the restructuring of the educational profession: Global and comparative perspectives*. Singapore: Springer.

Ou, Y. (2012). Reflections on the 'real-name recommendation system for principals of middle schools' in the independent enrollment of colleges and universities (关于高校自主招生中 '中学校长实名推荐制' 的反思). *Jiangsu Higher Education*, 2, 13.

Qin, J. (2019). The road to quality education in 2035: Monitoring-based diagnosis and improvement of academic performance in recent development zones (迈向2035优质教育之路:基于监测的最近发展区学情诊断和改进成效). *Shanghai Research on Education*, 11, 60–63.

Rasmussen, P., & Zou, Y. (2014). The development of educational accountability in China and Denmark. *Education Policy Analysis Archives*, 22(121), 1–22.

Ruan, J. (2016). *Guanxi, social capital and school choice in China: The rise of ritual capital*. Cham: Springer.

Sellar, S., & Lingard, B. (2013). Looking east: Shanghai, PISA 2009 and the reconstitution of reference societies in the global education policy field. *Comparative Education*, 49(4), 464–485. doi:10.1080/03050068.2013.770943

Shen, N. (2010). Quality monitoring of basic education: An analysis perspective of academic evaluation system, management and evaluation (基础教育质量监测:学业评价制度分析视). *Educational Science Research*, (7), 37-40.

State Council. (2010). *National medium- and long-term educational guidelines 2010–2020* (Original in Chinese). Beijing: Ministry of Education. Retrieved from http://www.gov.cn/jrzg/2010-07/29/content_1667143.htm

State Council. (2012). *Announcement of the establishment of a steering committee for the supervision inspectorate* (Original in Chinese). Retrieved from http://www.gov.cn/zwgk/2012-08/31/content_2214419.htm

State Council. (2014). *Opinions by the State Council on deepening the reform of the examination enrollment system* (Original in Chinese). Retrieved from http://www.gov.cn/zhengce/content/2014-09/04/content_9065.htm

Su, J. (2020). Changes in China's educational supervision system since reform and opening up (改革开放以来我国教育督导制度变迁). *Journal of Beijing Normal University (Social Sciences)*, 1, 30–37.

Tan, C. (2017). Chinese responses to Shanghai's performance in PISA. *Comparative Education*, 53(2), 209–223. doi:10.1080/03050068.2017.1299845

Teets, J. C. (2013). Let many civil societies bloom: The rise of consultative authoritarianism in China. *The China Quarterly*, 213, 19–38.

Wang, L., & Lewin, K. (2016). *Two decades of basic education in rural China: Transitions and challenges for development*. Singapore: Springer.

Xin, T. (2019). Study on the deepening reforms of education evaluation and establishment of a sound education evaluation system in China (深化教育评价改革建立良性的教育评价制度). *Tsinghua Journal of Education*, 40(1), 8–10.

Xin, T., Jiang, Y., Lin, C., Shi, B., & Liu, X. (2016). On the connotation characteristics and framework orientation of students' core accomplishment development (论学生发展核心素养的内涵特征及框架定位). *China Education Journal*, 6, 3–7.

Yang, J. (2001). New explorations of the theory and practice of education supervision in China in the past 20 years (20年来我国教育督导理论与实践的新探索). *Journal of the Northwest University (Social Science Edition)*, 38(2), 41.

Zhang, L. (2012). Summary of China-based quality monitoring of basic education (我国基础教育质量监测工作综述). *Journal of Hebei Radio & TV University*, 17(5), 97–99.

Zhang, W. (2019). Regulating private tutoring in China: Uniform policies, diverse responses, *ECNU Review of Education*, 2(1), 25–43. doi:10.1177/2096531119840868

Zhang, Y. (2010). Reforms on colleges and universities independent enrollment: Motivation, problems and countermeasures (高校自主招生改革的动因、问题及对策). *Peking University Education Review*, 2, 30–42.

Zhou, X. (2019). *Changed and unchanged: the transformation of educational policies on assessment and evaluation in China* (Doctoral dissertation). doi:10.1080/02680939.2016.1219769. sRetrieved from https://www.utupub.fi/handle/10024/148415

Zhou, X., Kallo, J., Rinne, R., & Suominen, O. (2018). From restoration to transitions: Delineating the reforms of education inspection in China. *Educational Assessment, Evaluation and Accountability*, 30(3), 313–342.

Zhou, X., Rinne, R., & Kallo, J. (2018). Shifting discourses of equality and equity of basic education: An analysis of national policy documents in China. *Nordic Journal of Studies in Educational Policy*, 4(3), 168–179.

10 Performance-based accountability in Brazil: Trends of diversification and integration

Dalila Andrade Oliveira and Luís Miguel Carvalho

Introduction

The chapter analyzes the emergence and consolidation of results-based and results-oriented modes of regulation in the federal state of Brazil, focusing on their manifestations: (a) the accountability policies formulated and implemented in several Brazilian states; and (b) the adoption of the Organization for Economic Co-operation and Development (OECD) Programme for International Student Assessment (PISA) by an important body of the Brazilian federal high administration – the Instituto Nacional de Estudos e Pesquisas Educacionais Anísio Teixeira (INEP) –, and the adoption of the 'PISA-based Test for Schools' at state and local levels. The analysis highlights the diversification and integration effects on public policies, resulting from the tension between transnational, national, regional and local regulatory dynamics.

Theoretically based on the 'multi-regulation' approach to education policy, and having as its main empirical basis the results of a dozen studies on performance-based accountability (PBA) policies in Brazilian states (see, for example, Oliveira, Duarte, & Rodrigues, 2019),[1] the chapter then unfolds into two separate analyses, concerning, respectively: (a) the mosaic of accountability policies in Brazil, focusing on the diverse types of accountability policy enactments in the country's Northeastern states; (b) Brazil's incorporation into the transnational circuits of 'datafication'. In the first case, the chapter depicts the intra-national diversification on PBA enactment at the state level. In the second case, the chapter shows the diverse effects of the adherence to international references at federal, state and local levels.

The chapter is organized as follows. In the first part, it summarizes the theoretical perspective. In the second, it presents the political and cultural contexts for the circulation and activation of results-based regulation in Brazil, highlighting two specific aspects the country which have considerable influence on its institutions – the characteristics of the Brazilian polity and the socio-economic inequalities between Brazilian regions. Thirdly, it analyses the emergence and consolidation of results-based regulation, focusing, on the one hand, on the accountability policies set in motion in Brazil; and, on the other hand, on the intensification and broadening of the use of international large-scale assessments (ILSA) as resources legitimated, by public authorities and federal, state and municipal experts, as valid for monitoring school systems. The chapter closes with a discussion of how these policies, which are currently in development, resonate with those policies that circulate internationally, especially through the agency of international organizations, with a particular focus on the OECD and PISA.

Performance-based accountability in Brazil through the lenses of multi-regulation and mobility

Theoretically, the chapter approaches performance-based accountability through the lenses of political sociology and comparative education. First, our analysis is informed by a political sociology that regards public policies as processes – and results – of the intervention of public authorities, through the normative production of such policies and the use of other policy instruments. In addition, there is a variety of state and non-state actors (e.g., bureaucrats and experts from the state technostructure, media, professional and union associations, philanthropic organizations, international organizations, and national and multinational companies), located at different scales (regional, national, local, supranational), who also take part in defining the common good and in determining how social processes should be coordinated, although such actors might possess different resources to exercise agency (see Commaille, 2004; Lascoumes & Le Galès, 2007). Secondly, the approach is also informed by theoretical elements that shape as a *problématique* the transfer, translation and transformation of policies, ideas, models, people, and practices, as signs of the mobility of social phenomena. These theorizations are richly synthesized in the well-known words of Robert Cowen (2009: 315), here paraphrased and applied to our subject: '*as [it]* performance-based accountability *moves, it morphs*'.

Within the policy sociology approach, the concept of multi-regulation helps to understand the complexity of educational policy processes by observing educational policies as resulting from plural agencies, located at diverse political-administrative levels (transnational, national and local) and in the context of different institutional arrangements, set into play by different types of instruments (normative, incentive, evaluative, contractual), and configuring different regulatory regimes (bureaucratic-professional, post-bureaucratic, neo-bureaucratic) (Barroso, 2005, 2018; Maroy, 2009; Maroy & Dupriez, 2000). The concept also invites us to observe the horizontal character and circularity of the multiple and interdependent relations of the various actors that intervene in public policies processes (Lascoumes & Le Galés, 2007).

From this perspective, it is important to capture the worldwide circulation of accountability policies in terms of its 'fluidity', 'multiplicity' and 'historical contingency', using Tom Popkewitz's words (2000: 6). Furthermore, it is needed to take the intensity and effects of the relations between the various instances of multi-regulation as matters that require 'proof' and not as *a priori* results of hierarchical connections (Carvalho, 2015). For these reasons, we focus here the mediation, reinterpretation and re-contextualization that mark the trajectory of discursive categories, organizational forms and technologies of government and management, related to the accountability policies that, since the 1990s, circulate – *move* – between social and political spaces, internal and external to Brazil, and participate in the transformations observed in teaching work (Oliveira, 2007).

Bearing in mind the existence of various variants of accountability (see e.g., Maroy & Voisin, 2013, 2014; Ozga, 2013; Verger & Parcerisa, 2017), we inscribe the phenomenon of the circulation of accountability policies within a *problématique* that aims to understand the processes and effects of the mobility of discourses, models, knowledge and instruments of accountability policies, by the (aforementioned) multiple and interconnected spaces of education policy. Following the formulation given to it by Cowen (2006, 2009), this *problématique* invites the questioning of what he calls *shape-shifting* – that is 'the metamorphoses of the institutions and social processes, which are mobile' (2009: 323) – around three interconnected concepts: the transfer of ideas and instruments of accountability variants in international and transnational spaces; the translation of ideas and instruments that, spatially transferred, are reinterpreted in each context; the transformation of ideas and (translated) instruments, in the course of their re-contextualization, either becoming indigenous or extinguishing (2006: 566).

The embracing of the notions of multi-regulation and shape-shifting for the analysis of the manifestations of accountability policies in Brazil has the following corollary: in the federal, state and municipal contexts, public policies materialize different models of accountability. Thus, in the third part of this chapter, a typology of these forms of deployment will be proposed, based on research carried out in the Northeastern states of Brazil whose political and social specificities are emphasized in the next pages.

Contextualizing the circulation and activation of results-based regulation in Brazil

As mentioned above, educational systems around the world have undergone important changes in the past three decades through the circulation of policies at the international level. This has a great influence on national contexts, with large-scale evaluation as their greatest instrument. Since they allow comparisons to be made between different countries and regions, such policies have been widely admitted in Brazil, given its size, its federal system and its great regional disparity.

In the midst of these changes, which demand answers based on criteria of effectiveness and efficiency defined at an international level, Brazil, through the federal government, principally the Ministry of Education, has mobilized states, municipalities and the Federal District to promote transformations in the management of public education aimed at achieving better performance in large-scale assessments. Key actors in this mobilization process are the INEP, the National Union of Municipal Education Directors (UNDIME) and the National Council of Education Secretaries (CONSED). In the national context, as in the international one, the movement and transfer of policies, through the production of comparative knowledge, seeks to motivate countries classified as 'experiencing difficulties' (i.e., with low educational performance) to be inspired by 'good practices'; this phenomenon has reinforced the rise of evidence-based knowledge. In the national context, the federal government, through actors such as the mentioned INEP, UNDIME and CONSED, seeks to encourage state and municipal managers to adhere to these logics. School systems are encouraged to respond for the sake of the country's economic development; simultaneously, it is expected that education will promote greater social justice through the inclusion of the most socially vulnerable. These policies reach the school context as requirements that education professionals must be responsible for, resulting in tensions and adaptations. School managers are the main subjects obliged to be accountable.

It is, therefore, a complex process that requires in-depth analysis of its determinants and dynamics. In the Brazilian case, it is also necessary to take into account local, regional and national specificities, understanding the extent to which they can be re-configured, responding to international trends (Ball, 2002; Carter & O'Neill, 1995). In this chapter, we highlight two such contextual specificities, as they are of substantial institutional strength: these are the characteristics of the Brazilian polity; and the socio-economic inequalities between Brazilian regions.

The structures of intervention by federal authorities in the educational field

Brazil is a federal republic composed of 26 states, the Federal District and 5,570 municipalities, entities that have relative autonomy, located in five geographical regions that present significant economic, social, cultural and political differences.

Brazilian education has a systemic organization with its competencies shared by the federal entities, defined in the Federal Constitution of 1988, that determined that the Union, the States and the Federal District are allowed to legislate concurrently, on education, culture, teaching and sport (Brazil, 1988).[2] These competences are regulated by the Law of Guidelines and Bases of National Education (LDB), Law no. 9.394/96. The primary role of the federal government in regulating education is made explicit in the first paragraph of article 8 of the LDB: 'The Union will be responsible for coordinating the national education policy, articulating the different levels and systems and exercising a normative, redistributive and supplementary role in relation to other educational instances' (Brazil, 1996).

The Ministry of Education (MEC), an executive body, and the National Education Council (CNE), a normative body, are the Federal Government institutions dedicated to the fulfillment of the functions and attributions of the federal public power in matters of education, involving the formulation and evaluation of the national education policy. In this sense, INEP plays a crucial role. As a federal autonomous organization linked to the MEC, INEP was created in 1937 to promote studies and research in education with the goal of supporting the formulation and implementation of education policies. However, throughout its history, especially from the beginning of the 1990s, its actions have been changing, focusing especially on conducting periodic assessments of the Brazilian educational system. INEP conducts statistical surveys and assessments at all levels and modes of education, in addition to being responsible for the administration of PISA in the country. From 2007 onwards, with the creation of the Basic Education Development Index (IDEB), INEP started to provide an indicator of 'quality of education' for all municipalities and states in the country. This indicator measures the level of school performance.

IDEB was established by the Education Development Plan (PDE) (Brazil, 2007), through Decree No. 6.094/2007, with the purpose of offering effective instruments for evaluation and the improvement of the quality of education to states, municipalities and the Federal District. This Decree provides for the Goals Plan and the All for Education Commitment, which includes 28 guidelines to be followed by states, the Federal District and municipalities with the participation of other entities and institutions of society. It also establishes the Plan of Articulated Actions (PAR) as a requirement for obtaining technical and financial support from the Union (Brazil, 2007). Therefore, the PDE inaugurates a new collaboration regime, reconciling the actions of the federal entities, primarily involving political decision, technical actions and the consolidation of the demand for the improvement of education indicators.

Considering the dimensions of the Brazilian educational system, the resources involved in this process that seeks to foster a 'new collaboration regime' were not negligible, which explains the great interest of municipal and state managers in meeting the expectations of the PDE. UNDIME was created in 1986 as an autonomous, non-profit civil association that brings together municipal education leaders. CONSED, the National Council of Secretaries of Education, also created in 1986, is a private, non-profit association that brings together the State and Federal District Education Departments. These two entities work in partnership and have great reach in the Brazilian educational context, since they are organized in all the country's states. An expression of this partnership is the *Colabora Educação* movement, which was created from a thematic table of the Consultative Council of the Inter-American Development Bank involving a set of private and philanthropic institutions, such as: the Natura Institute; Instituto Unibanco; Itaú Social Foundation; the All for Education Movement; the Lemann Foundation; Instituto Positivo; the Ayrton Senna Institute; and the Conceição Moura Institute. The Colabora Movement was created with 'the aim of strengthening governance and collaborative practices among federal entities within the scope of public education policies'.[3] Another important movement that emerged from the joint action of this partnership is the Movimento Nacional Pela Base, which expresses how such actors (UNDIME and CONSED) have been central to the process of conducting national education policy and how they have worked together with private entities directly influencing school contexts. Tarlau & Moeller (2019) consider that the National Common Curriculum Base (BNCC) became the most important educational reform initiative of the Ministry of Education between the years 2015 and 2017. Tarlau and Moeller (2019) suggest that this movement involved a broad arrangement in an accelerated process of policies that depended on the practice of philanthropic consent, that is, the use of material resources by foundations, knowledge production, media power and informal and formal networks to obtain the consent of various social and institutional actors to support a public policy. This movement benefited from the decisive participation of the Lemann Foundation, but involved UNDIME and CONSED as main actors. According to Tarlau and Moeller (2019), these foundations, like the Lemann, influence the consensus of state employees on which policies to adopt.

Inequalities as a social and political question

Brazil is the largest and most populous country in Latin America, but also one of the most unequal: it occupies the tenth position in the latest inequalities report of the United Nations Human Development Program (UNDP). With a population of about 207 million inhabitants and occupying almost half of the area that makes up South America, its educational system is characterized by great complexity and diversity, revealing hybridization processes, in the sense given by Canclini (1998) in *Culturas Híbridas*, when addressing processes related to the relationship between modernization and modernity, as well as tradition and modernity, in Latin America. According to Canclini (1998), the process of cultural hybridization in Latin America is characterized as the socio-cultural process in which structures or practices, which existed in separate forms, are combined to generate new structures, objects and practices. Since it is the trigger of combinations and unforeseen syntheses, this hybridity, for Canclini (1998), has marked the twentieth century in the most different areas, enabling developments, productivity and creative power distinct from the intercultural mixes already existing in the region.

The Brazilian educational system serves 48,455,867 students in basic education, according to the last School Census (Brazil/INEP, 2019). Of these, 39,460,618 attend public educational establishments. The Basic Education sector has 2,226,423 teachers and 181,939 schools. Despite this contingent of enrollment in Basic Education, some 2.8 million children and young people between 4 and 17 years of age are not attending school (PNAD/IBGE, 2015). The guarantee of the right to education comes up against very unequal socio-economic conditions, which have a regional expression in the country. According to the study, 'Scenarios of school exclusion in Brazil' (UNDP, 2018), out of the 1.5 million young people between 15 and 17 years old and who are out of school, many of them do not even finish elementary school (9 years of schooling), with 549,137 of them in the Northeastern region of the country.

In the same way, it is possible to say that working conditions among teachers also vary widely in different regions of the country. Salaries and working and career conditions are extremely unequal among professionals from different municipal and state public networks, including among those with the same training, qualifications and length of service. The same can be said about the school infrastructure, which varies according to the financial capacity of each municipality and state. (Oliveira & Vieira, 2012; Soares Neto, Jesus, Karino, Andrade, 2013)

Performance-based accountability in Brazil

On the manifestations of results-based regulation in the Northeastern states of Brazil

Since accountability policies result from the contractualization process in public education and have large-scale assessments as their main accountability instrument, we can say that, from the institution of the PDE in 2007, establishing as regulatory instruments the IDEB and the PAR, the federal government started to promote a results-based form of regulation of national education. Although the Brazilian states and municipalities enjoy relative autonomy to legislate on educational matters, the means developed from the PDE allowed the federal government to capture these federated entities and to regulate national education by defining the necessary metrics and the goals to be reached by states, municipalities and schools.

However, the adherence to PBA by these federated entities varies, even considering the prominent role played by UNDIME and CONSED as diffusers of government policies defined at the federal level; for different reasons, states and municipalities do not always respond in the same way or with the same commitment. However, the economic condition of the poorest states meant that in the end there is a degree of dependence and subordination of the state governments in relation to the education policies imposed by the federal government. According to a documentary study on educational policies underway in the nine states that make up the Northeastern region of the country (Oliveira, Duarte, & Rodrigues, 2019), it was possible to verify that despite the importance of the evaluation in these contexts, the states respond in different degrees and through different strategies to these policies. We can say that Brazil has developed since 2007 with IDEB a system of accountability in order to measure student performance and commit schools to the results achieved. This system is run by the federal government, but functions as a chain comprising the states, municipalities and schools.

Since the early 1990s, the culture of evaluation has been installed in Brazil through the institution of the National System for the Evaluation of Basic Education (Saeb). The National High School Examination (ENEM), created in the second half of the 1990s, and IDEB, are among the important indicators that were developed at the national level as instruments for the regulation of Basic Education and that ended up gaining the trust of society and, above all, of state and municipal governments regardless of their political affiliations. The belief in evaluation has grown enormously in the country in recent decades, which is revealed by the increase in its instruments, given the profusion of the development of many Brazilian states' and municipalities' own evaluation systems. Educational legislation also demonstrates the widespread acceptance that large-scale assessments and their indicators have with different sectors, as demonstrated in Law 13,005/2014, which establishes the National Education Plan (PNE), in its goal 7, which establishes as criterion for measuring quality the proficiencies of IDEB and, more specifically, strategy 7.11, which referred to PISA directly as the desired proficiency and as a quality criterion.

In the studies carried out on the educational policy of the states that make up the Northeastern region of Brazil, when seeking to establish parallels between their educational contexts, the centrality of the evaluation policies for Basic Education becomes evident, and, in particular, the importance attached to IDEB as a quality education reference. In the analysis of this material, the strong presence of evaluation policies stands out as a common feature in the nine states of the region as a strategy for improving education. Regardless of the political party composition of the state governments, the evaluation policy adopted follows the national orientation of reaching IDEB averages, as well as establishing, within states, their own evaluation systems. Concomitantly, the quest to improve their results in a context of enormous social inequality, as demonstrated in the states of the Northeast, has led to the adoption by their governments of strategies that vary from school reinforcement, the awarding of teachers and students, the extension of school hours, forms of involvement and the participation of professionals and family members in school management, among others.

From studies carried out on the educational policy of these nine states (Oliveira & Clementino, 2019), it is possible to create a typology (Table 10.1) of regulation of government action: States with high-, medium- and low-accountability systems.

We can thus consider that three states in the Northeastern region – Ceará, Paraíba and Pernambuco – adopt high-accountability policies characterized as 'high stakes'. In these states, test scores are used to determine punishments (such as sanctions, penalties, reductions in funds, negative publicity), praise (awards, public celebration, positive publicity), promotion or compensation (salary increases or bonuses for administrators and teachers). In the state of Ceará, for example, for students who reach the grade that leaves them at the ADEQUATE level, a laptop computer is offered as a 'bonus', and for teachers and staff from schools with 80% student participation in tests and 10% improvement in Portuguese Language and in Mathematics, the payment of a 14th salary in the

Table 10.1 Accountability systems adopted by state policies (in the nine states of Northeastern Brazil)

	High accountability	Average accountability	Low or no accountability
Normative action intensity	Strong	Strong	Non-existent or weak (evaluation rhetoric)
Strategy and devices	Action '*over*' the actors Bonuses and awards for results Sanctions and punishments[a]	Action '*with*' the actors Participative, with actors' involvement and commitment	Without explicit strategies or devices
States	Ceará, Paraíba, Pernambuco	Alagoas, Maranhão and Piauí	Bahia, Sergipe and Rio Grande do Norte

[a] As moral constraint for school managers and negative publicity.

year is guaranteed. In the state of Paraíba, it was instituted the 'Ficha' (form), applied to elementary and high school students in the State Education System who, during the month, skipped classes for five consecutive school days, or seven alternate days. This form is linked to the Bolsa Família program, for which the student assistance in 85% of classes is conditional to receiving the benefit. The 14th salary per year is offered to professionals in basic education schools in the state public network, as a prize for competence in school management and for the development of innovative and successful experiences in improving the quality of education that are reflected in improved performance in tests. The state also has a programme called the Prêmio Mestres da Educação (Master's of Education Award) that offers teachers a 15th salary a year as a reward for developing successful teaching practices. In Pernambuco, a contractual regime based on evaluation systems was instituted in 2008, with the adoption of the 'School Management Commitment Term' linked to the Educational Performance Bonus (BDE). It is, therefore, a contractual instrument agreed between principals (school) and the Pernambuco Department of Education (SEE/PE), in which the institutional performance goals to be achieved annually are established. This Term of School Management Commitment aims to guarantee the schools' engagement in the raising of educational indicators. School professionals who reach 50% of test proficiency are offered a bonus that is calculated proportionally to the achievement of the established goal.

We can consider as a second group of states those that make up a system of average or medium accountability, in which the incentives to improve performance are not directly addressed to teachers in the form of awards or sanctions, but through participatory strategies that seek their involvement and commitment. Alagoas, Maranhão and Piauí make up this group. In Alagoas, the Programa Escola 10 (School 10 Program) was created, with the purpose of guaranteeing the learning rights of Basic Education students from all public systems in the state. It is a concertation of the state government with the municipalities in order to improve the IDEB. The program aims to ensure that all public school students are literate in Portuguese and Mathematics by the end of the third year of elementary school, to reduce illiteracy and drop-out rates, in addition to reducing age-grade distortion (school delay). The actions include three axes: pedagogical monitoring, supply of teaching materials and periodic evaluations. In Maranhão, several programmes and actions were created to improve the IDEB, for example, the Plano Mais IDEB (More IDEB Plan), which sets strategies to strengthen secondary education and the improvement of educational indexes with a focus on continuing education, monitoring income and school flow, and in raising learning proficiency. With regard to continuing education, there is a focus on the subjects that are evaluated in large-scale tests, through the development of training in Portuguese and Mathematics. In Piauí, SAEPI, which is the state's own assessment system, serves as a reference for guiding work in schools. The secretariat offers workshops on data appropriation of SAEPI results for principals, coordinators and supervisors and guidance on how teachers can carry out pedagogical activities based on test results.

Finally, we can group the last three states – Bahia, Rio Grande do Norte and Sergipe – as those with either low accountability or a lack of accountability. This third group is characterized by adopting policies that, despite recognizing evaluation as the instrument of quality in education, do not have a very developed evaluation system, and in which no clear normative provisions were found that link actions directed at teachers by the secretariat with the pursuit of test results. These last two groups can be characterized by low-stakes policies which, despite the presence of evaluation systems, still implement low-risk testing, and thus have little impact on the lives of students, teachers and schools.

This typology helps us to understand how evaluation policies have been widely disseminated in the country, despite their reception being varied from state to state. Although it is not possible to explain these different forms of reception, we can nevertheless suggest that, more than the ideological or partisan orientations of the governments that adopt these policies, the local institutional structures, notions of progressivism carried to some extent by political actors, and also the degree of engagement of these actors in a political project converging to human capital theory, seem to be the most likely determinants.

Mobility and mobilization of ILSA in Brazil

The setting of results-based regulation in the Brazilian political and cultural space of education can be understood by taking into account how this modality of regulation emerges, socially and technically, in the transnational circuits that intensify the use – and the legitimacy of the use – of international large-scale assessments (ILSA) as proper resources to steer school systems and to support policies claiming for accountability. Two related phenomena, recent and crossing the different levels of Brazilian polity, will occupy our analysis in the next pages: the connections between INEP (the *federal* body responsible for the design and application of evaluation instruments to support the so-called quality education policies) and OECD's discourses and technical practices; the adoption, at the *state* and *municipal* level, of the PISA-based test for schools (PISA-S).

INEP and PISA: Inscribing the Federation into the world that counts

The discursive and technical connection between INEP and OECD is visible in the relationship that has been established between two of their main instruments, respectively, IDEB and PISA indicators. These connections have already·been addressed in studies by Villani (2018) and Villani & Oliveira (2018), based on an ethnography with INEP experts who participate in the PISA tests in Brazil, manifest themselves in Brazilian public policy matrix-texts, as well as in public policy processes.

In the first case, the inclusion of both indicators in the main national performance targets is significant: IDEB, which brings together school flow data and averages of student results in national tests, is registered in Goal 7 of the major National Education Plan, where it is stated that IDEB should reach the average value of 6, on a 10-point scale in 2022; and the improvement of the average of

Brazilian PISA results (in mathematics, reading and science) is one of the 36 strategies approved to achieve this goal. Furthermore, the improvement of PISA results is linked to a greater effort – the one of guiding Brazil to 'reach the educational level of the average of the OECD countries'.

Therefore, we are not just facing a case of 'adding' IDEB and PISA indicators within a political text, but a more complex connection, involving the re-composition of IDEB/PISA knowledge (statistical, above all) as well as organizational and social factors that involve both INEP and OECD. Regarding the relationship IDEB-PISA, INEP experts refer to a 'compatibility between distributions of proficiencies' registered in PISA and in the Brazilian national test (Saeb) that integrates the IDEB indicator (Brazil, 2014; Villani & Oliveira, 2018: 1352). This compatibility, detailed in an IDEB technical document, 'consists in identifying classifications of the scale of the SAEB that correspond to a specific performance in PISA (and vice versa)'.[4] Concerning the relationship INEP-OECD, they refer to socialization processes, within the context of the implementation of PISA in Brazil, including the training of INEP experts and the training that these experts then established, namely in universities and foundations involved with the production of educational knowledge (Villani & Oliveira, 2018: 1353).

However, this is not a linear connection process. Three aspects illustrate the complexity involved. On the one hand, regarding the relationship between IDEB and PISA, the indicators are not indisputably compatible due to the difference between the evaluated objects to which they are associated;[5] thus, for the experts involved, the technical sophistication currently achieved still seems insufficient (see Soares & Xavier, 2013). On the other hand, regarding the relationship INEP-OECD, INEP actors are not passive receivers of PISA, and they even take it as a legitimizing resource for promoting their status in public policy in Brazil, as much as their agency in national, regional and local spaces and in their interactions with decision-makers (see Villani & Oliveira, 2018: 1351–55). Finally, PISA does not fail to constitute a threat or a competitor to IDEB for an institutional reason: its cosmopolitan and politically decontextualized referentiality.

Several studies have indicated the effects of the existence of this pair of indicators – one national (IDEB), the other international (PISA) – on the processes of multi-regulation of education in Brazil (e.g., Almeida, Dalben, & Freitas, 2013; Oliveira, Duarte & Clementino, 2017; Oliveira & Jorge, 2015). Its effects have been described supporting the expansion of standardization, within the institutional regulation generated by the federal level, as well as reinforcing market-oriented regulatory processes at the local level. Thus, their regulatory presence has been associated with the intensification of federal pressure over state and municipal departments of education, schools and headteachers, teachers and families, in order to set performance goals based on the results in IDEB. And their regulatory presence has been related to the intensification of competitive mechanisms between public (state and municipal) and private schools.

Within this context, a new act of multi-regulation by results has been present in Brazilian education in 2017: the PISA-based test for schools (PISA-S).

PISA-S in Brazilian schools, municipalities and states: The route to transnational certification

Although referenced by INEP actors, as a demand from private organizations (see Villani & Oliveira, 2018: 1355), in its first pilot application carried out in Brazil, in 2017, PISA-S was mainly applied in the public sector – 33 of the 46 schools assessed were public schools – and having as main target the schools of the Municipality of Sobral (23/46). This municipality, located in the Northeastern state of Ceará, has shown high-accountability policies and is publicly acknowledged for the good results in national tests, with the city being referred to as a vivid example of the possibility of a high-quality public education in Brazil.

The implementation of the PISA-S pilot in public and private schools that had previously stood out in national assessments, resulted from a deliberate choice of one of PISA-S co-promoters (with the OECD) and sponsoring Brazil: the Lemann Foundation (see, for example, Fundação Lemann & Itaú BBA, 2012). This philanthropic organization is one of the main promoters of the *Todos pela Educação* (*All for Education*) movement; as suggested above, this is a coalition launched by actors from the business world (high finance and industry) that has been able to involve, since 2016, third sector and governmental actors around one overarching proposal: to reorganize public education in Brazil by prioritizing the introduction of quality standards (see Martins & Krawczyk, 2016, 2018). Significantly, when it comes to importing PISA-S into Brazil, the Lemann Foundation highlights the intended benchmarking effect: 'To contribute to the construction of policies based on data and evidence, the Lemann Foundation brought PISA for Schools to Brazil (…). The objective was to better understand the teaching systems of the teaching units that generate good results so that they can serve as inspiration and reference to other Brazilian schools.'[6]

Meanwhile, the PISA-S universe seems to be expanding in Brazil, finding new subjects and new partners. In its second application, in 2019, PISA-S was carried out in 300 schools in the state of São Paulo – the richest and most populous Brazilian state, whose capital was identified as the largest generator of wealth among all municipalities in Brazil in 2017 (IBGE).[7] The adoption of PISA-S by the public authorities of São Paulo was justified by two reasons: the introduction of 'important changes in the way of students learning in São Paulo', in the context of a utilitarian vocation given to the school curriculum; the gathering of information to support political and administrative decision-making.[8] In October 2019, an agreement was signed between the entity accredited by the OECD to manage the application of PISA-S in Brazil – the Cesgranrio Foundation (the private foundation responsible, for decades, for the application in Brazil of the main national exams for elementary and secondary education) – and a representative organization of the private sector, the National Federation of Private Schools, for the realization of PISA-S 2020.

In the argument justifying the adhesion of this sector to PISA (see for example, Pereira, 2019), once again the two main lines of argument above noted comes to the front. One, related with education and curriculum, envisions the student as a singular individual, proposes student-centred education, curricula based on competences and active learning, connecting the student with the so-called current and future daily life needs. The other, related to changes in educational systems governance and management, claims for practices aligned with international standards, benchmarking, results-based steering, claims which have long been in vogue in PISA frameworks and recommendations.

Finally, there has been an expansion of the nucleus of sponsors participating in the effort to implement PISA-S in Brazil. The presentation event of 2019 PISA-S is a symptomatic example of the variety of state and non-state actors, with diversified ranges of agency – municipal, state, federal, international – already involved in the Brazilian PISA-S.[9] This variety allows us to point out how this new OECD tool activates and legitimizes the presence of new regulatory spaces and multiple state and non-state actors: philanthropy organizations (those funding the programme); public and private expert organizations, from the fields of educational research and evaluation; heads of public schools; business education groups and heads of private schools; municipal and state authorities. These new intra-national ILSA-related spaces are contexts for regulatory agency, where material, informational, financial, and even symbolic (for example, status and reputation) resources are exchanged. Concurrently, new interdependencies are established; and new ways of understanding – what school education should be and how educational systems should be governed – are held. Together, these features seem to be reinforcing the knowledge/power of expert organizations and the positive status given to evidence-based policies.

Concluding lines: Trends of diversification and integration

In this chapter we have analysed the emergence of results-based regulation at the Brazilian federal polity. We focus on two manifestations that we consider representative of such a regulatory regime: accountability policies formulated and implemented in several Brazilian states; PISA adoption by an important federal high administration body (INEP) and PISA-S adoption at state and municipal levels. Our analysis sought to highlight the effects of international integration and intra-national diversification on public policies for education in Brazil, resulting from tensions between the transnational, national, regional and local regulatory dynamics. Having as its main empirical basis the results of studies on PBA policies in the Northeastern states, the most unequal region among the five geographical regions that make Brazil, we discuss the mosaic of accountability policies that are developed in these states, inducted by the federal government, manly through IDEB; and the Brazilian integration in transnational 'datafication' circuits, particularly in those take OECD's PISA as *the* reference for improving quality in education.

There has been a growing acceptance of evaluation in Brazilian society in the past decades, which can be noticed by the expansion and increment of tests, both those under the charge of INEP, at the federal level, and those developed in most states and in many Brazilian municipalities, with their own assessment systems. Facing these previous research observations, we seek to analyse the extent to which the connection between INEP's discursive and technical practices and the role played by other institutions such as UNDIME and CONSED have been responsible for the spread of the assessment instruments that support PBA in the states; and also the result of this in the adoption, at the state and municipal level, of PISA-S. Our hypothesis is that the expansion and consolidation of these policies are related to a regulatory process at the national level based on the mirroring of PISA as the great reference for quality of education that circulates internationally.

Among the strategies used for the implementation of a results-based regulation mode, the form of financing by the federal government through PAR, linking financial support to states to the adoption of the policies and metrics established by it, stands out as an important mechanism that explains to some extent the adherence of the states that make up the poorest and most unequal region of the country to these policies.

From a closer analysis of a specific region – the Brazilian Northeast – is possible to perceive that, to some degree, accountability policies are present in the educational context of the nine states analysed, always using IDEB as a reference for quality, showing a certain degree of adherence to regulatory policies emanating from the federal government and disseminated essentially through convincing state (CONSED) and municipal (UNDIME) managers. However, despite the intended homogenization of the assessment forms (through a single test and the same indicator, IDEB), we observe that there is differentiation in their reception in each context, ranging from the most accentuated forms of accountability to the mildest ones. These differences need to be better observed and analysed. Still, they may be indicating more or less resistance to the regulatory processes imposed from 'above' or 'outside', which may be related to the fact that this occurs in the Latin American context, already marked by hybrid cultures in the sense attributed by Canclini (1998).

Notes

1 Studies conducted at the research group Grupo de Estudos sobre Política Educacional e Trabalho Docente, Universidade Federal de Minas Gerais (Gestrado, UFMG) with CNPq funding.
2 More precisely, in article 24, item IX.
3 http://movimentocolabora.org.br (viewed December 8, 2019).
4 http://download.inep.gov.br/educacao_basica/portal_ideb/metodologias/Nota_Tecnica_n3_compatibilizacao_PISA_SAEB.pdf (viewed March 5, 2020). This implies to *a priori* accept as valid both the equivalence between the performance of Brazilian students in PISA and the performance of 8th grade students in SAEB, and the equivalence between the two tests. Then, it involves technical compatibility steps, described as follows: '[step one] identify which PISA note, called the reference note here, one wants to find approximate correspondence with in the SAEB, the scores corresponding to the median or the average obtained by students in the countries participating in PISA 2003, or the average of OECD countries. In the second step, from the distribution of students in PISA, the percentage was calculated of Brazilian students positioned above the reference grade. From this percentage it was verified that the grade separates exactly the same proportion of students in the SAEB]'.
5 The Brazilian test focuses on the school curriculum; PISA does not.

6 https://fundacaolemann.org.br/noticias/pisa-para-escolas (viewed December 23, 2019).
7 The biggest generators of wealth that year were: São Paulo (with 10.6% of the Brazilian GDP), Rio de Janeiro (5.1%), Brasília (3.7%), Belo Horizonte (1.4%), Curitiba (1.3%), Osasco, also in the state of São Paulo (1.2%), and Porto Alegre (1.1%).
8 https://www.educacao.sp.gov.br/noticia/sao-paulo-e-o-primeiro-estado-aderir-ao-pisa/ (viewed December 23, 2019). In addition to these schools, 40 other units of a technical education network in the same state (Centro Paulo Souza) and 36 schools linked to Fundação Bradesco (private sector) will have been evaluated.
9 The event ('International Conference – Launch – Pisa for Schools in Brazil') brought together, on June 13, 2019, representatives of the following segments: federal public authorities – National Education Council (body with normative, deliberative and advisory responsibilities to the Minister Education) and INEP (techno-structural body of the federal administration); structure credited to develop PISA-S in Brazil (Fundação Cesgranrio); financiers of PISA-S in Brazil (Lemann Foundation, Roberto Marinho Foundation, Airton Senna Institute, All for Brazil Movement), politicians and staff from OECD (Director of Education and Skills and staff from PISA for Schools); Municipalities (Ceará); public schools and groups of schools and schools in the private sector. http://pisaforschools.cesgranrio.org.br/#supporters (last accessed on December 26, 2019).

References

Almeida, L. C., Dalben, A., & Freitas, L. C. (2013) O Ideb: limites e ilusões de uma política educacional. *Educação & Sociedade*, 34 (125): 1153–1174.

Ball, S. R. (2002) Reformar escolas/reformar professores e os terrores da performatividade. *Revista Portuguesa de Educação*, 15 (2): 3–23.

Barroso, J. (2005) O Estado, a educação e a regulação das políticas públicas. *Educação & Sociedade*, 26 (92): 725–751.

Barroso, J. (2018) A transversalidade das regulações em educação: modelo de análise para o estudo das políticas educativas em Portugal. *Educação & Sociedade*, 39 (145): 1075–1097.

Brazil. (1988) Constituição da República Federativa do Brasil de 1988. Disponível em. http://www.planalto.gov.br/ccivil_03/Constituicao/Constituicao.htm.

Brazil. (1996) Lei nº. 9.394, de 20 de dezembro de 1996. Estabelece as diretrizes e bases da educação nacional. Disponível em. http://www.planalto.gov.br/ccivil_03/leis/l9394.htm.

Brazil. (2007) *O plano de desenvolvimento da Educação: razões, princípios e programas*. Brazil: Ministério da Educação.

Brazil. (2014) Lei nº 13.005, de 25 de junho de 2014. Aprova o Plano Nacional de Educação - PNE e dá outras providências. Disponível em. http://www.planalto.gov.br/ccivil_03/_ato2011-2014/2014/lei/l13005.htm.

Brazil. (2019) Instituto Nacional de Estudos e Pesquisas Educacionais Anísio Teixeira. Censo da Educação Básica 2018: notas estatísticas. Brasília, 2019.

Canclini, N. G. (1998) *Culturas híbridas: estratégias para entrar e sair da modernidade*. São Paulo: Edusp.

Carter, D. S., & O'Neill, M. H. (Eds.) (1995) *International perspectives on educational reform and policy implementation*. Bristol, PA: Falmer Press.

Carvalho, L. M. (2015) As políticas públicas de educação sob o prisma da ação pública. *Currículo sem Fronteiras*, 15 (2): 314–333.

Commaille, J. (2004) Sociologie de l'action publique. In: L. Boussaguet, S. Jacquot, & P. Ravinet (Eds.), *Dictionnaire des politiques publiques* (pp. 413–421). Paris: Sciences-Po.

Cowen, R. (2006) Acting comparatively upon the educational world: Puzzles and possibilities. *Oxford Review of Education*, 32 (5): 561–573.

Cowen, R. (2009) The transfer, translation and transformation of educational processes: And their shape-shifting? *Comparative Education, 45* (3), 315–327.

Fundação Lemann & Itaú BBA (2012) *Excelência com equidade: as lições de escolas que oferecem um ensino de qualidade aos alunos com baixo nível socioeconômico.* São Paulo: Fundação Lemann, Itaú BBA.

Lascoumes, P., & Le Galès, P. (2007) *Sociologie de l'action publique.* Paris: Armand Colin.

Maroy, C. (2009) Convergences and hybridization of educational policies around 'post bureaucratic' models of regulation. *Compare: A Journal of Comparative and International Education, 39* (1): 71–84.

Maroy, C., & Dupriez, V. (2000) La régulation dans les systèmes scolaires: proposition théorique et analyse du cadre structurel en Belgique francophone. *Revue Française de Pédagogie, 130*: 73–87.

Maroy, C., & Voisin, A. (2013) As transformações recentes das políticas de accountability na educação: desafios e incidências das ferramentas de ação pública. *Educação & Sociedade, 34* (124): 881–901.

Maroy, C., & Voisin, A. (2014) Une typologie des politiques d'accountability en éducation: l'incidence de l'instrumentation et des théories de la régulation. *Education Comparée, 11*: 31–58.

Martins, E. M., & Krawczyk, N. R. (2016) Entrepreneurial influence in Brazilian education policies: The case of 'Todos Pela Educação'. In: A. Verger, C. Lubienski e G. Steiner-Khamsi (Orgs.), *World yearbook of education 2016: The global education industry.* London. Routledge.

Martins, E. M., & Krawczyk, N. R. (2018) Estratégias e incidência empresarial na atual política educacional brasileira: o caso do movimento 'Todos Pela Educação'. *Revista Portuguesa de Educação, 31*: 4–20.

Oliveira, D. A. (2007) Política educacional e a re-estruturação do trabalho docente: reflexões sobre o contexto latino-americano. *Educação & Sociedade, 28* (99): 355–375.

Oliveira, D. A., & Clementino, A. M. (2019) As políticas de responsabilização na Educação Básica nos estados do Nordeste. In: D. A. Oliveira, A. M. Duarte, & C. L. Rodrigues (Orgs.), *A política educacional em contexto de desigualdade.* Campinas, São Paulo: Mercado de Letras.

Oliveira, D. A., Duarte, A., & Clementino, A. M. (2017) A Nova Gestão Pública no contexto escolar e os dilemas dos(as) diretores(as). *Revista Brasileira de Política e Administração Educacional, 33* (3): 707–726.

Oliveira, D. A., Duarte, A. M., & Rodrigues, C. L. (Orgs.) (2019) *A política educacional em contexto de desigualdade.* Campinas, São Paulo: Mercado de Letras.

Oliveira, D. A., & Jorge, T. (2015) As políticas de avaliação, os docentes e a justiça escolar. *Currículo sem Fronteiras, 15* (2): 346–364.

Oliveira, D. A., & Vieira, L. F. (2012) *Trabalho na educação básica. A condição docente em sete estados brasileiros.* Belo Horizonte: Fino Traço Editora, p. 468.

Ozga, J. (2013) Accountability as a policy technology: Accounting for education performance in Europe. *International Review of Administrative Sciences, 79* (2): 292–309.

Pereira, E. C. (2019, November 29) Pisa-S: Novos padrões para o ensino nas escolas particulares. *Gazeta do Povo* [Edição online], 18:37. Available at: https://www.gazetadopovo.com.br/opiniao/artigos/pisa-s-novos-padroes-para-o-ensino-nas-escolas-particulares/ (última consulta em 26 December, 2019).

Popkewitz, T. S. (2000) Globalisation/regionalisation, knowledge, and the educational practices. In: T. S. Popkewitz (Ed.), *Educational knowledge: Changing relations between the, civil society, and the educational community state* (pp. 3–27). New York: University of New York Press.

Pnad/IBGE (2015). https://www.ibge.gov.br/estatisticas/sociais/populacao/9171-pesquisa-nacional-por-amostra-de-domicilios-continua-mensal.html?=&t=o-que-e

Soares, F. J., & Xavier, F. P. (2013) Pressupostos educacionais e estatísticos do Ideb. *Educação & Sociedade*, 34 (124): 903–923.

Soares Neto, J. J., Jesus, G. R., Karino, C. A., & Andrade, D. F. (2013) Uma escala para medir a infraestrutra escolar. *Revista Estudos de Avaliação Educacional, 24* (54): 78–99.

Tarlau, R., & Moeller, K. (2019) 'Philanthropizing' consent: How a private foundation pushed through national learning standards in Brazil. *Journal of Education Policy.* doi:10.1080/02680939.2018.1560504

United Nations Human Development Program (UNDP) (2018) *Human development indices and indicators* [Statistical update]. New York: UNDP.

Verger, A., & Parcerisa, L. (2017) *Accountability and education in the post-2015 period: International trends, enactment dynamics and socio-educational effects.* Think Piece for the UNESCO Global Education Monitoring Report 2017. Available at: http://unesdoc. unesco.org/images/0025/002595/259559e.pdf (accessed 4 December 2019).

Villani, M. (2018) The production cycle of PISA data in Brazil: The history of data beyond the numbers. *Sisyphus Journal of Education, 6* (3): 30–52.

Villani, M., & Oliveira, D. A. (2018) Avaliação Nacional e Internacional no Brasil: os vínculos entre o PISA e o IDEB. *Educação & Realidade, 43* (4): 1343–1362.

Enactments and effects of accountability and datafication: Controversies and critical issues

11 A sociological analysis of the effects of standards-based accountability policies on the distribution of educational outcomes

Aaron M. Pallas

Introduction

This chapter discusses the contributions of standards-based accountability systems on students' educational outcomes, paying particular attention to the social distribution of these outcomes. Do standards-based accountability systems 'work', raising student performance, and shrinking the distance in the typical performance of members of different student subgroups? If so, can we specify the conditions under which these beneficial outcomes are observed?

Answers to these questions are not very satisfying. Because standards-based accountability systems typically have consequences for schools and the educators who work within them, there may be powerful incentives to work within, or occasionally outside, the bounds of the system to maximize students' reported performance in ways that do not reflect changes in students' underlying academic achievement. Reviews of the effects of standards-based accountability systems on student outcomes often boil down to expositions of the many creative ways that educators have sought to 'game the system'.

Moreover, even if we take test results at face value, the evidence regarding standards-based accountability on student outcomes is mixed, with studies finding benefits for some student subgroups in some grades on some subject assessments, in some contexts. The specific features of the accountability system design might matter, though I will only speculate about the likely implications of design features.

I begin by discussing test-based school and teacher accountability systems in the USA, with particular attention to No Child Left Behind. I then discuss the potential implications of test-based accountability systems for outcomes, including both the level of outcomes (e.g., excellence) and their social distribution (e.g., equity). I note that the recent shift from status- or proficiency-based measures of school and teacher performance to growth measures represents a fundamental shift in accountability system design, with implications not yet clear. There is more evidence on the effects of accountability systems on the level of student outcomes than on their distribution, and the effects described in the literature are heterogeneous, reflecting variations in policy design and implementation. I conclude with some potential lines of research for understanding the conditions under which standards-based accountability systems might matter, and these systems' indirect or unanticipated effects.

Standards and test-based accountability in federal education policy

No Child Left Behind

The first wave of what is now referred to as standards-based accountability, in which states and school districts gathered data on student performance, culminated in the bipartisan No Child Left Behind Act (NCLB), the 2002 reauthorization of the Elementary and Secondary Education Act of 1965. NCLB required states receiving federal funds to develop grade-level standards in reading and mathematics, and to assess students annually in Grades 3 through 8 in these subjects, and once in high school. Schools and school districts were to report the percentages of students meeting the standards (i.e., deemed proficient) on the state tests, and to set the terms for Adequate Yearly Progress (AYP) for all students, regardless of demographic subgroup, to be classified as proficient by the 2013–14 school year.

To be judged as meeting AYP, each subgroup in a school with sufficient numbers of students – defined by economic disadvantage, disability status, English Language Learner status, and race or ethnicity – had to meet the subgroup standards for AYP. If any subgroup failed to meet its AYP target, the school in its entirety was deemed to have not met AYP.

NCLB had a progressive set of sanctions for schools failing to meet AYP for two consecutive years. Such schools had to provide free transfers to students seeking to enroll in a higher-performing public school in the same district. Schools failing to meet AYP three years in a row were required to offer free tutoring to students. Continued failure to meet AYP would enable states to intervene, potentially closing schools, firing the staff, converting them to charter schools, or relying on another school turnaround strategy.

NCLB's attention to demographic subgroups was intended to illuminate the performance of students of varying backgrounds in schools and districts. No longer would they be able to hide behind high overall performance, masking substantial subgroup performance gaps. Presidential candidate George W. Bush, in a speech to the National Association for the Advancement of Colored People (NAACP), described festering achievement gaps as the residue of 'the soft bigotry of low expectations'. We should aspire for universal excellence, he argued, and hold all schools to the standard of bringing all children to academic mastery.

Politically, the 2013–14 school year was far away in 2002. It was easy to imagine that there was plenty of time to get to universal student proficiency, even though no diverse school system in the USA had successfully eliminated average performance differences among advantaged and less-advantaged social groups. By the 2010–11 school year, however, it was evident that there was a serious problem.

The Center on Education Progress at George Washington University estimated that over the period from 2006 to 2011, the percentage of public schools in the USA not making AYP had risen steadily from 29% to 48% (Usher, 2012). Six years into the implementation of NCLB, it wasn't working. US Secretary of Education Arne Duncan speculated that as many as 80% of schools would not make AYP in the 2011–12 year. Something had to give.

Thus, in September 2011, the Obama Administration offered to waive key provisions of the law – including the requirement of universal proficiency by 2013–14 and the law's accountability sanctions – for states that agreed to adopt standards for college and career readiness (such as the Common Core standards) and to initiate teacher and principal evaluation systems rating these educators in part on measured student performance. By 2014, the US Education Department had granted waivers to 43 states and the District of Columbia (Klein, 2014).

The Every Student Succeeds Act

Widespread dissatisfaction with NCLB, and its large federal footprint, led to the passing of the 2015 Every Student Succeeds Act (ESSA). ESSA continued annual testing of students in Grades 3 through 8 in reading and math, and once in high school, with reporting on results for demographic subgroups. States also were obliged to submit accountability plans, with goals for student proficiency on standards-aligned tests, English language proficiency, and graduation rates, and goals to shrink performance gaps among demographic subgroups. But the law provided states more discretion over the choice of accountability goals.

Most notably, ESSA granted states the flexibility to introduce new measures of school quality and student success beyond test scores and graduation rates. These were to be woven into a composite measure leading to a summative classification into at least three categories of school performance. ESSA also invited states to incorporate measures of student growth in reading and math performance at both the elementary and secondary levels into their state accountability systems.

Based on a school's location in the performance distribution within a state, it could be identified as a candidate for comprehensive support and improvement or targeted support and improvement. At least once every three years, schools are to be identified for comprehensive support and improvement based on being in the bottom 5% of impoverished Title I schools in the state; a high school with a four-year adjusted cohort graduation rate of 67% or lower; or a Title I school with consistently low-performing subgroups, even after the implementation of a targeted support plan.

Beginning in 2019–20, states are required to identify schools annually for targeted support and improvement if they have one or more consistently underperforming subgroups. Beginning in 2018–19, at least once every three years, schools with one or more low-performing subgroups are also to receive targeted support and improvement.

The law grants states discretion in the design of support and improvement plans. Common features are addressing inequalities in access to relevant school resources (including provision of Title I School Improvement funds); conducting a needs assessment, and the development of a school improvement plan; and relying on one or more evidence-based interventions.

It is too soon to assess the impact of ESSA on student achievement, and on trends in the distribution of achievement among student subgroups. Standards-based accountability systems in the USA and its states have not been very stable, changing with political winds and implementation challenges. Changing grade-level standards, test contractors, test difficulty, and thresholds for sanctions and supports are just some of the examples of system features that have changed substantially over the course of a policy's life cycle.

Most studies of the impact of standards-based accountability policies on student achievement are, then, studies of policies that are no longer in place, conducted in contexts that have changed over time. Unless one sought to replicate a previous policy, such studies have limited capacity to predict whether standards-based accountability policies 'work', or even how a particular policy might fare in the future. The impact evaluations do not yield generalizations about the likely effects of implementing standards-based accountability policies in novel settings and contexts.

Policy instruments and standards-based accountability

Standards-based accountability systems often feature a variety of policy instruments, such as capacity building, system changing and persuasion (McDonnell, 1994; McDonnell & Elmore, 1987). But mandates and incentives usually take the centre stage. Both of these instruments rely on a set of rules, laws or regulations stipulating a set of desired behaviours. The main distinction between them is whether uniform compliance with the rules is necessary, or whether it is acceptable for some targets of the policy to comply and others to fail to do so. Both mandates and incentives assume that policymakers have the requisite knowledge to specify rules that will have the desired consequences; the rules are precise enough to elicit the desired behaviours; and the penalties (or rewards) are valuable enough to compel or promote the desired behaviour (McDonnell & Elmore, 1987). Mittleman and Jennings (2018) refer to these consequences as 'accountability with teeth'.

Mandates and incentives are most effective when the desired behaviours are very specific, and, in the case of incentives, that the targets of the policy have no other legitimate ways of obtaining the desired rewards than by complying with the policy rules (McDonnell & Elmore, 1987). These are not always realistic assumptions, and governments may need to invest resources in the targeted organizations and individuals to create the capacity to produce the desired ends. As a policy instrument, capacity building is often complementary to mandates and incentives.

A simplified example may help. Suppose that the desired outcome is enhanced student performance on challenging standardized tests aligned with the Common Core curricular standards. If teachers have not had previous exposure to these standards, and how to teach to them, mandates and incentives may be for naught. Absent the legitimate means to ensure that students perform well on the assessments, teachers will either fail to teach more effectively, or seek alternative means to ensure students' high performance on the assessments, such as teaching to the test or more outright forms of 'gaming the system'. A mandate or incentive intended to produce greater effort from a policy target will be successful only if that greater effort is accompanied by the requisite knowledge of how to achieve the desired ends. Estimates of the impact of a high-stakes accountability system cannot easily be decomposed into the portion attributable to mandates and incentives, and portions attributable to other features of the system.

No Child Left Behind as a standards-based accountability system

Most analysts describe NCLB as a standards-based accountability system because of its use of standards, tests and incentives (Izumi & Evers, 2002). Examples of explicit incentives are bonuses in schools recognized as excellent, or threats of restructuring or closing low-performing schools. In contrast, implicit incentives are indirect, as when performance information spurs community pressure on schools to improve, either via exit, or voice (Hirschman, 1970).

Studies of the impact of NCLB on student achievement have contrasted the performance of states with standards-based accountability systems in place prior to NCLB with states whose systems were first implemented as a result of NCLB. Dee and Jacob's (2011) analysis, using state-level data on the National Assessment of Educational Progress (NAEP) to trace state-level trends prior to the implementation of NCLB through the NCLB period, illustrates this research design. They found meaningful effects on the math performance of fourth-graders, but no evidence of NCLB effects on fourth-grade reading achievement.

Educator responses to standards-based accountability systems

There is a strong presumption in the accountability literature that the targets of mandates and incentives change their behaviour in response to them, though not always in the ways that policymakers intend or hope for. That is the message of this next section, which discusses what is known as Campbell's Law, and the strategies that researchers have used to take it into account.

Campbell's Law

Much of the research on standards-based accountability has taken to heart Campbell's Law: 'The more any quantitative social indicator is used for social decision-making, the more subject it will be to corruption pressures, and the more apt it will be to distort and corrupt the social processes it is intended to monitor' (Campbell, 1979). Donald Campbell did not define *corruption*, but linked it to an indicator's validity: Does it measure what it is intended to measure? A corrupt measure might measure just a subset of the phenomenon it is intended to measure, or a superset, or something altogether different.

Campbell also did not specify the mechanisms that might yield corruption, although he noted that quantitative social indicators are produced via a social process, and that the actors involved in their production may have interests that result in corruption or distortion. He went so far as to implicate achievement tests in his account: 'But when test scores become the goal of the teaching process, they both lose their value as indicators of educational status and distort the educational process in undesirable ways … Achievement tests are, in fact, highly corruptible measures' (Campbell, 1979: 85).

This certainly *may* be true, but it is not evident that it must be so. An important distinction is between the use of test scores for monitoring and the use of test scores for social decision-making. Standards-based accountability systems such as NCLB use test scores for high-stakes decisions that have potentially powerful rewards and penalties for principals, teachers and schools. But test scores can also be used for monitoring purposes, without the immediate risk of positive or negative incentives. Monitoring can, however, have performative effects even in the absence of direct rewards or punishments.

The use of NAEP to evade Campbell's Law

NAEP, which provides a broad look at trends in the performance of US students over time, both overall, and for particular subgroups, has been used much more so for monitoring than as a basis for specific education policy decisions. Its design minimizes the risk of corruption. Because scores are not reported for individual students or schools, and cannot be attached to individual teachers, there are few incentives for manipulating who takes the assessment, or the performance of the test-takers. The assessment simply does not provide information to which consequences for individuals or schools could be attached.

Moreover, the NAEP design limits opportunities for 'teaching to the test'. Most NAEP assessments take about 90 minutes to complete, and are administered to randomly selected samples of schools within a state, and approximately 25 students within a school. Multiple-choice and constructed-response items are bundled into blocks, and blocks into the booklets of items to which students respond. Even though NAEP is a low-stakes assessment, it has long had design features using close supervision and monitoring to minimize the risk of score inflation.

Neal (2013, 2018) argues persuasively that it is unwise to use one assessment system to produce information about student performance for broad monitoring purposes and information about the performance of educators and schools that can drive school improvement. Campbell's Law suggests that any high-stakes consequences for educators or schools will lead to corruption, often in the form of coaching students on test-taking skills. Inevitably, he suggests, the prospect of rewards and punishments will propel the targets of policies to corrupt assessment indicators, to maximize their self-interests. Quoting Kerr (1975), Neal argues that it is a mistake to reward A, while hoping for B.

The heart of the problem: Incentives and self-interest

Robert Merton's (1938) strain theory is a useful framework for thinking about the potential consequences of mandates or incentives that are unattainable through normal means. Merton argued that society can place pressures on individuals to achieve commonly-accepted goals, even though they lack the legitimate means to do so. The strain induced by this mismatch between goals and means can propel individuals to rely on means that society might view as deviant. The classic example is an expectation for the poor to become prosperous through hard work and opportunity. Because opportunities are distributed unequally, not everyone in neighbourhoods of concentrated poverty will have access to legitimate means, and some will seek financial gain through activities deemed deviant or illegal, such as dealing drugs, or theft.

We often view those who resolve the strain created by a gap between goals and means as morally deficient. They have chosen to break the law, whereas others in similar circumstances have not done so. But in transposing this example to educators' responses to test-based accountability, assuming that teachers who cheat are just 'bad apples' may disguise the organizational preconditions supporting transgression.

This is a lesson of the Atlanta cheating scandal. In 2008, a dozen Atlanta public schools posted unusually high gains on the Georgia state assessments required by NCLB. Subsequent investigations revealed widespread evidence of cheating, leading to the indictments of nearly 35 educators, many of whom pled guilty to a variety of charges. Eleven educators stood trial and were convicted of charges such as racketeering, false statements, false swearing and influencing witnesses.

The racketeering charges reflected the concerted action in which teachers, testing coordinators and school administrators engaged, including weekend parties to erase students' wrong answers and replace them with right ones; teachers pointing to correct answers when standing next to students' desks; seating low-performing students next to high-performing students so the former could copy the latter's responses; and teachers changing their voice inflections while reading questions aloud to signal correct answers to students.

Why would educators engage in these behaviours? No one goes into education with the express intent of 'juking the stats' and behaving unprofessionally. Nor did the educators benefit personally from their crimes (in contrast, say, to a bookkeeper embezzling school district funds for personal use). Rather, the organizational conditions that enabled this cheating to occur involved a superintendent setting unrealistic goals about annual performance gains, and imposing a draconian system of rewards and punishments tied to school performance. Since there were no legitimate means to achieve the goals, and hence sidestep the punishments, educators acted outside the lines because they believed that they had to. Sociologist Diane Vaughan (1999) and others have referred to such behaviour as organizational misconduct.

Moreover, lines separating what is legitimate and what is not may be fuzzy. 'Teaching to the test' is not always recognized as a transgression; it has been the gap between performance on high-stakes and low-stakes tests, and evidence about score inflation (Koretz, 2009), that has led to that view. And if teaching to the test is acceptable, how bad is it to teach test-taking skills, review past exam questions, or even suggest to students that they reconsider their answers? These practices are neither clearly good nor clearly bad.

Less direct forms of corruption

Coaching is but one form of corruption of the measurement of student perfor-mance. The examples below are not exhaustive; there may be potential forms of corruption that have yet to be realized.

Selection of students who are assessed

Test-based accountability systems typically specify which students are to be assessed, and in which categories or subgroups they are to be classified. Schools and educators may be able to manipulate which students are tested, particularly those with disabilities, or those who are English language learners. Figlio and Getzler (2002) found that Florida schools reclassified low-income and low-performing students as disabled after the introduction of test-based accountability, and Cullen and Reback (2006) revealed that test exemption rates in Texas were responsive to a school's proximity to a particular accountability category. Jennings and Beveridge (2009) used longitudinal data from Houston to establish that students with higher scores on a low-stakes test (the Stanford 10) were more likely to take the Texas Assessment of Knowledge and Skills (TAKS) in the late 1990s and early 2000s. They found that the proficiency rate gap separating African-American and Hispanic students from white students was underestimated by about two percentage points for each group due to differential test exemption.

Focusing resources and attention on a particular segment of the test-taking population

In proficiency-based accountability systems such as NCLB, a key school-level per-formance metric is the percentage of proficient students in a subgroup, or overall. There may be powerful incentives to raise this percentage from one year to the next. Importantly, this directs educators' attention to those students whose per-formance can 'move the needle' to yield a higher percent proficient. In this sense, the performance of some students is more important to the accountability metrics than the performance of others. Students far below the proficiency standard in a given year are extremely unlikely to learn enough to surpass the proficiency bar, and thus boost the high-stakes performance indicator. Conversely, those students who are already well above the proficiency bar do not warrant special attention, as they will maintain the percentage of students who are proficient.

The students that provide the most leverage – and thus generate the greatest incentives for attention and resources – are those who are just below or just above the proficiency bar. Students just below the bar might, with some additional atten-tion and support, make enough progress to be classified as proficient, and thus influence the performance metric. Those students only slightly above the profi-ciency bar also warrant continued attention and investment because they might easily backslide below the bar on the subsequent state test.

Booher-Jennings (2005) found that teachers in Texas referred to such students as 'bubble kids', as they were on the 'bubble', or cusp, of proficiency. She suggested that because Texas rated schools based on the percentage of students who were proficient, teachers were motivated to focus on students who could be moved above the bar. Research on whether the accountability provisions of NCLB have led to a focus on students near the proficiency standard has been mixed. Ballou and Springer (2016) found that mathematics gains for students near the proficiency threshold associated with the implementation of accountability policies were no greater than those for students far below the proficiency standard. In contrast, Lauen and Gaddis (2016) find that in North Carolina, when academic standards in math and reading increased, educators had incentives to shift their attention away from low-achieving students, especially those in low-performing schools.

Focusing on predictable test content and form

In a series of studies, Jennifer Jennings, Dan Koretz, and their colleagues have demonstrated that in several states, the content of high-stakes standards-based assessments is often predictable from the content on prior years' exams. This predictability can yield what Koretz (2009) calls 'score inflation', in which gains over time on such assessments far surpass the gains in the underlying competencies the assessments are intended to address. Instances in which student performance over time on a high-stakes test rises much more quickly than performance on a low-stakes test raises the spectre of score inflation. The classic example is when changes over time on a state NCLB-style assessment greatly outpace the changes in the state's performance on the NAEP assessments.

Score inflation can distort estimates of student performance as well as the relative position of particular groups of students, such as students of colour or economically disadvantaged students. This is a particular concern if accountability systems place disproportionate pressure on schools serving such students, who historically have performed at lower levels than their more advantaged peers.

The design of most state assessments precludes a complete mapping of content standards onto the test items. There frequently are more standards than test items, and thus some standards will appear on a given test form, and others will not. Since the design of most state assessments calls for all students in a given grade and subject to take the same exam, so that students can be located reasonably precisely in relation to one another on the same proficiency scale, there will be uneven coverage of the standards. Thus, students' average performance on an assessment may not be representative of their mastery of all of the relevant standards.

NCLB-era assessments predictably emphasize some state standards to the exclusion of others (Jennings & Bearak, 2014). In New York, Massachusetts and Texas, which made item-level data available to researchers, students performed better on items tapping standards that were assessed more frequently in previous years than on items reflecting less-frequently assessed standards (Jennings & Bearak, 2014). This strongly suggests that teachers were targeting their instruction towards these frequently-tested standards, and in so doing, distorting student performance.

More direct evidence of this kind of targeting is shown by Koretz et al. (2016), who conducted a trial of 'self-monitoring' assessments, which incorporate audit

test items that are less susceptible to traditional test preparation. These researchers found evidence that there is score inflation on non-audit items, and that this
was especially salient for students who are on the cusp of proficiency (i.e., 'being
on the bubble') or who attend schools with high rates of poverty, both of which are
factors potentially associated with punishments.

The extent of this kind of score inflation, though, is a function of several factors,
including the 'bite' of the accountability system, the difficulty of achieving proficiency on the assessment, and students' location in the test score distribution.
Jennings and Sohn (2014) refer to educators focusing on test-specific skills as
'instructional triage'. This attention to the content and form of assessment items is
greatest for students near the proficiency threshold, and most common in the
lowest-performing schools, presumably the most vulnerable to penalties for not
meeting the accountability system expectations.

It is for these reasons that Mittleman and Jennings (2018) largely discount studies of the achievement effects of high-stakes accountability systems, whether the
focus is on the level of achievement or on its social distribution. The risks of corruption are sufficiently great, they argue, that it is not possible to distinguish the
effects of corruption from the less pernicious effects of accountability systems.
Nonetheless, researchers have sought to quantify the effects of standards-based
accountability systems on education outcomes.

The implications of standards-based accountability systems for educational outcomes

In this section, I examine how standards-based accountability systems might
affect educational outcomes. The level of performance of students in the system,
and whether the distribution of performance is fair or equitable, are enduring
public policy issues. There is no one way to think about either of these policy concerns, but the term 'achievement gap' has come to dominate the discourse about
the latter.

Proficiency vs. growth in standards-based accountability

The contrast between proficiency thresholds and growth models in standards-
based accountability systems is made more complex by the multiple meanings of
the phrase 'growth model'. In some cases, a growth model is one that pits schools
(or teachers) against one another, using statistical methods to simulate a level
playing field in which schools or teachers have a common starting point, and
examining whether the students of some schools or teachers perform significantly
higher or lower, on average, than similar students linked to other schools or teachers. In this kind of model, often referred to as a value-added model, there are
inevitably 'winners' and 'losers'; with a sufficiently large number of students, it is
likely that some schools and teachers will be identified as having a positive effect
on student achievement outcomes, and others identified as less effective.

In such models, the student outcomes associated with particular schools or
teachers are adjusted for students' prior achievement and social characteristics.

Since these factors often are associated with student performance on high-stakes assessments, the models attempt to adjust for these 'risk factors'. Risk-adjustment models reduce the likelihood of identifying some schools or teachers as more or less effective solely on the basis of the kinds of students they serve. The analogue in medicine is looking at the success rates of hospitals and surgeons for coronary bypass surgeries. One would not want to penalize a surgeon or hospital solely because they took on challenging cases where the odds of success were low. Ideally, the model removes any significant correlation between students' social backgrounds and school or teacher accountability ratings for the schools and teachers feeding into the model (cf. Leckie & Goldstein, 2019).

This is a different sense of the term 'growth model' than one that involves measuring growth in student performance from one year to the next, and judging whether that growth is above or below what is expected or desired. Whereas a value-added model will almost always have some schools or teachers classified as ineffective, it is possible for all schools to show growth in student performance from one year to the next, and thus possible for all schools to be classified as meeting a growth standard. But a great deal depends on how challenging the growth standard is. Whereas this kind of growth model does not statistically remove a correlation with students' social backgrounds, it is nevertheless the case that student achievement growth can be more challenging to promote in some schools than in others.

In contrast, there is clear evidence that the use of proficiency metrics in NCLB resulted in a much higher percentage of high-poverty schools being classified as not making AYP than was true for lower-poverty schools. Le Floch et al. (2007) found that in the early years of NCLB, schools that served higher concentrations of students in poverty, urban schools, and those with large numbers of children of colour were less likely to be classified as making AYP than their counterparts. For example, 57 percent of high-poverty schools (i.e., with 75 percent or more of the students in poverty) were classified as making AYP in 2003–04, compared to 72 percent of medium-poverty schools (with between 35 and 75 percent of students in poverty) and 84 percent of low-poverty schools (with fewer than 35 percent of students in poverty).

The association between school poverty status and accountability ratings in proficiency-based accountability systems is persistent. In Ohio, the achievement component of the summary school report card grades issued to school districts is based on student proficiency rates, as well as overall student achievement performance and chronic absenteeism. There is a clear gradient linking the average economic status of Ohio school districts and their report card grades. Exner (2019) reported that the median household income in Ohio districts receiving an A grade was $98,057. In contrast, the median household income in districts receiving a C grade was $59,969, and in districts receiving an F grade, the median household income was $36,342. Across Ohio's 608 districts, several measures of school district social and economic wellbeing were persistently linked to student proficiency rates, and thus the accountability report card grades.

Regardless of whether or not performance measures are calculated using proficiency levels or other metrics, such as growth over time, the proficiency level metric may distort estimates of group differences in performance. This is because the setting of a proficiency cutoff is necessarily arbitrary, and locating the cutoff at one point of the achievement distribution may yield different claims about the magnitude of performance differences among groups than if the cutoff is at a different location (Ho & Reardon, 2012).

This issue came to a head in reporting on the magnitude of the racial/ethnic achievement gap in New York City in the first decade of this century. Mayor Michael Bloomberg and Schools Chancellor Joel Klein pointed to proficiency rates on state tests to argue that the racial/ethnic achievement gap had shrunk substantially between 2002 and 2008. Elizabeth Green (2008), then a reporter for the *New York Sun*, sought to vet that claim with several scholars, including me, who questioned whether the evidence was consistent with it.

The New York City Department of Education argued that the Black–white and Hispanic–white achievement gaps had closed substantially between 2002 and 2008, relying on the percentage of students who were classified as proficient on the New York State achievement tests. In 2002, 41% of Black fourth-graders in New York City were classified as proficient, compared to 76% of white fourth-graders, a 35 percentage point gap. By 2008, though, the percentage of Black students classified as proficient had risen to 73%, and that of white students to 91%. Thus, the 35 percentage point gap in 2002 had shrunk to 18 percentage points in 2008, a reduction of about 50%.

This apparent reduction between 2002 and 2008, however, disguised the fact that Blacks and whites remained almost as far apart in the overall score distribution. The city's own calculations showed that the average Black student scored 0.77 standard deviations below the average white student in 2002, a gap that had shrunk to 0.68 standard deviations in 2008. The proportional reduction in this gap measure was about 12%, far less than the 50% reduction implied by the changes in percent proficient.

Differences of this magnitude are consequential, in ways that proficiency rates can disguise. Because the relative position of groups, and of the individuals within them, matters the most in how society selects and rewards individuals, comparably high proficiency rates may be misleading. Individuals are not selected for desirable positions in education and the economy based on surpassing an artificially low bar. Rather, there is a queue, in which those performing at the highest levels are selected first for the available positions. It is the ranking of individuals that matters, and getting everyone over the bar does not change those rankings, even if everyone's scores are going up.

Unintended consequences of standards-based accountability systems

Much of the attention that standards-based accountability systems receive is directed at the incentives for teachers to change their practices in the classroom, either by exercising greater effort, or by choosing content aligned with standards, or developing new teaching practices. But there are many other ways in which standards-based accountability systems might influence educator behaviour, some intended, and others perhaps less so.

For example, standards-based accountability might change teachers' working conditions, reducing classroom autonomy and the attractiveness of the job. Thus, teachers in districts and states might leave their classrooms at higher rates, and especially in schools that are most subject to accountability pressures, such as high-poverty schools. The evidence on these responses is mixed (Adnot et al., 2017; Brunner et al., 2019; Sallman, 2018). Too, standards-based accountability systems for teachers that rely on value-added models, and terminate teachers who do not perform well on these models, may weed out low-performing teachers, though at the risk of creating vacancies in the hard-to-staff schools from which they often are drawn (Adnot et al., 2017; Kraft et al., 2019). The weakened job security associated with standards-based teacher accountability systems may also affect the supply and quality of new teachers, in countervailing ways. Kraft et al. (2019) show a decline in the supply of newly-licensed teacher candidates accompanying the implementation of standards-based teacher accountability systems. But these new teachers often are drawn from more selective undergraduate institutions. Given the weak association between *ex ante* measures of teacher quality and student performance, the longer-term implications of this are unclear, even though there remain strong proponents of the view that we can fire our way to the top (Hanushek, 2009).

Publicizing standards-based accountability ratings for schools or teachers may affect the behaviour of parents, propelling them to value schools and teachers with high performance ratings, and shun those with lower ratings. Figlio and Lucas (2004) show that school report card grades in Florida affected housing prices for residences that were sold repeatedly over time. Similarly, Bergman and Hill (2018) showed that after the *Los Angeles Times* published teachers' value-added scores – akin to what an official standards-based accountability system would have generated – high-scoring students, typically from more advantaged socio-economic backgrounds, gravitated towards the classrooms of the higher-rated teachers within a school. Both lines of research suggest that the ability to access and make use of the performance information generated by standards-based accountability systems is not evenly distributed.

A final indirect or unanticipated effect of standards-based accountability systems is a weakening of the social compact between public school educators and their communities. In distinguishing between sanction-based accountability and trust-based accountability, Mansbridge (2014) suggests that incentives and sanctions crowd out a moral basis for action. Those educators who might otherwise choose to act based on a sense of professionalism or integrity may steer away from teaching, at least in settings that rely baldly on material incentives to drive people's work. Sanctions reduce initiative, creativity and flexible action, because they focus workers on adherence to quantitative metrics, not the 'real' goals, which are more diffuse.

Proponents of sanctions, though, argue that trust-based accountability has not addressed the serious problems of US public education. The search for short-term fixes leads naturally to mandates and incentives, rather than capacity building, which always has a longer time horizon. Sanction-based systems can also 'disrupt the highly integrated equilibrium based on self-interest or group interest', justifying a need for disruptive accountability in the face of stagnant student performance (Mansbridge, 2014: 63). At the least, she argues, systems might differentiate the monitoring of and sanctions for different agents (i.e., teachers and administrators), based on their prior performance.

Conclusion

I have noted a number of features of standards-based accountability systems that are relevant to studying their effects on the level and distribution of student outcomes. These include the variety of the policy instruments in these systems, and the centrality of mandates, rewards and sanctions. I also have discussed which students' performance is targeted by the accountability system, and the distinction between proficiency- or other threshold-based systems and those based on risk-adjusted growth models. The challenge level of the standards matters, as the bar can be set so high that it is impossible for educators to meet it via legitimate means. And the school context matters, as the types of students attending a school may influence whether a school will be judged as meeting the thresholds for positive ratings.

I also considered the distinction between different types of student assessments, most notably the high-stakes assessments that are held to be aligned with state grade-level standards, and lower-stakes assessments that may not be. An additional overlay on this is the fact that although state assessments may be consequential for schools and teachers, they rarely have direct consequences for individual students. Thus, student effort is another variable, as there is growing evidence of variation in effort that may affect the level of student performance (e.g., Gneezy et al., 2019). And schools and teachers may be subject to multiple accountability systems with conflicting standards, and even suffer from 'policy reform fatigue' (Dee & Dizon-Ross, 2019) when these systems change over time.

Ultimately, the challenge of research on the effects of standards-based accountability systems on the level and distribution of academic performance is twofold. First, researchers must relentlessly interrogate the mechanisms by which accountability systems, and the mandates, incentives and other policy instruments embedded within them, are intended to influence students' academic performance. Some mechanisms may be intended, whereas others may be unintended or serendipitous. Second, researchers will benefit from review of the features of standards-based accountability systems, including the criteria that trigger rewards or punishments and the challenge level associated with those criteria. As much as policymakers might crave summary claims that standards-based accountability 'works', the heterogeneity of system design makes such claims contingent.

Bibliography

Adnot, M., Dee, T., Katz, V., & Wyckoff, J. (2017). Teacher Turnover, Teacher Quality, and Student Achievement in DCPS. *Educational Evaluation and Policy Analysis*, *39*(1), 54–76.

Ballou, D., & Springer, M. G. (2016). Has NCLB Encouraged Educational Triage? Accountability and the Distribution of Achievement Gains. *Education Finance and Policy*, *12*(1), 77–106.

Bergman, P., & Hill, M. J. (2018). The Effects of Making Performance Information Public: Regression Discontinuity Evidence from Los Angeles Teachers. *Economics of Education Review, 66,* 104–113.

Booher-Jennings, J. (2005). Below the Bubble: 'Educational Triage' and the Texas Accountability System. *American Educational Research Journal, 42*(2), 231–268.

Brunner, E., Cowen, J. M., Strunk, K. O., & Drake, S. (2019). Teacher Labor Market Responses to Statewide Reform: Evidence from Michigan. *Educational Evaluation and Policy Analysis, 41*(4), 403–425.

Campbell, D. T. (1979). Assessing the Impact of Planned Social Change. *Evaluation and Program Planning, 2*(1), 67–90.

Cullen, J. B., & Reback, R. (2006). *Tinkering Toward Accolades: School Gaming Under a Performance Accountability System* (Working Paper No. 12286). Cambridge, MA: National Bureau of Economic Research.

Dee, T. S., & Dizon-Ross, E. (2019). School Performance, Accountability, and Waiver Reforms: Evidence from Louisiana. *Educational Evaluation and Policy Analysis, 41*(3), 316–349.

Dee, T. S., & Jacob, B. (2011). The Impact of No Child Left Behind on Student Achievement. *Journal of Policy Analysis and Management, 30*(3), 418–446.

Exner, R. (2019, September 17). See How Closely Ohio School Report Card Grades Trend with District Income. Cleveland.com.

Figlio, D. N., & Getzler, L. S. (2002). *Accountability, Ability and Disability: Gaming the System* (Working Paper No. 9307). Cambridge, MA: National Bureau of Economic Research.

Figlio, D. N., & Lucas, M. E. (2004). What's in a Grade? School Report Cards and the Housing Market. *American Economic Review, 94*(3), 591–604.

Gneezy, U., List, J. A., Livingston, J. A., Qin, X., Sadoff, S., & Xu, Y. (2019). Measuring Success in Education: The Role of Effort on the Test Itself. *American Economic Review: Insights, 1*(3), 291–308.

Green, E. (2008, August 5). 'Achievement Gap' in City Schools Is Scrutinized. New York Sun. Retrieved from https://www.nysun.com/new-york/achievement-gap-in-city-schools-is-scrutinized/83215/

Hanushek, E. A. (2009). Teacher Deselection. In D. Goldhaber & J. Hannaway (Eds.), *Creating a New Teaching Profession* (pp. 165–180). Washington, DC: Urban Institute Press.

Hirschman, A. O. (1970). *Exit, Voice, and Loyalty: Responses to Decline in Firms, Organizations, and States.* Cambridge, MA: Harvard University Press.

Ho, A. D., & Reardon, S. F. (2012). Estimating Achievement Gaps from Test Scores Reported in Ordinal 'Proficiency' Categories. *Journal of Educational and Behavioral Statistics, 37*(4), 489–517.

Izumi, L., & Evers, W. M. (2002). State Accountability Systems. In W. M. Evers & H. J. Walberg (Eds.), *School Accountability* (pp. 105–153). Stanford, CA: Hoover Institution Press/Stanford University.

Jennings, J. L., & Bearak, J. M. (2014). 'Teaching to the Test' in the NCLB Era: How Test Predictability Affects Our Understanding of Student Performance. *Educational Researcher, 43*(8), 381–389.

Jennings, J. L., & Beveridge, A. A. (2009). How Does Test Exemption Affect Schools' and Students' Academic Performance? *Educational Evaluation and Policy Analysis, 31*(2), 153–175.

Jennings, J., & Sohn, H. (2014). Measure for Measure: How Proficiency-Based Accountability Systems Affect Inequality in Academic Achievement. *Sociology of Education, 87*(2), 125–141.

Kerr, S. (1975). On the Folly of Rewarding A, While Hoping for B. *Academy of Management Journal*, *18*(4), 769–783.

Klein, A. (2014). *Arne Duncan Revokes Washington State's NCLB Waiver*. Education Week – Politics K-12. Retrieved January 29, 2020, from http://blogs.edweek.org/edweek/campaign-k-12/2014/04/washington_state_loses_waiver_html

Koretz, D. (2009). *Measuring Up*. Cambridge, MA: Harvard University Press.

Koretz, D., Jennings, J. L., Ng, H. L., Yu, C., Braslow, D., & Langi, M. (2016). Auditing for Score Inflation Using Self-Monitoring Assessments: Findings from Three Pilot Studies. *Educational Assessment*, *21*(4), 231–247.

Kraft, M. A., Brunner, E. J., Dougherty, S. M., & Schwegman, D. J. (2019). *Teacher Accountability Reforms and the Supply and Quality of New Teachers* (EdWorkingPaper: 19-169). Retrieved from Annenberg Institute at Brown University: https://doi.org/10.26300/7bcw-5r61).

Lauen, D. L., & Gaddis, S. M. (2016). Accountability Pressure, Academic Standards, and Educational Triage. *Educational Evaluation and Policy Analysis*, *38*(1), 127–147.

Le Floch, K., Martinez, F., O'Day, J., Stecher, B., Taylor, J., & Cook, A. (2007). *State and Local Implementation of the No Child Left Behind Act, Volume 3: Accountability Under NCLB – Interim Report*. Washington, DC: U.S. Department of Education.

Leckie, G., & Goldstein, H. (2019). The Importance of Adjusting for Pupil Background in School Value-Added Models: A Study of Progress 8 and School Accountability in England. *British Educational Research Journal*, *45*(3), 518–537.

Mansbridge, J. (2014). A Contingency Theory of Accountability. In M. Bovens, R. E. Goodin, & T. Schillemans (Eds.), *Oxford Handbook of Public Accountability* (pp. 55–68). New York: Oxford University Press.

McDonnell, L. M. (1994). Assessment Policy as Persuasion and Regulation. *American Journal of Education*, *102*(4), 394–420.

McDonnell, L. M., & Elmore, R. F. (1987). Getting the Job Done: Alternative Policy Instruments: *Educational Evaluation and Policy Analysis*, *9*(3), 133–152.

Merton, R. K. (1938). Social Structure and Anomie. *American Sociological Review*, *3*(5), 672–682.

Mittleman, J., & Jennings, J. L. (2018). Accountability, Achievement, and Inequality in American Public Schools: A Review of the Literature. In B. Schneider (Ed.), *Handbook of the Sociology of Education in the 21st Century* (pp. 475–492). Cham, Switzerland: Springer International Publishing.

Neal, D. (2013). The Consequences of Using One Assessment System to Pursue Two Objectives. *The Journal of Economic Education*, *44*(4), 339–352.

Neal, D. (2018). *Information, Incentives, and Education Policy*. Cambridge, MA: Harvard University Press.

Sallman, J. R. (2018). *Should I Stay or Should I Go? Teacher Retention in the Era of Accountability* (Unpublished Ph.D. dissertation). New York: Columbia University.

Usher, A. (2012). *AYP Results for 2010–11: November 2012 Update*. Washington, DC: Center on Education Policy, George Washington University.

Vaughan, D. (1999). The Dark Side of Organizations: Mistake, Misconduct, and Disaster. *Annual Review of Sociology*, *25*, 271–305.

12 Siren song: Performance-based accountability systems, effectiveness, and equity

Evidence from PISA in education systems in Europe and Canada

Annelise Voisin

Introduction

Accountability has emerged in recent decades as both an instrument to enhance effectiveness in education systems and a goal established as an 'icon of good governance' (Bovens, 2007, p. 449). Despite its multilayered dimension, accountability was quickly established in the education field as 'the process by which school districts and states (or other constituents) attempt to ensure that schools and school systems meet their goals' (Rothman, 1995, p. 189). Pushed by transnational policy discourses and narratives (Tröhler, Meyer, Labaree, & Hutt, 2014), and anchored in New Public Management principles (Hood, 1991), performance-based accountability systems (PBAS) emerged as a policy instrument to shorten the feedback loop between policymakers, schools and teachers and as a key strategy for raising student achievement (Ladd & Lauen, 2010). In a governing by numbers fashion (Ozga, 2009; Rose, 1991), PBAS call for the setting of national targets and performance indicators, the monitoring of students', teachers' and schools' performances in line with predefined standards and making actors (especially schools and teachers) accountable for test results.

A recent, but prolific literature has since developed, analyzing the consequences of new governing modes and processes in education (Fenwick, Mangez, & Ozga, 2014). A body of work analyzes the rise of new modes of governance in education in general, and of PBAS in particular, from a critical stance (Ball, 2003; Maroy, 2009). Emphasizing normative consequences, they bring up controversial elements regarding the rise of a new policy paradigm where education systems are considered as production systems (Maroy, 2009), and where 'schools are no longer shielded from the pressure of accountability and efficiency' (Meyer & Benavot, 2013, p. 11). Other bodies of studies, mostly conducted in the USA, analyze the effects of PBAS on student achievement, challenging the rhetoric of effectiveness surrounding their development with empirical evidence (Carnoy & Loeb, 2002; Hanushek & Raymond, 2005; Lee, 2008; Lee & Wong, 2004).

While there is no consensus to date about the capacity of PBAS to sustainably improve student achievement, quantitative studies that assess the relationship between PBAS and student achievement beyond the borders of the USA and of high-stakes accountability systems are scarce. In particular, PBAS' effects in education systems in Canada and Europe have been somewhat neglected. Recent literature nonetheless highlights the deployment of PBAS in these contexts (see Maroy, Brassard, Mathou, Vaillancourt, & Voisin, 2017 for Canada; Maroy & Pons, 2019 for France; Verger & Curran, 2014 for Spain; Croxford, Grek, & Shaik, 2009 for Scotland; Berényi, Bajomi, & Neumann, 2013 for Hungary; and Elstad, 2009 for Norway).

This chapter draws on the results of a quantitative comparative study that fills this gap in literature and goes beyond the classic distinction between high-stakes and low-stakes accountability systems (Carnoy & Loeb, 2002). Using the Programme for International Student Assessment (PISA) 2012 data, the study reports on the multifaceted nature of PBAS in education systems in Europe and Canada and assesses their associations with the degrees of effectiveness and equity. The following research questions were thus addressed: can we empirically determine cross-national patterns in the policy tools used and the forms taken by PBAS in education systems in Europe and Canada? Is there any significant relationship between PBAS and the degrees of effectiveness and equity in these education systems? Does this relationship vary depending on the favored tools and related forms of PBAS?

The chapter proceeds with a short review of evidence from cross-states and cross-national quantitative studies that assess the effects of PBAS on student achievement. The next section discusses the methods. The 'Results' section, present the main instrumental dimensions of PBAS and an empirical typology that highlights cross-educational systems patterns in this regard. Statistical associations between the forms taken by PBAS and the degrees of effectiveness and equity are then discussed. A final section considers key elements for discussion and presents a conclusion.

PBAS effects on student achievement, reviewing the evidence

The theory of action behind PBAS postulates that a greater focus on student results as measured by standardized testing in the light of clear standards will drive achievement while incentives systems will lead 'teachers to teach harder and students to learn more' (Ladd & Lauen, 2010, p. 427). Anchored in principal–agent theory, which considers actors as goal-oriented and value-maximizing (Bovens, Goodin, & Schillemans, 2014), PBAS emphasizes external devices such as standards (curriculum and performance), assessment tools, and symbolic and material incentives as the key levers for change (Maroy & Voisin, 2014). As actors are endowed with a calculating rationality, organizational constraints and incentives (and sanctions) systems should bring about a better alignment with organizational goals and ensuring actors' cooperation (Clark & Wilson, 1961).

Key studies carried out mainly in the USA have challenged these assumptions by measuring PBAS effects on student achievement, resulting in mixed and inconclusive findings. Cross-states econometric studies that use the National Assessment of Educational Progress data (NAEP – nationally representative data on student achievement across the USA) suggest that more stringent accountability systems may have a positive effect on student achievement (Carnoy & Loeb, 2002; Hanushek & Raymond, 2005). However, achievement gains appear to be greater in mathematics and for higher school levels and remain relatively weak and not stable over time (Carnoy & Loeb, 2002; Lee, 2008; Lee & Wong, 2004).

Moreover, there is little evidence of PBAS having an obvious impact in closing the achievement gap. Hanushek and Raymond (2005) suggest that the achievement gap between black and white students has widened in the USA since the introduction of high-stakes accountability systems, while Dee conclude that there have been 'reductions in educational attainment, particularly for black students' (Dee, 2002, p. 12). High-stakes accountability systems coupled with market mechanisms tend to increase social and ethnic segregation among schools (Hanushek & Raymond, 2005) and consequently may foster the stigmatization of low-performing schools and students.

International cross-national studies focusing on PBAS' and related tools' effects on student achievement also provide mixed findings. Wößmann (2005) concludes that students perform better in countries where central exit examinations and the public reporting of school results are coupled with greater school choice and autonomy. Schütz, West, and Wößmann (2007) conclude that there is a positive effect of external examinations on student performances although gains appear smaller for disadvantaged students. However, Yi and Shi (2018), using PISA 2012 data, found that the relationships between external accountability (national testing, publication of school results, sanctions and rewards based on student performances) and student achievement scores in mathematics are rather weak. Finally, Lee and colleagues (Lee & Amo, 2017) using both national (NAEP in the USA) and international data (TIMS and PISA) conclude that neither high-school exit examination nor high-stakes testing coupled with incentives for teachers have a positive effect on student achievement.

The bulk of the existing literature casts doubt on the capacity of PBAS to raise student achievement and close the achievement gap. Although specific forms of PBAS and related tools seem to contribute to an increase in average performance, the available evidence suggests that the issue is more complex, in particular with regard to equity. Literature indeed suggests that sanction-driven accountability systems potentially lead to the development of strategic behaviours (falsification of school results, educational triage, 'teaching to the test', etc.) (Heilig & Darling-Hammond, 2008; Reback, 2008). Overall, the evidence suggests that PBAS effects may vary according to the favoured policy tools and the forms they take. All of this points to the need to document the various instrumental configurations on which PBAS relies and to analyze their effects in this respect.

However, while the literature highlights great variations with regard to the favoured tools at the heart of PBAS according to the social, historical, cultural and structural specificities of education systems (UNESCO, 2017), few quantitative comparative studies have reported on their multifaceted nature, highlighting cross-national patterns and variations in the forms taken by PBAS, in order to assess their effects on student achievement. That is precisely what this study proposes to do.

Methods, sample and data

This chapter draws on the results of a cross-national study[1] that investigates the complex relationships between PBAS and student achievement in education systems little studied by quantitative comparative research. Using PISA 2012 data from 59 education systems in Europe and Canada (n students = 222,351), including the Canadian provinces, the member states of the European Union, Switzerland, Iceland and Norway, the study analyzes the system-specific regulation tools and accountability mechanisms at the heart of PBAS in these education systems and examines whether distinct forms of PBAS lead to distinct effects on their degrees of effectiveness and equity. The education system is therefore the main unit of analysis (when the data allow) whereas most of the comparative quantitative studies that have used PISA data worked at the country level, thus neglecting existing variations between autonomous jurisdictions, provinces or regions within the same country (as in the case of Canada).

Accountability measures

PISA 2012 provides rich information on school accountability, which was used to analyze the tools used and forms taken by PBAS in the 59 education systems under study. This information, collected at the school level (questionnaire filled in by headteachers), makes it possible to capture the accountability tools implemented within schools and for the external control of schools.

Seventeen variables were selected in the school database (Table 12.1). The first set of variables (1) provides information regarding the tools used at the school level for school improvement and quality assurance. The second set of variables (2) refers to the tracking of achievement data by administrative authority and/or their publication. The third set (3) refers to the uses of student results by schools. Finally, the last set of variables (4) provides information regarding the consequences attached to teachers' appraisal.

Principal component analysis (PCA) was used on these sets of variables to extract the principal components. Component scores were computed, providing information regarding the intensity of each principal component, interpreted as key instrumental dimensions of PBAS, in the 59 education systems. These principal components and related component scores (see below) therefore constitute the first set of accountability measures.

Based on component scores attributed to each education system, hierarchical cluster analysis (HCA) was performed in order to elaborate a descriptive typology of PBAS. The final number of clusters chosen was based on the dendrogram analysis (Appendix – Figure 12.) and the mean and standard deviation for each principal component within each cluster were computed to describe clusters' specificity (Appendix - Table 12.A2). The empirical typology and related PBAS types that emerged from our data therefore constitute the second set of accountability measures (Appendix - Table 12.A1).

Table 12.1 PISA 2012 – variables of interest

PISA 2012 – variables of interest

THEMES	Quality assurance and school improvement	Achievement data – accountability	Use of student assessment by school	Teacher appraisal
PROMPTS	*Which of the following measures aimed at quality assurance and improvement do you have in your school? (SC 39)*	*In your school, are achievement data used in any of the following <accountability procedure> (SC 19)*	*In your school, are assessments of students in <national modal grade for 15-year-olds> used for any of the following purposes? (SC 18)*	*To what extent have appraisals of and/or feedback to teachers directly led to the following? (SC 31)*
ITEMS	Experts consultation (over a period of at least 6 months) (Q09)	Achievement data – posted publicly (Q01)	To compare the school with other schools (Q08)	Changes in the work responsibilities that make the job more attractive (Q06)
	External evaluation (Q06)	Achievement data – tracked over time by administrative authority (Q02)	To make judgment about teachers' effectiveness (Q06)	Public recognition from headteacher (Q05)
	Internal evaluation (Q05)		To monitor the school's progress from year to year (Q05)	Change in the likelihood of career advancement (Q04)
	Systematic recording of data including teachers and student attendance and graduation rates, test results and professional development of teachers (Q03)		To compare the school with <district or national> performance (Q04)	Opportunities for professional development activities (Q03)
	Written specification of student performance standards (Q02)			Financial bonus or monetary reward (Q02)
				Salary change (Q01)

Effectiveness and equity measures

The degree of effectiveness (MEANM) refers to the overall mean scores in mathematics in PISA 2012 (Le Donné, 2014) while the degree of equity in education systems was assessed according to three measures of (in)equality of achievement within education systems – (1) the degree of (in)equality in outcomes, with the EO indicator estimating the achievement gap between top and lowest performers in mathematics); (2) the degree of (in) equality in education opportunities, with the EEO indicator assessing the effect of student family background on student achievement; (3) the degree of (in)equality of basic skills, with the EBS indicator estimating the proportion of students in each education system scoring below PISA Proficiency Level 2 (Table 12.2).

Analysis

Education system-level multiple linear regressions were used to investigate how the degrees of effectiveness and equity are related to PBAS (the forms taken and tools used). The first set of regressions models (Models 1, 2, 3) estimate the associations between each instrumental dimension of PBAS independently (PBASPCA1, PBASPCA2 and PBASPCA3) and the degree of effectiveness (MEANM) and equity (as measured by the EO, EEO and EBS indicators). In the second set of models (Models 4), the associations between PBAS types and the degrees of effectiveness and equity were tested.

Few control variables were introduced in the final model specifications. Based on previous empirical research, public expenditure on education as percentage of GDP (PUEXP) (Duru-Bellat, Mons, & Suchaut, 2004; Hallak, 1996), the social structure of education systems (SOSTR) (Mons, 2004) and the degree of horizontal and vertical stratification within school systems (HVSTR) (Dupriez & Dumay, 2005) were controlled for. However, the social structure of education systems is excluded from models where the EEO indicator is used as independent variable (the effect of family background on student achievement being taken into account in both indicators). The variables introduced in the models, their construction and types are summarized in Table 12.2.

In line with the theory of action of PBAS, accountability measures are expected to be positively associated with the degrees of both effectiveness and equity in education systems. However, some methodological issues should be borne in mind. First, the small sample size may have had a direct impact on statistical power, implying possible underestimation of associations tested. Moreover, the research design does not enable to control for reverse causality. Education systems with low levels of student achievement and degree of equity may have been more inclined to introduce more stringent accountability systems. Thus, this study does not allow conclusions to be drawn on the causal effects of PBAS with regard to the degrees of effectiveness and equity in education systems, but it does demonstrate the associations between them.

Table 12.2 Indicators introduced in models' specifications

Indicators	Description	Source
Degree of effectiveness (MEANM)	Overall mean scores in mathematics in PISA 2012	PISA 2012
Degree of (in)equality in outcomes (EO)	Interdecile ratio between top (decile 9) and low performers (decile 1)	PISA 2012
Degree of (in)equality in education opportunities (EEO)	Regression coefficient (r^2) linear simple regression with PISA index of ESCS as independent variable and student test scores in mathematics as dependent variable	PISA 2012 & OECD documentation (OECD, 2013; 2014)
Degree of (in)equality of basic skills (EBS)	Proportion of students who do not reach PISA Proficiency Level 2 in mathematics (lower score limit 420 – OECD, 2013)	
Instrumental dimension of PBAS (PBASPCA1, 2, 3 – see below)	Component scores for each principal component (extracted by PCA) attributed to each education system/jurisdiction	
Type of PBAS (Types 1, 2, 3 and 4 – see below)	PBAS types produced by hierarchical cluster analysis	
Public expenditure on education (PUEXP)	Public expenditure on education as percentage of GDP	World Bank
Social structure of education systems (SOSTR)	Overall variance in student economic, social and cultural status [PISA ESCS Index] within education systems [Mons, 2004])	PISA 2012
Horizontal and vertical stratification of school system (HVSTR)	Aggregate variable taking into account: 1) The number of tracks available at the end of compulsory schooling; 2) The proportion of students who have repeated at least one school year by the age of 15; 3) The extent to which students are grouped across schools according to their performances (intra-class correlation of performance [OECD, 2013])	PISA 2012 & OECD documentation (OECD, 2013])

Results

Instrumental dimensions of PBAS

The first series of analyses (PCA) enables us to extract three principal components interpreted as key instrumental dimensions of PBAS across Europe and Canada: (1) evaluation and outcomes monitoring; (2) incentives for teachers; and (3) external comparison and internal improvement mechanisms.

Evaluation and outcomes monitoring

The 'evaluation and outcomes monitoring' instrumental dimension (PBASPCA1) describing 48.74% of the variance, $\alpha = 0.885$) is constructed by seven variables (Table 12.3) referring to distinct instruments aiming at evaluating and monitoring schools', teachers', and students' outcomes. Student results are therefore at the cornerstone of a range of mechanisms aiming at improving the overall system outcomes. Figure 12.1 highlights great variations with regards to the intensity of this instrumental dimension within education systems.

Incentives for teachers

The 'teachers' incentives' instrumental dimension (PBASPCA2, describing 13.26% of the variance, $\alpha = 0.879$) has five variables referring to direct incentives linked to teacher appraisal (Table 12.4), with material incentives making the greatest contribution to this dimension which targets teachers at the heart of accountability

Table 12.3 Instrumental dimension of PBAS 1 – evaluation and outcomes monitoring

PBASPCA1 – *evaluation & outcomes monitoring*			
Items		*Loadings*	*Cronbach's alpha (α)*
39Q03	Data recording	0.857	0.885
18Q05	Use of student assessment to monitor the school's progress from year to year	0.821	
39Q06	External evaluation	0.743	
19Q02	Achievement data tracked over time by administrative authority	0.700	
18Q06	Use of student assessment to make judgments about teachers' effectiveness	0.695	
39Q02	Written specification of student performance standards	0.672	
39Q05	Internal evaluation	0.626	

Figure 12.1 Instrumental dimension of PBAS 1 evaluation and outcomes monitoring – breakdown by education system.

Table 12.4 Instrumental dimension of PBAS 2 – teachers' incentives

PBASPCA2 – *teachers' incentives*

Items		Loadings	Cronbach's alpha (α)
31Q02	Financial bonus or monetary reward	0.899	0.879
31Q01	Salary change	0.831	
31Q06	Changes in the work responsibilities	0.724	
31Q05	Public recognition from head teacher	0.648	
31Q04	Change in the likelihood of career advancement	0.645	

mechanisms. Figure 12.2 shows great variations with regards to the intensity of this instrumental dimension within education systems.

External comparison and internal improvement mechanisms

The last instrumental dimension, which we called 'external comparison and internal improvement mechanisms' (PBAPCA3, describing 8.97% of the variance, α = 0.767), is constructed from five variables (Table 12.5) referring to distinct mechanisms aiming at promoting external comparison of schools' performances and stimulating between-schools competition on the one hand (publication of student results, use of student results to compare the school's performances with other schools', etc.); and to school improvement strategies on the other (experts consultation, teacher professional development activities). Figure 12.3 highlights great variations with regards to the intensity of this instrumental dimension within education systems.

In summary, what is at stake is the very nature of the preferred policy tools that make it possible to distinguish among these key instrumental dimensions of PBAS, whose prevalence varies widely among education systems.

Typology of PBAS in Europe and Canada

Hierarchical cluster analysis allow distinguishing between four types of PBAS (with the dendrogram [Appendix] neatly suggesting a clear division into four clusters), highlighting shared patterns among education systems in Europe and Canada: (1) an accountability of lesser intensity; (2) an accountability that focuses mainly on evaluation and outcomes monitoring; (3) PBAS articulating performance monitoring and external comparison/internal improvement mechanisms; (4) PBAS privileging direct incentives for teachers.

The chart plots PBASPCA2 – Teachers appraisal (x-axis from 3.00000 to -3.00000) for the following education systems (top to bottom):

Ontario
Scotland
Saskatchewan
New Scotia
England & Wales & North Ireland
Alberta
New Found & Lab
British Colombia
New Brunswick
Quebec
Sweden
Norway
Croatia
Greece
Netherlands
Romania
Bulgaria
Slovak Republic
France
Slovenia
Denmark
Prince Edouard
Luxembourg
Iceland
Manitoba
Lithuania
Portugal
Hessen
Ireland
Navarre
Italy
Latvia
Hungary
Flanders
Estonia
Austria
Basque Country
Nordrhein-Westfalen
Catalunia
Poland
Balearic Islands
Madrid
Czech Republic
Bayern
Baden-Württemberg
Switzerland
Belgium (french & germ)
Finland
Cantabria
Rheinland-Pfalz
Asturias
Aragon
Andalousia
Niedersachsen
La Rioja
Extramadura
Murcia
Castile & Leon
Galicia

Figure 12.2 Instrumental dimension of PBAS 2 teachers' appraisal – breakdown by education system.

Table 12.5 Instrumental dimension of PBAS 3 – external comparison and internal improvement mechanisms

PBASPCA3 – external comparison and internal improvement mechanisms

Items		Loadings	Cronbach's alpha (α)
39Q09	Experts' consultation	0.783	0.767
19Q01	Achievement data posted publicly	0.772	
18Q04	Use of students' results to compare the school with district or national performance	0.716	
31Q03	Teacher appraisal – opportunities for professional development activities	0.709	
18Q08	Use of students' results to compare the school with other schools	0.605	

1. Accountability of lesser intensity – the most widespread type within Western European countries.

   The first cluster, which embraces twenty education systems (including those of Luxembourg, Prince Edward Island, France and Quebec), is characterized by what we have called an accountability of lesser intensity. The cluster means for each instrumental dimension are systematically among the lowest compared with other clusters, implying that key instrumental dimensions are significantly less developed in this PBAS type than in the others in our typology (Appendix, Table 12.A.1).

   For instance, the literature confirms that the French-speaking community of Belgium has witnessed the development of external evaluation and accountability policies (Maroy & Mangez, 2011), introducing policy instruments such as curriculum standards and national assessment (Eurydice, 2015). However, in the same vein as in France, where steering by results relies mainly on the triptych '[school] projects, evaluation, contracts' (Maroy & Pons, 2019) emphasizing bureaucratic accountability, regulation through results tends to be implemented less. It is nevertheless tending to develop, as in Quebec, where during the 2000s the results-based management policy introduced various tools (strategic planning and contracts based on performance objectives coupled with mechanisms for accountability to hierarchical authorities) in order to steer the system (Maroy et al., 2017).

2. Accountability favouring evaluation and outcomes monitoring – the Spanish regions, Iceland, Portugal and Finland.

   The second PBAS empirical type includes 17 education systems: the Spanish regions, Finland, Iceland and Portugal. It is mainly characterized by instrumental configurations oriented towards evaluation and outcomes

Figure 12.3 Instrumental dimension of PBAS 3 External comparison and internal improvement mechanisms – breakdown by education system.

monitoring and therefore clearly distinguishable from the first PBAS type, where this dimension is much less prevalent. Evaluation procedures and tools for monitoring schools' outcomes are therefore the main instruments used for the regulation of schools while accountability schemes operate mainly through the hierarchical chain.

For instance, in the 2000s, Spain has witnessed the introduction of education reforms aiming at ensuring quality and equity within the Spanish school system and at raising education outcomes (Verger & Curran, 2014). Oriented towards school autonomy and accountability, promoting school evaluation and large-scale assessment, new legislations and reforms, including the Education Law of 2006 (Ley Orgánica de Educación), introduced school evaluations, school development plans as well as regular evaluations of student achievement among the Spanish autonomous regions, although the latter do enjoy a great autonomy in the management of education (Glenn & Galan, 2011; Eurydice, 2015).

3. PBAS favouring external comparison and internal improvement mechanisms

This cluster formed by the majority of the Canadian provinces and Scotland (8 education systems) is based on instrumental configurations oriented towards evaluation and performance monitoring on one side, and school improvement and competition mechanisms on the other, with this cluster recording the highest mean for the latter dimension. This PBAS thus relies on a significantly wider range of tools than previous empirical types, combining tight performance monitoring and school competition mechanisms along with school improvement procedures such as expert consultation and teachers' professional development activities.

In Ontario, for instance, the performance management and accountability system orchestrated by the Education Quality and Accountability Office are based on a tight monitoring of students' results, measured through large-scale testing and reported publicly, with respect to performance standards (Jaafar & Anderson, 2007). School development planning and school improvement schemes such as experts' consultation and hiring coaches remain key levers to improve school management strategies and educational processes. Teachers whose professional development is an integral part of the 'performance appraisal system' (MEO, 2010), are expected to align their instruction and assessment practices with stated standards and outcomes (Earl, 1995, p. 50).

4. PBAS favouring direct incentives for teachers

Finally, the last PBAS type covers 14 education systems, including England, the Netherlands, Sweden and the majority of education systems within Eastern European countries. Relying on various instrumental configurations, this PBAS type is clearly distinct from other types because of the strong presence of incentives for teachers, an instrumental dimension weakly developed in other clusters. It thus combines a wide range of tools such as performance monitoring and accountability to hierarchical authority and the public with direct incentives for teachers. For instance, the literature highlights that PBAS in England relies on a highly sophisticated data production and management apparatus coupled with accountability schemes and market strategies foreseeing social and material consequences for actors. The system involves a close monitoring of performances (schools, teachers, students) in relation to benchmarks while different levels of action (central, intermediate, local), especially schools, are expected to produce and use achievement data to improve their performances (Ozga, 2009; Ozga & Grek, 2010). School evaluation procedures orchestrated by the Office for Standards in Education, Children's Services and Skills (OFSTED) target key outcomes (Rosenthal, 2004), while market and competition mechanisms (school choice, publication of students' results, etc.) put pressure on schools to attract the best students and to achieve better performance.

How PBAS relate with the degrees of effectiveness and equity: Mixed findings, negative associations

Do the distinct instrumental configurations and forms taken by PBAS in Europe and Canada affect the degrees of effectiveness and equity of these education systems? The results of multiple regression analyses that allow these questions to be answered are summarized in Tables 12.6 and 12.7.

With regard to PBAS instrumental dimensions, Table 12.6 shows a significant negative association between the teacher incentives instrumental dimension (Models 2) and the degree of effectiveness, and a positive one with the degrees of inequality in outcomes (IEEO) and of basic skills (IEBS). These results suggest that the higher the incentives for teachers, the lower the overall mean score in mathematics and the proportion of students who do not reach the minimum proficiency level, and the higher the achievement gap between top and low performers. In contrast, we found no significant association between this instrumental dimension and the degree of inequality in education opportunities (EEO).

Further, the external comparison and internal improvement mechanisms instrumental dimension (Models 3) appears to be negatively associated with the degree of effectiveness and positively with the degree of inequality of basic skills. In other words, the stronger this instrumental dimension of PBAS, the lower the overall mean score in mathematics and the proportion of students reaching the minimum proficiency level.

In contrast, the performance monitoring instrumental dimension (Models 1) seems to have no bearing on any effectiveness or equity indicators.

With regard to PBAS types, Table 12.7 shows that only the PBAS favouring direct incentives for teachers (Type 4) is significantly different from the

Table 12.6 Statistical associations between PBAS instrumental dimensions and the degrees of effectiveness and equity in education systems

	a) *Effectiveness (MEANM) (log)*	b) *(in) equality in outcomes (IEEO) (log)*	c) *(in) equality in educational opportunities (IEEO) (log)*	d) *(in) equality of basic skills (IEBS)*
MODELS 1	β	β	β	β
PBASPCA1	0.053	−0.114	0.071	−0.073
Performance monitoring				
PUEXP(z)	0.201	−0.006	−0.226†	−0.150
[Public expenditure in education]				
SOSTR(z)	−0.334*	0.349*		0.359*
[Social structure education system]				
HVSTR(z)	0.262	0.343*	0.526**	−0.074
[Horizontal & vertical stratification]				
F	3.144	6.676	12.755	3.005
R² adj.	0.129**	0.281**	0.378**	0.121*
MODELS 2				
PBASPCA2	−0.399**	0.291*	0.122	0.381**
Incentives for teachers				
PUEXP(z)	0.001	0.153	−0.224†	0.045
[Public expenditure in education]				
SOSTR(z)	−0.499**	0.447**		0.509**
[Social structure education system]				
HVSTR(z)	0.289**	0.366**	0.469**	−0.088
F	6.052	8.531	13.278	5.516
R² adj.	0.258**	0.382**	0.388**	0.237**
MODELS 3				
PBASPCA3	−0.268†	0.201	−0.053	0.280†
External comparison/ internal improvement				
PUEXP(z)	0.225	−0.012	−0.233†	−0.172
[Public expenditure in education]				
SOSTR(z)	−0.413**	0.386**		0.435**
[Social structure education system]				
HVSTR(z)	0.176	0.449**	0.475*	0.026
[Horizontal & vertical stratification]				
F	4.215	7.291	12.673	4.119
R² adj.	0.181**	0.303**	0.376**	0.177**

Statistical significance is noted by **$p < .01$, *$p < .05$, † $p < .10$

Table 12.7 Statistical associations between PBAS types and the degrees of effectiveness and equity in education systems

	a) Effectiveness (MEANM) (log)	b) (in) equality in outcomes (IEEO) (log)	c) (in)equality in educational opportunities (IEEO) (log)	d) (in) equality of basic skills (IEBS)
MODELS 4				
Type 2	0.149	−0.142	−0.072	−0.167
Type 3	0.098	−0.125	−0.210	−0.109
Type 4	−0.376**	0.172	0.018	0.349**
PUEXP(z) [Public expenditure in education]	0.028	0.089	−0.242†	0.013
SOSTR(z) [Social structure education system]	−0.577**	0.465**		0.591**
HVSTR(z) [Horizontal & vertical stratification]	0.363*	0.288†	0.375**	−0.172
F	4.584	5.258	8.253	4.200
R²	0.346	0.378	0.438	0.326
R² adj.	0.270**	0.306**	0.385**	0.249**

Statistical significance is noted by $**p < .01$, $*p < .05$, $† p < .10$.

reference category, namely accountability of lesser intensity, in terms of effectiveness and equity. PBAS Type 4 is negatively associated with the degree of effectiveness and positively with the degree of inequity of basic skills, while no significant relationship was found with other equity indicators and between other PBAS types and the degrees of effectiveness and equity. The overall mean score in mathematics and the proportion of student who reach a minimum proficiency level (PISA Proficiency Level 2) is therefore significantly lower in education systems favouring PBAS that relies on a wide range of tools, including direct incentives for teachers. It can therefore be hypothesized that the effects of the incentives for teachers and external comparison and internal improvement instrumental dimensions observed in the previous models (1, 2, 3) combine within this PBAS type to affect both the degrees of effectiveness and equity of basic skills downwards.

Finally, with regard to control variables, all models show a negative association between public expenditure on education and the degree of inequality in educational opportunities, suggesting a smaller effect of family background in education systems that make a greater budgetary effort in education. Furthermore, a more unequal social structure of education systems is systematically associated with lower degrees of effectiveness and equity (equalities in outcomes and of basic skills). These results thus reflect the strong effect of family background on student achievement. In the same vein, horizontal and vertical stratification in school systems is systematically associated with higher degrees of inequality in outcomes and in educational opportunities. Surprisingly, however, the former also seems to be associated with greater effectiveness, but only when the dimension regarding teachers' incentives is introduced in the models, a result that should be further explored in subsequent research.

Altogether, our findings suggest that although the relationship between PBAS and student achievement varies according to different instrumental configurations, PBAS are not associated with greater degrees of effectiveness and equity but, at worst, seem to affect the latter negatively. Moreover, our findings confirm that jurisdiction-level factors, namely the budgetary effort in education, the social structure and the horizontal and vertical stratification of school systems remain strong predictors of the degrees of effectiveness and equity.

Discussion and conclusions

This study provides evidence concerning key instrumental configurations and the forms taken by PBAS in education systems in Europe and Canada, and how they are associated with student achievement. Using PISA 2012 data, the study classifies education systems in Europe and Canada according to three key instrumental dimensions of PBAS that rely on distinct results-based regulation tools and accountability mechanisms and provides a typology of PBAS. Highlighting cross-national patterns and similarities among education systems, it then explores how PBAS are associated with effectiveness and equity in education systems in Europe and Canada and concludes that there are negative associations. This study contributes to the debate on PBAS in two ways.

A first key result concerns the results-based regulation tools and accountability mechanisms favored in education systems in Europe and Canada. Not only the range but also the very nature of system-specific regulation tools at play are undoubtedly a key feature that allows to distinguish between PBAS in these contexts. While key instrumental dimensions of PBAS discussed in this study rely on assessment and performance monitoring, either comparison mechanisms or incentives for teachers, the first two types of PBAS (1 and 2) in our typology rely on a more restricted instrumentation while the last two types (3 and 4) combine a wide range of tools and instrumental configurations. A first layer of interpretation relates to the classic distinction between high-stakes and low-stakes accountability systems (Carnoy & Loeb, 2002) that allow distinguishing between these two groups of PBAS (Types 1 and 2 on one side, Types 3 and 4 on the other). The latter two types of PBAS (Types 3 and 4) favoured in Scotland and the majority of the Canadian provinces, and in England and the Eastern European countries, respectively, are institutional set-ups that combine a wide range of policy tools in order to monitor and also control educational outcomes. They induce more pressure and higher stakes for actors, due to various material and symbolic consequences, than the two first PBAS types (Types 1 and 2).

Another layer of interpretation refers to the very nature of the policy tools favoured as the main drivers for change, which carry and enact distinct logics of regulation (Lascoumes & Simard, 2011). PBAS Type 4 relies on external devices coupled with material incentives systems as the main levers for change as the incentives theory commands (Clark & Wilson, 1961). The PBAS favoured in Scotland or Ontario (Type 3), however, multiply the objects (processes and outcomes), locus (external and internal) and forms of control (professional, hierarchical) in a logic rooted, we argue, in school effectiveness and school improvement frames. This PBAS combines pressure and support, in a capacity-building perspective (Fullan, 2007). Actors must align their practices and internalize expectations in accordance with benchmarks. The learning (individual and collective) process should favour the construction of 'value consensus about educational goals' (Broadfoot, 1996), sustaining the process of (cultural) change that seeks to modify existing norms, structures, and processes (Elmore, 2004, p. 11) in what some have called 'reflexive' accountability (Maroy & Voisin, 2014). Finally, Types 1 and 2 can be seen as two variants of 'soft accountability' systems (Mons & Dupriez, 2011). While both systems rely on external devices (standards, assessment tools) to steer the system and engage actors to reflect and improve processes when confronted with student results, the prevalence of accountability schemes and the range of tools enable to differentiate between the type 2 that relies on a wider range of tools than the type 1. Our study suggests thus going beyond the classic distinction between high-stakes and low-stakes accountability systems and also stresses cross-national and geographical patterns. Further studies are therefore needed in order to shed light on travelling models of accountability and processes of policy borrowing (Halpin & Troyna, 1995).

A second key finding that emerges from this study concerns the associations between PBAS and the degrees of effectiveness and equity, which vary according to the favoured instrumental configurations but remain mostly negative nonetheless. The teacher incentives instrumental dimensions and PBAS Type 4, which promote direct incentives for teachers in addition to a large set of instruments, are indeed associated with lower overall performance and lower proportions of students reaching a minimum proficiency level. This is an important finding that suggests that PBAS not only fail to bring the efficiency and equity in education systems that they promise but, at worst, also affect both efficiency and equity downwards. These conclusions support the findings of studies that cast doubt on the positive effect of more stringent PBAS on student achievement, such as those preferred in England or in Eastern European countries. However, as previously said, education systems that record lower levels of student achievement may have been more inclined to adopt tighter accountability systems. Subsequent studies that control for this bias are thus needed to observe whether PBAS actually cause a decrease in student achievement. Nevertheless, while our study sheds light on education systems little studied so far, such as those in Eastern European countries, it also extends discussions on PBAS beyond high-stakes accountability systems abundantly discussed in the literature, suggesting that other forms of accountability systems such as 'reflexive' or 'softer' accountability systems are not related to higher degrees of effectiveness or equity, at least in education systems in Europe and Canada. Overall, even though the accountability systems discussed in this study are based, we argue, on significantly different theories of change enacted by distinct regulations, they do not seem to make a significant difference in student achievement. It is, therefore, perhaps their common foundations and rationales that need to be questioned, such as an instrumental vision of change enacted by key instruments and driven by efficiency and effectiveness purposes.

To conclude, while PBAS are implemented worldwide, relying on rhetorics of effectiveness, equity, transparency and modernity and their popularity among policymakers seems unquestionable, previous research as well as the present study suggest that there is a need to adopt a critical stance to question the status of PBAS as an effective policy solution to improve student achievement and to tackle educational inequalities. It is clear that the effects of PBAS must be questioned in the light of the political objectives they are supposed to pursue. Although neither our large-scale quantitative study nor PISA data enabled us to shed light on specific policy objectives attached to the introduction of PBAS in the various contexts studied here, the present study conclude that they are not or, at worst, that there are negative associations with student achievement and with different figures of equalities of achievement nonetheless. However, a possible way forward would be to question the very meaning of accountability in education, its purposes and practices, putting at the very centre of the debate the notions of responsibility, answerability, professionalism and trust applied to all levels (central, intermediate, local) of education systems (Ranson, 2003). Although the very notion of accountability covers many meanings, how can accountability, rather than being an instrument of neo-liberal governance in pursuit of efficiency goals, be at the service of the functions of qualification, socialization and subjectification of education (Biesta, 2015)? How can accountability serve to build trust and to promote professionalism rather than being an instrument for control based mainly on power and compliance relationships? To what extent can accountability really be a means at the service of education? It seems to us that these questions constitute a set of issues that deserve to be further addressed.

Appendix: Hierarchical cluster analysis results

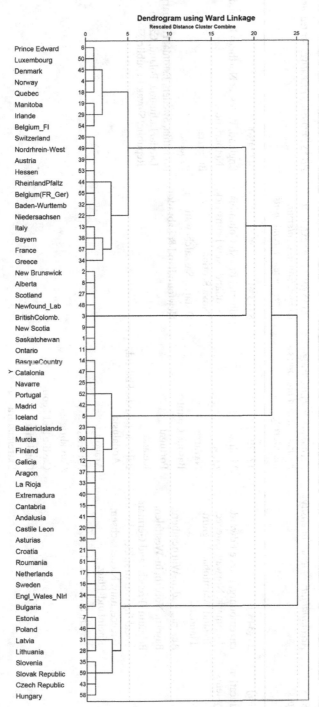

Figure 12.A.1 Dendrogram.

Table 12.A.1 Typology of accountability systems

PBAS types	Accountability of lesser intensity	Accountability favouring evaluation and outcomes monitoring	PBAS favouring external comparison and internal improvement mechanisms	PBAS favouring incentives for teachers
n (%)	20 (34%)	17 (29%)	8 (13%)	14 (24%)
Education systems	Luxembourg, Prince Edward, Denmark, Norway, Quebec, Ireland, Manitoba, Belgium Flanders, Austria, Baden-Württemberg, Bayern, Nordrhein-Westfalen, Belgium (French- and German-speaking communities), France, Greece, Italy, Niedersachsen, Rheinland-Pfalz, Hessen, Switzerland	Madrid Murcia Navarre Basque Country Portugal Iceland Balearic Islands, Finland, Andalusia Aragon Asturias Cantabria Castile and Leon Catalonia Extremadura Galicia La Rioja	Alberta, British Columbia, Scotland, New Brunswick, Nova Scotia, Ontario, Saskatchewan Newfoundland & Labrador	England, Wales, & Northern Ireland, Netherlands, Bulgaria, Croatia, Romania, Sweden, Estonia, Hungary, Latvia, Lithuania, Poland, Czech Republic, Slovak Republic, Slovenia

Table 12.A.2 Cluster characteristics – mean, standard deviation and significant differences with other PBAS types on each instrumental dimension

PBAS TYPES	EVALUATION AND PERFORMANCE MONITORING (PBASPCA1)			TEACHERS APPRAISAL (PBASPCA2)			EXTERNAL COMPARISON AND INTERNAL IMPROVEMENT MECHANISMS (PBASPCA3)		
	Mean	Standard deviation	Significant differences with other PBAS types*	Mean	Standard deviation	Significant differences with other PBAS types*	Mean	Standard deviation	Significant differences with other PBAS types*
1) *accountability of lesser intensity*	**-1.09**	0.65	< 2)* < 3)* < 4)*	-0.36	0.50	> 3)* < 4)*	-0.13	0.67	> 2)* < 3)*
2) *accountability favouring evaluation and outcomes monitoring*	0.81	0.55	> 1)*	-0.39	0.41	> 3)* < 4)*	**-0.89**	0.56	< 1)* < 3)* < 4)*
3) *PBAS favouring external comparison and internal improvement mechanisms*	0.49	0.49	> 1)*	**-0.96**	0.35	< 1)* < 2)* < 4)*	**1.67**	0.32	> 1)* > 2)* > 4)*
4) *PBAS favouring incentives for teachers*	0.30	0.63	> 1)*	**1.53**	0.57	> 1*) > 2)* > 3)*	0.31	0.69	> 2)* < 3)*

Note

1 For the original study, see Voisin (2017).

References

Ball, S. J. (2003). The teacher's soul and the terrors of performativity. *Journal of Education Policy*, 18(2), 215–228.

Berényi, E., Bajomi, I., & Neumann, E. (2013). Une expérience hongroise visant à gouverner par les nombres – genèse et évolution du Système National de Mesure des Compétences. In C. Maroy & Y. Dutercq (Eds.), *L'école à l'épreuve de la performance. Les politiques de régulation par les résultats*. (pp. 71–88) Bruxelles: De Boeck.

Biesta, G. (2015). What is education for? On good education, teacher judgement, and educational professionalism. *European Journal of Education*, 50(1), 75–87.

Bovens, M. (2007). Analysing and assessing accountability: A conceptual framework. *European Law Journal*, 13(4), 447–468.

Bovens, M., Goodin, R. E., & Schillemans, T. (2014). *The Oxford handbook public accountability*. Oxford: Oxford University Press.

Broadfoot, P. (1996). *Education, assessment and society: A sociological analysis*. Maidenhead, Berkshire (UK): Open University Press.

Carnoy, M., & Loeb, S. (2002). Does external accountability affect student outcomes? A cross-state analysis. *Educational Evaluation & Policy Analysis*, 24(4), 305–331.

Clark, P., & Wilson, J. (1961). Incentive systems: A theory of organizations. *Administrative Science Quarterly*, 6(2), 129–166.

Croxford, L., Grek, S., & Shaik, F. J. (2009). Quality assurance and evaluation (QAE) in Scotland: Promoting self-evaluation within and beyond the country. *Journal of Education Policy*, 24(2), 179–193.

Dee, T. S. (2002). Standards and student outcomes: Lessons from the 'First Wave' of education reform. Working paper PEPG 02-08: Swarthmore College.

Dupriez, V., & Dumay, X. (2005). L'égalité des chances à l'école: analyse d'un effet spécifique de la structure scolaire. *Revue française de pédagogie*, 150, 5–17.

Duru-Bellat, M., Mons, N., & Suchaut, B. (2004). Caractéristiques des systèmes éducatifs et compétences des jeunes à 15 ans. L'éclairage des comparaisons entre pays. *Les Cahiers De L'IREDU*, 66, 1–158.

Earl, L. M. (1995). Assessment and accountability in education in Ontario. *Canadian Journal of Education/Revue canadienne de l'éducation*, 20(1), 45–55.

Elmore, R. F. (2004). *School reform from the inside out: Policy, practice, and performance*. Cambridge: Harvard Education Press.

Elstad, E. (2009). Schools which are named, shamed and blamed by the media: School accountability in Norway. *Educational Assessment, Evaluation and Accountability*, 21(2), 173–189.

Eurydice (2015). *Assuring quality in education: Policies and approaches to school evaluation in Europe*. Luxembourg: Publications Office of the European Union.

Fenwick, T., Mangez, E., & Ozga, J. (2014). *World yearbook of education 2014: Governing knowledge: Comparison, knowledge-based technologies and expertise in the regulation of education*. New York: Routledge.

Fullan, M. (2007). Change theory as a force for school improvement. In J.M. Burger, C.F. Webber, & P. Klinck (Eds) *Intelligent leadership. Studies in Educational Leadership*, vol. 6. (pp. 27–39). Dordrecht: Springer.

Glenn, C., & Galan, A. (2011). Educational freedom and accountability for school quality in Spain. *International Journal of Education Law and Policy*, 7(1–2), 179–193.

Hallak, J. (1996). *Coûts et dépenses en éducation. Principes de la planification*. Paris: UNESCO IIEP.

Halpin, D., & Troyna, B. (1995). The politics of education policy borrowing. *Comparative Education*, 31(3), 303–310.

Hanushek, E. A., & Raymond, M. E. (2005). Does school accountability lead to improved student performance? *Journal of Policy Analysis and Management*, 24(2), 297–327.

Heilig, J. V., & Darling-Hammond, L. (2008). Accountability Texas-style: The progress and learning of urban minority students in a high-stakes testing context. *Educational Evaluation and Policy Analysis*, 30(2), 75–110.

Hood, C. (1991). A public management for all seasons. *Public Administration*, 69, 3–19.

Jaafar, S. B., & Anderson, S. (2007). Policy trends and tensions in accountability for educational management and services in Canada. *Alberta Journal of Educational Research*, 53(2), 207–227.

Ladd, H. F., & Lauen, D. L. (2010). Status versus growth: The distributional effects of school accountability. *Journal of Policy Analysis and Management*, 29(3), 426–450.

Lascoumes, P., & Simard, L. (2011). L'action publique au prisme de ses instruments. *Revue française de science politique*, 61(1), 5–22.

Le Donné, N. (2014). European variations in socioeconomic inequalities in students' cognitive achievement: The role of educational policies. *European Sociological Review*, 30(3), 329–343.

Lee, J. (2008). Is test driven external accountability effective? Synthesizing the evidence from cross state Causal comparative and correlational studies. *Review of Educational Research*, 78(3), 608–644.

Lee, J., & Amo, L. C. (2017). International and interstate analyses of student- and school-targeted accountability policy effects. In D. Sharpes (Eds). *Handbook on comparative and international studies in education* (pp. 3–22) Charlotte: Information Age Publishing.

Lee, J., & Wong, K. (2004). The impact of the accountability on racial and socioeconomic equity considering both school resources and achievement outcomes. *American Educational Research Journal*, 41(4), 797–832.

Maroy, C. (2009). Enjeux, présupposés et implicites normatifs de la poursuite de l'efficacité dans les systèmes d'enseignement. In X. Dumay & V. Dupriez (Eds.), *L'efficacité dans l'enseignement: promesses et zones d'ombre* (1st ed., pp. 209–224). Bruxelles: De Boeck.

Maroy, C., Brassard, A., Mathou, C., Vaillancourt, S., & Voisin, A. (2017). La co-construction de la Gestion axée sur les résultats: les logiques de médiations des Commissions scolaires québécoises. *McGill Journal of Education*, 52(1), 93–114.

Maroy, C., & Mangez, C. (2011). La construction des politiques d'évaluation et de pilotage du système scolaire en Belgique francophone: nouveau paradigme politique et médiation des experts. In G. Felouzis & S. Hanhart (Eds.), *Gouverner l'éducation par les nombres? Usages, débats et controverses* (pp. 53–76). Bruxelles/Paris: De Boeck.

Maroy, C., & Pons, X. (2019). *Accountability Policies in Education: A Comparative and Multilevel Analysis in France and Quebec*. Gewerbestrasse: Springer.

Maroy, C., & Voisin, A. (2014). Diversité des politiques d'accountability: l'incidence de l'instrumentation et des théories de la régulation des politiques. *Education comparée*, 11, 31–57.

MEO (2010). *Évaluation du rendement du personnel enseignant. Guide des exigences et des modalités*. Toronto: Ministère de l'éducation de l'Ontario.

Meyer, H.-D., & Benavot, A. (2013). *PISA, power, and policy: The emergence of global educational governance.* Symposium books: Oxford Studies in Comparative Education.

Mons, N. (2004). *De l'école unifiée aux écoles plurielles. Evaluation internationale des politiques de différenciation et de diversification de l'offre éducative.* (Doctorat en Sciences de l'Éducation), Université de Bourgogne.

Mons, N., & Dupriez, V. (2011). Les politiques d'accountability. *Recherche et formation*, 65.

OECD. (2014). *PISA 2012 technical report.* Paris: OECD Publishing.

OECD. (2013). *PISA 2012 results: What students know and can do – Student performance in mathematics, reading and science* (Volume I). Paris: OECD Publishing.

Ozga, J. (2009). Governing education through data in England: From regulation to self-evaluation. *Journal of Education Policy*, 24(2), 149–162.

Ozga, J., & Grek, S. (2010). Governing education through data: Scotland, England and the European Education Policy Space. *British Education Research Journal*, 36(6), 937–952.

Ranson, S. (2003). Public accountability in the age of neo-liberal governance. *Journal of Education Policy*, 18(5), 459–480. doi:10.1080/0268093032000124848

Reback, R. (2008). Teaching to the rating: School accountability and the distribution of student achievement. *Journal of Public Economics*, 92(5–6), 1394–1415.

Rose, N. (1991). Governing by numbers: Figuring out democracy. *Accounting Organizations and Society*, 16(7), 673–692.

Rosenthal, L. (2004). Do school inspections improve school quality? Ofsted inspections and school examination results in the UK. *Economics of Education Review*, 23(2), 143–151.

Rothman, R. (1995). *Measuring up: Standards, assessment, and school reform.* San Francisco: Jossey-Bass.

Schütz, G., West, M., & Wößmann, L. (2007). *School accountability, autonomy, choice and the equity of student achievement: International evidence from PISA 2003.* Paris.

Tröhler, D., Meyer, H.-D., Labaree, D. F., & Hutt, E. L. (2014). Accountability: Antecedents, power, and processes. *Teachers College Record*, 116(9), 1–12.

UNESCO. (2017). *Global accountability monitoring report 2017/2018. Accountability in education: Meeting our commitments.* Paris: UNESCO.

Verger, A., & Curran, M. (2014). New public management as a global education policy: Its adoption and re-contextualization in a Southern European setting. *Critical Studies in Education*, 1–19. doi:10.1080/17508487.2014.913531

Voisin, A. (2017). Systèmes d'accountability basés sur la performance - types, logiques instrumentales et effets sur l'efficacité et l'équité scolaires des systèmes éducatifs d'Europe et du Canada. Une étude comparative à partir des données PISA 2012 », Thèse de doctorat (Éducation comparée et fondements de l'éducation), Université de Montréal, 2017.

Wößmann, L. (2005). The effect heterogeneity of central examinations: Evidence from TIMSS, TIMSS-Repeat and PISA. *Education Economics*, 13(2), 143–169.

Yi, P., & Shin, I.-S. (2018). Multilevel relations between external accountability, internal accountability, and math achievement: A cross country analysis. *Problems of Education in the 21st Century*, 76(3), 318–333.

13 In and out of the 'pressure cooker': Schools' varying responses to accountability and datafication

Antoni Verger, Gerard Ferrer-Esteban
and Lluís Parcerisa

Introduction[1]

In educational research, performance-based accountability (PBA) systems have often been likened to 'pressure cookers' (cf. Agrey, 2004; Perryman et al., 2011; Tan, 2018). PBA puts high levels of pressure on schools by holding them liable for their performance, sanctioning underachievement and rewarding success. With high-stakes accountability systems in particular, underperforming schools experience higher levels of pressure, since continuous low performance has significant implications, from having restrictions placed on schools' pedagogic, organizational and economic autonomy to being forced into closure (Diamond, 2012; Kim and Sunderman, 2005; Mintrop, 2004). By exerting these and other types of pressures, PBA is expected to make schools more responsive to the achievement of centrally defined learning goals and more inclined to use learning metrics in their daily practices and decisions. Overall, PBA policies aim to schools more consciously aligning their instruction with the mandated curriculum, and more intensively using achievement data to identify learning gaps and define educational and organizational improvement programmes. Through the promotion of these changes, PBA systems not only aim to improve learning achievement in aggregated terms but also to ensure that schools (especially underperforming schools) pay sufficient attention to their most disadvantaged students.

Although the expectations with PBA are high, existing research shows that the impact of PBA on school organizations is rather uneven. Accountability instruments can generate a broad range of outcomes and responses, from altering the goals and organizational identity of schools to more short-term strategies and cosmetic changes, such as intensifying teaching to the test (i.e., focusing instruction on predictable test content and/or test formats) or narrowing the curriculum (i.e., dedicating more time and resources to tested subjects) (Au, 2007; Mittleman and Jennings, 2018). In the latter case, rather than aligning school practices with accountability expectations, such responses are more likely to decouple from them. Varying school responses to PBA are identified in both high-stakes and low-stakes accountability systems, as well as in countries where these systems have been installed for shorter or longer periods of time (see Candido, 2020; Diamond and Spillane, 2004; Landri, 2018; Maroy and Pons, 2019). Even in the US context, where decades of high-stakes accountability have turned schools into testing- and data-intensive organizations (see Mittleman and Jennings, 2018), schools' pedagogic and organizational responses are far from homogeneous.

Existing research tends to attribute the varying responses to accountability pressures to variables of a different nature, ranging from school leadership styles to the broader socio-economic contexts in which schools operate. However, to date, research has overlooked the role of subjective variables (such as school actors' perceived and experienced pressures) in the mediation and enactment of PBA. To address this gap, this chapter aims to analyze the production of different patterns of responses to PBA within schools from a policy enactment perspective. On the basis of a mixed-methods study conducted in Chile, we analyze how school actors' interpretations of and dispositions towards PBA, on the one hand, and their experienced levels of pressure, on the other, influence how they respond to the accountability regulatory system. As we will show, the responses to PBA that have been identified go beyond conventional alignment–decoupling dichotomy and include a more varying range of options. Our perspective is premised on the assumption that the way school actors respond to policy prerogatives is contingent on the way these actors make sense of PBA pressures and expectations within their broader social and institutional frameworks. In other words, the responses to PBA that we identify are the result of analyzing how school actors *perceive* and *live* accountability regulations in their reference contexts.

To build our main arguments, the chapter is structured as follows: in the first section, on the context of the research, we introduce Chile's long trajectory of experimentation with learning metrics and a broad range of related accountability measures. In the second section, we present our theoretical framework, where we highlight the importance of focusing not only on policy interpretation but also on perceived regulatory pressure to understand how policies are enacted. After presenting the methodology of our study in the third section, in the fourth one, we offer the main findings of the research in the form of a new categorization of school responses to PBA regulations. Finally, the conclusions highlight the key mediating role of subjective variables in the configuration of different patterns of school responses to PBA, and we reflect on the research and policy implications of our study.

Context of the study: Governing schools through performativity and markets in Chile

Chile is a country where PBA has a long tradition in the governance of education. Chile was an early adopter of national, large-scale assessments in education, the first of which was implemented at the start of the 1980s, in the context of an ambitious and drastic market reform promoted by the civic-military dictatorship (1973–1990). At that time, the main intention of the national assessment, known as the System for the Measurement of Quality in Education (SIMCE), was to inform school choice (Bellei and Vanni, 2015). Nevertheless, it was not until the restoration of democracy in the 1990s (specifically, in 1995) that SIMCE results started being publicly disseminated on a regular basis (first in the media and later on the Ministry of Education website). Since then, more and more functions and uses have been found for this standardized test. To start with, in 1996, the SIMCE became a fundamental component of a merit-based pay system for teachers, in which collective salary bonuses were attached to schools' performance (Mizala and Schneider, 2014).

During the early 2000s, the government implemented various compensatory programmes aimed at low-performing schools, to promote data use and school improvement processes (Falabella, 2020). This policy approach crystallized in the enactment of the Preferential School Subsidy Law in 2008. Under this scheme, the state gave an additional subsidy to schools for each 'vulnerable' student enrolled. As a condition of accessing this subsidy, schools accepted additional accountability measures. Schools were classified according to their SIMCE performance, and in the case of continuous poor performance, the state could impose sanctions which included the possibility of school closure (Valenzuela and Montecinos, 2017).

In 2011, a new Education Quality Assurance System (Law no. 20529) was created, whose provisions allow the Chilean state to adopt new data-intensive policy instruments and tools to inspect, evaluate and sanction all types of public and publicly subsidized private schools – not just those receiving the preferential school subsidy (Parcerisa and Falabella, 2017). Since then, schools have been classified in four performance categories (high, medium, medium-low and insufficient) according to SIMCE results, data on students' learning progress, and a set of personal and social development indicators.[2] Poorly performing schools are meant to receive pedagogical support and external evaluative visits from the Ministry of Education for a period of four years, and if their performance remains insufficient, schools can be closed. In parallel, the Education Quality Agency (EQA) has put a great deal of effort into making performance data intelligible and actionable for the elaboration of school improvement plans through various initiatives, online tools and training programmes.

In short, Chile is a country where both performativity and datafication, in interaction with market rules, have a great potential to alter school practices and to discipline teachers' behavior. Chilean education is a distinctive scenario within which to study the combined effects of market forces and different forms of administrative accountability pressure on educational organizations and practices.

Understanding the variation in school responses through enactment theory

Interpretation as a key moment in policy enactment

Enactment and sense-making theories are well suited to exploration of how school actors 'construct the demands of, and appropriate responses to, accountability systems differently' (Jennings, 2010, p. 229). Such theories broadly state that the way educational actors interpret and make sense of new policy mandates is key to explaining how such mandates translate into everyday practices (Ball, Maguire and Braun, 2012; Spillane et al., 2002). These theories do not portray teachers and principals as simple policy takers but as policy shapers who actively adapt, modify and reframe new policy prerogatives to suit their preferences and the needs and constraints of their particular school contexts. Following a policy enactment approach, school responses to policy instruments such as PBA will 'depend on how the aims and purposes ascribed to them, and the meanings and representations they carry, are perceived [and] understood [...] by key actors' (Skedsmo, 2011, p. 7). This does not mean that policy interpretation is mainly guided by instrumental rationality and causal beliefs. Principled beliefs, personal biographies, previous experiences or emotional scripts co-constitute the interpretive frames through which educators approach educational policy, and respond to it. Furthermore, policy interpretation, beyond an individual act, results from the interaction between school actors, and happens within a broader network that includes parents, the school owner, inspectors and external consultants, among others (Spillane et al., 2002).

Policy interpretation is key to understanding why some schools align themselves with new policy reforms, but others avoid implementing them. According to Malen (2006), school actors align with new reforms when they perceive that these reforms easily couple with their previous way of working and/or their particular or collective interests; the opposite is also true, and school actors with a more conflicting approach to a reform will be those that disagree with its main goals and/or instruments. School actors might dislike an educational reform due to concerns about its usefulness, validity or fairness, or out of concern that it goes against their interests (or the interests of students) or contradicts their professional values and educational beliefs. When negative interpretations predominate, schools tend to address the external pressure to comply with new regulations through dilution strategies and obstructive bureaucratic games, such as neglect, overt resistance or subtle adaptation (Malen, 2006). Some of these dynamics have been for instance observed in several francophone countries, where teachers justify ritualistic (but not substantive) adoption of accountability instruments because they consider that these instruments clash with their own notions of good instruction and student assessment (see Maroy et al. in this volume).

The role of actors' subjective perceptions of accountability pressures

PBA systems assume that the more pressure is exerted on schools, the more measures will be taken to enhance the educational quality of school provision. Pressure is likely to be exerted based on schools' performance levels; thus, schools on probation will be subjected to stronger and more coercive forms of accountability pressure. High levels of pressure may result in different responses, typically defined as alignment or decoupling, depending on whether the accountability expectations are met or not – with the latter usually being associated with tactical or symbolic responses in order to cope with regulatory pressures, at least in the short term (cf. Boxenbaum and Jonsson, 2017).

Research conducted in high-stakes accountability settings often concludes that schools exposed to coercive sanctions – which, not coincidentally, are those that tend to serve the most disadvantaged student populations or concentrate on students who are more challenging to teach (see Pallas, in this volume) – are those that more frequently adopt instructional tactics through which to inflate test results, without necessarily adopting 'deep' changes in pedagogy (Mittleman and Jennings, 2018, p. 481). Thus, schools facing higher levels of administrative pressure tend to intensify test preparation practices and the number of teaching hours dedicated to subjects evaluated externally; to focus further on so-called 'bubble students' (i.e., students who are closer to the proficiency cut-off score); or to track students according to their performance level in order to customize their training (Au, 2007; Mittleman and Jennings, 2018; Watanabe, 2008).

Accountability research typically assumes that pressure is equally high (once school performance is held constant), while contextual factors foster or hinder full implementation of school improvement policies. Specifically, instrumental responses may depend on factors such as school composition or performance levels (which, in turn, are related to composition). Schools' socio-economic and institutional characteristics define the limits of what is possible and desirable in terms of school improvement and performance, and how much pressure PBA exerts on them. For example, in deprived schools (where aggregate performance levels are likely to be lower and pressure is likely to be higher), school actors will be more prone to carrying out superficial strategies to increase scores in a short amount of time. Research also shows that privately managed schools tend to be more reactive to administrative accountability pressure than conventional public schools and articulate more instrumental responses (Berends, 2015; Zancajo, 2020).

Although we acknowledge that all these dynamics do indeed occur in PBA systems, we also assume that the reality of schools is highly complex, and it cannot be taken for granted that objective school characteristics alone determine the performative pressure that school staff experience. In our view, the intensity of administrative accountability pressures, which are objective in nature, is not constant, as is subjectively mediated. What makes schools reactive to the regulatory framework is not only the level of pressure that regulations and authorities exert (whether schools are put into the 'pressure cooker' or not), but also the pressure that school actors perceive, live and experience, collective and individually. School actors' perceptions thus, together with the characteristics of the school, play an important role in explaining divergent school responses to PBA.

But on which factors does the intensity of the perceived pressure depend? High-performing schools, and/or schools whose educational provision has a clear focus on academic excellence, will readily align with external PBA demands, so they do not necessarily perceive the PBA system as a source of pressure (see Keddie, 2013). Nonetheless, we expect that there might be teaching staff in well-performing schools who feel higher-than-expected performative pressure because their 'significant others' (i.e., their more direct competitors) are doing better than they are; or the school owner, the principal, families and/or teachers themselves might think that the academic results of the school have room for improvement.

At the same time, schools with poor levels of performance may have staff who do not experience high levels of performative pressure due to the fact that for moral, professional or pedagogic reasons they do not put academic achievement at the center of their work.

In short, school responses to regulatory environments are the result of complex policy enactment processes in which variables of a contextual and subjective nature interact. From a sense-making perspective, it follows that two subjective variables are particularly significant in terms of understanding different patterns of school responses to accountability pressure. The first is how school actors interpret and position themselves in the PBA policy debate, and the second one is the perceived level of performance pressure that school actors experience within PBA frameworks.

Methodology

Data

The data used in this research have been drawn from the REFORMED project database, which applies to a sample of countries, including Chile.[3] We have also used secondary administrative data provided by the Chilean educational authorities.

The Chilean database includes data collected from questionnaires administered to teachers (n = 1130) and school leaders (n = 200), distributed among 79 schools that were selected through a stratified sample strategy (Ferrer-Esteban, 2020). These questionnaires provide rich information about school contexts, the professional profiles of teachers and principals, school organization, teaching practices, use of standardized test data, perceptions of the PBA system and other teachers' beliefs (Levatino, 2020).

Method

The research follows a sequential mixed-methods design approach (cf. Teddlie and Tashakkori, 2006), which integrates two different empirical stages. The *first stage is eminently quantitative*. In this stage, we constructed school categories based on variables related to both attitudes and beliefs about PBA, and perceived performance pressure (as introduced in our theoretical framework). These school categories, in combination with school composition variables (socio-economic composition and performance), were then used to construct the school sample for the qualitative analysis.

During the *qualitative research stage*, we conducted interviews with teachers, principals and other school leaders. This phase was essential in order to identify (using the interpretative framework for the school categories) all those school-level practices that actors may adopt to deal with the accountability system. The manner in which these school practices are enacted (and the intensity) within each category allowed us to characterize and define varying school responses to performance-based accountability.

Quantitative research stage: Constructing school categories

This stage was carried out with the entire Chilean sample of schools (n = 79). The survey responses of all school actors involved (school leaders and teachers) were considered.

The first step was to identify broad categories of schools on the basis of attitudes and beliefs about PBA and perceived performance pressure. To construct composite indexes of PBA beliefs and performance pressure, we first identified the most significant variables in our survey database in order to capture each of these constructs through factor analysis. As a result of this analysis, the *PBA attitudes/beliefs* index is based on three variables related to both the perceived fairness and validity of the PBA system, as follows: (a) whether it is fair to measure school quality through the results of standardized tests; (b) whether it is fair to disseminate test results in the media and/or the internet; and (c) whether test scores reflect the efforts and ability of teachers. The index of *perceived performative pressure* includes variables relating to pressure from different account holders: the Ministry of Education, the EQA and the municipality (public schools) or school board (private schools).

From the intersection of the two indices, we then defined quadrants, which were used to frame the surveyed schools. Table 13.1 shows the frequencies of teachers and schools according to school categories, each of which covers between 22% and 30% of the sampled schools.

Qualitative research stage: Characterizing school responses

Qualitative fieldwork was conducted using a smaller sample of schools via semi-structured interviews with teachers and school leaders, covering similar topics to those of the survey. The schools for this stage were first selected taking into consideration their social composition (school vulnerability index, MINEDUC, 2019) and level of performance (Agencia de Calidad de la Educación, 2018). In Table 13.2, we can see how the selected schools for this stage related to our subjective categories (perceived pressure and beliefs about PBA), along with the indicators of social composition and performance. From Figure 13.1, it can be seen that the same schools are spatially distributed across the quadrants.

Table 13.1 Schools and teachers by performative pressure and culture

School categories	Teachers		Schools	
	Freq.	*Perc.*	*Freq.*	*Perc.*
High pressure and con-PBA	322	28.5	24	30.4
High pressure and pro-PBA	262	23.2	18	22.8
Low-pressure and con-PBA	249	22.0	18	22.8
Low pressure and pro-PBA	297	26.3	19	24.1
Total	1130	100	79	100

Source: Reformed database. Chile

Table 13.2 Schools of the qualitative stage

School	School SES	Performance category	Pressure/PBA approach
1	Low SES	Low-Medium	Low pressure, pro-PBA
2	High SES	High	Low pressure, pro-PBA
3	High SES	Medium	Low pressure, pro-PBA
4	Med-high SES	High	Low pressure, pro-PBA
5	Low SES	Insufficient	Low pressure, con-PBA
6	Med-high SES	Low-Medium	Low pressure, con-PBA
7	Med-high SES	Low-Medium	Low pressure, con-PBA
8	High SES	High	Low pressure, con-PBA
9	Med-high SES	Medium	Low pressure, con-PBA
10	Low-med SES	Low-Medium	Low pressure, con-PBA
11	Low-med SES	Low-Medium	High pressure, pro-PBA
12	Low SES	Medium	High pressure, pro-PBA
13	Low-med SES	Low-Medium	High pressure, con-PBA
14	Low-med SES	Medium	High pressure, con-PBA
15	Low-med SES	Medium	High pressure, con-PBA

Source: Reformed database. Chile

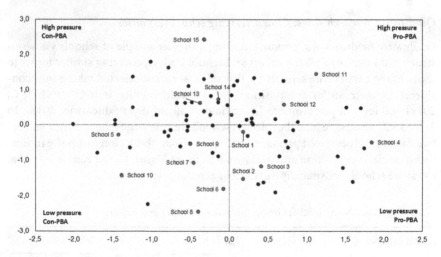

Figure 13.1 Distribution of schools according to school responses.
Source: Reformed database. Chile

Our typology of school responses was mainly defined and constructed through interview data, although administrative data and data from the survey were also used. The tables in the Appendix show more detailed information about the schools' main characteristics (namely, school ownership, socio-economic composition and performance) by quadrant but also in terms of PBA-related school practices (with a focus on data use and teaching to the test). The interviews enabled us to reconstruct and capture the narratives, rationales and logics of action that predominate in the different groups of schools, and to build patterns of responses to PBA accordingly.

All of the interviews with principals and teachers were transcribed and analyzed with a QDA software. To analyze the qualitative material, we combined the use of emerging and pre-established codes for key factors, the most relevant of which are as follows: school context and culture; leadership style; actors' opinions about PBA; knowledge about the quality assurance system; the importance given to test results; data use; test preparation strategies; classroom management practices; external support; and teacher autonomy.

Findings: School responses to accountability regulations

In this section, we present the most defining characteristics of our school categories, with a focus on depicting the responses to PBA that were found to predominate in each category. The resulting typology of school responses includes induced alignment, accommodation, fabrication, dilution and de facto opting out. Conceptually, this typology draws on previous categorizations of educational organizations' responses to regulatory pressures (see Coburn, 2004; Landri, 2018; Malen, 2006).

High pressure and pro-PBA: Induced alignment

In schools with a high level of perceived pressure and a more positive approach to PBA, we found that teachers and principals proactively embrace the mandate of PBA and put data-intensive instruments at the centre of the governance system of the school. The academic requirements for these schools tend to be high. In terms of the student population, schools in this category are predominantly 'middle class': almost three-quarters of their students are distributed between the second and third SES quarters (see Table 13.A.2). Both public and private schools are represented in this category, but private subsidized schools predominate. Specifically, 66.7% of the schools in this category are private subsidized schools.

These schools devote significant effort to incorporating the accountability mandate into not only instructional strategies but also broader pedagogic and management approaches. They do so not necessarily because they need to improve their learning achievement data (in fact, only 5.6% of the schools in this category obtain low results), but because they are externally pressured to improve their performance and/or reputation in the reference school market. This is why we describe the predominant response in this category as *induced alignment*.

Performative pressure is inflicted by the school owner to a great extent. As the principal of one private subsidized school pointed out, the school owner pressures them 'to achieve better results' on the SIMCE test because one of the central missions of the corporation is that its schools become 'top performing institutions'. Nonetheless, rather than being seen as stressful or frustrating, these pressures are regarded as 'necessary tensions' that trigger school change and activate internal improvement dynamics (principal, school 12).

Schools in this category tend to attach a lot of importance to SIMCE results and use them to identify learning needs and school improvement challenges. Almost 50% of the teachers in this category were found to be very positive about how much guidance the SIMCE gives them to help improve the quality of their teaching, while only 21.5% reported that test results are not used or are seldom used (see Table 13.A.5). Leadership teams and teachers use learning metrics as benchmarks and planning tools, and articulate and elaborate discourse on the importance of data-management practices.

> Look, actually, I think that they [SIMCE results] have affected my work from the perspective that they make an important point; you have to think about them. But you know that what I [get] from SIMCE is that when I see the distribution of results, I say: 'How many students are not learning?' and in reality, what drives me there is that this percentage or this number decreases. In my opinion, they are a new impulse to say: 'How do we make [that number] go down? How do we do it?' These [results] illuminate my tasks during the year, more than anything else.
>
> (Pedagogical coordinator, school 12)

In the schools where induced alignment predominates, test preparation practices are intensive, systematic and routinized. Teaching to the test is not only a remedial activity but an educational practice that permeates the educational dynamic of the entire school. Of the teachers in this category, 61.2% reported that they not only prepare their students for the test beforehand but throughout the whole year (see Table 13.A.4). 'Teaching to the test' is a common practice across different grades (beyond the SIMCE-assessed grades) and is strategically supported and reinforced by external testing services.

> We are working on the SIMCE courses with specific support. Ok? We work in the mode of the SIMCE questions, which means, let's say, … in certain ways …, preparing them [the students] to answer in a better way, ok?, in the courses that are evaluated by the SIMCE each year, which are always the 4th grade, and it varies in the 6th and 8th grades. Ok? [But it] is not only the teacher of the 4th grade; all teachers support, let's say, these reinforcements, in the collaborative work that … as I told you, characterizes us as a school.
>
> (Management team, school 11)

To sum up, schools' alignment with PBA in this category results from the coupling between an academic-oriented school ethos and an externally induced climate of pressure to improve school results. These are schools that regard learning achievement (and high academic standards) as being one of the main focuses of their educational provision.

Low pressure and pro-PBA: Easily accommodating accountability requests

Schools with a positive attitude towards PBA and which do not feel a high level of performative pressure are those that accommodate PBA regulations more readily. The schools in this category are predominantly private (68.4% are privately owned), and they enroll socially advantaged students (42.1% are in the first top SES quarter) (see Tables 13.A.1 and 13.A.2). Teachers in these schools have high expectations of their students and prepare them to access the best universities in the country. In terms of performance, 84.2% of these schools are distributed among the highest categories of achievement (see Table 13.A.3). Accountability regulations are convenient for these schools; rather than generating pressure, the regulations reinforce their educational and teaching approach. Thus, these schools easily accommodate the PBA regulations.

Order and discipline, and a culture of effort and academic rigour, are the main hallmarks of accommodating schools. These values are instilled into teachers by the school management team and, in turn, are instilled into students by teachers. These schools have a culture of continuous improvement and aim to boost their scores year after year. Nonetheless, their improvement plans can also be holistic, integrating goals and dimensions which go beyond learning achievement. Decisions about teaching strategies, materials and methods are centralized at school level. Some teachers in these schools miss the level of autonomy they had in previous placements and consider their job to be demanding and competitive. However, they also appreciate having clearly defined targets and goals, frequent meetings with school staff and regular feedback from the management team.

Test preparation is a common practice (with 55% of teachers in this category stating that it takes place throughout the year), but it is not necessarily seen as a strategy mainly focused on boosting test scores (see Table 13.A.4). Teachers in these schools realize that 'reinforcement activities' are more than just 'SIMCE simulations' (not fully focused on the SIMCE) and include, for instance, elaboration and delivery of lesson plans inspired by the most challenging SIMCE questions (teacher, school 3). They also do not feel the need to prepare for the SIMCE explicitly because doing well in the SIMCE 'should be like a natural process' if they do their job properly throughout the year (vice-principal, school 2).

Data use is highly routinized in these schools: 52% of teachers stated that SIMCE results guide all or most of their teaching, while 28% stated that SIMCE results are useful to a certain extent (see Table 13.A.5). Managers and teachers make numerous decisions at school level on the basis of performance data, not only to find room for improvement contingently but also to address more structural problems that might have been generated in previous years or in different subjects to those assessed by the SIMCE.

Accommodating schools are very positive about SIMCE data. They trust in the SIMCE's validity and believe that it provides a trustworthy representation of actual school performance. Staff in these schools feel that, if anything, the SIMCE should provide even more information and details, and they argue that they would like more time to analyze and discuss the data, and take further advantage of this information. Overall, accommodating schools have a very elaborated discourse on data use, and they can give numerous examples of how they use data in their everyday work.

> We use all the actions recommended by the system. The SIMCE tells us how to focus the question; that is, when we ask a question at an appropriate level, when we ask too [easy] questions ... there are teachers who use the tests as feedback; deliver the tests to the students [...]; then the teacher works [out] the questions. This works as a pedagogical space rather than as a learning or evaluation space ...
>
> (Pedagogic coordinator, school 1)

Low pressure and con-PBA: Between dilution and opting out

In the category of schools that perceive a low level of performative pressure and are openly critical about PBA, we found two distinct types of response: dilution and de facto opting out. These responses emerge in two drastically different school contexts, which is why it is difficult to characterize this category in terms of school performance, socio-economic composition and ownership. However, schools in this category share a low level of test-data use and a very low frequency of teaching to the test (with more than 50% of teachers in this category stating that they never conduct this practice) (see Tables 13.A.4–13.A.6 and 13.A.6).

Dilution

Dilution emerges in schools that feel a low level of performance pressure and do not put academic performance and metrics at the centre of their educational approach. The educational provision of these schools tends to focus on critical thinking, students' personal development and/or socio-emotional skills. Some of these schools define themselves as 'revolutionary', as in the case of school 6, whose principal is proud of having adopted a 'circular and integrative neuropsychological educational approach'. This principal made it clear that he is not averse to numerical data, but believes achievement data to be too narrow and limited to inform the most important school decisions. He has created his own data governance and assessment tools, which he considers to be more comprehensive and aligned with their pedagogical approach and beliefs.

Managers and teachers in these schools openly avoid using SIMCE data for competition purposes (see Table 13.A.6) or to assess and improve teachers' work (see Tables 13.A.4 and 13.A.6) because they believe that quality teaching cannot be developed under 'stress' and when students are put under 'high pressure' (teacher, school 7). Test simulations are not a frequent practice either. The owner and/or management teams of these schools do not ask teachers to intensify teaching to the test before implementation of the SIMCE, but some teachers nonetheless take the initiative to implement test simulations before the SIMCE as a way to familiarize their students with the rules and procedures associated with standardized test conditions. These teachers argue that they provide test preparation out of consideration for students' wellbeing on the SIMCE day, but not to inflate the results. Accordingly, test simulations are low-intensity and mainly happen in relation to SIMCE grades and subjects.

> [A]lthough it is not something that … they demand from me, we do a couple of essays as a matter of protocol, [so] they know who Marta [is], that she has to sit in a [certain] way, that you have to fill out an answer sheet, because it is not usual for us to use [these tests] here.
>
> (Teacher, school 8)

Overall, the schools where PBA pressures are diluted are well placed in the local education market, and their educational provision and their expectations are not mainly concerned with academic achievement. The combination of these factors counteracts performative pressures from the regulatory environment and allows them to develop educational, governance and data-management practices that they think better serve their educational vision.

De facto opting out

De facto *opting out* also emerges in schools that have low levels of perceived administrative pressure and are also critical of the accountability system. However, the logic of action and socio-material characteristics of the schools articulating this response are entirely different from what we saw in relation to policy dilution. Opting-out schools perform worse and enroll much higher rates of disadvantaged students. Rather than emphasizing alternative pedagogy, their educational approach emphasizes the importance of 'living together' and 'security'. These schools are located in disadvantaged neighborhoods where violence is a common concern among both parents and school staff. Families in these predominantly public schools do not have high academic expectations, and what they most value is the security that the school can give to their children.

> I believe that [the increase in student enrollment in our school] has to do with [our reputation] that … parents can rely on … [F]or example, they bring their children to the school with two eyes, a nose, and all his/her extremities, and at the end of the day we will deliver the same child back to them. I think that this creates confidence.
>
> (Principal, school 5)

Principals and teachers feel powerless in the face of the improvement requirements coming from the educational authorities. A central characteristic of this type of school is a low level of academic ambition, framed by the perception that given the socio-economic disadvantages of their students, there is no room to reverse poor SIMCE performance. Contrary to PBA expectations, in these institutional contexts, the threat of school closure does not translate into higher levels of performative pressure.

These schools rarely enact test preparation activities. Management teams do not advocate teaching to the test, and if test simulations are conducted, it is because teachers have decided autonomously to do so. For instance, one teacher told us that she voluntarily took the initiative to conduct a few test simulations before the SIMCE, but mainly for the purpose of familiarizing students with how answers are marked in standardized tests.

> Interviewer: Is the decision to not do SIMCE simulations yours or…?
> Teacher: Yes, it's mine.
> Interviewer: … or is it school policy?
> Teacher: No, it was mine; it was mine with my PIE [School Integration Program, in English] partner […] I think we did a test simulation, but it was [for the purpose of] marking the answers.
>
> (Teacher 2, school 5)

Another feature of these schools is a certain disaffection with learning metrics. School staff stated that data from standardized tests are decontextualized and misaligned with their educational focus, and that their professional judgement capacity as educators and related tools (e.g., 'class evaluations') (teacher 2, school 5) are more reliable than test data.

To conclude, de facto opting out should not be confused with overt or even covert forms of resistance. Far from being a type of conscious resistance or a policy dilution strategy, de facto opting out is a common non-reaction among schools operating in highly marginalized contexts, which feel powerless and resigned in front of unattainable improvement expectations. This response is thus characterized by indifference and passivity in the face of the external pressures generated by the quality assurance system.

High pressure and con-PBA: Fabricating better scores

Schools that experience high levels of performance pressure and are critical of PBA react to accountability regulations superficially and fragmentedly. Within this category, there are three main contextual features that stand out: a clear predominance of public schools (62.5%); low levels of educational performance (with 62.5% of schools in the low and mid-low achievement categories); and an overwhelming presence of disadvantaged students (with more than 90% of the students in these schools coming from the bottom and second quartiles) (see Tables 13.A.1–13.A.3). Despite the performance pressures faced by these schools and experience from different sources (educational authorities, school owner, etc.), they do not transform their core practices (namely their educational provision, their evaluation systems and/or their governance structures) as a response to such pressures. Instead, they adopt various practices and strategies to overcome accountability pressures but in a way that does not substantively alter their educational values and approach.

In these schools, learning achievement data are used moderately, mainly to define benchmarks and targets in core subjects and competences, but is not central to schools' evaluations of their teaching and planned educational improvement. Of the teachers in this category, 62% affirmed that SIMCE results do not provide useful guidance for improving teaching or that they do so only moderately (see Table 13.A.5).

The schools in this category are reactive to PBA, but instead of following the administrative expectations *verbatim*, they adopt partial practices to fabricate better results and, in a way, 'game' the system. They adopt many of these practices reluctantly, and are aware of the limitations and risks of doing so. To start with, fabrication schools are prone to focusing their teaching on the basic competences at the centre of the accountability system – so-called 'narrowing' of the curriculum. Nonetheless, despite the managers of these schools dedicating more teaching hours to the subjects externally assessed, with the clear intention of improving test results, they are also aware of the risks of these types of tactics and try to minimize them:

> I also have to [ensure] that this does not go to the other extreme, because in this… search to get positive scores, other subjects are also [cast] aside [like] music [and] art; then I give more literacy when I [should really have been doing] art. Or I do more math when I [should have been doing] music. I have to be … attentive that this does not happen.
>
> (Pedagogical coordinator, school 15)

Teaching to the test is, as could not be otherwise, another very frequent practice to boost test scores – with more than 50% of teachers reporting that they conduct this practice throughout the whole year, and more than 20% doing it just before delivering the SIMCE test (see Table 13.A.4). In these schools, test preparation materializes in numerous test simulations, in order to familiarize students with predictable test questions and the test format. As happens with narrowing the curriculum, the managers of these schools promote teaching to the test reluctantly and mainly in the grades covered by the SIMCE to try and minimize the risks. A common complaint, for instance, is the fact that 'instead of generating a pedagogical practice', standardized tests such as the SIMCE oblige them to engage in 'repetition of exercises to practice an evaluation style' (principal, school 13).

This is the only school category where we found that students' tracking was conducted with the explicit intention of boosting test scores, which is indicative of a fabrication response. When asked what they do to improve test scores, this principal stated:

> Well, the teachers have been very creative [a]nd … have developed several strategies. One of the strategies that has given us the best result is dividing the children into groups. For example, there are three third-grade courses. So, based on the results, we divide the children. Those who achieved the learning

objective, those who are average, and those who are low. [At certain times], the course structure is broken [into these groups] and the teacher who has greater competencies, because she has to have greater competencies, is the one that takes the low-performing students [...] This is what has been giving us the best results.

(Principal, school 14)

Tracking students seems paradoxical in a school that defines itself as 'inclusive', 'integral' and 'non-academicist' (principal, school 14). However, tracking is not a constitutive characteristic of schools' educational provision or philosophy but an experimental and pragmatic reaction to performative pressure, with the sole intention of making schools conform to performance expectations. Furthermore, as the principal of school 14 emphasized, tracking is only conducted in mathematics and literacy.

Conclusions

Schools do not respond to accountability regulations uniformly. This chapter shows that PBA regulations generate a broad and varying range of school responses, which go beyond conventional classifications mainly focusing on alignment vs decoupling or high-low fidelity implementation. Based on a mixed-methods study conducted in Chile, we identified five school responses to PBA, namely, accommodation, induced alignment, dilution, fabrication and de facto opting out. Our study does not imply that these are all possible or existing responses to accountability regulations. For instance, open and covert forms of resistance to PBA – which have not been identified in this study – are to be expected in a country like Chile, where quality assurance and accountability reforms have generated important debates, controversies and even public boycotting campaigns.

Our study highlights the mediating role of subjective variables in the enactment of PBA. Although interpretation practices have been considered important in previous enactment research, our study emphasizes the mediating role of perceived pressure in terms of understanding how and to what extent schools make sense of and react to external accountability prerogatives. Theoretically speaking, our research shows that the way policy actors translate and respond to policy mandates is contingent not only to interpretation dynamics, but also to the levels of pressure that actors experience to comply with the policies in question. We have tested this idea by developing a unique heuristic approach in which school actors' perception of accountability pressures and their conception of the fairness and validity of PBA have allowed us to build school categories, as a preliminary step to identify schools' varying responses.

This study perspective revealed that the levels of perceived pressure among school actors in terms of PBA systems vary significantly, and they do so partly independently of objectively defined pressure measures enforced by the educational authorities. The perceived pressure factor contributes to better understanding the non-linear and often 'unexpected' nature of school responses to PBA. The school responses we identified reveal that high-stakes accountability does not operate as a performativity device in all circumstances. Not all schools that authorities subject to the 'pressure cooker' experience high levels of performative pressure. Feeling powerless in the face of quality assurance expectations, being more inclined to please audiences other than educational authorities or embracing an academicist ethos are very different factors in nature, but all they help to take the pressure off schools.

We have also identified many schools where the staff experience strong performative pressure. This includes, counterintuitively, schools with satisfactory levels of performance. However, our data reveal that this type of pressure is especially strong within low-performing public schools with disadvantaged student populations. Teachers and principals in these schools tend to be critical of PBA regulations, and are those who more frequently resort to instrumental practices in an attempt to fabricate better scores and escape performance pressure. The fact that fabrication responses (and also opting out) predominate within schools serving disadvantaged students challenges to a great extent the equity and educational opportunity rhetoric of many accountability reforms.

The high levels of instrumental and fragmented responses generated by accountability pressures can compromise students' learning experiences. Indeed, alternative forms of accountability (process-based and/or oriented towards rewarding meaningful change) would be more meaningful for schools in the long term and less distracting than accountability systems that put an excessive focus on performance. However, advancing these alternatives in educational systems like the Chilean one is likely to be challenging as numerous accountability instruments, agents and expectations overlap (not always formally and not harmoniously), and accountability relationships have been shaped by threats and mistrust between key stakeholders reform after reform.

Appendix

Table 13.A.1 Share of schools by performative pressure and PBA approach, and ownership

School categories	Ownership			
	Public	Private-subs.	Private	Total
High pressure and con-PBA	62.5	37.5	0.0	100
High pressure and pro-PBA	33.3	66.7	0.0	100
Low pressure and con-PBA	38.9	55.6	5.6	100
Low pressure and pro-PBA	31.6	52.6	15.8	100

Source: Reformed database. Chile

Table 13.A.2 Share of schools by performative pressure and PBA approach, and socioeconomic level

School categories	SES quarters				Aggreg. SES quarters		Total
	Low	Low-med	Med-high	High	Low / low-med	Med-high / High	
High pressure and con-PBA	45.8	45.8	4.2	4.2	91.6	8.4	100
High pressure and pro-PBA	16.7	33.3	38.9	11.1	50.0	50.0	100
Low pressure and con-PBA	22.2	27.8	22.2	27.8	50.0	50.0	100
Low pressure and pro-PBA	26.3	10.5	21.1	42.1	36.8	63.2	100

Source: Reformed database. Chile

Table 13.A.3 Share of schools by performative pressure and PBA approach, and performance levels

School categories	Performance levels				Aggreg. levels		Total
	Low	Low-med	Med-high	High	Low / low-med	Med-high / High	
High pressure and con-PBA	33.3	29.2	37.5	0.0	62.5	37.5	100
High pressure and pro-PBA	5.6	27.8	55.6	11.1	33.3	66.7	100
Low pressure and con-PBA	5.6	33.3	50.0	11.1	38.9	61.1	100
Low pressure and pro-PBA	5.3	10.5	36.8	47.4	15.8	84.2	100

Source: Reformed database. Chile

Table 13.A.4 School categories and teaching to the test

School categories	Activities focused on preparing students for the national tests			
	Never	Month before	Whole year	Total
High pressure and con-PBA	26.81	20.65	52.54	100
High pressure and pro-PBA	25.57	13.24	61.19	100
Low pressure and con-PBA	50.23	17.67	32.09	100
Low pressure and pro-PBA	29.41	15.29	55.29	100
Total	32.44	16.89	50.67	100

Source: Reformed database. Chile

Table 13.A.5 School categories and data use (to improve teaching quality)

School categories	National test results provide useful information and guidance to improve the quality of teaching in the school			
	Not at all / a little	*Some*	*Much / completely*	*Total*
High pressure and con-PBA	36.0	26.1	37.9	100
High pressure and pro-PBA	21.5	30.1	48.4	100
Low pressure and con-PBA	48.5	22.6	28.9	100
Low pressure and pro-PBA	20.1	27.9	51.9	100
Total	31.2	26.7	42.1	100

Source: Reformed database. Chile

Table 13.A.6 School categories and data use (to assess teachers' work)

School categories	Uses of national test: to assess teachers' work		
	No	*Yes*	*Total*
High pressure and con-PBA	58.7	41.3	100
High pressure and pro-PBA	45.4	54.6	100
Low pressure and con-PBA	62.7	37.4	100
Low pressure and pro-PBA	44.8	55.2	100
Total	52.8	47.2	100

Source: Reformed database. Chile

Table 13.A.7 School categories and data use (to build reputation)

School categories	Uses of national test: to build reputation		
	No	*Yes*	*Total*
High pressure and con-PBA	59.9	40.1	100
High pressure and pro-PBA	52.7	47.3	100
Low pressure and con-PBA	73.5	26.5	100
Low pressure and pro-PBA	52.9	47.1	100
Total	59.4	40.6	100

Source: Reformed database. Chile

Notes

1 This work was supported by the European Research Council under the European Union's 'Horizon 2020 Framework Programme for Research and Innovation' [GA-680172 – REFORMED].
2 https://www.agenciaeducacion.cl/se-obtiene-la-categoria-desempeno/
3 See www.reformedproject.eu.

References

Agencia de Calidad de la Educación (2018). *Categorías de desempeño.* Santiago, Chile. Retrieved from: https://www.agenciaorienta.cl/

Agrey, L. (2004). The pressure cooker in education: Standardized assessment and high-stakes. *Canadian Social Studies*, 38(3), 1–12.

Au, W. (2007). High-stakes testing and curricular control: A qualitative metasynthesis. *Educational Researcher*, 36(5), 258–267.

Ball, S.J. (2003). The teacher's soul and the terrors of performativity. *Journal of Education Policy*, 18(2), 215–228.

Ball, S.J., Maguire, M., & Braun, A. (2012). *How Schools Do Policy: Policy Enactments in Secondary Schools.* New York: Routledge.

Bellei, C., & Vanni, X. (2015). The evolution of educational policy in Chile 1980–2014. In: S. Schwartzman (Ed.). *Education in South America. London* (pp. 179–200). London: Bloomsbury Academic.

Berends, M. (2015). Sociology and school choice: What we know after two decades of charter schools. *Annual Review of Sociology*, 41, 159–180.

Boxenbaum, E., & Jonsson, S. (2017). Isomorphism, diffusion and decoupling: Concept evolution and theoretical challenges. In: R. Greenwood, C. Oliver, T.B. Lawrence, & R.E. Meyer (Eds.). *The SAGE Handbook of Organizational Institutionalism* (pp. 77–101). London: Sage.

Candido, H.H.D. (2020). Datafication in schools: Enactments of quality assurance and evaluation policies in Brazil. *International Studies in Sociology of Education*, 29(1–2), 126–157.

Coburn, C.E. (2004). Beyond decoupling: Rethinking the relationship between the institutional environment and the classroom. *Sociology of Education*, 77(3), 211–244.

Diamond, J.B. (2012). Accountability policy, school organization, and classroom practice: Partial recoupling and educational opportunity. *Education and Urban Society*, 44(2), 151–182.

Diamond, J.B., & Spillane, J. P. (2004). High-stakes accountability in urban elementary schools: Challenging or reproducing inequalilty?. *Teachers College Record*, 106(6), 1145–1176.

Falabella, A. (2020). The ethics of competition: Accountability policy enactment in Chilean schools' everyday life. *Journal of Education Policy*, 35(1), 23–45.

Ferrer-Esteban, G. (2020). *Sampling Strategy.* REFORMED Methodological Papers No. 3.

Jennings, J.L. (2010). School choice or schools' choice? Managing in an era of accountability. *Sociology of Education*, 83(3), 227–247.

Keddie, A. (2013). Thriving amid the performative demands of the contemporary audit culture: A matter of school context. *Journal of Education Policy*, 28(6), 750–766.

Kim, J., & Sunderman, G. (2005). Measuring academic proficiency under the no child left behind act: Implications for educational equity. *Educational Researcher*, 34(8), 3–13.

Landri, P. (2018). *Digital Governance of Education: Technology, Standards and Europeanization of Education*. London: Bloomsbury Publishing.

Levatino, A. (2019). *Surveying Principals and Teachers in the framework of the REFORMED Project: Methodological Insights into the Design of the Questionnaires*. REFORMED Methodological Papers No. 2.

Malen, B. (2006). Revisiting policy implementation as a political phenomenon: The case of reconstitution policies. In: Meredith I. Honig (Ed.). *New Directions in Education Policy Implementation: Confronting Complexity* (pp. 83–104). Albany: State University of New York Press.

Maroy, C., & Pons, X. (2019). *Accountability Policies in Education. A Comparative and Multilevel Analysis in France and Quebec*. Cham: Springer.

MINEDUC. (2019). *Prioridades 2019 con IVE, SINAE, BÁSICA, MEDIA Y COMUNAL*. Santiago: Ministry of Education. Retrieved from: https://www.junaeb.cl/ive

Mintrop, H. (2004). *Schools on Probation: How Accountability Works (and Doesn't Work)*. New York: Teachers College Press.

Mittleman, J., & Jennings, J.L. (2018). Accountability, achievement, and inequality in American Public Schools: A review of the literature. In: Barbara Schneider (Ed.). *Handbook of the Sociology of Education in the 21st Century* (pp. 475–492). Cham: Springer.

Mizala, A., & Schneider, B.R. (2014). Negotiating education reform: Teacher evaluations and incentives in Chile (1990–2010). *Governance*, 27(1), 87–109.

Parcerisa, L., & Falabella, A. (2017). La consolidación del Estado evaluador a través de políticas de rendición de cuentas: trayectoria, producción y tensiones en el sistema educativo chileno. *Education Policy Analysis Archives*, 25(89), 1–24.

Perryman, J., Ball, S., Maguire, M., & Braun, A. (2011). Life in the pressure cooker–School league tables and English and mathematics teachers' responses to accountability in a results-driven era. *British Journal of Educational Studies*, 59(2), 179–195.

Skedsmo, G. (2011). Formulation and realisation of evaluation policy: Inconsistencies and problematic issues. *Educational Assessment, Evaluation and Accountability*, 23(1), 5–20.

Spillane, J.P., Diamond, J.B., Burch, P., Hallett, T., Jita, L., & Zoltners, J. (2002). Managing in the middle: School leaders and the enactment of accountability policy. *Educational Policy*, 16(5), 731–762.

Tan, C. (2018). *Comparing High-performing Education Systems: Understanding Singapore, Shanghai, and Hong Kong*. New York: Routledge.

Teddlie, C., & Tashakkori, A. (2006). A general typology of research designs featuring mixed methods. *Research in the Schools*, 13(1), 12–28.

Valenzuela, J.P., & Montecinos, C. (2017). Structural reforms and equity in Chilean schools. *Oxford Research Encyclopedia of Education*, 1–25.

Watanabe, M. (2008). Tracking in the era of high-stakes state accountability reform: Case studies of classroom instruction in North Carolina. *Teachers College Record*, 110(3), 489–534.

Zancajo, A. (2020). Schools in the Marketplace: Analysis of School Supply Responses in the Chilean Education Market. *Educational Policy*, 34(1), 43–64.

14 The performative to the datafied teacher subject: Teacher evaluation in Tennessee

Jessica Holloway and Priya Goel La Londe

Introduction

Globally, performance-based accountability (PBA) has become an education policy solution for excellence and equity (Smith, 2016). PBA is rooted in testing, evaluation and dis/incentivization as a means for steering teacher practice and defining teacher 'quality'. Advocates suggest such systems will improve teacher agency and student outcomes. Yet scholars have found these policies and practices produce a myriad of undesirable consequences for teachers and education more broadly. This includes diminished autonomy and reduced capacity for teachers to exercise professional discretion (Perryman, 2006, 2009), a narrowing of the curriculum, the stifling of collaboration, and cultures of distrust (Berliner, 2011; Hardy, 2018).

Stephen Ball's (2003) performativity framework has provided a useful lens for illustrating the impacts of such systems, especially in how teachers' subjectivities have been (re)shaped in the image of the market and managerialism. While metrics, data and dis/incentivism have been central features of performative systems for many years now, new data and digital techniques that change the relationship between data, the teacher subject and the site of intervention require new analytical tools for making sense of current conditions. Some scholars have looked to 'datafication' as a lens for understanding how digital platforms, big data and data surveillance are producing new conditions and possibilities within education (Bradbury, 2019; Selwyn, 2015; Williamson, 2017).

Of relevance to this chapter is the new 'datafied' teacher, whose practice, disposition and discretion are rendered as data and acted upon in similar, yet different, ways as the 'performative' teacher. We examine this new teacher subject in the case of the teacher evaluation system in Tennessee, USA. In 2011, Tennessee was one of the first states in the USA to implement a statewide performance-based accountability (PBA) system to evaluate educators through its Tennessee Educator Acceleration Model (TEAM). Using policy documents and reports, TEAM artefacts and instruments (e.g., accountability rubrics, value-added models, reports), and the CompassTN digital platform, we examine how performativity and datafication operate as complementary technologies of governance (cf. Foucault, 1991), but in ways that produce unique possibilities.

We begin the chapter with a background of US and Tennessee teacher-related accountability policies. Then, we articulate our theoretical framework that is informed by Rose (1999) and Foucault's (1980) concept of subjectivity, with performativity (Ball, 2003) and datafication (Kitchen, 2014; Lupton, 2016; Selwyn, 2015) forming the analytical lens through which we make sense of the evolving tools and techniques of teacher evaluation in Tennessee. In the second half of the chapter, we illustrate how performativity and datafication operate as complementary technologies of governance that produce a new kind of teacher subject – the datafied teacher.

Policy context – Teacher accountability in the USA and Tennessee

In the US, PBA's roots date back to the 1970s (with, for example, minimum competency tests), but the 2004 No Child Left Behind (NCLB) policy cemented PBA in the national education policy landscape. Focused squarely on test-based accountability, sanctions and rewards, NCLB mandated that states commit to objective measurement of student achievement. In turn, high-stakes testing, proficiency benchmarks, rankings, public identification of low performance, school closures and school reconstitutions all became commonplace across the USA. Perhaps the most outwardly visible contribution of NCLB to PBA was the introduction of measurement and incentives for the performance of subgroups.

Over time, through different policy solutions, PBA has intensified and drawn increasingly more on data surveillance as a means to hold students, teachers and leaders accountable for high performance (Amrein-Beardsley, 2014). This was particularly visible in the US$4.35 billion Race to the Top (RttT) federal-level grant competition, which marked the beginning of incentivist teacher and principal evaluation and formal, funded public-private partnerships towards the enactment of PBA. In RttT, states were encouraged to create school reform plans that employed a coherent PBA strategy, the adoption of common learning standards, school choice and teacher evaluation. While participation was optional, most states readily adopted performance appraisal systems that directly tied teacher and principal evaluation to student test performance (Collins & Amrein-Beardsley, 2012).[1]

An early winner of RttT funding, Tennessee became a formidable leader in the PBA movement. This was largely credited to their early creation and adoption of what would become America's most popular for-profit value-added model (VAM), which many states eventually adopted for their own RttT purposes (Amrein-Beardsley & Collins, 2012). Over the years, Tennessee has leveraged common dis/incentivist strategies, such as threats of school closure or reconstitution for failure to achieve performance benchmarks, as well as a voucher system to incentivize competition between schools. In the name of equity and excellence, Tennessee Governor Lee has advocated for incentive-based school reform under the premise that low-income children and families in low-performing school districts should have access to the schools of their choice. Despite mounting research showing that such approaches to accountability have led to a number of problems – from measurement (e.g., validity, bias) and ethical issues (e.g., fairness) to detrimental effects on collegiality and pedagogy (e.g., teaching to the test) – Tennessee continues its use of high-stakes teacher accountability to notionally achieve system-wide improvement.

Their latest iteration of teacher evaluation is called the Tennessee Educator Accelerator Model (TEAM), which is typical of most US teacher evaluation systems. The system – implemented in 2011 – is based on multiple measures of teacher performance, including rubric-based observations of classroom teaching, value-added measurement of student growth and teacher effectiveness, and rubric-based measures of teacher professionalism. These measures are combined for high-stakes personnel purposes, such as pay-for-performance, professional development and career advancement. Before describing the specific logics, components and instruments of TEAM, we use the following section to articulate the theoretical framework we used for making sense of the system.

Theoretical framework

Performativity

Stephen Ball – drawing heavily from Foucault's theoretical work on governmentality – offered a new way for understanding how top-down, managerialist forms of accountability were significantly (re)shaping teachers and teaching. In 'The teacher's soul and the terrors of performativity', Ball (2003) identified three interrelated policy technologies – markets, managerialism and performativity – that were re-constituting not only 'good' teaching, but also the teacher subject. Based on interviews with a group of England-based teachers and principals, Ball argued that new forms of accountability were transforming the means through which teachers were valued, professionalized and incentivized. In this new environment, traditional values associated with professionalism and collaboration were being replaced with values taken from the private sector, such as competition, individualism and 'what works' solutions (see also Lewis, 2017). Performance-based accountability systems, particularly those that were emerging in countries like the USA and the United Kingdom in the early 2000s, were acutely illustrative of the performative environment depicted by Ball (see also Holloway & Brass, 2018; Perryman, 2009; Wilkins, 2011). Borrowing from Foucault's concept of governmentality, rationality and technology, Ball defined performativity as such:

> Performativity is a technology, a culture and a mode of regulation that employs judgements, comparisons and displays as means of incentive, control, attrition and change based on rewards and sanctions (both material and symbolic). The performances (of individual subjects or organizations) serve as measures of productivity or output, or displays of 'quality', or 'moments' of promotion or inspection. As such they stand for, encapsulate or represent the worth, quality or value of an individual or organization within a field of judgement.
>
> (Ball, 2003, p. 216)

In other words, the technology of performativity (along with the technologies of the market and managerialism) operated as a new frame of power/knowledge that structured what was 'true' about teachers and teaching (cf. Foucault, 1980). Within this performative regime, the 'good' teacher is one who responds to external performance targets, subjects oneself to constant surveillance and who seeks continuous self-improvement. Various techniques of measurement, comparison and evaluation produce professionals who are 'calculative individuals' (cf. Miller, 1992) and who constantly work on themselves to be more competitive and more excellent.

Following Ball, many education scholars, across a number of contexts, have used the performativity framework to illustrate how the increasing ubiquity of targets, metrics and incentivisation has re-shaped the values and priorities of schools, as well as the ways that teachers conduct themselves. In the United Kingdom, for example, Perryman (2006, 2009) documented the influence of Ofsted inspections and the creeping 'panoptic performativity' of constant observation and audit. She argued that such regimes have fundamentally altered what teachers do and who teachers are because of how they are forced to perform for the inspections. In her investigation of a school's performance for such inspections, Perryman (2008) argued that '[I]t is through the increasing culture of performativity and accountability that conformativity, discipline and normalisation is ensured, as teachers learn to police themselves and to perform the successful inculcation of the normalised behavior' (p. 616).

In 2011, Wilkins – also out of the UK – provided a new view of how performativity was shaping teacher subjectivity. Coining the term 'post-performative', he was one of the first to document the contrast between veteran teachers who experienced an alternative version (i.e., pre-performative) of schooling and brand-new teachers who were not only trained within performative regimes at their universities, but also grew up in performative schools. By focusing on new teachers, Wilkins showed how the notion of 'professionalism' was being (re)constituted within the post-performative regime. While Ball's (2003) and Perryman's (2006, 2009) participants saw the techniques of performativity as undermining their professional judgement and autonomy, Wilkins' participants defined and embodied internalization of *professionalization* in ways that embraced the culture and practices of accountability.

In a similar way, Holloway and Brass (2018) drew on interview data collected ten years apart (in the USA) to document the shift of the performative teacher. Like Wilkins (2011), they also found significant differences between teachers of 2003 and teachers of 2013, with the most significant contrast being the teachers' acceptance of the performative culture. They argued that through an assemblage of material and discursive techniques and rationalities, teachers no longer viewed 'objectification, quantification, and measurement ... as antithetical to teacher professionalism, but as precisely what teachers need to know and monitor themselves, improve themselves, and fashion themselves as professionals' (Holloway & Brass, 2018, p. 20).

These studies offer a brief glimpse into how Ball's performativity has been put to use for making sense of contemporary accountability in schools.

Several others have developed, critiqued and expanded upon Ball's frameworks (e.g., Clapham, Vickers, & Eldridge, 2016; Englund & Gerdin, 2019; Falabella, 2014, 2016; Pratt, 2016), while others have drawn more heavily on other performativity theorists (e.g., Lyotard, Butler, see for example, Vick & Martinez, 2011). Together, these scholars have shown that the technology of performativity has normalized surveillance, compliance and hierarchical control of teachers and teaching. As schools are oriented to the ideals and logics of the market, managerialism and performativity, the teacher subject is simultaneously re-made in the image of standards, metrics and performance. Through processes of normalization, these conditions have produced particular possibilities for what teachers can do, who teachers can be, as well as what might come next. An emerging subfield of educational scholarship is grappling with these forward-looking questions, with a particular focus on how new forms of data, artificial intelligence and digital technologies are making possible a new type of teacher subject – the datafied teacher.

Datafication

As education is increasingly subjected to the 'data deluge' (de Freitas & Dixon-Roman, 2017), new thinking tools are necessary for understanding the roles of data, data technicians and online platforms in educational spaces, but also with how teacher subjectivity is affected. 'Datafication' offers a new lens for attending to conditions that are not easily captured by traditional market mechanisms and logics commonly found within performative regimes.

In the broadest sense, the 'datafication' of education can be thought of as the rendering of all aspects of schooling, students, teachers, etc., as data to be collected, analyzed, surveilled and controlled (Bradbury, 2019; Bradbury & Roberts-Holmes, 2017; Buchanan, 2019; Selwyn, 2015; Williamson, 2017). The 'datafied teacher', in particular, faces increased pressures to rely on numerical data (e.g., test scores, value-added model output) and evaluative tools (e.g., observation rubrics) to guide their pedagogical decisions and classroom practices (Bradbury & Roberts-Holmes, 2017).

In many ways, datafication and performativity point to similar problems associated with the 'governing by numbers' (Grek, 2009; Ozga, 2008), the excessive use of data to quantify and control teachers and their work, and (re)shaping of teacher subjectivities accordingly. However, the 'datafication' turn marks a distinct impact on education, as digital data techniques proliferate our reliance on, access to, and ability to capture more data about teachers and their practice than ever before. Datafication scholars warn that our fundamental understanding of individual people (in this case, teachers) becomes entangled with these data pictures (Lupton, 2018; Lupton & Williamson, 2017).

In other words, a teacher's data profile can become the object and subject of surveillance and control, perhaps even more so than the actual teacher (Thompson & Cook, 2014). Indeed, 'dataveillance' is pivotal to the establishment and growth of a culture of performativity and monitoring. It enables an understanding of teachers and students through 'algorithmic knowledge' (Lupton & Williamson,

2017, p. 786), as teachers and students are subjected to 'an ever-intensifying network of visibility, surveillance and normalization, in which their behaviours and bodies are continually judged and compared with others' (p. 786).

In the following sections, we describe our methods and analytical approach and then show how performative conditions and techniques in Tennessee's PBA system, TEAM, paved the way for algorithmic thinking and dataveillance to become key features of teacher accountability.

Methods and analytical approach

The empirical material for this chapter included publicly available policy documents and reports, as well as artifacts, instruments and digital platforms related to TEAM (see https://team-tn.org/teacher-evaluation-2-2/ for all publicly available documents). We analyzed TEAM evaluation rubrics, teacher and evaluator handbooks, frequently asked questions (FAQ) documents, observation and walkthrough guideline documents, scoring guidelines, templates and formulas, reports about value-added model (VAM) use, and technical support documents related to the online platform TNCompass (where TEAM data are collected, stored and accessed).

Analytically, we began with an open coding strategy (Saldaña, 2013) in order to gauge the scope of the data and to identify relevant sources for our research purposes. We then identified key features, instruments and logics of TEAM, using frequent analytic memos to track our ongoing sense-making and theorizing (Saldaña, 2013). Throughout all stages of analysis, we drew on Foucault's (1980) notions of governmentality and discourse, and Rose's (1999) notion of technologies of the self, to understand the ways in which: (1) TEAM emerged as a product of certain 'conditions of possibility'; and (2) how teacher subjects are shaped within such material and discursive parameters. Then, we brought together Ball's (2003) performativity with new thinking on datafication (Kitchin, 2014; Lupton, 2016; Selwyn, 2015) to trace the evolving emergence of data techniques, and to understand how performativity and datafication operate as similar, yet unique technologies of governance. This enabled us to understand how changing conditions might produce new kinds of teacher subjects.

Performativity and TEAM

The TEAM system features many of the logics and techniques of the performative regimes that have grown in popularity across the globe in recent decades. In particular, TEAM uses observations, feedback, student data and professional development as its main modes of accountability and professional support system. The system relies heavily on performative logics and techniques, such as market-based understandings of schooling (e.g., individualism and competition) and managerial practices of human resourcing (e.g., target-setting, top-down standards and evaluation). Similarly, teachers are subjected to ongoing surveillance and audit via frequent observations and walkthroughs, as well as ongoing, rubric-based evaluation, self-assessment and targeted professional development. According to the evaluation handbook, the model is designed to identify 'how teachers deliver instruction and what students learn from those lessons in order to gain complete picture of what goes on in the classroom' (Teacher Evaluation 2014). Teachers are also held responsible for their students' performance on annual standardized achievement tests. Below, we describe the key features of the system.

Level of Effectiveness (LOE)

The main element of the TEAM system is the Level of Effectiveness (LOE) score. All data – rubric scores, value-added measurement and student achievement – are combined to create an LOE scale score between 100 and 500. Teachers are then classified accordingly, ranging from 'significantly below expectations' to 'significantly above expectations'. Those who perform significantly below expectations are said to have 'limited knowledge of the instructional skills, knowledge, and responsibilities described in the rubric and struggles to implement them. He/she has little to no impact on student outcomes'. Those who perform significantly above expectations are said to 'exemplify the instructional skills, knowledge, and responsibilities in the rubric and implement them adeptly and without fail. He/she meets ambitious teaching and learning goals and makes a significant impact on student outcomes. Performance at this level should be considered a model of exemplary teaching.'

Student growth

Student growth, or the degree to which a teacher 'adds (or detracts) value' to a student's performance on the annual standardized achievement test, is the most important factor of the overall LOE. For teachers who teach test-subjects, 50% of their LOE is based on student growth (with the other 50% coming from their observation scores). What is more important, however, is that there is a '4/5 Trump Rule' that states teachers who score a 4 or 5 on classroom-level student growth can use their growth score to determine 100% of their LOE. In other words, the teachers can discard their observation scores *if* they score high enough on their student growth score. Additionally, evaluators are instructed to score the 'professionalism domain' of the observation component after testing is finished, so that 'all educators can remain focused on student preparation for state assessments'.

Surveillance and audit

Tennessee teachers are also subjected to ongoing monitoring and audit. Not only is their practice monitored in their classrooms via formal and informal observations, but their lesson planning, approach to assessment, professionalism and their ability to self-assess are also subject to audit. TEAM explains that the aim of observations is to 'focus on how teachers plan for instruction'. Teachers are asked to not submit lesson plans that are lengthy or developed solely for evaluation because then 'the feedback an educator receives on that plan is of limited utility'.

The model also calls for 'Unannounced Planning Observations'; in these cases, the evaluators can collect lesson plans after the classroom visit in order to assess how effectively a teacher plans for instruction.

The minimum required number of observations is based upon licensure status and evaluation scores from the previous year. At least half of the observations should be unannounced (conducted by surprise). These include a combination of observations and walkthroughs that total between 60 and 90 minutes. Teachers who previously scored a 5 on the overall LOE or the individual growth measure are required to have one unannounced, scored observation and two, 10- to 15-minute, un-scored walkthroughs. The TEAM guidelines say a walkthrough can focus on an area of refinement or an area of reinforcement. Walkthrough feedback guidelines suggest 'a brief, informal conversation, note, or email following the walk through to share immediate feedback is sufficient'.

TEAM also gives guidelines for conducting summative conferences that are designed to discuss evaluation results from the previous year. The required components of the summative conference include professionalism scores, observation data scores, growth and achievement data, and discussion of when and how overall scores will be calculated. Evaluators have the option to 'commend places of progress' and 'focus on the places in need of continued refinement'.

Coaching conversations are aimed at professional learning, but the conferences are prescribed (with templates and suggestion prompt-questions provided by TEAM). Specific recommendations for how the evaluators should conduct the meeting are described in the TEAM materials. For example, the guidelines tell evaluators to 'begin the conversation by communicating the purpose and goals to help reduce teacher anxiety'. The remainder of the conversation is to be focused on teacher growth and improvement.

In all, the TEAM evaluation system features many of the logics and techniques of the performative regimes that have grown in popularity across the globe in recent decades. What makes TEAM an interesting case to highlight, however, is its incorporation of new logics and techniques that are more closely aligned with what might be considered a datafication regime, as described next.

Datafication and TEAM

In this section, we describe two dimensions of the TEAM system that we see as making a distinct expansion of the performative regime. What we argue is that, as TEAM increasingly relies upon 'algorithmic thinking' and 'dataveillance', a 'datafication' lens is useful for making sense of the evolving environment.

Algorithmic thinking

As mentioned previously, Tennessee led the USA in implementing value-added models (VAMs) for purposes of teacher evaluation and merit pay. VAMs are statistical algorithms that operate by: (1) predicting how students should score on standardized achievement tests; (2) comparing their actual achievement score to the predicted score; and then (3) attributing the difference to the student's teacher.

In Tennessee, these scores are then used to make a number of personnel decisions, from performance-based pay to professional development, and even decisions about termination, retention or promotion. The means through which such predictions are calculated is based on large datasets that allow data analysts to group students according to 'like' testing histories. Using these historical trends, they then use a predictive algorithm to determine how much growth a student *should* make in a single school year. This approach to measuring student performance is meant to provide a more nuanced and unbiased view of a teachers' influence on student achievement (though research has shown VAMs are still biased and unreliable; see Johnson, 2015, for a review).

What we want to highlight in this chapter is the way in which the use of VAMs in Tennessee (like in many other US states) resembles a logic of 'algorithmic thinking' or 'algorithmic governance' that is increasingly (re)shaping nearly all aspects of social life, as well as schools (Beer, 2017; Benjamin, 2019; Introna, 2016; Kitchin, 2014; Lupton, 2016). VAMs, like other algorithms, make use of massive amounts of data in order to provide predictions about what might or should occur. In doing so, significant trust is placed in these algorithmic estimates for making important decisions about teachers and teaching (e.g., pedagogical decisions, decisions about intervention, personnel decisions). Similar to how a 'trust in numbers' (Porter, 1996) has underpinned much of education policy in recent decades (Ball, 2015; Grek, 2009), a trust in algorithms is, perhaps, even more problematic. For one, algorithms appear, and are often accepted, as even more 'objective' than simple measures of performance (e.g., proficiency scores) because they notionally remove human judgement and potential bias (e.g., by controlling for potentially confounding factors). However, as scholars of datafication have consistently reminded us, algorithms are designed by humans and, therefore, absorb all of the biases and judgements of the designers (Benjamin, 2019; Dixon-Roman, 2016). In terms of Tennessee's VAM, this is particularly troubling for two main reasons.

For one, SAS Analytics Inc. – the data analytics company that runs TEAM's VAM – is a for-profit company that maintains strict secrecy over their proprietary algorithm (see Amrein-Beardsley, 2008). As Pasquale (2015) has argued about the power of algorithms, it is their 'black box' nature that keeps us from fully understanding exactly how algorithms operate or how much we should trust their output. In the case of TEAM's VAM, public money is paying for a service that cannot be externally validated by the public. Despite this concern, as well as the fact that teachers are unable to interpret or use VAM data for informing their classroom practice (see Collins, 2014), and the fact that VAMs, in general, have shown to yield biased and unreliable output (Amrein-Beardsley, 2014; Johnson, 2015), Tennessee's trust in VAMs is clear given the stakes they have attached to VAM results. In doing so, what has come to be accepted as 'true' measures of student and teacher performance has been constructed not between a teacher and student, but by data engineers sitting at computers, miles away from the classroom.

This third-party involvement not only presents issues related to trust; it also raises questions about teacher expertise and authority. If teachers are no longer trusted to (1) 'know' their students and what their students have learned, or (2) to have a say in what should be valued and how it should be measured, then the professional discretion and status of the teacher is profoundly undermined. This is made worse as teachers are subjected to more enhanced levels of surveillance, which we expand upon next.

Dataveillance

Teachers in Tennessee have been under some form of surveillance for decades, and regular formal observations and informal walkthroughs have been a normal part of their accountability system since 2011. During observations and walk-throughs, evaluators would use paper rubrics to assess teacher performance and then hold one-on-one conferences to discuss the results of the assessment. With the new system, these same observations and conferences are performed, but the assessment is conducted on the online platform, TNCompass. On TNCompass, each teacher has a profile that contains data about their accreditation status, professional development status/goals, VAM scores and their observation assessment scores and notes. Teachers can access their own data profiles at any time (and are encouraged to do so), while school-level and district-level administrators have access to all teachers' data.

As mentioned previously, datafication increases schools' reliance on, access to, and ability to capture more data about teachers and teaching than ever before (i.e., the 'three V's' of volume, velocity, variety; see Selwyn, 2015). In Tennessee, data have been central to their accountability for many years. However, TNCompass changes where, how and to what ends data are collected, accessed and monitored. Previously, data were collected, stored and discussed in discreet units of time and place. For example, an administrator might keep observation data stored in a filing cabinet in an office, and then access and discuss that data with the teacher at specified intervals throughout the school year. If a district administrator wanted to access data about teachers, they would need to travel or call/email the school-level administrator to receive such reports. Now, as noted in the TNCompass access guidelines, both school- and district-level administrators can access these data anytime, anywhere. District-level administrators also have the ability to modify data records, if they can provide evidence for the change. This enables a more ubiquitous and continuous form of monitoring that some have described as 'silent control' (Orito, 2011; see also Selwyn, 2015) or 'digital rule' (Jones, 2000).

Even though numbers and metrics have played a significant role in shaping teachers and teaching for many years, which is at the heart of Ball's (2003) performativity, dataveillance creates a new set of conditions whereby a teacher's data profile – sometimes called 'data doubles' or 'data shadows' (Selwyn, 2015, p. 73) – can become the main site of inspection, intervention and control (Thompson & Cook, 2014). This shifts the inspectoral gaze from the physical body to 'bodies of data', while simultaneously shifting priorities to improving data, rather than other educative practices (see Hardy, 2019; Lewis & Holloway, 2019). In Tennessee, the weight of these data has had significant consequences for teachers, including whether they will keep their jobs. Thus, we can imagine a new kind of teacher subject – one who is not only performative, but datafied.

From the performative to the datafied subject

Foucault (1988) reminds us that individuals are not simply objects of an oppressive power, but also subjects who actively engage with 'technologies of the self, which permit individuals to effect by their own means, or with the help of others, a certain number of operations on their own bodies and souls, thoughts, conduct, and way of being' (p. 225). In other words, as individuals are subjected to a given set of conditions that define what is true and 'real', they use material and symbolic norms, techniques and discourses to 'know' themselves and to optimize their success, quality, happiness, and so forth.

Foucault was interested in how discourses worked to produce particular types of people as 'docile subjects' (Foucault, 1984). He sought to understand the relationship between discourses and the formation of subjects as determined (and re-determined) over time by types of knowledge available. He wrote that 'what we should do is show the historical construction of a subject through a discourse understood as consisting of a set of strategies which are part of social practices' (Foucault, 2000, p. 4, as cited in Davies & Bansel, 2010, pp. 5–6). What is important to note here is that the subject is not a passive individual who has discourses done to them. Rather, subjects are part of the discourse and part of the construction of themselves as subjects in relation to the discourse.

This is at the heart of the performativity work that has been so influential in the field of education policy sociology over the past two decades (Ball, 2003; Perryman, 2009). As Ball (2003) once famously remarked, performativity does not just change what teachers *do*, but it also changes who teachers *are*. His point is that the logics and techniques of performativity – e.g., individualism, competition, numerical understandings of teaching and learning, self-responsibilization – provide the material and symbolic means for teachers to know themselves, and for them to know how to be 'better' versions of themselves. Over time, we have seen these practices and techniques become normalized, insofar as teachers have begun to embody performativity as the way to be and to practice as teachers. In an onto-epistemic sense, performativity has served as both the reality and the knowledge about what it means to be a 'good' teacher and to know what 'good' teaching looks like (see also Holloway, 2019).

As new datafied logics, techniques and discourses emerge and overlay those of performativity, we must be attuned to the ways in which such conditions create new possibilities for the teacher subject. Indeed, datafication makes available a complementary, but different, onto-epistemic framework for being, thinking and doing (see also Lupton, 2018). For the performative teacher, the site of surveillance and intervention remains on the physical body and in physical spaces (e.g., in the classroom, during one-on-one meetings, during professional development workshops). However, for the datafied teacher, the main site of surveillance and intervention becomes the data profiles, or the 'data doubles' (Selwyn, 2015), of the teacher (e.g., VAM data stored on TNCompass).

This dataveillance creates the ability for teachers to be subjected to what Jones (2000) referred to as 'digital rule'. Specifically, Jones argued that digital technologies, like those seen in TEAM and TNCompass, enable a new form of controlling individuals 'from a distance'. Data profiles can be accessed anytime and anywhere by those who have been granted privileges to do so. Usernames and passwords supplement classroom doors and personal interactions. Teachers have no way of knowing when or how often they are being 'monitored', and thus must prioritize their data profiles over their interpersonal engagements in the classroom (see also Thompson & Cook, 2014). In this way, there are certainly performative elements of datafication. Thus, we want to stress our point that performativity and datafication should not be viewed as discrete and separable technologies of governance. Rather, datafication should be seen as a complementary technology that is operating with performativity, but also establishing a new language and set of conditions that transform the teacher subject into something *of* data, rather than oriented *to* data, as is seen in the performativity framework.

Concluding discussion

Bradbury (2019) critiques datafication for the 'loss of complexity, issues of reliability, the impact on pedagogy' (p.18), which echoes what others have said about the undesirable outcomes of PBA more generally (see, for example, Berliner & Biddle, 1996). In many ways, performativity established the conditions that have made datafication possible. However, in saying that, we want to stress that the two are not separate, or operate in a necessarily linear way. While performativity may have preceded datafication in a technological sense, the two are really dependent upon one another. Indeed, there are performative elements of datafication, just as there are datafication elements of performativity. For example, the hyper-focus on data and metrics is a key feature of both performative and datafied regimes. Similarly, what makes performativity and datafication so powerful is surveillance and the knowledge that teachers are under constant and ubiquitous monitoring (and self-monitoring).

As we described with the history of PBA in Tennessee, testing and dis/incentivism have been central elements of teacher accountability for decades. Over time, this way of conceptualizing teachers and orienting their practice in terms of numbers and metrics has normalized the logic that teachers and teaching should be understood in terms of numbers, and that our knowledge about teaching practice should be grounded in numerical data. In other words, as teachers come to know themselves and their success as that which can be calculated by tools like rubrics and VAMs (see Holloway, 2019), the move to collect and store such information online is of relatively little shock to the system.

Thus, we note that part of what makes the datafication of teaching possible is the fact that much of our contemporary life is similarly intertwined with datafied understandings of ourselves and our surroundings. From smart-watches and smart-homes that track all sorts of data about our physical location, health and other personal activities, to apps that track productivity, mood, eating habits or almost anything imaginable, we have become accustomed to using data, charts and algorithms to know all sorts of information about ourselves. Therefore, it is easy to imagine how this same logic translates into the classroom, where data and numbers have featured prominently long before smart technologies were even thinkable.

Indeed, in today's environment, there is an inescapable intimacy between humans and technology, and data assumes more and more concrete importance in our everyday environments (Lupton, 2016). Schools cannot escape this. Thus, we are not arguing that technology is always pernicious, or that digital technology makes performativity worse. Rather, we argue that in order to fully capture the changing conditions and the effects these conditions have on teacher subjectivity, we need to think with both performativity and datafication frameworks. What we identified in this chapter are some of the possibilities that have emerged in response to such technological advancements, while drawing attention to how these changes might affect what it means to be a teacher.

As we have shown in this chapter, Michel Foucault and Gilles Deleuze have been significant sources of inspiration for performativity and datafication scholars in education. However, we see a need to think more carefully about matters often left out of analyses that draw from these frameworks, especially within the field of education. Race and gender, in particular, are rarely addressed explicitly in the datafication of education literature. Therefore, we urge scholars in this area to engage with theoretical and methodological tools that deal more intentionally with how data practices produce and (re)produce categories of 'difference'. Feminist and black feminist theorists have much to offer – see, for example, Benjamin (2019), Dixon-Roman (2016), and D'Ignazio and Klein (2020). Ultimately, we call for researchers to consider the subtle, and not so subtle, ways that datafication is shaping schools, teachers and students, as well as the relationships, priorities and possibilities that might accordingly emerge.

Note

1   In the 2015 replacement of NCLB with ESSA, there are two significant changes, both in the vein of moving away from the undesirable results of PBA observed since the 1970s. First, states must have a measure of school quality or student success, apart from test-based achievement and graduation rates. Second, the USDOE can neither prescribe school or teacher sanctions, nor can it mandate a teacher evaluation system. The return to state-level flexibility and the introduction of more varied measures of accountability was met with the hope that the disastrous effects of TBA on students, families, teachers and leaders and on the aims of education could somehow be reversed, or at least slowed.

References

Aldrich, M. W. (2018, October 11). Teachers getting better under Tennessee's controversial evaluation system, says new analysis. *Chalkbeat*. Retrieved from https://www.chalkbeat.org/posts/tn/2018/10/11/teachers-getting-better-under-tennessees-controversial-evaluation-system-says-new-analysis/

Aldrich, M. W. (2019, September 10). A renewed debate in Tennessee: Should schools be judged by how much students know, or how much they grow? *Chalkbeat*. Retrieved from https://docs.google.com/document/d/1dAYbiMYpm2bzoaypgv2NuPFLKp5MGjwS8z2Aa3YwQZk/edit?folder=1p3_qAo5fUO6jKHZz78l9gj7km2DmZ2aI#

American Reinvestment and Recovery Act (ARRA) (2009). Retrieved from http://www.gpo.gov/fdsys/pkg/BILLS-111hr1enr/pdf/ BILLS-111hr1enr.pdf

Amrein-Beardsley, A. (2008). Methodological concerns about the education value-added assessment system. *Educational Researcher, 37*(2), 65–75.

Amrein-Beardsley, A. (2014). *Rethinking value-added models in education: Critical perspectives on tests and assessment-based accountability*. New York: Routledge.

Amrein-Beardsley, A., & Collins, C. (2012). The SAS education value-added assessment system (SAS® EVAAS®) in the Houston Independent School District (HISD): Intended and unintended consequences. *Education Policy Analysis Archives/Archivos Analíticos de Políticas Educativas, 20*, 1–28.

Ball, S. J. (2003). The teacher's soul and the terrors of performativity. *Journal of Education Policy, 18*(2), 215–228.

Ball, S. J. (2015). Education, governancse and the tyranny of numbers. *Journal of Education Policy, 30*(3), 299–331.

Benjamin, R. (2019). *Race after technology: Abolitionist tools for the new Jim Code*. New Jersey: John Wiley & Sons.

Berliner, D. (2011). Rational responses to high stakes testing. *Cambridge Journal of Education, 41*(3), 287–302.

Berliner, D. C. (2013). Problems with value-added evaluations of teachers? Let me count the ways. *Teacher Evaluation, 48*(4), 235–243.

Berliner, D. C., & Biddle, B. J. (1996). The manufactured crisis: Myths, fraud, and the attack on America's public schools. *Nassp Bulletin, 80*(576), 119–121.

Bradbury, A. (2019). Datafied at four: The role of data in the 'schoolification' of early childhood education in England. *Learning, Media and Technology, 44*(1), 7–21.

Clapham, A., Vickers, R., & Eldridge, J. (2016). Legitimation, performativity and the tyranny of a 'hijacked' word. *Journal of Education Policy, 31*(6), 757–772.

Canon, K. S., Greenslate, C., Lewis, J. L., Merchant, K., & Springer, M. G. (2012). *Evaluation of Tennessee's strategic compensation programs: Interim findings on development, design, and implementation*. Nashville: Tennessee Consortium on Research, Evaluation, and Development. Retrieved from http://www.tnconsortium.org/projects-publications/compensation/

Collins, C. (2014). Houston, we have a problem: Teachers find no value in the SAS education value-added assessment system (EVAAS®). *Education Policy Analysis Archives, 22*(98), 98.

Collins, C., & Amrein-Beardsley, A. (2014). Putting growth and value-added models on the map: A national overview. *Teachers College Record, 116*(1), 1–32.

Darling-Hammond, L. (1997). Toward what end? The evaluation of student learning for the improvement of teaching. In J. Millman (Ed.), *Grading teachers grading schools. Is student achievement a valid evaluation measure?* (pp. 248–263). Thousand Oaks, CA: Corwin.

Davies, B., & Bansel, P. (2010). Governmentality and academic work: Shaping the hearts and minds of academic workers. *Journal of Curriculum Theorizing, 26*(3).

D'Ignazio, C., & Klein, L. F. (2020). *Data feminism*. Cambridge: MIT Press.

de Freitas, E. & Dixon-Roman, E. (2017). The computational turn in educational research: Critical and creative perspectives on the digital data deluge. *Research in Education, 98*(1), 3–13.

Dixon-Roman, E. (2016). Algo-ritmo: More-than-human performative acts and the racializing assemblages of algorithmic architectures. *Cultural Studies? Critical Methodologies, 16*(5), 482–490.

Englund, H., & Gerdin, J. (2019). Performative technologies and teacher subjectivities: A conceptual framework. *British Educational Research Journal, 45*(3), 502–517.

Falabella, A. (2014). The Performing School: The Effects of Market & Accountability Policies. *Education Policy Analysis Archives, 22*(70), 1–29.

Falabella, A. (2016). Do national test scores and quality labels trigger school self-assessment and accountability? A critical analysis in the Chilean context. *British Journal of Sociology of Education, 37*(5), 743–760.

Foucault, M. (1980). *Power/knowledge: Selected interviews and other writings, 1972–1977.* New York: Vintage.

Foucault, M. (1984). *The Foucault Reader.* New York: Pantheon.

Foucault, M. (1988). *Technologies of the self: A seminar with Michel Foucault.* Massachusetts: University of Massachusetts Press.

Foucault, M. (2003). *The Essential Foucault: Selections from Essential works of Foucault, 1954–1984.* New York: The New Press.

Foucault, M. (1991). Governmentality. In G. Burchell, C. Gordon, & P. Miller (Eds.), *The Foucault effect: Studies in governmentality* (pp. 87–104). Chicago: University of Chicago Press.

Grek, S. (2009). Governing by numbers: The PISA 'effect' in Europe. *Journal of Education Policy, 24*(1), 23–37.

Hardy, I. (2018). Governing teacher learning: Understanding teachers' compliance with and critique of standardization. *Journal of Education Policy, 33*(1), 1–22.

Hardy, I. (2019). The quandary of quantification: Data, numbers and teachers' learning. *Journal of Education Policy,* 1–20.

Holloway, J. (2019). Teacher evaluation as an onto-epistemic framework. *British Journal of Sociology of Education, 40*(2), 174–189.

Holloway, J., & Brass, J. (2018). Making accountable teachers: The terrors and pleasures of performativity. *Journal of Education Policy, 33*(3), 361–382.

Introna, L. D. (2016). Algorithms, governance, and governmentality: On governing academic writing. *Science, Technology, & Human Values, 41*(1), 17–49.

Johnson, S. M. (2015). Will VAMS reinforce the walls of the egg-crate school? *Educational Researcher, 44*(2), 117–126.

Jones, R. (2000). Digital rule: Punishment, control and technology. *Punishment & Society, 2*(1), 5–22.

Kitchin, R. (2014). Big Data, new epistemologies and paradigm shifts. *Big Data & Society, 1*(1).

Lewis, S. (2017). Governing schooling through 'what works': The OECD's PISA for Schools. *Journal of Education Policy, 32*(3), 281–302.

Lewis, S., & Holloway, J. (2019). Datafying the teaching 'profession': Remaking the professional teacher in the image of data. *Cambridge Journal of Education, 49*(1), 35–51.

Linn, R. L. (2001). The design and evaluation of educational assessment and accountability systems. CSE Technical Report 539. University of California, Los Angeles. Public Law 107-110 (No Child Left Behind). Retrieved from https://www.k12.wa.us/esea/NCLB.aspx

Lupton, D. (2016). The diverse domains of quantified selves: Self-tracking modes and dataveillance. *Economy and Society, 45*(1), 101–122.

Lupton, D. (2018). How do data come to matter? Living and becoming with personal data. *Big Data & Society, 5*(2), 1–11. doi: 10.1177/2053951718786314.

Lupton, D., & Williamson, B. (2017). The datafied child: The dataveillance of children and implications for their rights. *New Media & Society, 19*(5), 780–794.

Miller, P. (1992). Accounting and objectivity: the invention of calculating selves and calculable spaces. *Annals of Scholarship, 9*(1/2), 61–86.

Orito, Y. (2011). The counter-control revolution. *Journal of Information, Communication and Ethics in Society, 9*(1), 5–19.

Ozga, J. (2008). Governing knowledge: Research steering and research quality. *European Educational Research Journal, 7*(3), 261–272.

Pasquale, F. (2015). *The Black Box society: The secret algorithms that control money and information.* Cambridge, MA: Harvard University Press.

Perryman, J. (2006). Panoptic performativity and school inspection regimes. *Journal of Education Policy, 21*(2), 147–161.

Perryman, J. (2009). Inspection and the fabrication of professional and performative processes. *Journal of Education Policy, 24*(5), 611–631.

Porter, T. M. (1996). *Trust in numbers: The pursuit of objectivity in science and public life.* Princeton: Princeton University Press.

Pratt, N. (2016). Neoliberalism and the marketisation of primary school assessment. *British Educational Research Journal, 42*(5), 890–905.

Public Law 107-110, No Child Left Behind Act of 2001, January 8, 2002. As of June 7, 2010. Retrieved from http://frwebgate.access.gpo.gov/cgi-bin/getdoc.cgi?dbname=107_cong_public_laws&docid=f:publ110.107.pdf

Rose, N. (1999). *Powers of freedom: Reframing political thought.* Cambridge: Cambridge University Press.

Saldaña, J. (2013). *The coding manual for qualitative researchers* (2nd ed.). Los Angeles, CA: SAGE.

Sanders, W. L., & Horne, S. P. (1998). Research findings from the Tennessee value-added assessment system database: Implications for educational evaluation and research. *Journal of Personnel Evaluation in Education, 12*(3), 247–256.

Selwyn, N. (2015). Data entry: Towards the critical study of digital data and education. *Learning, Media and Technology, 40*(1), 64–82.

Smith, W. C. (2016). *The global testing culture: Shaping education policy, perceptions, and practice.* Oxford Studies in Comparative Education Series: Symposium Books.

Stecher, B. M., Holtzman, D. J., Garet, M. S., Hamilton, L. S., Engberg, J., Steiner, E. D., Robyn, A., Baird, M. D., Gutierrez, I. A., Peet, E. D., de los Reyes, I. B., Fronberg, K., Weinberger, G., Hunter, G. P., and Chambers, J. (2018). *Improving Teaching Effectiveness: Final Report: The Intensive Partnerships for Effective Teaching Through 2015–2016.* Santa Monica, CA: RAND Corporation. Retrieved from https://www.rand.org/pubs/research_reports/RR2242.html

Taubman, P. M. (2010). *Teaching by numbers: Deconstructing the discourse of standards and accountability in education.* New York: Routledge.

Tennessee Department of Education (2013a). *Teacher evaluation in Tennessee: A report of year 1 implementation.* Retrieved from http://team-tn.org/wp-content/uploads/2013/08/Year1-Evaluation-Report-TNDOE.pdf

Tennessee Department of Education (2013b). *Teacher evaluation in Tennessee; A report of year 2 implementation.* Retrieved from http://team-tn.org/wp-content/uploads/2013/08/yr_2_tchr_eval_rpt.pdf

Tennessee Department of Education (2014). *Tennessee value-added assessment system.* Retrieved from http://www.tn.gov/education/data/TVAAS.shtml

Tennessee Department of Education (2015). Tennessee Consortium on Reforming Education. (2013). Educator evaluation in Tennessee: Initial findings from the 2013 first to the top survey. Retrieved from http://www.tnconsortium.org

Tennessee Department of Education (2017). *Every student succeeds act: Building on success in Tennessee.* Retrieved from https://www2.ed.gov/admins/lead/account/stateplan17/tncsa2017.pdf

Tennessee Educator Accelerator Model (2014). *Teacher evaluation.* Retrieved from http://team-tn.org/evaluation/teacher-evaluation/

Thompson, G., & Cook, I. (2014). Manipulating the data: Teaching and NAPLAN in the control society. *Discourse: Studies in the Cultural Politics of Education, 35*(1), 129–142.

US Department of Education (1965). Elementary and Secondary Education Act. Retrieved from http://www.ed.gov/esea.

US Department of Education (2009). *Race to the top: Executive summary*. Retrieved from http://www2.ed.gov/programs/racetothetop/executive-summary.pdf

Van Dijck, J. (2014). Datafication, dataism and dataveillance: Big Data between scientific paradigm and ideology. *Surveillance & Society, 12*(2), 197–208.

Vick, M. J., & Martinez, C. (2011). Teachers and teaching: Subjectivity, performativity and the body. *Educational Philosophy and Theory, 43*(2), 178–192.

Wilkins, C. (2011). Professionalism and the post-performative teacher: New teachers reflect on autonomy and accountability in the English school system. *Professional Development in Education, 37*(3), 389–409.

Williamson, B. (2017). Learning in the 'platform society': Disassembling an educational data assemblage. *Research in Education, 98*(1), 59–82.

Yettick, H. (2014). Researchers advise caution on value-added models. *Education Week, 33*(32), 10–12.

15 Enactments and resistances to globalizing testing regimes and performance-based accountability in the USA

Bob Lingard

Introduction

There is much evidence to suggest that over the last 20 years or so many schooling systems around the globe have introduced standardized testing (National Large-Scale Assessments – NLSAs), often of a census kind. The case of the USA dealt with in this chapter is a case in point, with such testing being conducted at the subnational state level, but in response to federal requirements. The first significant federal requirement for such testing at Grades 3 through 8 was President G.W. Bush's *No Child Left Behind Act* (2002), further reinforced by President Obama's *Race to the Top* legislation (2009). These were high-stakes tests linked to performance-based accountability (PBA[1]) for teachers, schools and systems. There has been a less robust federal agenda on such matters under the Trump Presidency with more commitment to 'states' rights' in education and a strengthened focus on further privatization.

In many systems these high-stakes tests and performance-based accountability complement international large-scale assessments (ILSAs) such as the OECD's Programme for International Student Assessment (PISA). PISA is a sample test which has become influential in national education policy in participating nations. At times, national tests have been introduced explicitly as a complement to the ILSAs (Kamens and McNeeley, 2010; Kamens, 2013). It has been suggested that an international comparative reference is a necessary complement to national testing to ensure an accurate measure of trends in systemic performance (Schleicher and Zoido, 2016, pp. 379–380).

These national and international large-scale tests are indicative of a new mode of educational governance, the conjoining of the 'global eye' with the 'national eye', in Novoa and Yariv-Mashal's (2003) insightful description. Comparison is central to this new mode of governance and enables layers of public accountability. The significance of these large-scale tests in educational governance has also been enabled and enhanced by the creation of data infrastructures (Anagnostopoulos, Rutledge, and Jacobsen, 2013) and greater computational capacities, which have also witnessed the datafication of educational governance in many school systems across the globe (Williamson, 2017).

It must be said, however, that these matters always play out in path-dependent ways in specific nations, as do resistances to them at various political levels within the nation, as this chapter will demonstrate in respect of the USA. In terms of ILSAs and the broader work of international organizations, powerful nations such as the USA have more capacity to resist, than do, say, developing nations in respect of something like PISA for Development (PISA-D) tests and the UN's Sustainable Development Goals (SDGs).

One can argue that high-stakes standardized testing, both national and international, has become part of a new mode of performance-based accountability (PBA), with teachers, schools, systems and ministers of education being held to account through comparative performances on these tests. The work of the OECD and national policy impacts of comparative performance on PISA league tables has also worked to globalize educational accountabilities (Lingard et al., 2016) and construct modes of 'mutual accountability' (Novoa and Yariv-Mashal, 2003).

The globalization of this particular mode of top-down, test-based accountability has been facilitated by the global infrastructures linked to international large-scale assessments; indeed, Sassen (2007) has argued that globalization is actually the creation of global infrastructures. Elsewhere, she also argues that the global and the national (and, I would add, the subnational) should not be seen today as discrete, mutually exclusive entities; rather, 'they significantly overlap and interact in ways that distinguish our contemporary moment' (Sassen, 2001, p. 260) with the global embedded within the national. The global and the national today constitute, and are entangled with, each other. Yet, as this chapter will demonstrate, there has been something of a right-wing political backlash against perceived global impacts and thus vigorous attempts to reassert the national. This is evidenced in the rearticulation of new forms of nationalism and ethno-nationalist identity politics that reject cultural pluralism and the super diverse ethnic populations of most present-day developed nations and resent the elites who have benefitted from globalization. Instead, ethno-nationalist politics prioritize the interests of the dominant ethnic group and its culture over all others (Bonikowski, 2017). These politics are very apparent in President Trump's America First stance, his strong opposition to multilateralism, his endorsement of anti-immigration and anti-globalization sentiments and a desire to return to a mythical 'ethnically pure' USA of the past (Schertzer and Taylor, 2020).

There is a real danger of reifying the global and the education work of the OECD in respect of global tests and accountability developments. The global is, often inaccurately, thought of as 'abstract, homogeneous, structural, and without agents or agency' (Robertson, 2018, p. 36). Sassen (2001, 2006, 2007) has disaffected us of that view of the global, showing the complex and multifarious imbrications of the global, the national and the local and how the national has been central to the constitution of the global, as well as the work of international organizations such as the OECD, and that the global sometimes works with subnational entities and vice versa. Sobe (2015) argues persuasively that we should not take the global as an a priori given, and instead, in relation to the OECD's education work, see it as constituting the global in education rather than simply reflecting it. De Sousa Santos (2006, p. 396) has posited that 'there is no originally global position; what we call globalization is always the successive globalization of a particular localism'. Top-down, performance-based accountability is one such example of this: in de Sousa Santos's (2006) terms, we see a localism globalized (globalized localism) and when this Anglo-American apparatus of accountability is taken up and proselytized by an international organization such as the OECD and then taken up by other nations, what we see is the localizing of a globalism (localized globalism). Top-down performance-based accountability within national systems might be seen then as the localizing of the Anglo-American approach to accountability (Lingard and Lewis, 2016). Thus, while there might be some seeming and apparent material and discursive global convergence of education policy (Rutkowski, 2007), globally circulating policy ideas from international organizations such as the OECD always play out in path-dependent ways and thus differently within nations (Carvalho and Costa, 2014).

Nation-states are thus not passive in the use and impact of ILSAs; at times, ministries of education actively use such data to legitimate and drive their own reform agendas (Takayama, 2008). Grek (2020) has argued convincingly that the relationships between the OECD and national policy developments in education should not be seen as 'hierarchical, linear and hegemonic', but rather the idea of entanglements might better grasp these relationships. The complex, multiple spatialities of globalization have reconstituted the various directionalities and character of global/national/local relations/imbrications (Sassen, 2001, 2006, 2007; Amin, 2002). It is these entanglements, evident in changing US relations with the OECD's testing regimes and in local resistances to PBA in New York State, that are the dual concerns of this chapter.

Powerful nations like the USA are very often the source of globalizing localisms (e.g. PBA), while the USA also has been the most powerful actor (both covert and overt) in the work of the OECD, more broadly and specifically in education. They were the central actor in relation to the OECD's creation of PISA in the late 1990s, with the first test administered in 2000 (Henry et al., 2001; Pizmony-Levy, 2013). As Haas (1990, p. 57) observed, all international organizations, including the OECD, have their own superpower 'capable of playing a hegemonic role if it chose to do so'. The USA chose to play this hegemonic role in the late 1990s, pushing for the creation of what became PISA. As the chapter will demonstrate, more recently and in the context of President Trump's anti-multilateralism, the USA has been very critical of the OECD's expansionary aspirations for their testing regime. Here we see a collision between the USA's changing global role, and the more active actor role of the OECD as an agent of globalizing educational accountabilities.

This chapter will begin by succinctly outlining the enhanced role of the OECD's education work and its future ambitions and impact. This documentation will show how the OECD's testing work has contributed significantly to the global in education policy, particularly through their constitution of the globe as a commensurate space of measurement. This documenting of the OECD's ambitions in relation to their education work, particularly testing, will demonstrate how the OECD has become a policy actor in its own right, as well as being a node in a network of power relations. Yet, as the analysis will demonstrate, the nation-state and subnational political units nonetheless remain important in education policy in both enacting and resisting PBA.

All of these global policy changes in education have occurred against a seeming post-Cold War consensual backdrop of neo-liberal globalization and marketization. However, as the chapter will show and as has been noted already, more recent backlashes to this mode of politics and governance have seriously challenged this smooth consensus. These challenges to the apparent hegemony of neo-liberal globalization are having significant policy effects in some nations and are potentially beginning to affect the smooth expansion of the OECD's education agenda, particularly in relation to testing and its ambitions for it, as will be shown in the case of the USA.

It is this backdrop that will frame the analysis of US resistance to the OECD's globalizing and expansionary testing regime and to parental resistance to performance-based accountability. In a sense, these broad political developments have ensured that we need to rethink in more sophisticated and empirically based ways the multifarious relationships between the global, the national and the local and reject any simplistic one-way, top-down account of these relationships. These backlashes also raises questions about the ever-changing workings of the nation in education policy and continuing significance of the politics of schooling at subnational levels. On the latter, the chapter will also document opposition to PBA in New York State.

The work of the OECD: Globalizing testing regimes and performance-based accountability

There is a broad literature outlining the history of the OECD as an international organization (e.g. Woodward, 2009; Carroll and Kellow, 2011). The point needs to be stressed that from the outset the OECD was a project of the USA, created in terms of its geopolitical and economic interests. Its membership has grown considerably since its creation in 1961. It now has 36 members, up from the original 20, with the imminent ascension to membership of Colombia as the 37th member. Membership now requires commitment to a market economy, liberal democracy and, more recently, human rights.

There is also a considerable literature on the changing role of education at the OECD (Henry et al., 2001; Pizmony-Levy, 2013; Ydesen, 2019), where it became a separate directorate in 2002 and restructured as the Directorate of Education and Skills in 2012. With the end of the Cold War, the OECD strengthened its global presence, dealing with non-member nations and also participated in some projects of UNESCO on a broader global stage (e.g. PISA for Development tests linked to outcomes measures for the SDGS) and collaborated with the EU. The history of education at the OECD and a considerable body of research (e.g. Lingard and Sellar, 2016) would suggest that in the contemporary world it has become a policy actor in its own right, not merely the expression of the policy desires of member nations, the usual self-descriptor proffered by the OECD. International comparative data such as PISA have become very important in the post-Cold War role of the OECD. This is very evident in education with an expanding testing agenda, a manifestation of the OECD's actor role. The OECD actor role in education is also linked to the strengthened significance of education and skills across the whole of the OECD and of performance data in relation to these matters.

As noted already, under pressure from the USA, in 1997 the OECD launched what was to become PISA, first administered in 2000 and every three years subsequently, with 32 participating nations in 2000, 79 in 2018, with 88 participants expected in PISA 2021, now postponed to 2022 because of the global Coronavirus pandemic. The development of educational indicators and PISA was largely in response to pressures from the USA.

The success of PISA and its enhanced global coverage are also indicative of the alignment of such comparative performance data with developments within nations, including national testing, the usage of data, PBA and so on. These national policy developments have also been facilitated by the education work and soft power of the OECD and the seeming epistemic alignments between the dispositions of OECD and national policymakers in education (Lingard, Sellar, and Baroutsis, 2015). The OECD has been a persuasive actor in the introduction by so many nations of national or subnational census testing. Declining comparative PISA results, for example, were important contexts for the introduction of national testing in Australia in 2008, and also for President Obama's *Race to the Top* policy and top-down, performance-based modes of accountability in the USA, instantiated in the education work of the states.

Elsewhere, it has been shown that the OECD is seeking to expand the scope (what is measured), scale (number of participating nations) and explanatory power of its testing work (Lingard and Sellar, 2016). The expanding scope of PISA has seen the inclusion of some non-cognitive measures into the tests, beyond the original scientific literacy, mathematical literacy and reading literacy, and with the move to online testing the potential for analytics to be applied to log file data. Another significant example of expanding scope is the inclusion in 2012 of a measure of financial literacy, and in the 2018 PISA of a measure of global competence, linked to notions of global citizenship. It is significant here that the USA did not participate in this measure in 2018. The expansion of the scale of PISA is indicated clearly in the increasing numbers of participating nations, with the ambition for more than 100 participants in the future. Explanatory power is linked to the OECD's long-term desire to link PISA data and the OECD's Teaching and Learning International Survey (TALIS) (Sorensen and Robertson, 2019) to get at the 'holy grail', as one OECD interviewee put it to me, of educational research, namely what pedagogies make the most difference to student learning.

In addition to these ambitions, the OECD has also developed other tests with PISA as prototype. These include the Programme for International Assessment of Adult Competencies (PIAAC) (PISA for adults/16–64 year olds), PISA for Development, which will be linked to the main PISA scale in 2021 and used as part of the outcome measures of the UN's Sustainable Development Goals, specifically SDG 4 (2015–2030), PISA for Schools, which sees the OECD reaching topologically inside nations directly to schools and local school authorities and these reaching out to the OECD (see Lewis et al., 2016), the International Learning and Child Well-being Study (IELS) (Baby PISA) for 5-year-olds and the new PISA4U, a school improvement tool for schools (Lewis, 2019). This is an expansionary and ambitious testing agenda and a further indicator of the policy actor role of the OECD.

The education work of the OECD has been important in constituting a global education policy field and global education policy (Lingard and Rawolle, 2011), achieving this emergence through its testing and review capacities and through the practices of soft power. The OECD's impact works through suasion, through the creation of mutual accountabilities via comparative test results and league tables, through the impact of its broader testing regimes, through examples, and through epistemological and infrastructural governance and the constitution of an epistemological community between OECD and national policymakers. The OECD has been influential in proselytizing the notion of school autonomy linked to systemic test-based accountability mechanisms. As noted to this point, a specific mode of educational accountability, that is, schools, teachers, and systems being held to account, is the Anglo-American model of top-down, test-based accountability, which has also filtered into the OECD's discourses in a somewhat more nuanced way. This mode has become a globalized localism, with its polysemous character allowing vernacular expressions of its manifestation in specific national schooling systems.

The impact of PISA has also been enhanced and legitimated through the concept of 'PISA shocks', where PISA test results are contrary to national self-evaluations of schooling systems. The PISA shock in Germany following release of PISA 2000 results in late 2001 precipitated a real policy shock in Germany (Grek, 2009). Hartong (2018) has documented in a granular fashion the impact of this shock on schooling policy in Germany, with subsequent moves to implement hitherto resisted modes of performance-based accountability. We see here the impact of the PISA shock and the localizing of a globalized localisms via the OECD. PISA shocks in England and the USA following the stellar performance of Shanghai on PISA 2009 had different impacts in the USA and England (Sellar and Lingard, 2013). At the time, of course, these systems had extant top-down, performance-based modes of accountability, yet this PISA shock did not result in changes to this mode of accountability; rather, the shock in the USA strengthened federal government support and demand for PBA.

Resistances to globalizing testing regimes and performance-based accountability in the USA

Backdrop to US cases

As already noted, PISA was developed by the OECD after much pressure from the USA on the organization in the context of growing concerns about education standards that stretched back to President Reagan's *A Nation at Risk* (1983) report. However, until PISA 2009, this ILSA had had little impact on US schooling, reflecting the dispersed structure of schooling in the USA in which schooling was 'controlled' and administered more at state and local levels than at the federal level. Nonetheless, globalization and a human capital framing of schooling policy pushed a stronger federal presence under the Obama Presidency. As stated above, Shanghai's outstanding performance on PISA 2009 precipitated a PISA shock in the USA with this being a focus of President Obama's 2011 State of the Union Address (see Collins, 2012). In an earlier *New York Times* story on 2009 PISA (December 10, 2010), President Obama was also quoted as saying that the USA's comparative poor PISA performance, especially when compared with that of Shanghai, was the USA's twenty-first century 'Sputnik moment'. One policy response was the commissioning of a report from the OECD/National Centre on Education and the Economy (NCEE) on high-performing PISA systems and what could be learnt from them. President Obama's *Race to the Top* (RTTT), pressure for states and school systems to develop data infrastructures and integrate them within and across states, and the use of test data for teacher performance-based accountability purposes, must be seen in the context of the USA's poor PISA performance and the 2010 PISA shock. Interestingly, some states subsequently paid to participate in PISA as part of their responses to *Race to the Top* demands for systemic test-based accountabilities and data infrastructures.

The point to note here in relation to the two cases of resistance outlined below is: the USA was centrally involved in the creation of PISA by the OECD and that until the 2009 PISA, this test had little policy impact there. Furthermore, the 2010 PISA shock, at least during the Obama Administration, strengthened the role played by test-based data and test-based accountabilities for schools and systems. Under the Trump Administration, that policy pressure has weakened and the political focus has been more on expanding Charter Schools and the usage of vouchers with a less focused concern with national and subnational testing and ILSAs. Indeed, with regard to PISA, as will be illustrated below, some criticisms are now beginning to be articulated.

Resistance to test-based accountability in New York State

Here the opposition in New York State to high-stakes testing and top-down, test-based modes of accountability (TBA/PBA)[2] will be documented, focusing on the work of two grassroots, parent activist groups: Long Island Opt Out (LIOO) and New York State Allies for Public Education (NYSAPE) (see Lingard et al., 2017, pp. 63–71; Hursh et al., 2019; Lingard and Hursh, 2019). High-stakes testing has been a part of US schooling for some time, but the federal endorsement and demand for testing strengthened considerably from President Bush's *No Child Left Behind* (NCLB) implemented from 2002 and subsequently with President Obama's *Race to the Top* (RTTT) (2009), which linked testing to the Common Core State Standards in Literacy and Maths. The complexity of federalism in US schooling is evident here in that the Common Core was developed and endorsed by the states, but was the basis of the tests required by RTTT. As argued above, importantly the backdrop to RTTT and many of its requirements of the states was the USA's poor PISA performance, and specifically the 2010 PISA shock; a manifestation of the complex contemporary imbrications of the global, national and local as suggested by Sassen.

These reforms resulted in testing at all grade levels from 3 through to 8 and was to be used for school accountability, teacher accountability and evaluation (a version of PBA). These reforms also provoked considerable opposition to both the high-stakes testing and this mode of PBA. They also provoked the creation of both NYSAPE and LIOO, which have had considerable success in the numbers of parents opting their children out of the tests, 20% across the state in 2015, 22% in 2016, with more than 50% of parents in the two Long Island counties of Nassau and Suffolk opting their children out in these two years. While the numbers have declined since, a considerable number of parents continue to opt their children out of the tests with impact on the usefulness and validity of the tests. A specific strategy of both groups was to increase the numbers of those opting out so as to limit the usage of the test for their intended purposes.

The membership of these two opt-out activist groups is very middle-class, highly-educated, mainly white women from high-income families, with 45% of the membership teachers (Pizmony-Levy and Green, 2016). This large teacher membership is because of the seeming ambivalent attitudes of the teacher unions across the state in relation to the *Race to the Top* reforms, which President Obama had packaged as a new civil rights agenda. Interestingly, until the 2016 election of President Trump, while most of the membership of the two groups were Democratic voters, there were considerable numbers of Republicans also involved, particularly on Long Island. These two differently aligned political groups opted out for different reasons; the Democrats saw high-stakes testing as reducing the quality and width of the schooling provided, rejected the notion of teacher evaluation and accountability based on the tests, and were also critical of the ways in which these reforms opened opportunities for edu-businesses to participate in schooling for profit. Republican opposition was focused more on the incursion of the federal government into what was regarded as the domain of local communities and politics and support for local control of schooling through school boards and the like.

Opting out has had some noticeable successes deriving from their very well-informed, grassroots activism, an activism which effectively utilized social media, and functioned horizontally within communities and vertically to pressure the State Board of Regents, the State Department of Education and local administrations. Their successes include changes in the membership of the Board of Regents, including the Chancellorship. A good number of opt-out supporters have also been elected to school boards. The group successfully opposed the *InBloom* reform, which was a collective response across a number of states, including New York, to President Obama's RTTT, which demanded that school systems develop data infrastructures to handle test results and to work with PBA. *InBloom* was opposed by the parents because of the involvement of edu-businesses in the creation of the required infrastructures, their collection, management and analysis of student data with the possibility for on-selling of this data for profit to third parties. There was also the related concern of data privacy. On this point, the NYSAPE website listed amongst the reasons for supporting opting out was that, 'State tests will serve as a vehicle for corporate digital learning platforms, data mining and privatization'. In relation to high-stakes testing and PBA, the website also noted that, 'All state-based tests must be computer-based by 2020'. Here we see the opposition of the parent activists to the broader corporate reform agenda in schooling. The opt-out movement in New York State has also achieved a moratorium on the usage of test results for teacher evaluation and performance-based accountability.

President Trump's election has witnessed a federal government more focused on expansion of privatization and charter school numbers and the introduction of vouchers. This has also precipitated some divides in the movement as tensions have arisen between the Democratic and Republican membership of the movement, as the more progressive membership wants to mobilize opposition to the broader politics of the Trump Presidency. The leadership of the movement has also become increasingly concerned about privately provided online curricula, pedagogy and assessment, as part of their opposition to the corporate reform agenda.

A new US stance on the OECD's globalizing testing regime?

The rise of ethno-nationalism and populist nationalisms in much contemporary politics was alluded to earlier and can be situated against the ongoing depredations of the 2008 Global Financial Crisis, the collapse of manufacturing in developed nations with real impact on industrial rust-belt cities, and the substantial growth in inequality (Piketty, 2013). It can also be seen in some nations' responses to the climate emergency and the Coronavirus pandemic. This kind of politics has been very evident in the presidency of Donald Trump in the USA. President Trump opposes multilateralism, evident for example in the USA's withdrawal from the Paris Agreement on climate change and emissions reductions, and stresses instead the significance of the national, as, for example in the exhortation of 'America First' and 'Make America Great Again'. This opposition to multilateralism is also apparent in the US's withdrawal from the WHO in the context of the pandemic. President Trump emphasizes national sovereignty in America's interest and supports bilateral nation-to-nation agreements, rather than global multilateralism. Global free trade, the norm during the dominance of neoliberal globalization in the period following the end of the Cold War, has also been challenged by this presidency; for example, think of the tariff wars with China and the reworking of North American Free Trade Agreement (NAFTA). Thus, President Trump, while accepting the neoliberal, market economics for domestic US politics, has challenged to some extent the post-Cold War global policy consensus.

This new politics, including in the USA, relates to the seeming loss of some economic sovereignty, with culture, national identity or ethnos being one aspect over which national governments have retained sovereignty (Appadurai, 2006). Here we see a structural reason for the rise of ethno-nationalism and populist nationalism. It is important to note, though, that this politics always plays out in path-dependent ways in any given nation.

Appadurai (2006) has argued that there have been two tropes of neoliberal globalization. The first of these is the apparent loss of economic sovereignty, the backdrop to the dominance of a human capital construction of education policy, an approach strongly sponsored by the OECD globally and evident in their talk of the emergence of a 'knowledge economy'. The OECD's stance is that the apparent loss of economic sovereignty makes education the most important economic policy for nations in the production of the quantity and quality of human capital necessary to ensure the global competitiveness of putative national economies.

On the loss of economic sovereignty, Appadurai observes,

> The virtually complete loss of even the fiction of a national economy, which had some evidence for its existence in the eras of strong socialist states and central planning, now leaves the cultural field as the main one in which fantasies of purity, authenticity, borders, and security can be enacted.
>
> (Appadurai, 2006, pp. 22–23)

Additionally, Appadurai (2006) argues that, 'The nation-state has been steadily reduced to the fiction of its ethnos as the last cultural resource over which it may exercise full dominion' (2006, p. 23). The nation-state, however, retains the capacity to instigate neoliberal market-driven policies (Carnoy, 2016) and this capacity is essential to the creation of a global economy. The new ethno-nationalism and populist nationalisms are political and policy responses to these two central tropes of neoliberal globalization. This new politics has had effects in schooling with renewed emphasis on producing national citizens, and, as will be argued, has had impact on the USA's stance on the OECD's education work, specifically testing.

The argument here is that the context of the new politics outlined above has seen the reassertion of the national in education policy in some nations and has also witnessed some rescaling of education polices. On the latter, think of the creation of a national curriculum in Australia's federal political structure (Lingard, 2018), of the creation of the Common Core State Standards in the USA, of the national curriculum and testing regime in England and the weakening of the role of local authorities. We also need to understand, as Grek (2019, p. 269) points out, that global policyscapes demand willing actors within nations: 'Interdependence is the new game in town.' However, despite the interdependence of the global and national in education policymaking today, she argues that we are currently witnessing a new 'sort of education protectionism'. She defines this as 'a folding back of internationalism in favour of a retreat to a nostalgia for education as a guarantor of patriotism, nationalism and the old, pre-globalization, "golden days" of the nation-state' (p. 20).

This is the context of severe criticisms of PISA that have been proffered by Mark Schneider (2019a, b, c, d), director of the US Department of Education's Institute of Education Sciences. It is almost as if President Trump's politics, and in particular his strident anti-multilateralism, have provided a space for these criticisms to be aired. This is a confirmation of how important context is to policy approaches. Schneider has been very critical in a number of addresses of the

OECD's expansionary ambitions for their testing regimes, particularly PISA. The significance of Schneider's stinging criticisms must also be put in the context of the USA being the main mover that pressured the OECD to develop what has become PISA. As noted throughout, PISA might be seen, in the first instance at least, as a US-driven agenda; the OECD's hegemonic power getting its ways, as it were. It should also be recognised that the USA's National Assessment of Educational Progress (NAEP) was the model on which PISA was based. These factors make Schneider's criticisms even more significant.

Schneider's criticisms might be seen overall as offering a critique of the OECD's desire to expand the scope, scale and explanatory power of PISA and its links to PBA of various kinds. He has been very critical of what might be seen as the over-reach of the OECD. Specifically, Schneider has been critical of: the expansion of the numbers of participant nations in PISA and future OECD ambitions in this respect; the perceived reduced usefulness of the PISA data given the expanded participant numbers; the inclusion of PISA for Development nations in the 2021 PISA round; the usefulness of the socio-economic survey of schools associated with PISA student tests for developing nations; the lack of a thorough research base to some of the new test items (e.g. the measure of global competence in the 2018 PISA); and the costs of the three-year PISA cycle (see Engel and Rutkowski, 2018). He also suggested that if participant numbers were smaller and only involved developed nations that maybe with computer-adaptive testing PISA might become a continuous assessment rather than operating in a three-year cycle. With that possibility, he would like main PISA to move to a five-year test cycle. All of this is argued to be in the interests of the USA: America First in respect of the OECD's testing regime.

This is a substantial set of criticisms that provoked responses from the chair of the PISA Governing Board, leading Australian education policymaker, Michelle Bruniges (2019a, b), who acknowledged that the views of governments change. Nonetheless, she defended the technical competence of the tests. In response, Schneider stressed that the USA was still supportive of PISA, but he also offered further criticisms, particularly of PISA for Development. He also questioned the impact of PISA's global growth on the validity and technical quality of the tests and suggested that his criticisms stemmed from the OECD's failure to discuss the implications of the ambitious expansion of PISA, especially in relation to its scope and scale. His criticisms here might be seen as a critique of the OECD taking on an actor role and working well beyond the interests of the USA.

Conclusion

The chapter has shown how the rise of high-stakes testing and PBA in the USA was situated in the same context as the USA pressuring the OECD to create what became PISA. That pressure was situated in the *longue durée* following the *Nation at Risk* report. A strengthening of that agenda in the first decade of the twenty-first century must also be contextualized against the USA's poor comparative performance on PISA, particularly in relation to the USA's PISA shock in 2010, following Shanghai's stellar performance on PISA 2009. Yet, as this chapter has shown, there has been considerable bottom-up, grassroots opposition to PBA as in the case of the opt-out movement in New York State. The specific administrative structure of US schooling with much local input has been a central factor in the grassroots organization and some successes of the bottom-up opt-out movement in New York State to high-stakes testing and performance-based accountability.

Tensions between the expansionary ambitions of the OECD in relation to PISA and other components of their testing regime have been shown to be indicative of a more ambitious actor role of the OECD. This has now come into tension with the USA's view of these ambitions. This is very interesting, given that the USA is the most significant global player at the OECD and was the nation that actually pushed for the creation of PISA. President Trump's strident opposition to multi-lateralism and rearticulation of populist nationalism and ethno-nationalism appear to have given a senior policymaker the contextual space to proffer criticisms of the OECD's expansionary plans for testing. The critiques have been technical ones related to the ways the expansion of PISA is seen to reduce its relevance to the USA. Yet, as with all policy articulations and exhortations, there is always a political context and here it has been argued it is President Trump's anti-multilateral America First approach.

Eccleston (2011, p. 248) has observed that the political authority of an international organization 'is at its zenith when its rational/technical agenda aligns with prevailing social values and sentiments'. This has been the case to this point it would seem as OECD-supported performance-based accountabilities have been put in place around the globe, including in the USA during both the Bush and Obama presidencies, and when PISA and national testing have grown in significance across the globe. Clearly, the OECD's technical agenda regarding PISA has been critiqued by the director of the US Department of Education's Institute of Education Sciences and that agenda in the USA is now also apparently not in alignment with prevailing politics and social values and sentiments of anti-multilateralism, anti-globalization and ethno-nationalism. Yet the director also stated the USA remains committed to PISA, suggesting perhaps an ongoing contretemps between the OECD's testing agenda and that of the USA concerning who should be framing the former. This is indicative of the complex interweaving of the global and the national and the multidirectionality of such relations, of the global in the national and the national seeking to reframe the global. There is, of course, substantial resistance to prevailing populist politics and a presidential election might see a rearticulation of the ever-changing and complex imbrications of the global with the national, and indeed with the local.

Notes

1 In this chapter, performance-based accountability is taken to be synonymous with test-based accountability (TBA).
2 This case study research was funded by the New South Wales Teachers Federation (Lingard et al., 2017). The research interviews in New York were conducted with Professor David Hursh of Rochester University. Also see Lingard and Hursh (2019) and Hursh et al. (2019).

References

Amin, A. (2002). Spatialities of globalisation. *Environment and Planning A: Economy and Space*. 34, 385–399.

Anagnostopoulos, D., Rutledge, S., and Jacobsen, R. (Eds.) (2013). *The infrastructure of accountability: Data use and the transformation of American education*. Cambridge, MA: Harvard Education Press.

Appadurai, A. (2006). *Fear of small numbers: An essay on the geography of anger*. London, UK: Duke University Press.

Bonikowski, B. (2017). Ethno-nationalist populism and the mobilization of collective resentment. *British Journal of Sociology*. 68, S1: S181–S213.

Bruniges, M. (2019a). What we're getting right with PISA. *Education Week*. February 6.

Bruniges, M. (2019b). Response: Allowing more countries to participate in the PISA exam enables innovation and fosters diversity. *The 74's Newsletter*. March 11.

Carnoy, M. (2016). Educational policies in the face of globalization: Whither the nation state? In K. Mundy, A. Green, B. Lingard and A. Verger (Eds.). *The handbook of global education policy*. Oxford: Wiley Blackwell: 27–42.

Carroll, P. and Kellow, A. (2011). *The OECD: A study of organisational adaptation*. Cheltenham, UK: Edward Elgar.

Carvalho, L.M. and Costa, E. (2014). Seeing education with one's own eyes and through the PISA lenses: Consideration of the reception of PISA in European countries. *Discourse: Studies in the Cultural Politics of Education*. 36: 638–646.

Collins, R. (2012). Mapping the future, mapping education: An analysis of the 2011 State of the Union Address. *Journal of Education Policy*. 27, 2: 155–172.

Eccleston, R. (2011). The OECD and global economic governance. *Australian Journal of International Affairs*. 65: 243–255.

Engel, L. and Rutkowski, D. (2018). Pay to play: What does PISA participation cost in the US? *Discourse: Studies in the Cultural Politics of Education*. DOI: 10.1080/01596306. 2018.1503591.

Grek, S. (2009). Governing by numbers: The PISA 'effect' in Europe. *Journal of Education Policy*. 24, 1: 23–27.

Grek, S. (2019). The rise of transnational education governance and the persistent centrality of the nation. *Bildungsgeschichte International Journal for the Historiography of Education*. 2: 268–273.

Grek, S. (2020). Facing 'a tipping point'? The role of the OECD as a boundary organisation in governing education in Europe. *Education Inquiry*. DOI: 10.1080/20004508.2019. 1701838

Haas, E. (1990). *When knowledge is power: Three models of change in international organizations*. Berkeley, CA: University of California Press.

Hartong, S. (2018). Towards a topological re-assembling of education policy? Observing the implementation of performance data infrastructures and 'centres of calculation' in Germany. *Globalisation, Societies and Education*. 16, 1: 134–150.

Henry, M., Lingard, B., Rizvi, F., and Taylor, S. (2001). *The OECD, globalisation and education policy*. London: Pergamon-Elsevier.

Hursh, D., McGinnis, S., Chen, Z., and Lingard, B. (2019). Resisting the neoliberal: Parent activism against the corporate reform agenda in schooling. In L. Tett and M. Hamilton (Eds.). *Resisting neoliberalism in education: Local, national and transnational perspectives*. Bristol: Policy Press: 89–102.

Kamens, D. (2013). Globalization and the emergence of an audit culture: PISA and the search for Best Practices and Magic Bullets. In H. Meyer and A. Benavot (Eds.). *PISA, power, and policy: The emergence of global education governance*. Oxford, UK: *Symposium Books*: 117–139.

Kamens, D. and McNeeley, C. (2010). Globalization and the growth of international educational testing and national assessment. *Comparative Education Review*. 54, 1: 5–25.

Lewis, S. (2019). Historicizing new spaces and relations of the OECD's global education governance: PISA for Schools and PISA4U. In C. Ydesen (Ed.). *The OECD's historical rise in education: The formation of a global governing complex*. London: Palgrave Macmillan: 269–289.

Lewis, S., Sellar, S., and Lingard, B. (2016). Pisa for Schools: Topological rationality and new spaces of the OECD's global education governance. *Comparative Education Review*. 60, 1: 27–57.

Lingard, B. (2018). The Australian curriculum: A critical interrogation of why, what and where to? *Curriculum Perspectives*, 38, 1: 55–65.

Lingard, B. and Hursh, D. (2019). Grassroots democracy in New York State: Opting out and resisting the corporate reform agenda in schooling. In S. Riddle and M. Apple (Eds.). *Re-Imaging education for democracy*. New York: Routledge: 239–255.

Lingard, B. and Lewis, S. (2016). Globalization of the Anglo-American approach to top-down, test-based educational accountability. In G. Brown and L. Harris (Eds.). *Handbook of human and social conditions of assessment*. London: Routledge: 387–403.

Lingard, B., Martino, W., Rezai-Rashti, G. and Sellar, S. (2016). *Globalizing educational accountabilities*. New York: Routledge.

Lingard, B. and Rawolle, S. (2011). New scalar politics: Implications for education policy. *Comparative Education*. 47, 4: 489–502.

Lingard, B. and Sellar, S. (2016). *The changing organizational and global significance of the OECD's education work*. In K. Mundy, A. Green, B. Lingard and A. Verger (Eds.). *The handbook of global education policy*. Oxford: Wiley Blackwell: 357–373.

Lingard, B., Sellar, S. and Baroutsis, A. (2015). Researching the habitus of global policy actors in education. *Cambridge Journal of Education*. 45, 1: 25–42.

Lingard, B., Sellar, S., Hogan, A., and Thompson, G. (2017). *Commercialisation in public schooling*. Sydney: New South Wales Teachers Federation.

Novoa, A. and Yariv-Mashal, T. (2003). Comparative research in education: A mode of governance or a historical journey? *Comparative Education*. 39, 4: 423–438.

Piketty, T. (2013). *Capital in the twenty-first century*. Cambridge, MA: Harvard University Press.

Pizmony-Levy, O. (2013). *Testing for all: The emergence and development of international assessment of student achievement, 1958–2012*. PhD thesis. Indiana University.

Pizmony-Levy, O. and Green, S.N. (2016). *Who opts out and why? Results from national survey on opting out of standardized tests*. New York: Teachers College, Columbia University.

Robertson, S. (2018). Researching global education policy: Angles In/on/out. In A. Verger, M. Novelli and H. Altinyelken. (Eds.). *Global education policy: New agendas, issues and policies*. London: Bloomsbury: 35–54.

Rutkowski, D. (2007). Converging us softly: How intergovernmental organizations promote neoliberal educational policy. *Critical Studies in Education*. 48, 2: 229–247.

Sassen, S. (2001). Spatialities and temporalities of the global: Elements for a theorization. In A. Appadurai (Ed.). *Globalization*. London: Duke University Press: 260–278.

Sassen, S. (2006). *Territory, authority, rights: From medieval to global assemblages*. Princeton, NJ: Princeton University Press.

Sassen, S. (2007). *A sociology of globalization*. New York: W.W. Norton.

Schertzer, R. and Taylor, E. (2020). Nationalism: The ethno-nationalist populism of Donald Trump's Twitter communication. *Ethnic and Racial Studies*. DOI: 10.1080/01419870.2020.1713390.

Schleicher, A. and Zoido, P. (2016). *The policies that shaped PISA and the policies that PISA shaped*. In K. Mundy, A. Green, B. Lingard and A. Verger (Eds.). *The handbook of global education policy*. Oxford: Wiley Blackwell: 374–384.

Schneider, M. (2019a). Is PISA a victim of its own success? *Education Week*. January 31.

Schneider, M. (2019b). PISA is a unique resource for testing educational attainment of 15 year olds in 78 countries. *The 74's Newsletter*. February 25.

Schneider, M. (2019c). Where is PISA headed? *Education Week*. February 26.

Schneider, M. (2019d). My response to essay rebuttal. *The 74's Newsletter*. March 13.

Sellar, S. and Lingard, B. (2013). Looking East: Shanghai, PISA 2009 and the reconstitution of reference societies in the global policy field. *Comparative Education*. 49, 4: 464–485.

Sobe, N. (2015). All that is global is not world culture: accountability systems and educational apparatuses. *Globalisation, Society and Education*. 13, 1: 135–148.

Sorensen, T. and Robertson, S. (2019). Ordinalization and the OECD's governance of teachers. *Comparative Education Review*. DOI: 0010-4086/2020/6401-00XX

de Sousa Santos, B. (2006). Globalizations. *Theory, Culture & Society*. 23: 393–399.

Takayama, K. (2008). The politics of international league tables: PISA in Japan's achievement crisis debate. *Comparative Education*. 44, 4: 387–407.

Williamson, B. (2017). *Big data in education: The digital future of learning, policy and practice*. London: Sage.

Woodward, R. (2009). *The organisation for economic cooperation and development (OECD)*. London: Routledge.

Ydesen, C. (2019) (Ed.). *The OECD's historical rise in education: The formation of a global governing complex*. London: Palgrave Macmillan.

Index

Bold locators indicate **tables**. *Italicized* locators indicate *figures*.

Printed in the United States
By Bookmasters